About THE ULTIMATE GAME

- On October 28, 1985, Bhagwan Shree Rajneesh, the self-described "rich man's guru," founder of a spiritual movement that grew phenomenally from humble beginnings in India to a multinational, multimillion-dollar enterprise, headquartered in Oregon, was arrested by U.S. federal agents in Charlotte, North Carolina, on charges of thirty-five felony violations of immigration law and flight to avoid prosecution.

- That same day, Ma Anand Sheela, Bhagwan's personal secretary and chief administrator of his far-flung empire, who had left Oregon a month before amid a flurry of charges and countercharges of crime and corruption within the organization, was arrested in West Germany to be extradited to the U.S. on a charge of attempted murder.

- On November 14, 1985, Bhagwan appeared in federal court to plead guilty to two of the immigration charges against him. He was given a ten-year suspended sentence, five years probation to be served *outside* the U.S., and forced to pay $400,000 in fines and court costs. He immediately left the country.

- On November 22, 1985, Bhagwan's followers announced that the Oregon property, Rancho Rajneesh—100 square miles with facilities for housing 5,000—would be put up for sale. The asking price: $40,000,000. Also offered: an airplane, mobile homes, satellite TV equipment, a complete beauty salon, gambling tables, and place settings for 20,000.

- On July 22, 1986, Ma Anand Sheela was sentenced in U.S. District Court in Portland, Oregon, for charges that included attempted murder, assault, arson, and wiretapping.

Bhagwan Shree Rajneesh's vast, American-based "experiment" was finished.

What was the twisted path that led from the peaceful, idyllic Ashram in Poona, India, to an armed camp in Oregon? How did a high-principled spiritual movement that inspired countless followers worldwide and that had fostered breakthrough contributions to psychology, agriculture, scientific research, and the arts sink into a morass of paranoia, disillusion, corruption, and even violent crime?

Now, Kate Strelley, for nine years an insider with Bhagwan Shree Rajneesh's organization, provides an insider's look at the movement's meteoric rise to worldwide fame and riches and its equally dizzying fall from grace.

The following pages examine the key players in the unfolding drama, particularly Bhagwan Shree Rajneesh and Ma Anand Sheela, as well as inner workings, strategies, and tactics—the ultimate game plan—that made the Rajneesh movement a global religious phenomenon. What was the source of its wealth? Why were thousands attracted to the movement, and what were the internal machinations and external forces that brought about its collapse? How does Bhagwan Shree Rajneesh continue to exert an influence over many followers even in the wake of shocking disclosures? Bhagwan's underlying philosophy hints that he may not yet have played his final hand in THE ULTIMATE GAME.

THE ULTIMATE GAME

THE ULTIMATE GAME

The Rise and Fall of Bhagwan Shree Rajneesh

KATE STRELLEY

WITH ROBERT D. SAN SOUCI

1817

Harper & Row, Publishers, San Francisco

Cambridge, Hagerstown, New York, Philadelphia, Washington
London, Mexico City, São Paulo, Singapore, Sydney

FIRST EDITION

Library of Congress Cataloging-in-Publication Data

Strelley, Kate
  The ultimate game.

  1. Rajneesh, Bhagwan Shree, 1931-
2. Strelley, Kate.   I. San Souci, Robert.
II. Title.
BP605.R344S77   1987   299'.93   86–43021
ISBN 0-06-250821-0

---

87 88 89 90 91 HC 10 9 8 7 6 5 4 3 2 1

Whatever words you may speak, let them be truth.

Once you decide to be a disciple, you enter into another world—a totally different world of the heart, of love, of trust. Then it is a play: in fact, it is the ultimate game in life. You have played many other games; this is the last. You have played at being a husband, being a wife, mother, brother, being rich, being poor, being a leader, being a follower—you have played all the games . . .

This is the last game. After this game, games stop, game-playing stops. . . . Only you are left—neither the Master nor the disciple exists there. . . .

Bhagwan Shree Rajneesh
The Art of Dying

Contents

Preface

Since the writing of this book Bhagwan has returned to the original site in Poona. Messages have gone out to all *sannyasins* to send donations and return to live and work once again in the Ashram.

It is amazing just how many people have chosen to return, together with many new people. It would seem the cycle continues.

There are only a few more years before Bhagwan can return to America, and so far the Ranch has not been sold. Sheela will be released around that time and it will be interesting to see what happens. As you can see the story is certainly not over yet.

This book has given me a chance to go over the past, especially the way I viewed life and the players in it. It would take another book to describe the way I view it now. In many ways what I had always considered confronting life was really a denial of it. I would like to thank everyone over this last year who helped me to see these things and how I have misinterpreted their ways through my rather egotistical eyes.

A very special thanks to Antonio for making me see things the way they really are rather than how I would like them to be. Thanks, too, to my immediate family, whom I don't feel I have really appreciated until now. I know that some of what has been written here they have never had knowledge of and may even hurt them. For this I am sorry, but I hope that now it is all out in the open, they will be able to put it all behind them, too. I hope the future will not be quite so sensational but more relaxing and enjoyable.

This is a true story, but I have changed the names and details of people I knew at boarding school and in the commune in England.

Welcome to the Carnival

In November 1985 I left Ashland, Oregon, for Thailand, to die in peace. In one piece. Throughout the preceding year I had been pulled apart by events surrounding the collapse of Rajneeshpuram, near Antelope. Even my diagnosis of lymph cancer, discovered the previous summer, had not been enough to keep a host of people from making demands on me.

I was separated from my husband at the time, staying on at our ranch, Cold Mountain. I had chosen not to reside in the Rajneeshee commune, and had begun to build a life in Ashland. Even so, I continued to be confidante to Ma Anand Sheela, for whom I had been secretary and a friend in India before the commune moved to the United States.

Because of my long years of service at the Rajneesh Ashram in Poona, and subsequent duties as administrator for Rajneesh Centers in both London and Boston, Sheela continued to count on me for a variety of long-distance services. This continued almost to the moment she fled Oregon to seek asylum in Germany.

As the situation at the Ranch near Antelope worsened—with reports of racketeering, violations of immigration and naturalization statutes, and bizarre murder plots on a mind-boggling scale—U.S. government agents contacted me to work with them as an "insider." Finally, Bhagwan Shree Rajneesh summoned me himself, shortly after Sheela's flight. He asked my help in sifting through mountains of records and to help fill in gaps where documentation was missing.

I felt battered on all sides by people who were utterly insensitive to my own health crisis. Still, I attempted to find the path between betraying trust and justice. As the accusations flew thick and fast, and the truth grew increasingly elusive, I decided to give priority to my health.

For a time I tried an alternative course of treatment at a wheat-grass farm, which involves a life-long commitment to strict dietary disciplines. Though the prospect of a permanent diet of wheat-germ, bean sprouts, and raw vegetables seemed increasingly less appealing, what really hit me was the realization that I no longer had a thirst for life. The uncertainty, disillusion, and bitterness that engulfed me at the end of ten years of deep commitment to Bhagwan and his experiments in India and America had sapped the last of my reserves. I felt a huge part of my life—a part of *me*—had been wrenched away. Still, the Ranch tugged at me, forever trying to reinvolve me in the morass it had become.

One evening I found myself looking around and thinking, Wait, I'm going to die. *I want a chance to live my dying.*

I refused to continue my involvement with the drama on the Ranch, which was slipping into the melodrama of a poorly written police show.

I made up my mind to go to Thailand to die.

Earlier I had planned an extended visit to Thailand. I am particularly fond of a stretch of beach on an island there, which has always brought me a feeling of peace, serenity, and joy. It was the ideal place to go for this ultimate meditation. I had become so involved with the Rajneesh community that I fancied only death would give me the rest I so desperately hungered for. It simply seemed easier to die than to live.

Once I had made my decision I was able to look on the process of dying as an experience that could bring me deep spiritual awareness, which would help me as I continued my journey through lifetimes of rebirth. It's only when you face the fact that you're going to die that you can put your death in the perspective of a meditation on the profoundest questions of existence.

I was reading *The American Book of the Dead*, which I felt would be the ideal meditation to go out with. I've always taken everything to the limit, and this was my opportunity to turn the process of dying itself into the ultimate meditation. Ironically, for the first time in my life, I thought I knew where events were taking me: The fact of death was inevitable.

I spent the better part of a year becoming aware of these processes in my body. It was a logical extension of my own tendency to turn everything into a meditation; and anyone who meditates continually lives with the awareness that one day he or she is going to die.

My illness presented me with the all-too-rare opportunity to know, in advance, that my body was already caught up in the ultimate process. I could observe this process as it unfolded, come to terms with it in stages, and use each stage to bring me to a heightened sense of self-awareness and understanding.

I told a few people what I was doing. My closest friend extracted a promise that I would call her when I knew that I had reached the point where I could no longer endure the pain. By that time I would have meditated enough, and gone through the "death moment." I would have discovered all I could about myself and the business of dying. I had already gone through stages of denial and self-pity during the first terrible days and nights after I had learned of the cancer. I felt ready now for inner reconciliation, tranquility, and enlightenment.

I planned to be in Thailand about a year before I sent for my friend. She would come, then, to be near me at the end. *The American Book of the Dead* stresses that it is important to have a practitioner who will remain with you, and help talk you through the process. This helper sets up a *mantra*, a chant reminding you to surrender, to let go of things that bind you to this lifetime. Such a *mantra* is continued up to eight hours after the actual moment of death. During this crucial time the spirit has the opportunity to leap for the light that means escape from the wheel of *dharma*, or rebirth. But freeing oneself utterly for that transcendent "falling upwards" requires a singleness of concentration; a practitioner by the bed helps one escape the cords that tie the spirit to the physical world.

I returned to Thailand, found a tiny hut on an island four hours from the mainland, fell in love with it immediately, and settled in. The ever-changing ocean, beyond a beach of clearest white sand, provided a spectacular backdrop as I began my meditations. As far as I was concerned I had already made my peace with the world; and anyone whom I had overlooked I included in a general prayer to the cosmos, asking forgiveness of my sins and wayward moments. I acknowledged whatever hurt or trouble I had created in the world, then let it go. This was the start of true peace. As each seemingly more perfect day flowed by, I used the sound of the waves to bring myself into harmony with the moment. But events have a way of turning out far differently from the way one anticipates.

One afternoon, while I was sitting on the beach, reading a book, a young man who had gotten lost on his motorbike came up to me and wanted to begin talking. His name was Antonio.

For a full minute I wouldn't look at him. I kept my eyes on the page in front of me, while clearly thinking to myself, *Go away, I've chosen to die. I am not going to be dragged out of this.* I tried to concentrate on the sound of the waves very near my feet, to let their muted roar drown out the distraction of words. I wanted done with talk; I had been nearly talked to death in Oregon; I wanted to finish out my days in the silence of my own being.

Finally, my resolve broke and I looked up. In that instant I felt life as a kind of persistent energy, like the waves on the beach of shimmering sand, letting me know it wasn't quite done with me, for all I had made up my mind I was done with it. Once again life was having a laugh at my expense—telling me that the moment I had everything wrapped up neatly in my mind, it was going to be unraveled.

Impulsively, I decided to seize the opportunity and see where it might lead. I changed my *sarong* and bikini top for a tee-shirt and black tights with yellow stripes. Then I climbed aboard my new friend's motorbike for an adventure that lasted all afternoon. When I told Antonio of my illness, he treated it like the sort of thing that could be dealt with later—simply one of those problems in life that get blown out of proportion.

He came back the next day, and the day after that.

We became inseparable. We journeyed throughout Thailand, Malaysia—here, there, and everywhere. Finally, Antonio's holiday ended. He had to return to Milan, and he asked me to come with him.

I originally planned to go for only two weeks. Then, I promised myself, I would return to Thailand, I promised myself, to my life-meditation, which Antonio had so unexpectedly, so wonderfully, interrupted.

The highlight of the trip to Italy was my first experience of Venice Carnival. The whole city became a Renaissance wonderland filled with magic, lavish costumes, colors, and music. Most striking was the fact that, during Carnival, no one talks except in the briefest word or phrase. People become totally the character they are playing. Talk would shatter that illusion. It reminded me of the time I had spent in the Ashram: We were silent there, apart from speaking what was termed "the needful." We would move past each other, very much as I remember dancing through the streets of Venice, everything communicated in a glance.

The night before I was going to leave, Antonio and I danced in St. Mark's square. I really felt I had stepped into another world, yet one that was tantalizingly familiar. I felt as happy as I had felt at the Ashram before things fell apart—when everything was fresh and new, and I walked around wrapped in the world I discovered inside its walls.

Around us everybody wore masks or had their faces painted and wore the most elaborate costumes. The lilt of waltzes mingled with the splash of water in the canals. I recall thinking how the sea that had given birth to the city and sustained its commerce would also be the death of it one day. Venice was sinking. Streets that had been dry when Antonio and I walked on them earlier in the day were taking on water by the time the Carnival was in full swing.

My sense of the city was so very alive. Yet thoughts of time and the sea, mingled with thoughts of my own imminent departure for Thailand, encroached upon it relentlessly.

I must have gone very far into my reverie. It took me a moment to answer Antonio when he asked, "Why don't you stay?"

His straightforward question touched me on many levels. It seemed to ask me to stay with him in Italy—but also to ask me to stay in this world, in this life. I felt a surge of energy run through me, sweeping aside the exhaustion that plagued me so much of the time.

"Yes, I will," I said, because there was no other answer I could give.

So I stayed with him. Two weeks later he insisted that I go have another battery of tests in the local hospital. Those first tests were good; I was doing much better. Subsequent tests proved that the illness was in complete remission.

During this uncertain but increasingly hopeful time, I had begun to give more and more thought to the book I had often dreamed of writing: a full account of my experiences with Rajneeshpuram in Poona, India, and in Antelope, Oregon.

Such a book, I felt, would give me a chance to clarify my own understanding of the extraordinary ten years I had been a *sannyasin*, a follower of Bhagwan Shree Rajneesh; a participant in a spiritual experiment that took him and so many around him from a glimpse of ultimate wisdom to the pain, folly, and in some cases corruption, that signaled a tragic fall from grace.

I had begun thinking about it the night of Venice Carnival. In the midst of so much excitement, so many impressions touching my senses—teasing masks, fragrances of perfumes and freshly baked pasta, music and laughter—so profound an awareness of vast influences touching my life and world, I found myself caught up in a rush of vivid memories about my life in the Rajneesh community.

Leaving the Ashram had been like walking away from a disorienting, orange-tinted dream. I had been cut off from the world a long time. I had lived in a fairy-tale kingdom of heightened awareness, beauty and sensuality, emotional and intellectual intensity. When that dream world had turned nightmarish, I felt ripped-off, drained, in doubt that anything could be salvaged.

Now, in Venice, afloat on the magic of Carnival, I realized once again how alive I could be to the world around me. I was deliciously aware of every color, fragrance, and sound around me. I could glance in a man's eyes and see his story; I could read volumes in a woman's single, graceful laugh or gesture.

And so much of this—so much of what made me the person I was here, in the moment—was something I had carried away with me from my years as part of the Rajneesh community. For all the waste and failure and corruption that marked the collapse of Bhagwan's extravagant dream, some of us managed to take away some good things with us—flowers among the ruins, you might say.

From time to time I had talked of writing a book about my experiences. But when friends would ask me when I was going to get down to putting words on a page, I would put them off, saying, "It doesn't feel right . . . that part of my life isn't finished yet."

In Venice I found myself on the brink of a new beginning. But it was a beginning that signaled an end to a large portion of my life. The Rajneesh chapter needed some sort of closure, some summing up and reflection to discover what those years in India and elsewhere had meant to me. In one sense this book is a meditation on those extraordinary years.

Now, for the first time, I feel able to look at *all* sides of the experience: to acknowledge and let go of negativity and to affirm the positive experiences I had undergone.

I feel I've been growing through the twenty-six years of my life toward this book. My progress has sometimes been one step forward, then two back. The last ten years, the years spent as a part of the Rajneesh community in England, India, and America, are especially significant.

This book is a way of sharing with people my understanding of the world and how it works. I'm not claiming to be a teacher, or to have answers to the great questions in life. I simply feel I've learned some things—good and bad—that are worth passing along.

So much of my life has been a time of taking, in one way or another. I've done pretty much everything under the sun, including things that might shock a number of people. But it was all a part of getting here and becoming who I am, now, in this moment. I like to think that this book marks a turning point, a way to give back to the world some positive part of my experiences.

That so much of what I discovered came during my sojourn with the Rajneesh community gives a unique perspective to matters; but the troubling or inspiring things my experiences taught me about human nature and the human spirit are, I feel, universal.

Here, then, is the book. . . .

Part 1

SINGAPORE: THE GURDJIEFF EXPERIMENT

CHAPTER 1

Under Arthur's Stone

My parents met in an unusual way. My mother left her home in Hereford, England, when she was very young, and joined the British foreign service. My father was also working for the foreign service at this time. They met in Thebes, Egypt, at the feet of the Sphinx.

On reflection I think that the image of the sphinx is properly symbolic of much about both my earliest years with my parents, and my life since I left home under not the happiest of circumstances. "Being the supreme embodiment of the enigma," writes the Spanish artist Juan Eduardo Cirlot, "the sphinx keeps watch over an ultimate meaning which must remain for ever beyond the understanding of man." Much about the way my parents raised me was—and to some extent, remains—enigmatic to me.

My father had an approach to life that dictated how I was brought up. My father's goal in life is to participate in what he might call "the ultimate game." This sense of becoming the very best player you can, and setting the stakes as high as you dare, this was very clearly communicated to me early on. Life is not merely a challenge to you, but a series of challenges you set yourself—always testing yourself, pushing yourself, never being satisfied with one goal, but pushing on toward the next. You must use each encounter as a learning experience, assimilate the lesson, and apply that knowledge of yourself and how the world works to reach the next level of the game.

It is this idea of gamesmanship that allows me to see someone like Sheela, the power behind the Rajneesh throne, in a morally neutral light. What others might decry as amorality, I tend to see in the context of someone else's perception of the "game," its goals, its rules. It might not reflect my own sensibilities and how I play my own particular life game; but I can see it as a *variation*, rather than a *deviation*. Each one of us has to play the game our own way, because that's a crucial part of our own essence and evolution.

I know a lot of people would say, "No, no, it's wrong." But I know from the way I've been chosen to view life, from what I learned from Rajneesh, and from reading about the mystical teacher G. I. Gurdjieff, that there are people who "play" in the world on this basis. There's excitement in it—and an almost religious feeling of reaching toward fulfillment, exceeding the limits of the daily, the humdrum, the complacency with the little (or the much) that life tosses our way.

I think that Gurdjieff's philosophy sustained and encouraged people like my father in a lifestyle that is resistant to patterning, fraught with uncertainty and even risk; a lifestyle so much at odds with the majority of people who seek security, undisrupted schedules, and a way of living that lets them tune out the disturbing, the unresolved, the paradoxical. Most people want to think that life is a tidy package. They're very suspicious of surprise and avoid risk at all costs. Gurdjieff, who died in 1949, saw just such "living on the edge" as a way to rise above routine existence and achieve a new sense of alertness, renewed vitality, and a higher level of consciousness. Gurdjieff was an admitted influence on Bhagwan, and many of his ideas and ways of working with his followers paralleled much of what Bhagwan taught.

A few years ago I lived in a commune with someone who had spent a good deal of time with one of Gurdjieff's main disciples. He talked of a person who had carried out the "perfect" robbery as an extreme working out of the Gurdjieff formula for living a life as intensely as possible. It was all done with an eye to "the game," to bring oneself to such a heightened point. To a certain extent I saw this same idea at work in the Rajneesh organization—not a jewel theft as such, but the execution of the ultimate plan without any compromise or failure. The goal was never possession or ego gratification, the way a jewel thief might later boast that he had the world's most flawless emerald. It's just "the game"—and never to lose, as a thief wants never to get caught, is the ultimate.

In many ways my ability to appreciate the essence and importance of this game helped me function all the years I was at the Rajneesh Ashram, both in Poona and Oregon. If one can accept the game on its own terms, and not impose one's point of view on what form the game should or should not take, then one can tolerate many things. This, I think now, explains how Bhagwan might have been able to condone drug dealings and other illegal activities. From this point of view where Sheela, Bhagwan, and the rest fell down, quite simply, was in getting caught.

It will be interesting, in the wake of Bhagwan's deportation and Sheela's court convictions, to watch and see if they will regain their old energy once more and wriggle onto the next square of the gameboard.

My mother's family was well known in the farming culture of England. It was a good family, but she wanted more. So she moved to London, did some secretarial work, and then joined the foreign service. She was in her early twenties when she met my father and later married him in Cyprus.

My father also came from a solidly middle-class background, though I have had a much harder time piecing together his history. He is extremely reticent on the subject, as he has always been about so much. He remains an enigma to me.

Grandfather spent much of his time traveling the world. On the few occasions when he would come to visit, he would never talk much about things he had seen or done. My father had been evacuated from London during the war and spent much of his time separated from his parents.

I identified myself with my father. I always sensed my mother, on the other hand, as warm, sweet, loving—but somehow at one remove from this most important sector of my life. While we were living in Singapore, one of the many exotic places in which I spent my youth, my mother would give dinner parties, entertaining, trying to be as "normal" a mother as living in such an exotic locale would allow.

Here in Singapore my father and I were something different, special; in many ways we lived in a world into which no others were invited. I had almost no friends in those days. My sisters were away at school in England; my father was often gone for long or short periods of time.

My father tailored my school lessons to draw me out, letting my own inclinations, rather than a rigid curriculum, dictate the direction of my study. If he was in the middle of teaching math, and I had a question about English, he would immediately switch for me. And if he didn't know the answer on the spot, he made it *our* business to find out right away.

I loved being taught in that way. He always stimulated my sense of inquiry; as a result I acquired a broad range of knowledge.

My father never indulged in chatter. When we were together we would talk about things that interested me. I remember coming to my father when I was quite young, perhaps seven or eight, and saying that I believed that there was a way to communicate with other people that wasn't telepathy, but a way of combining vocal and visual signals. Even then I realized that using words alone limited your ability to make another person see something just the way you are seeing it, rather than filtered through and so distorted by their own experience. I understood that misunderstandings would be inevitable because, without a more exact way of communicating, people would always be interpreting what was said rather than really getting my meaning.

So I came to my father with this problem, and we discussed it for a long time. I remember telling him at one point that what I was talking about was really the idea of opening another sense, so that people would not only understand what I was saying, but would actually see what I was seeing in the moment.

In our pursuit of the answer to this question I became fully aware, for the first time, of my father "stretching" my mind—and his own. We were moving into a field that wasn't simply history or math—though I always had to keep up my lessons in these areas. I remember getting very impatient with him for making me continue math drills, when I wanted to give all my energies to the joint project I called "sound and vision."

At that time I sensed new channels of awareness opening between us. This heightened awareness seemed to expand out to include others. I had a dog named Zsa Zsa, my only playmate. I found I was able to attune myself to her, and later to plants, frogs, and snakes, which I kept as pets. I feel that I was able in this way to comprehend something of their experience of their world.

My parents would not dictate to me how I was to see the world. I guess this was all part of the "experiment." I would never be told there was a God or there wasn't one, that Jesus had existed or he hadn't. I would be given information, sometimes tantalizingly limited, that this was what people thought about the subject. But it was up to me to inquire further, to formulate the questions that would eventually let me form my own conclusions. I realize now this was to make me expand what I believe from a nonconditioned position.

Now I can look back on that time and see something of what the "experiment" was all about. You would bring a child into the world, but you wouldn't force-feed it predigested information, like boxes of goods in a supermarket. Give it just enough clues as to what might be, then let it pursue its own course of inquiry and arrive at its own con-

clusions. Who knows what might be discovered: perhaps the same answers that others have formulated, which would certainly be sugges-
tive in itself. Or, freed from the constraints of certain ways of thinking,
such an inquiry might lead to wonderful new knowledge and ways of
perceiving the world.

My world was a silent one: the underwater kingdom (I swam in the
ocean nearly every day from one to five, as part of my regimen), the
plant and animal world near the house. But other children were absent,
and there were very few adults around. Even so, I sensed very quickly
that my father and I perceived our world in a very different way from
my mother and Tina, the household servant.

My understanding of the way that I grew up and lived was "normal." I never questioned that my two sisters went away to school and
came back twice a year, while I never did. One of my clearest memories
was of my sister suddenly coming home in a very flowered dress (this
was the 1960s, when the Beatles were at their peak). She played "Hey
Jude" on the record player while she danced a kind of "slouchy" dance
to it—almost mesmerized.

When I first heard that music I really began to wonder why my two
older sisters were off studying in England, while I stayed behind with
my parents in Singapore. What was wrong with me? But it seemed impossible to stay pensive, being a child growing up in Singapore with
the sunshine.

It wasn't until I was about sixteen that I even got a hint from my
father that, in actual fact, the life that I had lived in close contact to him
up to eleven had been strongly influenced from his own philosophical
beliefs, the details of which, even now, I can only surmise. It is my belief that this reticence arises from the conviction that the "work" involved is something that is simply not discussed.

Years later, I confronted my father. I had just returned to England
from a brief visit to India, where I had met Rajneesh and decided to
stay on at the Ashram at Poona. One day, while we were driving in the
car, I was talking to my father about how brilliant Bhagwan was, and
how he often quoted someone named Gurdjieff. I asked my father,
"Have you ever heard about this man?"

My father turned to me with the kind of affectionate smile a parent
reserves for a very precocious child—in my case, a child who had been
in India a few months, heard a few words from somebody, and was
suddenly the world's authority on every master who ever existed. Our
eyes met, and I'll never forget that look he gave me: It was the sort you

get from someone who knows a whole lot more than you do about some subject about which you presume to know a good deal. This was my first dose of humility. It was my first full understanding that I didn't know everything—and I certainly didn't know everything about this man sitting beside me in the car.

To this day I am uncertain about where and how my father first encountered the teachings of Gurdjieff. From time to time he would attend meetings about which little, if anything, was said. I don't know who else was involved, but I am fairly certain that on these occasions he met with other adherents of similar opinions.

My mother always told me never to ask where he was going. She did mention that only men were allowed to attend these meetings, but I've never known how accurate that information was. These meetings continued all through my childhood; then, about five years ago, he stopped attending. For reasons that he has never made clear, he decided that he wanted nothing more to do with these meetings.

My feeling is that he became disillusioned. I saw him go through the same sort of thing I saw others go through when they left the Ashram and Bhagwan. I guess you would call it a kind of self-doubt. I view that as a very healthy thing, but I know just how devastating it can be.

For a time, he seemed to me like a dead man. He'd never been a very talkative man, but his silences had always been *alive*. Now, they were only dull, closed, uncomfortable.

Then, last year, he suffered a mild heart attack. This happened while I was at the wheat-grass farm. Over the years we had touched upon the inevitability of death. But when Mary called to tell me what had happened, I was shocked at the sudden thought that my father wouldn't always be around.

And it brought into focus how far our relationship went beyond father-daughter. I tried to explain to Mary that I felt my father and I had said our good-byes—for this body, at any rate—by the time I was nine.

And then he had another heart attack in June of 1985, and I did return home. We spent a few incredible days together—borrowed time. We had already had all the time we ever needed together in this lifetime, and these few days that happened along were just out of this world.

We went together to a place outside Hereford called Arthur's Stone, which is where King Arthur was supposed to have undergone his initiation into the Druid mysteries. It is a ring of standing stones with a lid of stone upon it. The initiate would spend some time in a chamber in solitary meditation, then come down a passageway into the ring. This would represent his passage through a "birthing channel" to his next phase of awareness. It is also reputed to be the place where Arthur will reappear when he is brought back into existence at some unspecified future time. It is a magical spot to which still clings some power of those old rites over which Merlin was said to preside.

My father and I sat under the stones that afternoon and listened to the rain beat down. I picked up a small stone (which I still have) that I found nearby. It fit neatly into the palm of one hand. I was holding my father's hand with the other.

In that instant I seemed to feel the totality of my father as he sat beside me. Maybe, for a moment, we achieved the extrasensory communication that I had dreamed about as a child. I shared all his strength, all his presence, the substance that I had only been able to see in fragments before. He was no longer outside of me as father or friend or anything else: He was a part of me. I shared not only his strength, but his wonderful clarity.

And these words formed in my mind: *Whatever words you may speak now, let them be truth.* I realize that those words can be construed in many different ways. But my understanding of those words in that particular moment had nothing to do with truth meaning lies, or truth on this level, but truth for the whole purpose. I don't know how better to put it. It was as if I was reading his mind. And, hard as it is for me to interpret truth for myself, how can I presume to know what another person's truth is? In the "not-knowing" I can begin to see Bhagwan, Sheela, and so many others.

I only know that for a moment, under this magical stone, I understood what our relationship had been about—what this man, and his beliefs, and his "experiment" were about. It was a moment of pure enlightenment, when you see clearly how the whole of eternity telescopes into a single moment. I understood that I had never, in spite of miles and years, been separate from this being, this man. We were a totality.

In Zen they say, "Be here now." That doesn't mean be just in this one moment, but be here in the fullness of this moment and in the fullness of all moments which simultaneously exist, past and future, in any dimension. It means being fully in this moment, recognizing that there is no other moment.

Those words that crystallized in my mind told me to pay attention to truth, as we know it, to our full capacity, only in the present moment. If you open your being you're opening yourself to the ultimate truth, which has nothing to do with this plane, which feels to me merely the appetizer. It bursts beyond the realm of bodies, and talking, and seeing, and our interpretations of these things.

In that instant I understood all that my father had brought me to in this moment—my weird childhood, all the things that had happened to me before I encountered Bhagwan, and my own experiences in India, Oregon, and elsewhere. And Arthur and Merlin, the rain pouring down, and the rich smells of the Herefordshire soil and grass and trees, the wet megaliths around us—these were all a part of this moment, while we sat dry under Arthur's Stone.

CHAPTER 2

Singapore

My earliest real memory is of being on the plane going to Singapore. I must have been two and a bit. My sister Sarah, who was a year older, was beside me. We were traveling in one of those huge, old, propeller-driven craft. The walls were bare metal with seats bolted in place in the most functional fashion.

In those days it took twenty-four hours to travel from London to Singapore. As we flew one propeller came on fire, but they continued on. No one seemed unduly alarmed; it was a British plane, and everyone seemed to feel that there was nothing to do but "get on with it"—"it" being the business of staying aloft until we reached our scheduled destination.

But the clearest part of the memory was the moment we got off the plane in Singapore. I remember the smell: It was hot, humid, totally unlike the cool air I had breathed all my short life in England. At first you can hardly breathe, then you feel yourself opening up to it as a new sensation. It's something that's peculiar to the Orient; a mixture of animals, vegetation that's hot, saturated in water, and overripe—but still pleasing.

The sky was so blue; the lush vegetation massed everywhere; the wonderful, bright flowers everywhere. One huge plant in particular appealed to me immediately: the broad-leaved one called "elephant ears." This was always my favorite; years later I was delighted to discover them growing abundantly on the grounds of the Rajneesh Ashram in Poona.

Singapore represented open space. I remember our house clearly. In the front a row of pillars supported a generous veranda. About twenty-five feet from the foot of the porch was a palm tree; beyond the tree the ground would drop away sharply to a clear, flat plain beyond, stretching away to the west.

One image in particular stands out from that time. It was my father standing next to a palm tree, framing the setting sun, and shouting, "four times six" or "three times nine" as he drilled me in my multiplication tables. I would be sitting cross-legged on the concrete lip of the drainage ditch, dug against monsoons, with my feet dangling into the trench, my dog sitting beside me. I would answer Father with half my mind—the other part would be totally caught up in the vision of the huge, orange sun, in the center of sky burning red.

Sometimes my father would get impatient with me, because I would lose concentration to the sunset brilliance. When he became angry he would never shout or speak to me in a harsh way, but a certain *inflection* in his voice would cut through all my end-of-day dreaming. I would only have to glance at him to get what he was thinking.

Once settled into the house in Singapore, we immediately got into a routine: when he could, my father tutored me from eight in the morning until twelve noon; then, from one until five, my mother would take me out to the ocean. They had experimented with a plastic bubble-like apparatus that was used to help youngsters not yet able to have an air tank strapped onto them learn the rudiments of diving. It wasn't snorkeling: An air hose, running up to the surface, assured a steady supply of oxygen, while weights kept you always beneath the surface, until an adult pulled you out.

So, for four to five hours a day, my reality was the underwater world, which was just color. Shoals of rainbow-tinted parrot fish with their funny little mouths, sea anemones and urchins—all these creatures became, for me, friends. I would speak to them silently; communicating with them without speaking became a huge part of my world. This ability get in touch with nature or other people has never left me to this day.

A lot of what I initially felt with Bhagwan echoed my sensations in that wonderful, mysterious, silent undersea world. A belief that you could understand without words, a sense that you could share so much with looks, touches, feelings. Even today I tend, by choice, not to speak a great deal; I can sit for hours and hours not talking, perfectly content—actually feeling disturbed if too much talking is going on around me. I prefer to live very silently.

I can recognize now that this isn't the "usual" way people function in the larger society; I can appreciate that at times it makes friends actually uncomfortable. But for so long as a child I thought this was the way the world functioned. Later, in India, working at the Ashram, I spoke very little when my duties did not require it; and this was never commented upon, because silence was so much the order of the day there. Many people had come there from America and Western Europe to learn how to be silent; but for me it came naturally. It wasn't until I *left* the Ashram that I discovered this was a discipline that most people had to impose on themselves. Over the years it has become so much a part of my being that I find I cling to it, because that silence is the key that continues to open doors to new understandings and joy.

As a child I would walk in the back gardens, which were far more wild than the front or sides. The latter were more carefully manicured to protect household members from snakes; but the back was let go somewhat.

When I was about seven I sat in my hideaway built of wood scraps and covered with daubs of paint. I was alternately checking over the box of "treasures" I kept there—odds and ends I had collected for years—and watching a pitcher plant that grew nearby.

The pitcher plant is carnivorous, like a Venus flytrap; it has a flower that looks like a pitcher with a lid. As I watched a fly landed on the top of its sticky surface; the fly tried to escape, but was held in place. The more it struggled, the more it got caught up with the sticky goo. If it had flown away the moment it had landed, or had simply relaxed and gradually worked its way free, it would have been safe. Instead it began to struggle more and got covered with the goo, and finally just dropped into the pitcher, where the enzymes cupped there would digest the insect.

Suddenly, I broke off the pitcher plant's flower and ran back to the house, where I found my mother in the kitchen. I said to her with a kind of desperation, "Tell me what we're here for."

I felt an intense—almost a *passionate*—need for an answer that made sense of such things. Watching this fly in its death throes I felt that my awareness had burst open—but I didn't know what to make of it all. I didn't have the answers inside me. I had the sense of having seen something beyond the limits of myself, the house, the grounds, the world as I knew it. I felt wide open, vulnerable, in touch with something that frightened and threatened to overwhelm me.

My poor mother, meanwhile, was trying to calm me down and get a grasp on what I was fussing about. She grabbed my hand and held my wrist, while I tumbled out my story of the fly and my life-or-death need to know *that very minute* what was going to happen to me.

She said, "Well, you're going to grow up and get married and you'll have children—"

I didn't even let her finish the word "children," before I started shaking my head *no, no, no*. I knew that what was involved was a whole lot more than that.

By this point my father had come into the room and was staring at me. But his look told me he couldn't answer me, either. It was the first time I could remember him being unable to tell me what I needed to know. And in that moment I sensed that, in this one realm of probing for the answers to the deepest questions in life, we had become equals: We didn't know.

It was my mother who saved the day. I had grown even more desperate when I discovered my father didn't have the answers I needed. Still holding my wrist, she knelt in front of me and said, "I don't know what it is that you see, but all I know is that you have to live to find out." Those words sustained me through days more difficult than I could ever have imagined.

I treasured those special moments when all three of us were together. I also had a friend in Tina, the household servant; her son, Sayanudin, was the only child I played with, and he only visited a few times a year. When he did, I would dress up as a little Malaysian girl with a *sarong*.

Tina was about five feet four inches tall, with dark brown skin and even darker brown eyes. She had the softest skin; when she would touch me, her fingertips were like velvet. I felt, if I were careless, that I could go right through her fingers like poking through a soap bubble. It wasn't just that she was delicate on the surface: her whole being was soft, relaxed.

She was a "smiler" who could laugh with a hearty, cackling laugh that was beautiful in its own way, and magic in the way it always made me want to laugh, too. She was a Malaysian woman, and wore her jet-black hair tied back in a tight bun. She was always trying out different styles on my own long hair.

The *sarong*s and *sarong-cabaya*s, the little tops she wore, were bright batiks; they set off her beautiful figure. She had generous breasts, a tiny waist, flat stomach, and trim hips. There was so much grace in her movements that I loved watching her perform even the simplest tasks: cooking, bringing water into her own quarters, whatever. A *sarong* forces you to move very differently from Western skirt or slacks, but she turned its limitations into a source of what I like to think of as fluid grace.

Though I remember my childhood in Singapore as essentially happy, its intensity could frustrate me at times; yet this intensity was so much a part of me that I never really wanted to be free of it. It was something of the same intensity I later found and liked in the Ashram. But it also made one horrific incident almost unbearable for me.

The Vietnam War was going on while I was growing up in Malaya. One day I went with my parents to swim at Jason's Bay, on the coast. Most of the time we would swim in nearby freshwater pools. It was all very idyllic, but also very wild.

On the afternoon walking near Jason's Bay, I came upon two iguanas, facing off and locked in a fight to the death. These carnivorous lizards travel in packs. A single one is not dangerous, I had been told; but if a pack spots a wounded animal they can go into a frenzy and tear it to bits.

I was still a bit nervous when I went into the sea. I swam a good way out, toward what I thought was a clump of driftwood. But the nearer I got, the more terrible the smell from it was. Finally, the odor drove me back to the beach, where I told my father about it.

He swam out to investigate and discovered a grisly sight. This "clump" was actually five or six women and children, strung together. They had been carried all the way down the coast from Cambodia by the currents. Each had been shot through the head. When I heard him talking about what he had discovered, the awfulness of it rushed over me with an intensity unlike anything I had felt before. Up to this time I had never been near death; my upbringing had kept me terribly sheltered.

I was about five at the time, but I was suddenly filled with the need to know what war was and why it happened. That smell made what I later heard devastatingly real to me. Because the mind blots out horrific things, I think that the image that comes to mind now may be equally made up of parts of photographs I saw considerably later in *Life* magazine. But from the moment I realized what I had almost touched on Jason's Bay, and understood that such awful things had happened and were continuing to happen, I felt something die in me.

I could no longer feel secure, could no longer see my world as safe, when horrors could literally wash up at your doorstep. And matters were brought home even more as war orphans were routed through Singapore en route to adoptive parents in the United States and elsewhere.

One little girl came to stay with us for a week before she was to go to America. It happened to be the Chinese New Year, which has always been an exciting, magical time for me. I would look forward for months to the firecrackers and lion dances and parades in the streets. It was one of the few nights I was allowed to stay up late and accompany my parents into the city proper.

The whole of Singapore was a wonderful carnival. We would sit on the side stalls and eat the *satay* sticks, barbecued pork done with cucumber and onions and covered with a peanut sauce—a treat I was allowed on this night.

I walked hand-in-hand with my Vietnamese friend. Though we couldn't speak each other's language, we got on quite well just exchanging glances. We'd only been together for a week, but we'd become real friends. I'd had so few children around that I delighted every minute in showing her things and sharing things with her. This night was the highlight for us both.

But when they set off the firecrackers, everything changed. I clung to her hand and, for an instant, I shared the total horror she was feeling. She was screaming and screaming and holding her hands over her ears. Later I found out that her parents had been shot to death in front of her; the firecrackers that night had yanked her back to the moment when the armed men had come in and executed her mother and father. As I held her hand, I was in this moment.

The next day she pointed to my parents and made gestures like someone shooting a gun to show me what had happened; then she acted out how she had hidden herself when she was afraid they would come back to kill her.

When her terror entered me at that moment, it made the terror of war real to me. Even though my days would continue happy enough on the surface, my sleep would frequently be plagued with nightmares of war.

Part 2

ENGLAND

CHAPTER 3

Not So Golden School Days

We lived in Singapore until 1970, when I turned eleven. At that time my father was transferred back to England, and we moved to Nottingham. It was the beginning of the end of my childhood.

When we first returned to Britain I begged and begged to be allowed to go to boarding school, as my sisters had done. At first my parents said no, and I had to fight to convince them. When they agreed I discovered that, to go to a private school, you had to take a "common entrance exam" and another exam called "the eleven-plus," which is a general grading evaluation. I took the "eleven-plus," and passed without a problem. For the "common entrance" I sat in the exam room in the local normal school. When I finished I thought I had passed. But the headmaster called me in when I had turned back the papers and asked, "How did you feel about the exam?"

"Fine," I replied.

He gave me an odd look, and asked me again how I felt. When I had assured him that I was feeling quite well, he dismissed me. But I later found out that I had written few if any words on the paper. Now, I can only guess that something in some part of my brain was telling me that I didn't *really* want to go to the same school my sisters had gone to.

I was given a battery of psychological tests before I was allowed to take the exam again. This time I passed without a problem. But I had already missed qualifying for the school my sisters had gone to. Instead, my parents found another school.

The minute I walked through the door I announced, "This is where I want to go." At that point it was the idea of going away to school, rather than the school itself, that had caught my fancy.

My experience there was, in a word, *horrific*.

Preparing to go away to school was very exciting for me. I had a trunk that had to be packed with the required six pairs of underwear, a day dress and a night dress, indoor and outdoor shoes, and so forth. And my name had to be sewn into all these things.

Watching my sisters pack their trunks with new clothes and things had always fascinated me. Now I had my very own trunk to fill with my own new school wardrobe. My favorite were the brand new clean shoes—probably because I hadn't worn shoes all those years in Malaysia. So these became as magical as the "red slippers" in the children's story that has always been one of my favorites.

But it was all wonderful: my six pairs of black socks and six pairs of white socks, a silk shirt for Sundays, a Sunday suit, one hat for Sunday and another for everyday, and gloves. And the "tuck"—the sweets you're allowed before half-term, and which you replenish at that time. Then there was the pocket money to allow fifty pence per month, doled out in weekly allowances.

I loved the ceremony of packing it all inside the trunk. I felt I was getting ready to go to a wonderful new world—nor was I in the least worried about it, since my sisters always seemed very happy going off to school themselves.

My arrival, however, was a rude awakening.

The school had lovely grounds, because the whole place had once been a private estate. There was one building where we went to class, and another that was the dormitory. The latter was a gorgeous old house. The buildings were surrounded by beautiful gardens filled with bright flowers and trees. There was also a tennis court and a swimming pool.

I fell in love with the place immediately.

Up the steps we went, my father holding one end of the trunk, me the other. I was so proud of everything. The matron directed us to my bedroom, which I would share with three other girls. It had big windows that looked out over the tennis court and gardens.

The school was filled with people: parents and guardians and all the other girls, back from summer holiday. The other students were all unpacking their trunks and greeting each other because they had already been together for a year, having begun at age ten. I was coming in at eleven, and knew no one, so I was pretty much ignored. But that didn't bother me: I had grown up with so much silence and alone so much of the time, that this seemed no more than to be expected.

I enjoyed watching this incredible movie all around me. I remember saying to my mother, "You must go now." I wanted to be on my own to drink in all this unfamiliar activity: girls running here and there, comparing new clothes, sharing stories about what they'd done that summer.

Part of the newness was the idea of dividing my life into sections: holidays and school term; attending classes in forms; fitting into the complex pattern of the routine.

I sat very gingerly on the bed, sorting through my precious things. Each item was brand new because we'd only just arrived from Singapore, and I had no store of winter clothing. Then I made a ritual of putting things away in the drawers or hanging them up in the closet that had been assigned to me.

It hadn't occurred to me how strange it was that none of the three girls who were to be my roommates had spoken to me. I just continued about my own tasks very quietly, while their mothers made their goodbyes. Earlier, one of the mothers had led us in a round of introduction, so I knew that I had a pair of Susans and a Leslie as roommates. But that was all the exchange we'd had.

As soon as the mothers were gone the energy in the room changed abruptly. No one said anything, but I could feel the hostility from the other three girls. Shortly after, I found that I had been "sent to Coventry," an English phrase that means you're not being spoken to.

Something inside me said right away, *You've got to get out of here.* I felt panicked, cornered, for the first time in my life. And I knew that I had put myself in this situation by insisting that I had to go away to boarding school.

My roommates continued to talk among themselves, pointedly cutting me dead. Because I was so backward socially I couldn't deal with their hostility. And I blamed myself for having done something to bring it down on myself, when, actually, they would have done the same with *any* stranger assigned to room with them. I retreated into myself and took my living energy from looking out the window at the plants and grass. Dinner that evening was a blur to me.

When I came back to the room, and pulled back the covers to get ready for bed, I found someone had left a note on the sheet. It was done in red felt pen on a ruled notebook page. It had my name on it.

My first reaction was joy. I decided that at least one of my roommates wanted to communicate with me, maybe wanted to become my friend. I unfolded the letter. I could feel the two Susans and Leslie all watching me, because they had returned to the room shortly after I had.

I sat on the edge of the bed to read the note. It warned me, "Don't

think that by sharing a room with us, that we're going to have anything to do with you. Make sure that you don't ever put any of your
things near our things. The only reason you're here is that your parents
don't want you, and we don't want you if they don't want you."

More followed that was just as hateful. I felt totally on the spot,
reading their letter while they stood and looked at me. My first reaction was an overwhelming desire to cry, but I stopped it. For the first
time in my life, I felt a part of me inside turn to steel or ice. I understood that my only hope was to retreat into my own world and continue in my own world. I would accept their terms. It never occurred to
me to fight with them or to try to communicate with them in any way.

Because my own character and upbringing had left me without certain social skills, I decided they were going to have to communicate
with me to change this state of affairs; I simply hadn't any ideas for
breaking through that wall of hostility by myself.

It was downhill from that point on.

Socially, I was retarded; academically, I was ahead of my school-
mates—the worst possible situation. I was disliked by others my age
because of my "unusualness," and because subjects like math and English came so easily to me. The classroom environment and the rigidly
followed study plans were nothing like the way I had been taught by
my tutors and encouraged—at least by my father—to let my mind jump
from subject to subject in pursuit of some idea.

I developed severe migraines soon after my arrival. Now, looking
back, I'm inclined to think that these were a way to escape my increasingly unhappy circumstances.

Inevitably, I suppose, I became a rebel. I realized that although
these people could control me by trying to limit me, they were really
very limited themselves. And if you blew those limits you'd blow them
out of the water too.

So I began to test those limits. I quickly grew to understand that
they were so many straw creatures: Their only strength was in banding
together to support each other. Individually, they had no real *being*. I
categorized them as "morons," who had no awareness beyond what
had been drummed into them by rote. They lived their lives according
to what others expected of them or told them to do. They disliked me
for no other reason than that it was the thing to do when someone who
is a stranger or who doesn't act a certain way turns up in their midst.

I remembered the day of the pitcher plant, when I demanded that
my mother tell me why we were living and what we were meant for.
She had tried to tell me I'd go to school, meet boys, get married, raise

children—and that was the end of it. That answer hadn't helped me all those years before. Now I found there were hundreds of people here that believed this. I felt excluded, because those limits didn't exist for me. And so I got into a lot of trouble.

Not long after I arrived, I met a girl named Suzzane, who is still my best friend. She was two grades above me, but she became my savior.

One evening, when I had come to the end of my tether, I had found a private corner of the garden to have a good cry. I rarely allowed myself to do this, so I was really howling. Suzzane, who had sneaked out for a forbidden cigarette, discovered me crying and crying. Without a word she came over and put her arms around me. It was the first bit of tenderness I'd had in something like six weeks.

She rocked me in her arms until I got all the tears out of my system. At last she said, "That's it: It won't happen any more." I took her at her word—after all, she was two years older—thirteen. *Her eyes are my own eyes*, I thought. And that pretty much cemented our friendship in my mind.

Suzzane was beautiful. She had long, very straight blond hair—so pale it almost seemed white—and incredibly blue eyes. She had huge breasts—I remember that very clearly because, at the time, I had no bust at all. She wore thick glasses, but she also had contact lenses. And this intrigued me because, until then, I'd never really known anyone who wore glasses. I was always trying to borrow them and wear them, though I never could see a thing through them.

Perhaps what struck me most was her earthiness. She would throw her head back and laugh a great laugh that would set her breasts and bottom jiggling. When she smiled her whole face would come alive, so you'd feel you just had to smile in return. Though she was very English she had a wonderfully clear, light-olive skin. Put me in the sun and I'll break out in a minute in freckles and a bright red nose; but Suzzane never turned up a single freckle to spoil her lovely complexion. I thought of her as a "sun goddess," because she'd go so bronze from its rays.

She was brilliant, with physics and chemistry her strongest points. Academically, we were very well-matched. Up to that point I hadn't encountered anyone at school who wanted to "dance" with John Donne or math or any of the other subjects I loved to explore. We would explore these subjects, which stimulated us both—though we always maintained our rebellious, earthy, mischievous side, too. We found the other brains at the school boring. We amused ourselves over problems of pure math and philosophy. I remember our having an earnest discussion on the question of whether, if you broadened your mind totally to the infinity of numbers, you could create a vacuum and so become enlightened.

We did our grandest thinking under the tree where we had first met and become the best of friends. Along with philosophy, she and a couple of others introduced me to cigarettes. Those sessions in the shade of our favorite tree were some of the few bright spots in what was becoming an increasingly bleak landscape for me.

I continued to be unpopular and to get in all kinds of trouble. I passed all my exams—not because I studied, but because I was so far ahead of my classmates in most subjects. All during this time I was trying to convince my parents that I had made a mistake, I really shouldn't be at boarding school. Even the shoes that had seemed like the "red slippers" hurt my feet, making me feel clamped in irons. Having my feet done up in stiff leather and shoelaces, when I had been used to going barefoot or wearing flip-flops, was really *hell*.

The cold weather got to me; I could never sort out which skirt I was supposed to wear at which time of day or which class I was supposed to be going to. I was always in trouble for what I thought were the *stupidest* things; I could never relate to how anyone could take so seriously whether I was wearing blue gloves or had lost my gloves or whatever. I couldn't see why people would pin so much on these things, because I had always felt that material things never had much importance in the world. Now, suddenly, a matter as small as the ribbon on my Sunday hat or losing the shilling for the collection plate assumed vast importance. It all seemed bizarre to me; and the fact that I had to go to church on Sunday rubbed me the wrong way. I'd never had to do *that* before.

More and more, I began to feel that I was paying a price for the freedom that I had had in Singapore. I felt like I was in jail. I couldn't adapt, so I grew more and more depressed. My whole task became to convince my parents that I didn't belong in this boarding school.

A few weeks after I had arrived at school my father and mother moved on to Belgium. Somehow, I muddled on until the Christmas holiday, when I went home. "I love learning, I really, really do," I told them, "but I can't live this way. I'm dying."

By this point I was on antidepressants from the doctor, tranquilizers for being hysterical, and having migraines that were so painful and so intense that I wanted to kill myself to put an end to the agony. But the worst was that nobody at the school seemed to have any love in their hearts. Everyone was so clinical. The teachers were all spinsters who would never give you a hug or a really sympathetic listening-to or show the least affection.

One day I was lying in bed with a migraine. I had a wet towel over my eyes so that I didn't have to see the light. And I heard my three roommates, who didn't like me at all, deliberately making as much noise as they could. I wanted to shout at them, "You're driving me crazy; why can't you leave me alone?"

With this image in mind, I tried to convince my folks that I would do just fine here if I didn't have to *live* here. If I could come here for classes during the day, and have an apartment and nanny in town—*that* would be the ideal solution.

But that was out of the question. I think that my parents hadn't really realized that it was too abrupt a change to put me through, taking me from one extreme to the other. Perhaps their own uncertainty made the question of what to do with me that much more difficult.

I suppose I was something of an embarrassment to them both. I was so keyed up that it was more like one long, hysterical outburst. I wasn't able to sit and reason with them because of my own emotional overload. I would try to explain things rationally; but within a moment my emotions would run away with me, because I felt so desperate. My father had never seen me like this, and he had no idea how to deal with me. I had always been a calm child, though maybe a little highly strung—even the nightmares about war had triggered only horror and sadness, but nothing like this hysteria.

He and my mother chose to believe the headmistress, who had told them I was hysterical, obnoxious, out of control. I knew that people were getting the impression that *this* was the kind of person I really was. I couldn't see what they were seeing. All I knew was that there was this person inside me screaming and saying, "Please, there's been a terrible mistake, this is not who I am, but I don't know how to show you."

I felt like I was living in a nightmare. It was as if I was in a bubble, and all these terrible things were happening around me. I was still the person I always was, but I couldn't communicate this to anybody. It was like the whole world had gone nuts, and I had no way of bringing it back on course.

I had lost all my ways of communication and my feeling of centeredness. At moments I felt pure hate for my parents; but it would change quickly so that I saw them as very weak. This made me feel stronger, and let me begin to find my center again.

I decided that I was getting into more and more of a mess the more I involved my parents in my life. They seemed to be adding to my confusion. So I eliminated them, wrote them off. I was actually quite unemotional about that. When I returned to school I was already detaching from them, consigning them to their little corner of Belgium and their letters that arrived once a week—and which I quite often never bothered to open.

As for my teachers, they were just "over there." I used them to get the information I wanted; but, personally, there was nothing there for me. The headmistress existed only as someone whose office I had to sit outside of, wait to be called into, and walk away from after being told off for breaking some sort of rule. Pretty soon I "got" the way this system of punishment worked. You call the person in, you try to demoralize them, and then they leave. This only worked until I realized that this was all that was going to happen to me. Straightaway my rebelliousness got worse, because I knew that there was really nothing they could do to me beyond the lectures and the vague threats of punishment.

Part of my growing mischievousness was a tendency to push, push, push, waiting for someone to push back. But they didn't and they didn't and they didn't. I could stay out all night, and nothing would happen. I'd be called on the carpet the following day, and the headmistress would extract a promise that I wouldn't do this again, and I'd be dismissed.

The worst punishment they could think of was to make me stay in a classroom and do extra schoolwork—which I loved. That way, I got more of the teaching that I was thirsty for, and I didn't have to integrate with others.

Now I felt stronger. The things that had seemed crushing before couldn't get to me. Moreover I was teamed up with Suzzane, who was a rebel for her own reasons. And we added a third to our group when a new girl transferred into Suzzane's class. Her parents were Indian, but she had been born and raised in England.

She never seemed particularly interested in Indian culture. This disappointed me just a little, because I still remembered the Kipling stories about India from growing up. Except for the rich color of her skin, she seemed as English as Suzzane or myself.

Although she was only thirteen years old, we soon found out that this new girl was very well acquainted with grass. Though I was only eleven, I found smoking it helped me escape from my problems.

With my two friends, and our shared secret, I got through the Easter term much more easily. Still, underneath everything, was the intense feeling that I had to get out of that place. But I could not come up with any clear idea how to do it. I wasn't scared of the world "outside," because I didn't really know it. I realize now that was the one thing that saved me, and later let me do the things that I did. I wasn't indoctrinated with fear of the world. I had already traveled extensively, and I had never seen any limits on the world inside me.

I returned home to Belgium for the Easter holiday. Both my sisters were there this time, and we traveled a bit through Europe as a family. I was subdued much of the time—in large part because I was on even heavier doses of tranquilizers, prescribed by a doctor. This visit seemed remarkably uneventful, given the hysterical conditions over Christmas. I felt as ill at ease at home now as I did at school.

That holiday I broke all ties with my parents. Most children have an emotional link with home that stops them from doing most of the things they fantasize about doing—like packing a bundle of clothes and running away from home. Perhaps the final straw was that I had now alienated myself from my family.

The summer was also quiet, but now I had a real change to look forward to. In the fall I would be allowed to go into town to shop on weekends, accompanied by a senior girl. And Suzzane was a senior. To my mind this was the first step in the process of "getting out," as I called it.

I traveled around Europe with my parents a good deal during the summer holiday, and I had quite a nice time. But I felt sad: I knew I was leaving. I had no idea how; I had no idea when; but I sensed that I was leaving these people. In everything we did I felt a *good-bye*.

I returned to school for winter term. That first weekend I went with Suzzane into town. We didn't do much but window-shop and have lunch and sightsee, but I felt freer than I'd felt in ages.

The second weekend Suzzane went off with a newfound boyfriend, and left me to my own devices. I was quite happy, and went along to a record shop. The main floor was general-interest music; downstairs was reggae and other "black" music. That's where I headed, because I loved this sound. You could feel it. Listening to it, I felt I was communicating in a way that I hadn't since Singapore. Something in this music was bringing me back to life.

The salesman behind the counter was bopping in place to the music. He was about five feet nine inches, a bit skinny, with big blue eyes framed by bushy eyebrows and dark, curly hair. He had a neatly trimmed beard and a moustache. And he was dressed in "punk" fashion—long before this was really happening. He wore bright green

skintight trousers with bright red leather "kickers." His shirt was a
deep royal blue set off with a canary yellow tie. He was a rainbow, and
I thought he was just beautiful. His name was Simon.

We looked at each other, and his face broke out into a smile. I was
in heaven, thinking, "At last, I've met another real human being." For
a minute we just kind of danced to the music, and I was gone. We began to talk, and out of the blue he asked me if I wanted to go see *Hamlet*
the following weekend.

"Sure," I answered, without the least idea how I was going to do it.
We weren't allowed out at night. But I had already made up my mind
that I was going to the play.

Later I met Suzzane. On our way back to school I told her about Simon and his invitation. Suzzane's boyfriend was a Welshman whose
mode of transportation was a converted ambulance. Another classmate
of hers had become Suzzane's friend because she was dating Suzzane's
boyfriend's best friend. Together, we cooked up a scheme to get me out
to see *Hamlet*—and give them an evening out with their Welsh boyfriends. Because school was so boring to us, we really threw ourselves
into it.

The logistics were difficult. We had to arrange to get out of the
building past the matron on patrol, skirt the gardens and tennis courts
(which were well lit and overlooked by too many windows); and slip
through the main gate without alerting the gardener (a man we'd nicknamed "Weed"), whose cottage had been the gatehouse at one time.

Suzzane and her classmate friend lived on the second floor, so they
had to slip down an indoor fire escape to the kitchen. I had to slip out
of my room on the ground floor without alerting my roommates, who
still didn't like me at all. Then we had to go out the back door past the
rabbit hutches, and begin skirting the edge of the grounds, which were
huge. We were all dressed in nightshirts with our day clothes underneath, so that if we did run into anyone in the dormitory they
wouldn't guess what we were up to.

We had to dart across one stretch of open lawn, praying that no one
would spot us from inside. Just on the edge of this, while we were getting ready for the dash to freedom, the classmate dropped out. Now
she was faced with the business of getting back without getting caught,
and maybe blowing the whole adventure. And we were already running late, what with getting nervous, and stopping, and changing
plans on the spur of the moment.

But Suzzane and I decided we had to get on with it, because our
friends would be waiting down the street for us in the ambulance. We
took a breath and ran the last stretch to the shadow of a rhododendron

bush, beside the gate. I could feel my heart pounding, so I kept repeating, like a mantra, "Be the watcher, be the watcher. Just relax, just relax." This had all come from my childhood awareness and it helped calm me down.

Somehow we got the heavy gate open without alerting Weed. Then we ran down the little lane toward our getaway car, hoping that we wouldn't run into anyone on the street. It was a tiny village and everyone knew the school and its students; they would surely report us if they saw us.

We found the ambulance without being found out ourselves. When we arrived Suzzane went off with the Welshmen, while I went off to meet Simon at the theater.

I don't think I saw the play at all. I was infatuated with Simon, all wrapped up in him; and, I think now, I also sensed that he was going to be my escape. I can see now that I was already playing the game. I was in a detached mode where, although I was feeling very deep emotion, I wasn't ruled by it. I felt my life was going forward again, and that what I felt for Simon was a bonus—not the only goal.

After the play we went for a drink. Then he took me back to meet Suzzane and the ambulance at the point we had agreed upon earlier.

During *Hamlet*, I had already made up my mind that Simon was going to be my lifeline out of boarding school. I hadn't told him anything yet, but there wasn't the least doubt in my mind that he would go along with me—or that I could make him go along with my plan.

Somehow, we managed to sneak back inside the dormitory without getting caught. It was almost four o'clock in the morning, and we had to come back through the front door because the back entrance was locked.

After that I felt better at school, because I knew I was getting out. I had a secret; and with a secret you're strong. Of course I told Suzzane, because she was going to have to help me. But neither of us told anyone else.

The pieces all began to fall rather neatly into place. One of the day girls was having a party, and six of us were given weekend passes to go and stay the night at her house.

I invited Simon to the party. Afterwards, I coerced him into taking me back to his apartment. Although I had no formal training in sexual matters, I think a woman's instinct—and a man's, for that matter—instructs you in how you can use that power for your own purposes. Though I was still very young, and a virgin, with no clear sense of all that I was getting myself into, I knew this much: You could certainly get what you wanted from a man this way.

CHAPTER 4

Black Plastic Days

Simon shared a place with an artist, who was a lot of fun. I liked him a lot. There were always works of art in various stages of completion around the place.

At first we all lived together quite happily. I found the apartment beautiful: They had painted the counter in the kitchen red, the table was blue, everything was bright, primary colors. If you got inspired you could always paint another piece of furniture. There were a lot of prints of David Hockney paintings on the walls. I loved the whole environment.

I didn't go out very much, because we knew people would probably be inquiring about me. One day, after I'd been there about three weeks, I did chance going out, but returned home sooner than I had expected. I found Simon shooting up.

Up to that point, apart from the grass I'd smoked earlier, I really had no idea what drugs were. I didn't know that there were truly "bad" drugs, like heroin, as well as "kind of okay" ones, like pot. I was really intrigued with what he was doing. I begged him to let me try it for myself. "It's not for you," he told me. "What do you mean?" I asked. "If you can do it, I can do it."

He had just shot up, so he wasn't in much of a state to argue. Finally he just mumbled, "Okay, okay, okay." Then he did it to me, and I *loved* it. I didn't have any trip on me about whether heroin was "good" or "bad." I wasn't taking a great deal; but, for a body as young as mine, it hit hard. As I continued to shoot up, things started going downhill.

One other thing happened to change my circumstances: I came home one night to find Simon and his roommate in bed together. This didn't bother me particularly, since it was one of many things I had had no training about. My parents had always steered away from the subject of sex. Also, at this time such subjects were very much avoided when young children were around. Finally, I suppose, the notorious British reserve about such things added to the general silence.

I just naturally climbed into bed with them; and our relationship continued as a threesome. This state of affairs continued for almost two months, and I loved it. I was very happy with the arrangement.

Then the roommate seemed to get a little jealous, and things began to fall apart. In the face of the growing tension and imbalance, I felt myself losing the control and strength that had been so much a part of my decision to run away and to begin this new life.

I decided it was time to move on. I had been there about nine weeks, all told—and much of it had seemed good to me at the time.

It had also been a colorful time for me. I had become a part of the punk scene that was just emerging. I used to wear black-plastic trash bags—they were the in thing—with safety pins strung together as a belt.

I had my long hair dyed red, blue, and green in three sections. I went outrageous, and I *loved* it. I felt I was splashing my whole world with color—my hair, my clothes, the apartment where I was living. After all the drabness, the rules and regulations of the boarding school, I let the color in my soul run rampant.

I had made my decision to leave, so I hitchhiked down to London. It was the end of November and very cold when I arrived. I found my way to Earl's Court, which in those days was surrounded with "squats," derelict houses where drifters stayed for a day or a week or forever. I moved into one of these.

The tawdriness of things never really affected me, because I was still very much in my own world. I had blotted out most of the year at school. In fact, it's still hard for me to remember any negative sides of my stay in London. Looking back I can say, God, you must have lived in a pigsty. But my memories are of being able to take an old jar, pick a few daffodils, and watch it transform even the grungiest quarters into something nice and comfortable.

I've always had the ability—whether in the squats then, or the Ashram later—to not see what I didn't want to see. The time in London was even more blurry, because I was still on drugs. I wasn't at all selective; drugs were so free and easy that I bounced from smack to barbiturates to LSD to whatever, day to day. It seemed to make no difference to me.

Everything seemed spacey, adrift, in flux; time became so uncertain that I can't even say for sure precisely when I moved from London to

Oxford. At some point, though, I settled into a garret apartment in Summertown, in southern Oxford.

My favorite hangout was a record store (I seem to be drawn to these shops). It was below ground in a place called the Corn Market. There I met Christopher. He ran the store for a man I had never seen, but whom I later knew as Ian. Pretty soon I had gotten myself a part-time job, working there a few days a week, earning just enough money to live.

One of the steadier customers was a man whom I got to know over coffee. He asked me, "How would you feel about going over with me to Amsterdam, picking up some magazines, and bringing them back?" I thought, *Why not?* It seemed easy enough, and the money he was offering seemed really good.

So I went across with him. The magazines were pornographic. In those days the British anti-pornography laws were quite strict; the Dutch laws, by contrast, were *quite* incredible.

Making that run from Felixstow to Rotterdam became a regular thing. Because I looked so young and innocent, I was able to waltz through customs with bundles of magazines. At the time border agents never really bothered to check the trunk of your car. Later, when I was carrying contraband across to England, I never got stopped at all.

I think part of what protected me was my feeling that I couldn't be caught: I never felt guilty about what I was doing. I didn't feel I was doing anything wrong. I had lived in a "no-judgment" atmosphere—and, certainly, none of the people I was meeting were doing anything to change my mind about matters. "Good" was accomplishing what you set out to do, and "bad" was failing to deliver or getting caught. It was all as simple as that.

During the time at Oxford I kept in touch with Suzzane. She lived with her mother in the midlands. They had a wonderful high, old house, filled with staircases.

Her mother, Marion, was in trade. The place was hung with burgundy drapes and furnished with exquisite antiques. I felt I could explore for days on end and never see more than a fraction of the things there. She could tell me a story about each thing I picked up.

Marion was an elegant woman with clear olive skin, long blond hair, graceful tapering fingers, and deep blue eyes under eyebrows plucked to a thin line. She always had a lit cigarette in hand or within reach.

I felt Marion liked me without putting any conditions on me.

Through all of that time, when I was out of touch with my family, and embarked on a life that was growing more risky every day, there was a place to come home to that kept me from becoming hard.

I could drop in on them any time and be assured of a warm welcome, plenty of good food, and real companionship. Marion took life on her own terms; she dated who she wanted, made friends of anyone she found interesting, and opened up the world of her memories to Suzzane and me. She never probed too deeply into my lifestyle, or tried to impose her own set of rules, although if she would have been aware of how I was living she would have.

In her house, for a short time, I could become the child I had forgotten. The place was filled with warmth, noise, laughter, *magic*. Her parents also lived in the house; they were a real family. And when I went to visit, I became part of that family too.

Life continued quite differently for me back in Oxford.

I transported the bulk of contraband in the trunk of my car. I never had the least problem until one night in Oxford. I was speeding, and got pulled over by a policeman. I remember thinking, *Oh, God, this is it,* because I had just come from the Netherlands.

He made me climb out of the car. In England, if an officer stops you for speeding, he can routinely search the vehicle. So this policeman said, "I'd like to look in the trunk of your car." And I said, "Oh, yes, of course." I stood there talking while I fumbled for the key to the trunk (I was high on something at the time, too). Abruptly, he said, "Okay, you can go." He never even bothered to look in the trunk. It was as if he had forgotten all about it—which was incredibly lucky for me, because I hadn't made any effort to hide the stuff at all.

I decided to stop running it myself, and began to hire others to transport it for me, while I ran my own show. And I kept in touch with Simon, who would sell it up in Derby—I had really quite a network going. I would take delivery on what came in from the Netherlands, and would distribute it to people who came to my apartment to pick it up, and I never got busted once.

However, a frightening tragedy woke me up and put an abrupt end to that phase of my life.

I was going out at the time with a man named Steven. Late one evening we were in a field just outside of Summertown. He had never taken heroin before, and he wanted to do it. I kept saying, "No, there's no point." But he nagged me—very much the way I had begged Simon to let me try back in Derby. He said that he wanted to score it himself—there's very much a ceremony involved with use of this drug—

so he went off with his friend John.

They came back a little later with the junk they had got, and only two syringes. We were still in the field, and they insisted on shooting up first. So they did. But the stuff had been cut with rat poison.

Steven died in my arms. John died halfway to the road, trying to get help.

Somehow I found my way back to my apartment. A friend told me when the funeral was going to be held. I demanded to know whether something was going to be done about it. And my friend just looked at me, a bit surprised, and said that the parents wanted it all hushed up, so that's that. The whole incident was just forgotten.

That, for me, was another turning point. I remember sat in my apartment and told myself, *Either you stop now, or you go into it completely.* Up to that point I had wanted to find out how far I could push my body, how far I could push *everything* in the world, before something would stop me—death, or some great hand from somewhere, or a voice that would say, "This is the limit, and you've reached it." But it never seemed to happen, so I pushed a little further.

For about three months after Steven died, I threw myself into whatever drugs I could get my hands on. I'd made a great deal of money during these years, but I'd never spent it on anything. I had no bank accounts: The money was all just *stuffed* into the apartment—there were piles and piles of cash everywhere.

After three months I moved into another district of Oxford (though I continued paying rent on the other apartment). This place was so tiny that you could only open the door part-way before it ran into the bed. It had a little two-ring hotplate and a record player.

I brought only two records with me whan I moved: Patti Smith's *Horses* and *Radio Ethiopia*. And I stayed in that apartment for months without leaving. I just listened to one side after the other of these records. During that time I felt my mind going through one transformation after another. It was, in many ways, the most intense experience I had ever undergone.

A friend brought me food enough to live, and a barbiturate, which I had become totally dependent upon. I'll always associate those blue-and-red capsules with that time in my life. The only food I would eat was fried rice and bean sprouts covered with soy sauce.

I had only this narrow bed, and the small window that didn't give much light. I would lie there all day, listening to these records over and over, with the record player on automatic repeat, so I didn't even have to get up and lift the needle.

The changes I went through during this period were incredible. At times I seemed able to leave my body. I felt I was engaging in experiments of self-understanding and silent communication that reminded me of my days in Singapore.

But, where that earlier time had somehow involved all the colors of the rainbow, this time in Oxford gave me the overwhelming impression of *black plastic* everywhere. Maybe that came from listening to the vinyl records over and over. During that time, I went through the dark side of being in silence with myself.

Then, though I don't remember exactly what prompted me to get out of the apartment, I *do* recall reaching the decision to go out. I was thin to the point of ghastliness. I wore tight-tight bluejeans, black over-the-knees boots, and a sloppy joe sweater that was red, blue, and green—to match my hair. I walked out of the apartment, and never went back again.

For two days I just wandered around Oxford. My parents were living just outside of Oxford.

I hitchhiked to London, where there was a Lou Reed concert on. I bought a ticket and took my seat. When the curtains opened, the stage was covered with hundreds and hundreds of TV sets. Lou Reed came onstage—he was in *his* heroin-blotto days at the time—stumbled, picked himself up, and sat down on the edge of the stage. He began singing "Satellite of Love," about how he loves to watch things on TV.

He could hardly sing. At that point I stumbled into the bathroom myself, deciding I needed a hit of something. I remember the white, white tile, the highly polished wood of the door, and the white porcelain door handle. I was standing in the stall, all set to shoot up, with all the stuff unwrapped, when I heard a voice inside me say, *If you do it now, you're no longer innocent.*

And I really "got it."

Without any great drama, I just turned away from the toilet, left everything where it was, walked out of the restroom, and out of the concert hall. I went to Victoria Station, which was very near where the concert was. And I remember wondering, "Where do I go now?"

Leaving Singapore had been one phase; school was another; now this phase was finished for me. All the money I had, with the exception of a couple of hundred pounds in my pocket, was back in Oxford. But a return to Oxford merely to pick up the cash was no longer an option. London felt like no option either. It was time for a complete move, but my mind kept revolving around the question, "Where do I go now?"

In that moment I realized that, through everything so far, I had still hung onto a quality of innocence. Something in the core of my being hadn't been corrupted. All I knew was that I had to go *someplace*; I needed an environment. I didn't realize I would have withdrawal symptoms, that physical uprising that happens when you stop heroin cold turkey. Somehow, I thought I could just walk away from it all.

I made my way to the M-1 motorway, and began hitchhiking north to Nottingham. I spent the night traveling, and got up there just before morning. I went to a squat that I had used before—a huge old Victorian stone house, with huge rooms.

Luckily the man who helped start me in all this was one of the persons living there. I told him I needed a room, and what I was trying to do. By this time—it was four and a half hours or more since I'd left the junk behind—I was beginning to sweat and go into withdrawal. I realized it was going to hit me hard, and the fact that I hadn't eaten anything in ages wasn't helping.

He found me a room, but I quickly realized I wasn't going to be able to go through this alone. All the people around me were junkies, or people who weren't going to want to be around someone who was going through withdrawal. Someone, I was sure, would simply knock me up with something to keep me quiet, once things had run their course a bit further.

Somehow I hung on, and kept myself from disturbing the other squatters. But things were getting worse. On an impulse, I made my way to a phonebooth, got my father's number through information, and called the house. He answered the phone and I said, "I'm in Nottingham, and I really need your help."

And he said (though the full impact of it didn't hit me until weeks later), "I know. I'll be right there."

I went back to the house, and this man stayed with me until my father came. After that, it's all a bit of a blur; but I remember my father picking me up, putting me into his car, and driving me back down to a hospital, where he signed me a drug rehabilitation program.

Before I went to the hospital, my father took me home for a few days. It was a strange and difficult time for all of us.

My sisters were away at school—I didn't see them again until years later. It was a very difficult time for my mother; to suddenly have me turn up in the condition I was in filled her with relief, resentment, and downright confusion. I felt it was harder for her to deal with the things I had done during these years than it would have been to know I was dead. It took us quite a few years before we could communicate with each other. On those infrequent occasions when I would go to spend a weekend with them, the tension, the endless searching for *something* to say to each other that wouldn't open a new wound or reopen an old one, was nearly unbearable.

My father remained aloof. I couldn't get him to say more about those things he had hinted at when he had gathered me out of the squat. He concentrated on keeping the uneasy peace between my mother and me; but whatever closeness we had shared that night was gone. At times I thought I had only imagined him saying he had been aware of what I had been going through with the drugs and all.

It was always a relief to return to my place at the detox center. Those visits home reinforced how far I had come from that phase of my life, and the fact that I was in a clean-up program signaled the closing of yet another chapter. I felt on the brink of something new and exciting, though I hadn't the least idea what it might be. But I had the certainty that whatever was coming next was going to be extraordinary— and I knew that I was going to throw myself wholeheartedly into the next round of playing the game that my life had been from the first.

One day my father came to visit. Right off I asked him, "Was I dreaming that you said, 'I know'? And how did you know where the house was? I didn't tell you."

He indicated that he had also been in touch with one of the people there.

This blew me away; but, when I tried to get more out of him, he refused to say anything else.

So I began what was supposed to be a long "clean-up" program.

This hospital's drug rehabilitation program involved going cold turkey. I was assigned to a room, and my hair was cut as a kind of visual reinforcement that I was no longer involved with the world of junkies, longhairs, that whole subculture. I still remember the shock of waking, seeing myself in the mirror, and asking myself, *Who is this?*

We also had to do therapy groups. One of the psychiatric nurses in my small therapy group was a *sannyasin,* and he was also extremely attractive. We got to know each other and like each other. After only a few weeks in the program, he asked me if I would like to spend a weekend at his home. This was totally illegal in terms of nurse-patient relationships, but it didn't faze me in the least. I liked this person; he was open in a way that was all too rare.

So, one weekend I went to visit him. I had to forge a letter from my parents to the hospital saying that I was going to spend the weekend at their home. This was an easy deception, because my folks lived so close that the postmark on the letter was no cause for suspicion. The letter said that I would be taking the bus, that my parents would meet me, and so forth. Since I would usually call my parents, rather than the other way around, there was little likelihood they would find out what I was up to. I *was* taking a risk, but the business of risk-taking has never stopped me once I've decided on a course of action.

My friend had given me directions for finding his home. When I got off the bus I discovered the address I had been given was a beautiful sixteenth-century farmhouse. It is in a tiny old village with two pubs, a local school, a church, and picturesque little cottages.

For a few moments I stood by the gates, where the bus had left me, and stared at the white farmhouse with black trim. Just beyond the gate were two red-brick barns, and, past another barn at the back, gardens that seemed to go on forever.

But I couldn't see anybody around. I went up to the front door and rang the doorbell, but I still couldn't get any answer. So I opened the door, and stood facing a large stairway and a hall running back to a kitchen. After a moment a woman with dark hair started down the stairs. As soon as she saw me, she said, "Oh, you must be Kate," and made me feel right at home.

This woman put her arm around me and led me back to the kitchen, which was warm after the cold winter weather outside. I asked her where my friend was, using the name I knew him by at the hospital. She said, "Oh, his name's *Kamul*."

I soon found out that the farmhouse was a commune—at this point I didn't even know what a commune was! In the commune members were followers of an Indian guru or teacher named Bhagwan Shree Rajneesh. They were called *sannyasins*, "seekers of enlightenment." In Hinduism, a *sannyasin* is one who has given up all worldly attachments and values— including the ego, represented by words like "I" or "mine"—in favor of a life of meditation, which brings you to zero, "no-mind."

It seemed that at the hospital, a lot of the nurses were *sannyasins*, although they didn't make it generally known while they were working.

Of course I knew nothing of any of this. The name "Kamul" didn't surprise me much—none of the names did. I think it was because I had grown up in Singapore, where one often heard names like those the *sannyasins* had. I guess too that everyone I met was wearing the red or orange clothing that Rajneesh followers wore, but this really didn't register. They didn't have a lot of money, so most of the clothes were well-worn or faded and didn't seem at all different from the semi-hippie clothes I had been used to seeing. Anu told me Kamul had gone to the pub to play darts, but was due back very shortly. She invited me to sit down while she went on fixing dinner.

I wandered into the dining room off the kitchen, and discovered a long, long table with fourteen chairs around it. I thought, *Kamul certainly has a large family.* I still didn't get it. The walls were lined with shelves jammed with books. I ran my fingers lightly along row after row of volumes, delighted, recalling my fascination with literature and learning.

I pulled one book off at random and settled into an armchair in one corner that faced out tall windows into the garden. The book I had picked out was *The Mustard Seed*, by Bhagwan. I looked at the front, which was a picture of Bhagwan, and thought to myself, *I know this man.*

I opened to the first page, began reading, and quickly discovered that I liked it very much. I felt like I was coming home; perhaps it reminded me of something I had heard years before. I finished that page, then closed the book and began rocking in the armchair, feeling very much at peace.

Anu was in the kitchen, making two monstrous shepherd's pies in big stainless steel pans. The place had energy, yet it was very, very quiet. An Old English sheepdog, Eric, wandered in and sat at my feet. A jar of freshly picked wildflowers rested in the center of the table. Everything felt homey, comfortable, cared for.

Slowly, people started to drift in toward the kitchen. They added to the warmth I felt about the whole place. My impressions were of light, laughter, dancing, and especially singing. There was a piano, and we sang all sorts of tunes that I hadn't heard for years, like, "My old man said follow the band . . ."

Kamul and I had the whole weekend together, and it was wonderful. We spent it going to the pub or walking in the country. Because there were fourteen people and two children in the house, it was lively pretty much all the time. I enjoyed every minute.

On Sunday night I returned to the hospital and the next morning I went to group. Kamul was there, but of course, we couldn't say anything to each other. Sitting there, I began to realize just how important Kamul was becoming to me. I felt like I had discovered my first pure love relationship. It was nothing like I had experienced with Simon or anyone else; it was like a fresh beginning. I felt I was just growing into becoming a woman.

In group there were hippie junkies and housewife junkies and alcoholics and people with all sorts of other problems. I found myself getting caught up in an idea of "us" and "them." I had had this weekend, filled with light and laughter, which I couldn't talk about; I had to sit in therapy with people who could only talk about problems.

But the groups proved a good training ground for the game. Up to then, though I had been extremely successful by worldly standards—at least in terms of making money and not getting caught—I had never really felt I was moving the pieces in the world I was creating. But, sitting in these groups, I discovered a new skill.

I found that I could actually *know* what these other people were like inside. I would become empty in myself, and *become* that woman or that man across from me or beside me in the group. I could become them so completely that I felt I had actually lived their lives up to that very minute. As time went on I found I could tell an extraordinary amount just by reading faces or noticing the clothes people wore or the way they moved. Some of this, I'm sure, came from my early training; but I used my time in those groups to fine-tune these skills.

One woman in group was plump, but very sexual in her way. She had peroxide-blond hair and huge eyes. I nicknamed her "Bunny," because that was what she was to me. You could just imagine her in frilly things, mating with her rather plump husband, just as bunny rabbits might.

She was in for drinking and suicidal tendencies, but I recognized that she was a playful, colorful person who had kept running up against a dead, colorless world. She didn't have the strength to go out and really live; she let the world run over her like a big black tire and grind all the life out of her.

The group leader was bald on top but he had wispy sidehair, and hairy ears and nostrils. He also had an endearing smile. Every now and again he would doze off during group, then wake up suddenly with an "Um, um," and ask, "What would your mother say to this?" This was his pat answer to cover his lapses. We developed a very warm friendship in our silent communication.

I was infatuated with Kamul, but I couldn't forgive him for spacing out in group. I seemed able to forgive the leader; but I always felt Kamul should be more vibrant and either inject more into the proceedings himself, or at least wake people up more.

Another member of the group who especially interested me was Sara. She was addicted to Valium. She had been an airline hostess, and was married to a rather mundane man. I had seen him once or twice, on those occasions when a husband or wife was brought into the group. You could only read apprehension in her eyes, most of the time. But sometimes I could get her out into the garden and we'd sit, and I'd get her to laugh. She had a beautiful laugh, but she would shut it down almost as fast as it began.

She had raised two children, but had grown more and more dependent on Valium. She just couldn't cope. She wasn't cut out to be a housewife; to her, being an air hostess was glamorous. It was easy to picture her flirting with her passengers, keeping them happy, traveling to all sorts of places and loving every minute of it.

Sara was one of those people who had built her life on "shoulds." Her children were delightful, but she might much better have been an aunt to them—flying in from exotic places, bringing them little gifts, taking them to tea or the cinema. But it wasn't her energy to be a mother, doing the washing and cleaning and cooking.

I could actually experience who she was. I could move into the persona of each member of my group. I could see that Sara needed to start by forgiving herself, permitting herself to say, "I can't be your wife and I can't be your mother: What I need to be is a playgirl of the skies. That's my dance in this world."

She went home one weekend and tried to kill herself by jumping out of the bedroom window. When I saw her again, she had had electric shock treatment. I couldn't get her to smile ever again; she was just like a machine. It really sickened me to hear them say, "She's better now."

As I moved through these various personas, a certain part of me kept saying, It's not going to happen to me. I knew that I had my own dance to dance. But I could see that unless I could learn to become an adept at moving through the spaces that ran between these weird, "normal" people, I'd be trapped in their world.

Unless I could learn to play the game, put on the different faces and disguises, keep the secret dancer inside me hidden, I felt I would be destroyed. This was the beginning of the survival training I knew I was going to need to make it in the world. With this understanding came the first glimpse of how I could learn to move people as pieces in my game plan.

One man in the group was a logician, and he had short-circuited on being a logic computer. Another man, a time-and-motion manager, was a truly kind man. He would sit with his hands on his belly, like Mole in *The Wind in the Willows*. He was married to a shrew who spent her time nagging at him, and he was obsessed with guilt.

All of these people had failed in their different ways to dance or play the game. These sessions were like school for me: I did not have to go out into the world to learn what to do or not to do; these people had lived these lives for me. I learned from their failures some of the steps I could take toward success in my own life.

On another level I learned to understand at a glance what "demons" or "angels" ruled these people, and to intuit what would make or destroy them. This helped make clear to me the ground rules that would help *me* play the game: what to bring into my life and what to let go that would allow me to dance my dance without causing ripples that might ultimately come back and drown me.

I would often get sad and depressed moving in and out of other people's skins; I could see that their potential for laughing and dancing was tremendous, but they'd been born into the wrong world or time. They'd picked a hard road to follow with their beings.

Somehow, I managed to keep some laughter in me—not laughter *at* people, but *with* them. The detox center was part of a mental hospital, and things sometimes were surreal. Sometimes people with no clothes on would get lost and wander into the midst of our little psychodramas.

I really began to appreciate how I'd been brought up; I began to see that I really had a hell of a gift just being me, because of what I was getting out of these situations.

Later in the week Kamul invited me back to the commune for the next weekend. I went through the same business of forging a letter from my parents to get myself released. Then off I went and had a wonderful time.

I became especially friendly with a woman called Seema. When she smiled, she had beautiful dimples, and her eyes twinkled. She was a kind of earth mother. Her feet were always solidly in touch with the ground, as though she were drawing strength from it.

On Sunday I went into the meditation room. It amuses me now to realize that, even then, I *still* didn't know that these people followed a man named Rajneesh. Nobody talked about it much in those days; it hadn't become the big deal that it did later.

Everyone in the room was hugging Kamul and crying, so I asked what was going on. Seema told me that he was going to India to be with his master. "Who's his master?" I wanted to know. She told me, "Bhagwan," and showed me a picture.

"You mean this man's alive?" I asked. I guess I assumed that to have his picture on the book meant he was dead. But I didn't think much more about it, because I was so upset that Kamul was going away.

So I rode up with him on the bus to Reading, where he was to leave for the airport. Just before he left he wrote on a slip of paper:

17 Koregaon Park

Poona

India

I thought this address was some house where he was going to stay. It never dawned on me that this was where Bhagwan was. I had just assumed his "master" was the sort of teacher who would float in and out of a town or city. I really didn't know much about it at all.

The next day I went back to group, listened to everybody's problems again, and decided that, without Kamul, I couldn't take any more of it. So on Wednesday morning I walked out of the hospital for good.

I hitchhiked to Oxford, where I looked up a good friend named Clive. I told him I wanted to go to India, and he gave me about fifty pounds. Then I hitchhiked up to the university, because Suzzane was there. I brought her the records I had, and a coat, and a rainbow-colored tee-shirt. (These were the things my father had gathered up from my apartment and brought to me when I was in the hospital. When he went to my apartment, no money was found, and he had to spend an afternoon scrubbing graffiti off the walls.)

I told Suzzane I was going to India to follow this man, Kamul, whom I loved. As a token gesture she bought all my stuff. She gave me over one hundred pounds.

After that I went back to the commune, because they had told me the door would always be open to me as a friend of Kamul's. They gave me a warm welcome, and were delighted that I had decided to go to India. But I started to cry, because I couldn't afford to go. The ticket was something like two hundred pounds, and I'd had to spend a part of what Clive and Suzzane had given me traveling up and back.

I was still crying when the phone rang. It was Clive. He could tell I was upset and asked me why. When I explained about the ticket, he said, "Don't worry, it's all taken care of. You shouldn't be in pain like that." He gave me the balance of the money I needed.

I spent two days at the commune. As a kind of farewell party the night before I was flying out, some of the people there took me up to Oxford for a Joan Armatrading concert.

The next day I flew off to India. I still had my passport from when I was eleven—they're good for ten years. The only instruction my friends gave me was this: When I got to Bombay, I was to go to Dada Taxi rank, and ask to go to 17 Koregaon Park.

Part 3

POONA, INDIA: THE ASHRAM

CHAPTER 5

17 Koregaon Park

I got into Bombay around ten o'clock in the morning, after an exhausting flight from London. The year was 1976 and I was fifteen years old.

As I stepped off that plane, closing my eyes and breathing in the warm, moist air, my childhood years came flooding back. It was as if the ocean, which had once been such a friend to a younger me, rushed back, washing away the barnacles accumulated over the years. I felt welcomed and awed by India, which has played host to so many of the great masters: Buddha, Bodhidharma, and more recently, Mahatma Gandhi, a man who found peace in his own being. *Yes,* I told myself, *this is a new beginning.* In a few hours I'd be joining my friend Kamul, and this land would be the place for us to follow our individual paths—and, at the same time, discover ourselves as a couple.

I selected a likely looking vehicle from those drawn up at Dada Taxi rank. These taxies are the only conveyances that will make the drive to Poona, a semi-industrial city about one hundred miles southeast of Bombay. The taxi driver and I immediately began the usual haggling over the fare. Though this is actually fixed, anyone who has traveled in Asia—or Mexico, for that matter—knows that this is one of the delightful, obligatory games that everyone seems to have a good time playing. It doesn't matter whether you're traveling first-class or steerage—out here, you're on your own! Fortunately, memories of my early years in the Orient returned; I knew how to conduct such business.

The game, typically, was over when both the driver and I had lost our voices. I had also managed to scrape the palm of my hand raw from beating on the cab for emphasis, and suffered a touch of sunstroke. But I hadn't done too badly: The price was only a little above what I had been told I should pay.

The moment we struck our bargain and I was aboard, the taxi driver took off. Feeling the cab lurch and listening to it rattle along, I can't say

I was sure I was going to make it—but I was excited to be underway and moving closer to my goal with every heart-stopping sway or near-collision.

The road to Poona is breathtaking—well, not the road itself (*that* leaves something to be desired), but the landscape it winds through. On either side lie bright-green rice paddies. As the road climbs higher, tall trees of deeper green mark the fringes of uncultivated jungle; through their massed trunks you can sometimes glimpse impressive waterfalls, cascading down into gullies, roaring into streams that will provide a major means of travel, irrigate fields, serve as laundry for countless villages and cities, and refresh hot and thirsty multitudes.

As the taxi rocketed along the road I found it was better not to look ahead—I was apt to see a huge, gaily painted lorry bearing down on me. But whether I looked or not, I was flung first to one side of the cab, then the other, as the driver narrowly avoided disaster by swerving to the side of the road.

I was able to get beyond a fervent prayer that I and my life were not about to part company. Then I was able to spare some compassion for a poor woman, dressed in an old, patched *sari*, who looked as if she was about to lose her hold on the water jug balancing on top of her in the wake of nearly being run down by my taxi.

As far as the driver was concerned, the crisis was over. Still shaking, I looked back along the road to see the lorry bouncing into the distance, ready for upcoming near-misses. Painted across the receding rear doors the inscription "Horn Please" was just visible through the dust it raised. It reminded me of a flirtatious woman sashaying along inviting wolf whistles—or a bully seeking applause for a game of "chicken" in which he has bested someone with less nerve (but more brain).

Righting her water jug, the woman in the patched *sari* continued on her way as if she had no part in this little drama. A quick inventory proved that I was still in one piece—and hoping to remain that way. With a great deal of relief I realized that the driver's frantic gestures were not signaling another imminent accident, but our arrival on the outskirts of Poona.

The taxi ground to a halt outside 17 Koregaon Park, where Bhagwan had begun his commune in 1974. I paid the driver our agreed-upon fare and wriggled out of the plastic seat, which by then felt half-melted in the afternoon heat.

It was now about two o'clock, the hottest part of the day. As the taxi roared off I began to take in my surroundings. I was standing at the midpoint of a short street, punctuated with tall banyan trees on either side. Many of these framed the gateways to elegant houses. Later I learned this had been a "Hill Station," a district built as residential housing for Army Officers when the British Raj flourished.

Looking over the hedgerows that lined the street, one could see the tops of what must have been very grand houses in Queen Victoria's time. Although many of them now seemed unkempt, they still managed to convey a very "Somerset Maugham" quality to me.

Directly in front of me were two huge teakwood gates. They were carved with elaborate flowers whose centers were engraved brass. The gates were supported by white marble gateposts and surmounted by a marble archway, in the center of which hung a huge crystal chandelier. Black marble letters, inset into the archway, spelled out the inscription: SHREE RAJNEESH ASHRAM. Beside the legend was the symbol:

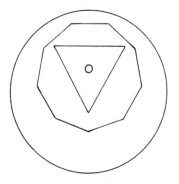

Stretching away from the gates in either direction were the beginning of what would later be impressive hedgerows. At this time, however, the shrubbery was barely four feet high, and looked oddly out of proportion to the massive gates.

Through the gates I could see a broad path of poured cement studded with polished pebbles in brown, slate gray, and earth-toned reds, giving a feeling of richness. Bordering the path were poinsettias, elephant ears, hibiscus, pansies, and other plants. The breeze blowing back toward me from the gardens felt refreshing; this was because the grounds were kept so well watered that the rising dampness from the flower beds cooled and moistened the normally arid air.

Twin gatehouses of white marble, round with teak roofs, faced each other just inside the gates. One was the reception; the other, which hadn't been completed, was going to be the bookstore.

Everything—the colorful flowers, the green grass and leaves, the revitalizing breeze—wove together in an instant to suggest to me *new beginnings.*

I'm not sure how long I stood there just staring, lightheaded from my trip, absorbing the sights and smells and sounds, before a man came to open the gates. He was a very tall, solidly built, good-looking Indian Sikh, wearing cotton *dhoti*, baggy pants, a loose tunic, and a turban—all of bright orange. He reminded me of films like *The Jungle Book* and *Gunga Din*; everything had a wonderful, fairy-tale quality—or that freshness and clarity that you'd expect to find on a movie set.

I later learned his name was Sant. He was looking at me with huge eyes, but I couldn't read anything in his expression. It was not threatening or particularly inviting—just calm, open, attentive. He gave an impression of solidness, of being truly grounded.

I didn't expect him to speak English but I thought I'd give it a go anyway, having no other option at hand. I picked up my bag, took a few steps toward him, and asked, "Do you know a person named Kamul? He should have arrived a few days ago. He's expecting me—only, maybe not quite so soon."

Sant looked down—he was a good deal taller than me—and fixed me with his eyes. Then, without uttering a word, he pointed me along the footpath in front of me. Still feeling as though I were playing a role in a film (although not at all sure of the part), I once again picked up my single, small bag and headed in the direction he'd indicated.

To the left of me, at the end of a small branching path that ran beside the bookstore-to-be, was the start of Buddha Hall. (Later on the names for all the parts of the Ashram were explained to me. Every building was named after a saint or mystic; it was interesting to discover, on reflection, that each department housed in these structures took on the character of its namesake in one way or another.)

At the time of my arrival Buddha Hall was a concrete rectangle enclosing an area only a third of the size it was to become later, when the Ashram grew to its full capacity. Then the structure was roofless; the walls were not complete; iron reinforcement rods jutted up against the intense blue sky. Already, however, the flower beds around it had been laid out, and some of the plants were in bloom.

Beyond the partially completed hall were Buddha Hall huts. These tiny buildings has been thrown up quickly to house the growing numbers of people living on the grounds, until the more elaborate dormitories were completed. The huts were bamboo frames supporting walls of woven sheets of split bamboo called *shitiva*. Each had a thatch of bamboo rushes.

On my right, beyond the border of shrubs and flowers, was a quarter-acre with the beginnings of a lawn and rock garden. The center of this area was a circular pool with jets around the circumference that created a fountain, shooting plumes of water high into the air. Although it looked a little out of place, set amongst the newly planted seedlings it gave a promise of what a beautiful garden this would be when all the plants were fully grown.

This appealing corner of the Ashram was named Rada gardens. The Hindu religion honors Rada as Krishna's consort—he represents the feminine side of the male, she represents the male side of the female. And, through mutual exploration, they are said to have reached *nirvana*.

As Krishna became more and more aware of himself and the forces surrounding him, he was supposed to have been able to manifest miracles, creating wonders from thin air. There are hundreds of these tales, but my favorite has always been the legend that, as he became enlightened, he brought into being a great silver-and-blue waterfall from the sky. As it touched the ground it turned into a stairway, which Krishna and Rada ascended to heavenly bliss, freed forever of the confines of the body.

Once a year the Hindus celebrate the enlightenment of the two, commemorating the belief that these heavenly persons continually shower their bliss upon the earth from worlds beyond.

Turning from Rada gardens on that first day I was immediately confronted with wide steps sweeping up to the main entrance of a building, whose white walls shimmered in the hot sunlight. As I shaded my eyes against the glare I could make out plate-glass doors framed in dark teak. To the left of these the name KRISHNA HOUSE was carved into the stone. On either side of the stairs were massed elephant ears and blossoms nearly bursting with color in the intense sunlight.

Mounting to the terrace outside the doors I glanced to my right, where I could look in through floor-to-ceiling plate-glass windows to an office. A large desk of light-colored wood faced two generously cushioned armchairs; the more severe chair behind the desk was set on a dais.

Eager to find Kamul, I pushed through the doors and into the reception area just inside. The only furnishings were a table and very comfortable-looking chairs lining the walls on either side. Through a glass door on the right I got another view of the office. A long room off to the right was filled with desks, and I soon found out it was the accounting office. Krishna House was the administrative nexus for the whole Ashram—the place that was expected to—and *did*—create miracles on a regular basis.

The first thing I noticed as I entered was the air-conditioning. No other buildings in the Ashram—with the exception of Bhagwan's room in Lao Tzu House—were air-conditioned. The contrast with the warmth and humidity outside made me feel I'd entered a new kingdom.

From the moment I had stepped through the main gates I was aware of the tranquility about the place—and, at a deeper level, a thrill, a vibration. Everyone I talked to later recalled this double sensation of calmness shot through with energy.

Several women were working in the reception area—all of them characteristically beautiful and moving with a grace that turned each step, each gesture into a work of art. Later I was able to recognize how long someone had been at the Ashram by the depth of grace and the simplicity of movement they displayed.

Even people who might normally be considered ordinary seemed to radiate a special kind of beauty. It was a phenomenon I was able to watch happen in myself over the years I lived in Poona. The more relaxed and content I became, the more I could feel myself glowing and discovering a previously unknown beauty that was revealed in my movements, my voice, even my face.

In the Ashram the rhythm of our bodies, our tone of voice, even our facial expressions would reveal just how centered and completely in touch with ourselves we were. This was a whole language of being I was to become fluent with over the years—one that would enable me, and other adepts in this art, to effect changes in people and guide them in situations they might not normally have put themselves in, and responses they might have thought themselves incapable of at other times.

The more involved I became with the day-to-day workings of the Ashram, the clearer it was that this creation of an atmosphere of serenity, physical beauty, *perfection* in even the smallest details was part of the game the Ashram's key players were engaged in. Controlling how the Ashram and its inhabitants were perceived by the world at large set the groundwork for all dealings with that world outside the walls—the major gameboard.

One receptionist greeted me, came over, put her arm around my shoulders, and guided me to a soft, comfortable chair. Under that cool touch my feelings of being hot, dusty, weary, sloughed away. Even the weight of the case in my hand suddenly seemed less. I relaxed completely into the welcoming cushions and just sat, watching the efficient yet unhurried activity around me, noting that all the women in the offices wore long, flowing dresses in various shades of saffron. These were not robes but handsomely styled garments, which in their very design and fluidity reflected harmony and grace. These women seemed supremely relaxed, content, and confident.

They wore no makeup; their hair was generally worn long. From the coloring of their hair and skin, and the shape of their eyes, it was easy to see they represented a variety of nationalities. Together they gave an impression of health, vitality, *aliveness*—all overlaid with a deep sense of peace.

I had only the haziest idea of the work that was going on around me. I was here for one reason: to find Kamul. Though I had seen the words SHREE RAJNEESH ASHRAM at the gates, I didn't know what an "Ashram" was. Though I had seen the name Rajneesh on the copy of *The Mustard Seed* back at the commune, I had forgotten it in all that had happened between that moment and my arrival in Poona. Also, at the commune, people spoke of "Bhagwan" rather than "Rajneesh." Even the orange clothing all around me in Krishna House didn't register.

I guessed the place was a monastery of some sort. The saffron-colored garments reminded me somewhat of the robes worn by Buddhist monks and nuns. And, like those Asian temples I had visited as a child, the Ashram brought time to a halt. I lost track of how long I actually sat in the reception area.

The greeting and acceptance without questioning that were extended to me (I later understood) came from the fact that I was wearing a *mala* around my neck; this necklace indicated I was a follower of Bhagwan. The *mala* is a familiar part of many Eastern religious traditions, where each of its 108 beads is used as a counter for repeating a particular *mantra*, a sort of hymn or prayer, somewhat in the fashion of the Christian rosary. In the Ashram its use was symbolic, the outward sign of a disciple. It had been given to me by Seema as a going-away present when I left England to follow Kamul. She told me it would keep me safe in my travels, so I wore it as a kind of lucky charm. Though everyone else I had met so far at the Ashram was wearing a *mala*, it didn't dawn on me that this had guaranteed me a warm welcome. Everyone assumed from the first I was a *sannyasin*, and knew what the place was all about.

After a while I began to think they had forgotten me. Everyone was preoccupied with tasks, and I felt uncomfortable about interrupting. Impatiently, I pushed through the doors back outside, thinking I'd have a look around for myself.

Seated on the thick bannister beside the steps was a Greek woman, whom I later knew as Mukta—and who was one of Bhagwan's confidantes. She was an older woman with long grey hair, which she piled upon her head for coolness. "Hullo," she greeted me in a deep, slow, raspy voice, looking up from the clipboard she had been studying. In heavily accented words she asked, "Are you looking for something?"

"Yes," I replied, "I'm looking for Kamul. Do you know him?"

"No, but *he* might know where he is."

"Oh," I said, a bit confused, "Who is *he?*"

"Why, *Bhagwan*," she said, clearly surprised at my question, "You can go and ask *him.*"

"Fine," I said, "Where do I find *him?*"

She stared at me for a moment, but only said, "Well, you can wait a few days and go and see *him.*"

"But I don't *have* a few days," I explained. "I've come all the way from England, and I want to find Kamul. If you think *he* will know, then I'd like to see *him now.*" I assumed that she was referring to someone who knew everything that was going on—like the town gossip.

"Well, actually, you could go this evening," she drawled.

"Okay," I agreed, sensing that this was the best arrangement I was going to be able to make.

"Go home and take a shower. Wash your hair and freshen up. Make yourself feel good. Then, tonight, you can come there—" she pointed around the corner of Krishna House along the path to a pair of huge, black wrought-iron gates. "Wait outside those at six o'clock," she told me, "and someone will take you in."

I nodded, then asked, "Is there a place I can stay?"

"Go back to the main gates," she said, "The people there will be able to help you."

I thanked her, and went back to the front gate reception. They asked me what my budget was (I had about fifty pounds left), then directed me to a place called the Blue Nile in town. As I left I noticed Sant was still standing there, for all the world like a mummy from an old Hammer film. For some reason I got the impression that he was smiling inside.

I didn't know it, but those first moments at the Ashram had sealed my involvement in its life, its growth, and the game. I had a feeling of well-being, joy, *belonging*. From somewhere a bird called out with the same distinctive hoot that I had heard so many years before in the botanical gardens in Singapore. My fondly remembered childhood years and this new, yet familiar, present flowed into each other. This continuity closed over the unpleasant years in between like water smoothing jagged stones. I felt healed, whole, and excited—standing at the threshold of an extraordinary experience I wouldn't turn away from, whatever shape it took. I was certain that I was going to find Kamul, but I also knew I wanted to discover more about this strange new world.

I got into an Indian rickshaw just outside the main gates. It was a motorscooter with a light metal pod built onto the back. The metal reached to about waist height, with just a framework supporting a cloth sunshade above. During monsoon they roll plastic flaps down the sides to keep the rain off. The vehicle is traditionally painted black with a yellow stripe running around the middle of it.

As we rolled along the driver constantly sounded his Klaxon horn to clear the way. That was the characteristic sound of Poona: hundreds of these horns all going off simultaneously. People always sounded their horns, whether there was a need or not. Because the driver would push the scooter's tiny engine to the limit, you were always aware of it straining for that extra burst of speed. Changing gears is an art the rickshaw drivers have never mastered; any shift up or down produces a loud grinding sound.

They take corners at full speed, so you're continually thrown from side to side of the passenger pod. The driver is off in a cloud of dust the minute you set foot in the cab. You're forced to shout directions over the noise of the engine and the horn. I don't know how many times I had to scream "Blue Nile!" to him before he figured out my destination.

Tucked into little panels in the side of the pod were religious pictures. They included likenesses of Christ, the Virgin Mary with the child Jesus in her arms, Rada and Krishna embracing love. They were all done in glossy, bright, air-brushed colors, with huge kohl-accented eyes, and framed with elaborate borders—odd patterns that carried over even to the swaddling clothes the Infant wore. A closer look revealed Mary had a caste mark in the center of her forehead.

We roared through the otherwise sedate Koregaon Park, filled with stately old houses set on large plots of land. Ancient, tall banyan trees overhung everything; there was enough breeze to start the leaves rustling and keep things pleasantly cool.

Once the rickshaw left the boundaries of Koregaon Park, however, we hit mayhem. Suddenly there were cows on the road. Beggars on the road edge kept up continual *mantras* of "Blind, ten *paises*" (there are 100 *paise*s to the rupee). Dust was heavy in the air. All around, what green-ery had struggled to establish itself had been burnt lifeless by the sun.

This was the world that flashed past as my rickshaw screeched down M.G. (Mahatma Gandhi) Road and around to the Blue Nile.

The hotel was a one-story, ramshackle affair, made up of bits and pieces from other buildings. I walked up a short staircase that must have come from a private house. Eight-foot wooden uprights support-ed the pressboard walls; these were inset with windows that also had clearly come from another structure. Someone had begun to paint it sage green but had never completed the job, so there were patches of paint here and there that suggested a bit of betel nut had gotten mixed in with the attempt.

The sign announcing BLUE NILE had a background that looked like an ad for the Bahamas. There was blue sky, an expanse of ocean with whitecapped waves, sandy beach, and palm trees in abundance. I was amused and delighted by the image.

Someone had made an attempt to start a garden on the strip of ground separating the hotel from the road. Elephant ears and a few other plants struggled halfheartedly in the heat and dust.

The hotel was off by itself; the nearest buildings were a cluster of beggars' shacks across the road. Whoever had built the Blue Nile had been sparing with the nails, because the whole structure swayed as I walked across the tiny lobby. A young Eurasian woman sat behind a formica-topped desk. She informed me the charge was five rupees a day. I realized that, even at such a modest rate, I couldn't stay indefi-nitely; I was also a bit surprised because, in those days, you could man-age for a year in India on my fifty-pound bankroll.

But I was tired, excited, and savoring the familiar strangeness of it all. The last thing I wanted to do was quibble over a room rate—al-though the hostess was probably disappointed at not having the oppor-tunity to refine her haggling skills. So I registered, and she led me back through a maze of pressboard cubicles to my room.

Nothing in India is ever done straight ahead or on grid; I've never understood why, but things always turn out far more complicated than you'd expect. None of the closed doors I passed was hung true or quite reached to the top of the doorjamb. On the outside of each was a steel latch-and-eye arrangement so that guests could use their own padlocks to secure the room. The irony was that you could rattle the whole struc-ture with little effort—and probably pull it down around your head if you really wanted to put some muscle into it.

I had requested a "large" cubicle, which meant a "double" bed (in actuality, a twin). My corner room also held a chair with missing slats, a wardrobe (which helped make the room "deluxe"), and a piece of mirror stuck on the wall. The bed was covered with a thin bedspread done in a mix of bright colors suggesting a funky tartan.

The room opened into a large common area that featured a sink in one corner. Water from the basin simply dropped down to a hole in the floor beneath, and dripped down to ground level. Patrons of the little restaurant that had established itself under the hotel proper were treated during meals to an erratic waterfall from this arrangement.

Around the corner was the shower, which consisted of a metal storage tank for collecting rainwater. A pull-chain would open a panel long enough to give you a quick dousing; you'd lather up; then give a second tug on the chain for a rinse. Beyond the shower stall was the door to a veranda that was dotted with plants in pots.

For me—in love, drifting amid the sights and sounds of Poona, hovering on the brink of a new life—the Blue Nile was magic. An Indian was always hovering near the veranda. You could call out "*chai*" (spicy Indian tea) or "papaya juice," and he would fetch it for you straightaway—sort of like room service. It added to my sense that I had entered an enchanted kingdom where everything would be mine for the asking.

The fatigue from my journey had become a kind of pleasant fuzziness by this time. In this state of blissful weariness I unpacked my little bag, took a shower, then stretched out on the bed. I was in paradise. I was thrilled to be who I was, where I was. A friend who visited me a bit later at the hotel saw only the squalor of the place. But I only saw a beauty in it; I loved the craziness that daubed paint on walls with no logic whatsoever, put heavy-duty locks on rooms built of kindling, and let you call for *chai* on a whim, and know that someone, somewhere was already running to get it for you.

All through the afternoon I drifted between sleeping and waking. At one point I went out and bought a *lungi*, which is like a *sarong*—a soft, woven fabric that felt lighter than air after the regulation dresses at boarding school and the heavy tweeds and flannels one was obliged to wear as fall turned to winter in England. I selected one in orange because I recalled the women in saffron dresses who had moved so gracefully through the offices of Krishna House.

My bed looked like an old hospital bed. I lay there listening to the murmur of people passing up and down the hall, or opening and shutting doors, which set my walls shaking. Then I would get up, go out to the veranda, hold onto the railing, and just breathe in the sun, the warmth, the smells, the sky, the dust, the feeling I was close to Kamul and had come home.

So much in me needed expression that first day. I sat in my room writing little passages or drawing sketches of things that had caught my fancy. It all was a part of my joy at being in this moment.

Still later I walked down the road to a juice stand to purchase a fruit pulp. It was mixed with buffalo cream, which gave it a rich, distinctive flavor. Sometimes they would just top a glass with a dollop of this cream. The pulp would be mixed up with ice, and sold from a kiosk. This kiosk stall was necessary to establish one's claim to be a "merchant."

But the stand itself was only a facade—and, as I later came to know, this was indicative of both India and the Ashram. The kiosk would display tasteful arrangements of fruit, designed to appeal to the eye; but everything happened *behind* the scenes. They don't want the Westerners to see how things are actually prepared because Americans and Germans in particular wouldn't touch foods that were prepared so unsanitarily.

A prospective customer looking around the corner of the stand would see an Indian—very often a child—jabbing away at a block of ice with icepicks in both hands. If a chunk of ice flew out of the pan into the dirt, he would quickly retrieve it and toss it back with the rest of the ice. All the time there might be chickens pecking in the dust, goats grazing, or naked infants playing nearby.

Tin tables and tin chairs were set up in front of the kiosk. Had I been in the mood I could have whiled away the afternoon, sipping a fruit pulp and watching the world pass by along M.G. Road.

But I returned to the hotel when my glass was empty, noting with surprise how many Westerners were staying at the Blue Nile. I didn't realize that most of them were here to visit the Ashram or were actually a part of it. Many of them weren't wearing red or orange, but had heard of Bhagwan and had come to see what he and the Ashram were all about.

I didn't speak to anyone, choosing to enjoy in silence the river of impressions flowing over me.

So the day drifted along. By late afternoon I felt refreshed and impatient to return to the Ashram. When it got near four o'clock I dressed myself in a long orange skirt and white tee-shirt that Seema had given me, combed my hair, and took a rickshaw back to the Ashram.

CHAPTER 6

Bhagwan

I returned to the Ashram at about a quarter to six. The sun was setting and everything had a golden glow. The path and bushes and trees looked like they'd been sprinkled with gold dust. Everything had cooled off by this time. Walking along, I felt clean and light.

A haunting music was in the air—someone was playing a *hakamachi* flute of bamboo. A few moments later I heard the strains of a *sitar*, and the beat of a *tabla*.

A lot of other people were also gathered outside the black wrought-iron gates, so I knew we were going to a meeting of some sort. Behind the gates I could make out a sign that read, "Shoes and Mind are to be left here at the gates . . ."

Beyond the ironwork the greenery was lush—not at all like the tentative growth in the freshly laid-out gardens or the recently planted hedgerows. The foliage was thick and high and gave off the heady smell of greens upon greens upon greens. Past the black metal gates the path was loose pebbles, soft to walk on.

Once the gates were opened we walked single-file past two women. Although I didn't realize it until later, they were actually smelling each visitor to be sure no perfume, aftershave, cigarette smoke, or any other fragrance clung to him or her. These were offensive to Bhagwan—grounds for exclusion from his presence; Bhagwan was said to have severe allergies, and couldn't tolerate any strong scent.

I was still wearing the *mala* Seema had given me, so everybody automatically assumed I knew the rules of the game. It was blind luck (and poverty) that kept me from splashing on a little *eau de cologne* that night—which would have barred me from admittance to Bhagwan's presence. No one had warned me that a touch of scent would have put an end to everything the moment the "sniffers" detected it.

As far as I was concerned I was still simply going to ask some guy

about Kamul. I was also still, on some level, walking through my early
childhood days. Subconsciously, I had already made up my mind that I
was *not* going back to the West, though I had no plan for the future—or
any idea, even, that it might be possible to stay at the Ashram.

Pebbles crunched softly underfoot; birds called from deep inside
the bowers; the air was steamy because the gardens had just been watered, and the ground was still warm from the residual heat of the sun.
Through the massed leaves—almost a jungle—I could just see a gleam-
ing white corner of Lao Tzu House, Bhagwan's house. It was a large,
two-story building—the heart of the Ashram.

Everyone automatically became silent. The vegetation that turned
the path into a tunnel seemed to absorb whatever sounds our feet
made. Where the path curved around the corner of the house, a man
came forward and signaled for us to follow him. Further along the
path, I could glimpse an open-air auditorium built out from the side of
the building we were skirting.

Everything was white marble. An extension of the roof of Lao Tzu
House overhung the stage, which was the focal point of the amphitheater. I later learned that Bhagwan's bedroom was that part of the residence immediately to the right of the hall. In the center of the stage
was a white armchair; to the side a door led into the building proper.
The main section of the hall that was given over to seating was roofless, though the partial roof gave me the feeling of being enclosed.

I was asked my name at the gate, and one of the young women dutifully wrote it down without comment.

We all filed in and sat wherever we chose. That night there were
only about fifteen people in addition to myself. I chose a seat up front
that was sure to give me a good view of whatever was going to happen;
it was directly opposite the door leading back into Lao Tzu House. Because the door was open, I could see down a stretch of corridor into a
room lined with bookcases.

I sat there, mildly impatient, aware that everyone around me was silent and expecting something important to happen at any moment. My
recollection of that time is both of an eternity passing—and only a few
minutes. The marble floor underneath me felt cold, but not too
uncomfortable.

Suddenly the light went on, then off, in the room to the right of the
open doorway. Something seemed about to happen, so I watched the
doorway and the corridor beyond.

At that exact moment I became aware of what looked like a light
moving down the passageway, which commanded the attention of the

entire gathering. You could feel the anticipation that electrified the whole hall: I found every jot of my being drawn totally to that rectangle of light. Without having the least idea *what* I was looking at or for, I knew that I wanted to experience *all of it*.

Gradually, a face with a dark beard and hands folded in *namaste*, the Hindu gesture of thank you, prayer, and much more, materialized inside the light—seeming to float as independent objects. Then the surge of brightness resolved itself still further, and I could distinguish the white robe the man wore. It was so long, and still so much of the background whiteness, that for a moment he seemed to me to be floating like a ghost in a Japanese painting. The ghost reveals its nature by having no visible feet—it is a visitor in this reality, who has no essential connection to this physical world.

In actual fact Bhagwan had simply come around a corner and started walking down the corridor toward the stage. But, as with so much I later experienced in the Ashram, even this simple entrance was magical, dreamlike, somehow outside of time. To me it was as if some extraordinary being had materialized, atom by shimmering atom, in front of me.

He had a grin that was at once warm and inviting and Cheshire Cat sly—as though he were pleased and a bit embarrassed to see so many people gathered in the hall. At the same time I had the impression that he was barely able to contain a wonderful joke which he might share with us—or be about to play on everyone present.

At that moment, without any prompting, I straightened my back and folded my own hands into *namaste*; my heart jumped. I felt myself giving him the biggest answering smile my face was capable of. Even then I had the sense that it wasn't Bhagwan who gave me the feeling I was feeling: It was like looking at a mirror. In that instant, I felt I was coming home—not to the Orient, not to India, not to Poona, but to *myself*.

Now I could make out a woman behind him. This was Vivek, his constant companion, following at a respectful distance. Her eyes were downcast in her pale face framed by long, straight dark hair.

Bhagwan advanced to the edge of the stage and slowly turned, right to left, surveying everyone seated in the auditorium. Then he settled himself into the armchair, his jet-black eyes still fixed on his audience. There was such a fluidity to his movements that he hardly seemed to be moving at all.

Bhagwan always seemed to take away your reference points—anything could have been possible. It reminds me of the Zen story in which a Roshi and a disciple are sitting, observing a flag fluttering in the breeze. The Roshi turns toward the disciple and asks, "Is the flag moving by itself? Is the wind moving the flag? Or is it your moving mind?"

Two women seated themselves cross-legged on the floor beside the armchair. The woman I had spoken with earlier in the day, Greek Mukta, was on his right; the tiny, intense Indian woman I would come to know as Laxmi sat on his left. She wore an orange scarf and kept glancing at a list she was holding in front of her. Vivek knelt between Laxmi and Bhagwan, a little behind Laxmi.

Bhagwan's bodyguard Shiva, a Scotsman with long, frizzy red hair, sat behind the guru and watched the crowd. The way the light fired his hair, burned white-hot on Bhagwan's robe, drew out the red-orange of Laxmi's scarf and gave everything a dreamlike intensity. Though I didn't know the term at the time, I was sitting in on my first *darshan*, a "meeting with the Master."

Laxmi began reading off names from her list. As each name was called the person would come forward to sit at Bhagwan's feet. Depending on the reason for the *darshan*, Bhagwan would either offer a comment to the *sannyasin* in question, or actually lean forward to bestow a touch, a small gift, or a word of encouragement. All this time, I was watching things like someone in a dream, present, yet still dissociated from events. This was how I later came to live my life in the Ashram; a participant fully engaged in the game, but never losing that sense of also being an outsider, an observer.

I hardly heard anything that Bhagwan was saying to individual *sannyasins*. What I do remember is watching him, and being aware of the animal and bird sounds outside the auditorium. I was particularly fascinated by Bhagwan's hands, which seemed, in their rapid, graceful movements, to speak a silent language all their own. Bhagwan several times referred to his hands in later lectures; when I began working in the Ashram office, I learned to read hands and gestures as a way of assessing where a person was at. I also learned that the Tibetans claim you can actually hypnotize a person with *mudra*s, ritual hand movements. I intuited the language of those hands; and that first evening it brought me a warmth and a heightened sense of belonging.

For a time he talked with various people; then, to my surprise, I heard my own name called out by Laxmi. Since I was still mainly concerned with finding Kamul, I walked on up, deciding this was the most direct way of getting information.

I sat down in front of Bhagwan, as I had seen others sit. I said nothing because I had seen that he was always the first to speak. But I was impatient to ask about Kamul. After a moment, he said, "So, you've made it at last."

This surprised me even more than being summoned to center stage; but, before I could answer, he went on, "It took you a while to get here—but not as long as most people. You've lived your life passionately and intensely to this point, so that now you're empty and ready to continue from here inward."

He paused for a moment, then added, "Your name is Ma Prem Avibha. This means 'Infinite Burning Love.' Your energy is such that you are a candle burning from both ends into the center until, ultimately, you will burn out and disappear. In the beginning, as this flame burns, it burns as a yellow flame, without too much of a center, yet still hot. As you continue more and more on the inner journey, the flame will become a blue flame, one with a definite cone to it, with the hottest part at its center. This is you; this is the meaning of your name."

I was lost in those grave-laughing eyes now. I could feel myself nodding as he went on, "The way you manifest yourself is through love, but people will be scared of you and will run away. But all you have to do is keep burning and burning in your own light, and that's the only business you have here."

I must admit that, all the time he was talking, I forgot Kamul, forgot planet earth, forgot *everything*. He spoke so beautifully, his words touched me so deeply, that I felt he had always known me. The rhythm and tone of his words more than their content seemed to speak to me at some deep level. It interests me that people have mentioned just how much power Bhagwan could manifest through his tone and verbal pattern. I know I felt that at my first *darshan*: I felt he was communicating directly to my spirit, reawakening it, inviting me to come back into the arena and play the game on a level I had never experienced before. I heard him as an ageless spirit speaking directly to some equally ageless part of myself, appealing to me to come out and dance my dance, while assuring me he would provide the home and the means for such dancing to happen.

I got locked into his black eyes; the pupil of his eyes had become almost as large as the irises, edged with just a thin line of dark, dark brown. They were like well openings, floating in the purest whites imaginable.

They almost made me think of the eyes of Kaa the serpent, in the film of Kipling's *The Jungle Book*. But where the gaze of the snake might make you feel fear, Bhagwan's look displayed only the timelessness,

the power, the wisdom that the ancient serpent embodied. His eyes
were warm, mutable, whatever you wanted them to be. For a moment I
felt I could borrow his eyes, look at myself, and see a potential in me
that I had never really grasped before. He seemed to loan me his eyes
just long enough to let me see myself more favorably than I'd ever
done up to this point—since another can see your strong points (and
your weak points) most clearly, and can give you the objective assessment you lose trying to look from the inside out.

Bhagwan's eyes were the key to much of his personal power.
"When I initiate you into sannyas," Bhagwan commented in a lecture
later published in The Secret of Secrets, "I want to look into your eyes, I
want my eyes to dig deep into your eyes to have a contact there, because behind your two eyes is the hidden third eye. If the third eye is
contacted . . . I know a disciple has come: if it is not contacted, then I
only hope that you will become a disciple some day. In that hope, I
give you sannyas."

Laxmi handed Bhagwan a sheet of paper; on this he inscribed my
new name, then signed it at the bottom. On the back he wrote in English what the name meant. Then he touched me in the center of the
forehead, where the "third eye" is supposed to be located. Through it
all I remained in a dream-state, accepting without question everything
that was happening to me.

I remember sitting there while he told me about my new name, and
where I had come from, and what the future held for me. When he
paused, clearly waiting for my reply, my words startled me even as I
said, "I can't wait for the day I can leave you." Somehow, in that moment, I looked into myself and acknowledged, Yes, this person had something that I could use to learn more about myself, but he is not the key to my
being.

Bhagwan chuckled at my answer. Then he said, "Tomorrow, you
move into the Ashram and start work in the office."

My immediate response was, "Work?" At this, the whole auditorium burst into laughter. "I've never worked before in my life," I protested. Nothing seemed less attractive to me at that moment. After that,
I said, "But, actually I'm looking for someone named Kamul; you don't
know where he is, do you?"

For me, the whole spell had been broken by the single word work. I
remembered the only reason for my visit to Poona: to find the man I
loved.

Now everybody in the amphitheater was roaring with laughter;
Bhagwan himself laughed, and said, "No, no, I have no idea." He an-

swered quite kindly, but I felt like a precocious child who had just asked an adult a totally off-the-wall question. The reply was loving, but it also put me in my place.

I forged ahead, saying, "I came here because I thought you'd be able to tell me where he was, and that's who I've come to see." All the while the audience kept on laughing, because they'd all come to see Bhagwan; while I, sitting at the feet of the Master, was only interested in some romantic attachment.

Nor did I realize at the time how extraordinary it was that I was being offered a job and a place to live at the Ashram. I wasn't aware that this was an unusual event—that people had to work and work and work to find their way even to a food pass that would guarantee them one meal a day. Here I was, being offered more than most *sannyasins* could hope for in a year, and still primarily concerned with the whereabouts of Kamul.

"Now that you've arrived," Bhagwan added when the laughter had died away, "you can just relax and be here." That was the end of my encounter; Shiva quickly moved forward and hustled me back to my seat.

I was not aware of any arrangements being made to move me into the Ashram. But what he said was noted and would be put into effect without any further ado. This sort of thing indicates how dreamlike the whole place was. Somehow, things like this always got taken care of.

I sat through the rest of *darshan*, but was so wrapped in my own thoughts that I had no sense of what went on after my meeting with Bhagwan. Nor did I have any clear sense of what the Ashram was or how it worked. Most people never did find out how the place worked.

When *darshan* ended I went back to the Blue Nile. My head had hardly touched the pillow before I was sound asleep.

The next morning I returned to Krishna House determined to find Kamul. The moment I entered the reception area I was told that I was now to be in the office—just as Bhagwan had indicated the evening before. The person I was to work for was Ma Yoga Vidya. First, however, I was to be shown to my new room.

I checked out of the Blue Nile, fully expecting I would move right back in the probable event that no accommodations were ready for me at the Ashram. Surprised, I followed one of the receptionists to the room assigned to me in one of the dorms.

When I opened the wardrobe I discovered three new bright orange dresses on hangers evenly spaced apart, two pairs of orange *zoris* on the floor, plus a comb, toothbrush, toothpaste, scentless soap and shampoo, nail clippers, and a lacquered bamboo hairpin or skewer (almost like a single chopstick in appearance), which was a standard part of hair-dressing at the Ashram. These items were all lined up on a shelf with the sublime precision of a Zen artistic arrangement.

The room itself was very pleasant; it was furnished with a bed on the floor, a mat beside it, and a small meditation stool. Above the bed was a clean, clinical three-tier shelf with green curtains that could be drawn across it. There was a single window opposite the bed.

The bedspread matched the green curtains on the shelving; the sheets underneath were a tone that matched the bedspread—as did the mat. Bed, mat, stool were laid with attention to harmony and exact right angles. Even the smallest details contributed to a feeling of unity. I came to understand very quickly that this outward consistency exist-ed as a subtle reminder to keep watch on our inner consistency.

All elements of life in the Ashram community reflected this con-tinuity. If you were in a green-themed room your meditation cushion for sitting in the lecture hall would also be that color. The pillow would always be set in a certain place. I later came to realize that not all the rooms were assembled in this way—though all were uncluttered and aesthetically set out. These particular rooms were the handiwork of the woman Deeksha, who later became a formidable power and a close friend of mine. At the time, however, I was doubly impressed by the feeling that the whole room had been lovingly composed, and imagined each room in the Ashram had been given the same treatment.

Although all the clothes were orange at that time—the color of sun-rise, of a new beginning—the style of clothing would always be appro-priate to one's duties and place in the Ashram. I'm not sure why I didn't question any of it at that point. The idea of working there seemed no more appealing than it had the night before. But there was a sense of certainty on the part of everyone else that overrode any argu-ments even before they could form in my mind—let alone be voiced.

Shortly after this I met Ma Yoga Vidya. From the first moment I met her something warned me that I wasn't going to get on with this wom-an at all. She sat me down at a little corner desk with an old typewriter and told me that I was to be a typist. The in-basket on the desk was piled with notes for items to be ordered from Indian supply houses: gardening shears, carpentry tools, woodworking supplies, and so forth.

One basic form letter served as a model and it introduced me to the idea of always speaking of myself in the third person. A standard letter would run, "Beloved Swami Gee"—this was the Hindu equivalent of "Dear Sir"—then the word "LOVE" just below. This was followed by several more blank lines before the body of the letter, which might run, "Thank you for your catalog of August 20, 1976. We lovingly request your earliest deliverance of gardening shears at 120 rupees per half-dozen, with stainless steel blades . . . " What followed would be a full description culled directly from the catalog. It would be absolutely specific on what the advertisement had said. This would leave us a way to get back if there was the least element that failed to perform as promised or failed to deliver every feature as described.

This was my first step in learning to play the game inside the Ashram. We left no room for anyone to wriggle out of the description they had put in their catalog or newspaper advertisement.

This precision grew out of the total immersion in the job at hand that was demanded of everyone in the offices at Krishna House—and, indeed, throughout the whole Ashram. The simplest tasks became an exercise or meditation—using the work at hand as a means of dissolving the ego and emptying the mind, which is the first step in opening yourself to enlightenment. I quickly became so immersed in the routines of the place that I soon began speaking of myself in the third person. At the same time we were expected *every moment* to be attentive to our immediate circumstances, letting the impressions flow through our "unencumbered" consciousness, paying attention to the information about ourselves and our world these would provide.

As observer, I was constantly forcing myself to be aware of the different dimensions of even the most routine situation. Not only was I communicating with the person to whom I was writing; but I was also observing myself. To accept anything less than absolute correctness *at every point* was, according to the directives in Krishna House, to fail at giving myself *totally* to the work of being the best typist, supply clerk, or whatever was my potential. And failing that was, on another level, a holding back, a lost opportunity to move toward enlightenment.

I would constantly challenge myself: *This is who you say you are in the moment, this is how you present yourself, now bring the two into harmony. Line up those elements: be absolutely clear in every dimension in which you manifest yourself.*

All letters concluded with, "Love and His Blessings." I would then type in "Ma Yoga Laxmi" and sign my name for her.

Of course, it took me a while to assimilate these lessons and to turn the business of letter-writing or other office work into an automatic meditation.

That first morning my head was still spinning at my overnight transformation from seeker of Kamul to secretary in the Ashram. The world, in my experience, didn't operate in such a way that from 6 P.M. one evening to 8 A.M. the following morning you suddenly find yourself moved into new quarters, supplied with new clothes, and working at a job you'd never even asked for.

From the day I moved in it was made clear to me that *nothing* was *mine*. No one spelled this out in so many words, but I noted the absence of words like *I, me, my*. Everything was *we* or *ours*. Lapses were never commented on directly, but I was aware of a subtle judgment about the degree to which I was failing to let the ego dissolve, and would find myself noting it in others. Alternately, I learned to speak of *the* desk or *the* typewriter paper. Even one's body was to be viewed as somehow separate from oneself. Birthdays were referred to as "body birthdays," and these were distinguished from *"sannyas* birthdays," commemorating the day you officially became a disciple of Bhagwan.

The only personal pronouns encouraged were *he* and *his*—and these used only in reference to Bhagwan. (We always referred to *Him* with a capital "H" when writing letters.) The world of the Ashram was divided into *him* at the center, and a constellation of *thes* in attendance.

I wasn't much of a typist, having taken only a few lessons around Oxford in England along with a bit of shorthand. I was even less cut out for office work. Within an hour I was bored and longing for a cigarette. Since smoking was not allowed in the Ashram at all, I was told that I would have to go out to the front gate before lighting up.

I lingered as long as I felt I could, then returned to *the* desk, and continued typing letters—pausing every few minutes to white-out an error. I worked steadily until noon when, I had been informed, I was to go to someplace called Jesus House for my meal. I hoped that I might spot Kamul there.

The dining hall was fairly primitive in those days: Two long trestle tables held the food; you set what you wanted on a stainless steel *thali* tray. I took mine outside to Jesus Gardens to dine; a few people had done this, while others sat upstairs in Miriam Canteen, or took trays to their rooms. There weren't very many people at lunch; only about thirty to thirty-five people lived and worked full time at the Ashram, though the grounds covered five acres.

People didn't talk a lot, even at meals. I was left to myself, which suited me fine. I spent most of the lunch hour looking around at my new surroundings and keeping an eye out for Kamul. The gardenswere beautiful; they—like Jesus House itself—had been part of the original estate that had been rented by the Ashram. Krishna House and Lao Tzu House also had come with the property.

I drifted back with the other office workers and halfheartedly took up my typing. As the pile of completed letters grew, I began to feel better about things. I also kept reminding myself that they were giving me room and board, so a little typing didn't seem too much to pay.

At the end of the day I turned in my folder of letters to Vidya, and sat while she went through them. I had followed all the instructions—making three copies, putting the flap of the envelope over the top, arranging the finished paperwork with the precision I was growing aware of in every aspect of the Ashram.

In the office you followed instructions *to the letter*, whether it was the most efficient method of doing something or not. You didn't question procedures, you didn't think—you simply *did*. In the process you learned to drop a part of your mind.

Vidya went through each letter one at a time. She held each sheet of paper up to the light to see if she could find any white-outs, strike-overs, or erasures. When she spotted the tiniest correction she would rip up the letter or envelope, telling me I would have to redo it the next day. Any mistake in punctuation or spelling—deriving from my inadvertent use of British style and spelling rather than the American forms the Ashram followed—were also destroyed.

In short order some thirty finished letters were reduced to one, and the envelope for that was disposed of as flawed. A lot of people who came to the Ashram later thought this sort of obsessive attention to detail and perfectionism only happened toward the end, when things began to get crazy. From the outset, however, *total awareness* was the order of the day. When you operate on this level day in and day out, you learn that perfection is not something that comes from the mind; as soon as you begin to think about something, mistakes creep in. Success in the office was measured by the degree to which you could surrender yourself to perfect completion of the tasks you had been assigned.

I remember thinking to myself, *This isn't going to be the little cup-of-tea-and-gameshow niche I thought I'd found.* It was clear—in spite of all the stress on detachment, on not passing judgment, on not letting feelings interfere with the work—that Vidya had taken an immediate dislike to me. I felt the same about her. This worried me somewhat, because she was already established in the office hierarchy. But I was self-aware enough to appreciate that I'd come through so much already that losing this job wouldn't hurt me. I decided that whatever happened would be my *karma*, and all I could do was let matters run their course.

So I carried on unhappily for a few days. Working with Vidya I felt that same sort of uncomfortableness that I felt all the time I was at boarding school. I put far more energy into settling into life at the Ashram, and looking for Kamul.

I found him quite by accident three days after I started work. At that time there was no central list of everyone who was visiting the Ashram—only of those who were living and working inside. My work hours were long, and I often went back to my room too tired to do more than collapse and sleep. I also assumed that everyone who had come to be near Bhagwan would eventually pass through the offices in Krishna House.

This was exactly what happened. When he had gotten over his initial surprise at discovering me tapping away at my typewriter, Kamul and I had an emotional reunion. He asked how I'd gotten there, and I eagerly filled in all the details. But when I got to the part about Bhagwan assigning me a job and a room, I felt him take a step back from me emotionally. That was my first clear sense that people in the office were regarded as special—and that, having been personally directed to Krishna House by Bhagwan, I might be viewed as special in my own right.

To myself, I was just who I'd always been. I insisted that he could move in with me. But he hesitated, saying that wasn't possible. I wasn't about to accept that, after I had followed him all the way from England. "What do you mean it's not possible?" I demanded, "*Of course* it's possible!"

Without waiting for any more protests, I took him by the hand and went to Vidya. "This is Kamul," I told her, "the person I came to find. It's all right for him to move in with me, isn't it?"

She replied, "No, it isn't."

I shrugged and said, "Then it's quite simple: I'm moving out. I want to be with Kamul, and he wants me to be with him. Don't you?" I asked him, suddenly realizing that he hadn't said anything to Vidya.

"Yes, of course," he said. I could still sense a trace of hesitancy in his voice. The fact that I was now denying the room Bhagwan had bestowed on me added to his sense that I was someone special.

As for me, seeing him again had only confirmed how very much in love I was. I had Kamul; and neither Vidya's all-too-evident disapproval, nor the fact that I was rejecting more than most *sannyasins* dared to hope for, mattered in the least.

CHAPTER 7

Music House and Groups

That evening I packed up my things and moved in with Kamul. He lived in one of a cluster of huts on the grounds of the Music House, which accommodated some of the Ashram musicians and even Bhagwan's astrologer, Kabir. These people, although they had an active role in the Ashram, supported themselves. Kabir, for example, would draw up natal charts and, for a small fee, give interpretations. People were very creative with their cottage industries—making handbags or clothes, giving Tarot readings, or even baking Western-style cookies, which everybody craved!

For a few days, I only went to work on a hit-or-miss basis; nobody challenged me. Anyway, wasn't I simply living up to my name, fanning the flames of love?

Although Kamul had arrived a week before me, his *darshan* didn't occur until a week after we had been together. At that time Bhagwan told him to sign up for three groups.

One of the foundations of the Ashram was its group therapy. The fees paid by participants (and virtually all *sannyasins* were required to take groups at some point) provided a steady source of income. At the same time these sessions introduced them to the routine and language of the Ashram—and, I came to realize, began the process of breaking down the ego and will so that you could be more easily manipulated by the office and other authority figures.

The official reason was much more high-minded. "The groups that I give you are really devices to go through a turmoil . . . ," Bhagwan said in a lecture (quoted in *The Secret*).

The psychological purpose is only minor; the spiritual purpose is major. The spiritual purpose is to bring your whole turmoil to the surface. All your doubts, all possible doubts that you have carried for many lives have to be brought to the surface, because only from the surface can they evaporate and disappear.

They have to be brought out of your conscious, unconscious, collective unconscious . . . The Master's whole function is how to help you die as an ego, and all kinds of means and methods have to be used.

Kamul was given the encounter group and a psychological exploration group (*vipassana*), which explored personality through the light of the twin disciplines, silence and inner awareness. Last (but certainly not least in my book!) was *tantra*, the sex group. "*Tantra*," Bhagwan said, "is the method to encounter your sexuality, your sensuousness."

My feelings were in turmoil as I stood there outside Lao Tzu gate, having just been informed of this latest development by Kamul, who was still beaming from having been with the Master. I had a "serene" smile plastered on my face, but a far different scenario was taking place inside. In my mind's eye, I was undergoing a transformation worthy of the "Exorcist": Two very sharp horns had sprouted on top of my head and I was tightening my grip on a red-hot pitchfork that had suddenly appeared in my hands.

Had that little angel who represents the voice of reason not whispered in my ear that moment, I might have been responsible for the corpses of one blissed-out, orange-shirted young man, and a small old man with a grey beard and a long white dress.

Now that interior screenwriter was providing me dialogue. I thought to myself, *So this is what the old boy means by "coming in the back door"!*

To the mental image of Bhagwan, watching with hands folded, Cheshire Cat grin half-concealed by his beard, I said, very sportingly, "*You certainly woke me from a blissful sleep. Score one for you!*"

Back to myself, frantically wondering, *How do I retrieve the game plan? If I say "No" to Kamul or argue, he'll simply say, "That's your own jealousy speaking"—which I admit—and he'll still do the group.*

Would I do better arguing the issue cooly and calmly, carefully building the case that Kamul doesn't need the group? No, that will never work: you can't win an argument by disagreeing with the Master's command. I know enough to know that's the number-one rule around here.

By now my inner self was wringing her hands and pacing furiously, suggesting, *Hide his money—No: he'll only borrow it back from me. Strangle him? Yes, I could happily do that right now.* The devil was back, immediately replaced with the calming voice, *No, I might regret it tomorrow.*

The me inside grew fanciful. *I know! I'll find some sort of herb that'll make it seem like he has some kind of social disease. Yes, that's the best idea. It will keep Kamul out of* tantra—*and give him a good scare! Only, how would I find out about that? And it probably doesn't exist anyway!*

And, finally, I consoled myself, *Anyway, I'll think of something.* I felt like Scarlett O'Hara, scheming to get Rhett Butler back, knowing, "There had never been a man she couldn't get, once she set her mind upon him," and vowing, *I'll think of it all tomorrow, at Tara. I can stand it then. Tomorrow, I'll think of some way to get him back. After all, tomorrow is another day.*

With that happy thought firmly implanted, I left the theater of my mind and returned to the meeting outside Lao Tzu House, determined to be genuinely happy for Kamul, who really was glowing from his *darshan*—and just as determined to figure out a solution that would make me just as happy (though for exactly the opposite reasons).

But several things had become clear to me during the run through of my mental cinema.

I was reminded of just how firm Bhagwan's control of most *sannyasins* was. There was no way to challenge his word head on: The best you could do was hope to be creative enough to get around him—using some back door or side door—just as I envisioned him as doing. His explicit word was carved in granite (or, in keeping with the Ashram setting, Carrara marble might be the more appropriate image). This authority was passed along through the office, where any "suggestion" Sheela or Laxmi or Arup made carried the full weight of Bhagwan's say-so. But the chain of command extended further yet: into one's own mind.

In time, with proper training (either in group or, in my case, working in the office, which functioned in many the same ways as group), the "alchemy" (as Bhagwan called it) began to work on you, making you less and less trusting of your own instincts, reasoning, and emotions, and more and more pliable to manipulation by the office or the Master. Your own mind was artfully guided into a series of preconditioned ways of thinking that always challenged doubt or defiance and nudged you toward surrender to Bhagwan's will.

I had already assimilated enough of this to make me question an emotion like my jealousy. Still on the cusp between the independence I had known outside the gate, and conscious efforts to drop the ego and surrender, I wasn't yet ready to give up my jealousy or Kamul without a struggle. At the same time I was admitting to myself that jealousy was not a valid reason for forbidding Kamul to join the *tantra* group, and probably indicated a defect in my own psychic makeup.

Once Kamul became involved with the groups I could see just how fully indoctrinated he was becoming. First, his language changed. He began to refer to himself in the third person—"I want" or "I don't want" were simply not to be used. If I suggested going to Miriam Canteen or into Poona for a meal, and he wasn't in the mood, he'd say, "Kamul doesn't feel to go and eat in this moment." He became fully articulate in the Ashram lingo, and would say to me things like, "Why can't you *surrender* to the fact that I'm doing the *tantra* group?"

In a more subtle way I could see just how closely he identified with his group leaders, who were perceived as mediums for Bhagwan. His verbal language and his body language both reflected this loss of ego. Ma Anana Suda was a mulatto from New York City, with a streetwise way of walking and talking. When Kamul would come out of a *tantra* session with her, he'd be "mucking" along, talking with a born-and-bred-in-the-Big-Apple accent. On the other hand, when he worked with Ma Predeepa, an upper-class Englishwoman who led the *vipassana* group, his accents would turn strictly Mayfair and his walk would reflect this group leader's grace and refinement.

This type of identification would later be transferred unconsciously to department heads, to the office, and, ultimately, to Bhagwan. At the same time the "absolute trust" (again, Bhagwan's phrase) the group taught participants actually was a lesson in obedience and surrender to authority. It also implanted certain automatic responses that could be— and were—used to manipulate people. For example, a certain tone of voice or turn of phrase used by the group leader to indicate approval or disapproval would be used by people in the office to squelch an argument or get something done.

Many groups were "no-limit"—whatever happened was fine. Because the groups were so intense people learned to go with the group leader's wishes and the will of the group. The process was fairly simple, and highly effective. To use an extreme example, if a woman announced that she wanted to be hugged by the other members of the group, and the group leader agreed to the proposal, everyone would be expected to join in. If someone held back the group leader would single that person out to be "nailed" by the group. That person would become the victim of the group's verbal (and in some rare cases, physical) abuse—which was terrifying. When twenty-six people and the group leader in an enclosed space suddenly zero in on you, your response is total fear. You could walk out of the group, which meant you might as well keep on walking out the gates of the Ashram. Or you could stay, take what was dished out, take in the messages, and, as Bhagwan would have it "go with the flow" (though he was always directing the course of the stream).

The therapy sessions stripped you of all reference points except dependence on the group itself. Those inner guideposts we all have would be broken down or redirected, so that you either found yourself moving ahead on El Camino Bhagwan, slipping back into doubt and fear, or simply running in circles when you hit one of those intersections where you tried to find a way to resolve the conflict between your own best interests and the will of the tribe.

You would never blame group leaders for your difficulties or accuse them of being abusive: They were all too skillful for that. You were reminded over and over that they served only as a mirror—and, as such, they were merely reflecting your own inner discord and doubt. Again, it was stressed that not taking the group experience to the limit was to deliberately handicap yourself: Groups were for *your* benefit and ultimately existed only to help *you* improve *yourself*. But they also tapped into sources of doubt then self-torment and, finally, blissful acceptance of the group's wishes and an abiding terror of ever falling out of step with the group's wishes.

That fear carried over at a deep, subconscious level into daily life in the Ashram. Any refusal to go along with the group (the commune) or the group leader surrogate (a supervisor) would bring the words, the body language, the tone of voice that prompted the conditioned fear/self-doubt reflex.

I guess you can say that it amounted to a form of "brainwashing"—all in the guise of liberating yourself, moving toward enlightenment, deepening relationships. In point of fact this new "freedom" was actually a powerful form of mind control. When your turmoil was at the greatest, and your reserves of self-esteem, self-defense, and logic had been beaten down, the group dynamic flooded you with a sense that in the group and in the higher authority of Bhagwan was your only real hope for security, serenity, happiness.

A comment made by Gurdjieff in 1915 (quoted in P. D. Ouspensky's *In Search of the Miraculous* and used as an epigraph in the limited edition of *The Sound of Running Water: A Photo-Biography of Bhagwan Shree Rajneesh and His Work* published by the Rajneesh Foundation in 1980), reveals both the goal of groups and, by its placement in the latter book, something about the centrality of groups in the *sannyasin* experience. In part, it states,

A group must work as one machine. The parts of the machine must know one another and help one another. In a group there can be no personal interests opposed to the interests of others, or opposed to the interests of the work, there can be no personal sympathies or antipathies which hinder the work.

The groups also were a training ground for secrecy that was the norm everywhere in the Ashram. Nobody talked about what went on inside the group except in the vaguest sort of way: "I really learned a lot about myself." There was no crossover of specific information when someone went from, say, a *tantra* group to a *vipassana* group. This training applied to all situations: Someone from the office would never gossip about office business with anyone from another department. Even the office itself became increasingly segmented, the right hand *never* to know what the left was doing.

The office subtly shaped the collective personality of the Ashram, while letting it appear that everyone had total freedom. Few ever realized how carefully molded they had been from the moment they entered the gates or took their first encounter group.

The groups also served a very practical function. In those early days groups served as one of the primary sources of income for the Ashram. People were responsible for paying their way; they were not, at this time, expected to turn over everything to the Ashram in return for being kept. Whatever happened, the Ashram wouldn't help. You took care of yourself and each other.

When you were assigned a group, you would go to the booking office to secure a place. You would then have to pay the full amount within a week. Thirty or forty people were living inside the Ashram, but hundreds were living outside the walls. Each of these would be assigned an average of three groups to take—though it wasn't unheard of for people to be taking as many as six at a time. A group might easily have twenty-five or thirty members; the average cost was $200 to $300—for that time, in India, this meant a substantial amount of money. This side of things was already a good business.

I had little luck coming up with a way to win Kamul back. It quickly became clear to me that he regarded Bhagwan and the Ashram as the end-all and be-all of his existence—a position his ongoing group work constantly reinforced. Frustrated though I was, I continued to regard Kamul as the focus of my new life, and avoided (as much as was humanly possible) any confrontations that might jeopardize our relationship. And the Ashram environment thoughtfully provided a way of taking my mind off my problem: I was reminded continually to throw myself into my work, and that did help bleed off a lot of potentially explosive negative energy.

Life in the Ashram had a timeless quality. Every day I would check the date countless times to be sure that what I was typing onto the letters was absolutely correct. But the passage of time was so irrelevant that I stopped thinking of dates as anything other than *codes* one included to help with referencing and filing paperwork. I can vividly remember events, but I still have a hard time linking these up with any particular dates. This sense of time wasn't peculiar to me; many other people who worked in the Ashram have reported a similar sense of time-distortion or detachment from the sense of *when* that frames each instant of existence outside the Ashram.

This was a big part of the Ashram's appeal for me: I had entered a never-never-land where time ceased to exist. Cut off from use of clocks and watches, we learned a new way of telling time: We marked the progress of the day by lecture; breakfast, which came after lecture; work; *darshan*, in the evening; work again; and sleep. Time was a collective awareness within the Ashram walls—almost a new biorhythm we attuned ourselves to.

There you no longer saw yourself as the familiar "I"—instead, you discovered yourself as *being, energy, light*; you spoke a whole new language; you thought in concepts utterly alien to the world outside 17 Koregaon Park. It was refreshing to step into a new world, a new consciousness, even a kind of asexuality, when all the familiar barriers and definitions were broken down. Our shoes and minds had, indeed, been abandoned at the gates.

Some of the ideas I encountered were familiar to me from my training as a child growing up in Singapore, but life in the Ashram refined them to an extraordinary degree. I began to live as two entities occupying a single point in space and time: I was the *watcher*, always observing from a point of detachment; and I was this *being* called Avibha, the creature who moved—the machine, the body, the person, the focus of the emotions.

This process of viewing the self as disconnected from anything but the immediate, intense experience of being freed us from the rule of *ought*s and *must*s and immersed us in the world of *is*. We were trained to keep all our options open, because limiting these for any reason— morality, religion, duty—would hamper our growing into self-awareness, self-fulfillment, and, ultimately, enlightenment. This openness kept us continually questioning ourselves and everything around us.

We took nothing for granted. With the same intensity that had once led me, as a child, to dream of finding a new color, I now questioned everything—even the familiar colors. I would wonder if what everyone else saw as "green" was really the same thing that *I* called "green." If we could swap eyes, I wondered, would we find that what we had agreed was "green" was actually "blue" for you?

The further I pursued this line of thought, the less certain I became of *anything*. Later, I no longer knew whether I was a man or a woman in the spiritual sense—though I could not deny that I was, at present, living in a woman's body. It was as if all the cards I had been dealt at birth had been tossed into the air and could recombine in an infinite number of ways.

Question yourself was the overriding principle. This didn't mean questioning outside yourself—or determining what someone else was doing. If you *did* question another, you did it in reference to yourself, not looking at that other in a judgmental way. In this way all encounters, all experiences, became a way to self-understanding.

The Ashram deliberately created situations that took people beyond pat answers and familiar circumstances. For example, a man who was a noted psychiatrist or therapist in the West might well be given toilets to clean immediately upon his arrival at the Ashram. If he understood the lesson properly he might begin by thinking, "Vidya is an idiot for assigning me such duties," but he would quickly be guided to move beyond this to look at what was happening in himself and to ask, "Who do you think you are? How come you're still attached to this idea of who you were last week ... or five minutes ago ... or one moment ago? Who are you now? You're a toilet cleaner, so bring all that you've known and experienced into this moment of cleaning toilets—but simultaneously drop all that you've been. Become one with the toilet brush, and simply disappear." The idea was not to let anyone assume that they were any longer what they were when they first came into the Ashram.

Not long after I'd moved in with Kamul, I was transferred to the cleaning staff. This was one of only two brief instances when I didn't work in the office. I was elated to be away from my desk and free of the tension of working under Vidya.

The cleaning staff at that time was run by two women, Paras and Shanti. Paras had dark, wavy thick hair; Shanti had long, blond curly hair. Paras was solidly grounded and deliberate in her movements; Shanti was a dancer, always in motion. Paras wore severely cut, straight-line dresses; Shanti wore fancy bodices over wide skirts that would puddle around her when she sat—almost like Victorian hoopskirts. There was always something ethereal about her: She reminded me of a doe or nymph. Her conversation leapt about; she often made up her own words on the spur of the moment; but I found I could have the most delightful conversations with her once I accepted that usual forms and content did not necessarily apply.

At that time the cleaning staff hadn't been organized into a proper department; they simply kept their supplies in a cupboard. Shanti and Paras were in the latter's room at Jesus House when I first met with them to find out my new duties.

In the office the feeling was sterile, hard—machine-like is the word that most easily comes to mind. It was all highly efficient, but with the odd antique part: more like a well-tended old upright manual typewriter than a modern electric model. For all the smooth operation people saw in the office, I knew that, behind the scenes, things were often done in a distinctly quirky fashion and cemented by the force of several strong personalities—most notably Laxmi and, later, Sheela.

Just walking along the pathway from Krishna House to Jesus House that first morning lifted a weight from me and let me breathe again. The smell of fresh, green, growing things stirring slightly in the breeze cleaned out my brain, which had begun to feel metallic.

Part of that feeling of heaviness was due to the fact that I had put on a good deal of weight since my arrival at the Ashram. I had been decidedly thin upon my arrival at Poona; now, like the majority of women, I was tending more decidedly toward the Rubenesque figure. Plump was beautiful there—a far cry from the mannequin-ideal I had left behind in England.

At Jesus House someone directed me to Paras's room. It was tiny, but she had decorated with a few carefully chosen knicknacks that gave it warmth and personality. Nobody ever had many things; to have more than about five such items—a bud vase, a diary, Western soap or toothpaste as opposed to the standard issue—was unusual.

Paras was reclining on her bed with the shades drawn. She had draped a *lungi* over her, as she leaned her head on her hand. A half-consumed pot of tea sat on a side table. Her shoes had apparently been kicked off, to land where they would—very different from the office, where shoes would be kept at right angles to the baseboard, toes always touching the wall.

Shanti was sitting beside her. She had one foot folded under her, lost in the billows of her skirt, the other foot dangling so that her toe could touch the floor.

The office couldn't function without a fine line of tension; the atmosphere in Paras's room was anything *but* tense. I sensed immediately that I was going to like my cleaning duties, whatever they turned out to be.

I hesitated in the doorway; but Paras waved me in, crying, "Well, come in, come in, come in."

At this point, although I'd seen a lot before coming to India, I had been very much a loner. I'd certainly never had women friends, with the exception of Suzzane and her mother. Here, I suddenly met grown women whose openness made it clear from the first that, although I was just over fifteen, I would be treated as an equal. It was very different from the standoffishness of the office. These two were relaxed, confident in their femininity; they were *real women*. Looking into their eyes I saw a roundness, a wholeness, that was entirely lacking from the office staff.

The office demanded that those who worked there drop their "personality"—which in terms of the quest for enlightenment meant the essence that each of us comes into this world with as an individual. This was viewed by the powers-that-were in the office as something negative. A short time around Paras and Shanti, however, let me see that this "essence" was the uniqueness we have in this life and any other life that we may move into. At the time I was frustrated with myself for thinking too often in such "egotistical" terms; the friendship I developed with Paras and Shanti began opening me up to the value of my own uniqueness.

I had arrived just before lunch. They asked me what I was doing, and I told them that I had been reassigned out of the office. "Far out," they said in unison, in what I immediately spotted as American accents. Compared with a British accent, an American one is much rounder, "laid back." I thought of their accents not so much in terms of what their backgrounds might be, but primarily as being appropriate to their being round Venuses.

I also felt shy and a little out of place, like a child sneaking downstairs and being allowed, briefly, to be a part of her parents' dinner party. The more I saw how self-confident they were, the more I felt like an out-of-place child. They manifested the beauty, the joy of the Ashram that could happen when we fully got in touch with our own beings. I felt these two women had reached that inner point of discovery and delight; I realized how new I was at the game—and how far I was from feeling such ease and self-assurance.

We sat in the sunlight in Jesus Gardens, eating and talking and sometimes just sitting quietly to listen to a bird singing or savor the warmth of the day.

After that Shanti suggested that I should start by cleaning someone's room in Eckhart House. First she supplied me with a bucket, two rags, a sponge, a bottle of cleaner, and a broom; then she took me into the room. Like all the others in the Ashram, it was perfectly square and held a bed, triple shelving, a meditation cushion, and a floor mat.

Shanti positioned herself in the center of the room, and began animatedly to instruct me in the proper way to tidy a room. "Now, when you clean a room, you don't just walk in and start to scrub anywhere. You have to remember: You're not just cleaning the outside, you're cleaning the *inside* of yourself. You begin in the middle of the room; you just stand for a moment and look. Then you *turn*"—here she demonstrated, twirling in place, her skirt spinning around—"and you look from the top on down and down and around and on the shelves. Then you go to the bed and you roll up the bed"—these were very light coconut mattresses—"and you take your broom and you sweep underneath." She illustrated all this with quick, graceful movements, for all the world like an impromptu ballet. In one continuous movement she lifted the mattress, swiped underneath it, and lowered it back into place. She had made the whole business of cleaning an art—one which I never really mastered, seeming always to be able to raise more dust than I could get rid of.

She explained to me that there was a system for cleaning as rigid as any we had followed in office procedures. One cloth was to apply cleaner; one was to wipe clean; these were *never* to be mixed up. One soap was for the floor of the bedroom; one soap was for the floor of the bathroom (this room was one of the few that had a private bath attached). There was a special cleaner for the toilet bowl; another for the basin; another spray for the mirror. Each of these required their own pair of cloths or a "scrubby"—orange for the basin, blue for the bowl. As a final step I was to add a bit of chlorine to the water in a jug and use it to disinfect things, since disease was always a problem in India— and even the Ashram, with its strict rules of hygiene, was not immune to cases of typhoid, hepatitis, or dysentery.

Shanti would never dream of deviating from the way she had been instructed to do things; and she simply assumed I would do things exactly as *she* had trained *me*. Shanti would never use the wrong cleaning cloth for mischief as I would sometimes do to keep from going nuts with the systems-within-systems on which the Ashram operated. Reviewing this "treasure trove" of cleaning supplies, one part of me was amused at the obsessional way Shanti approached the whole business.

Of course, things were never *yours:* You outfitted yourself with the necessary supplies each day from the general store. However, one *never* mixed the supplies assigned to Eckhart House with those delegated for cleaning Krishna House. If you lost an item you had to go to "supply," put in a formal request, and explain what had happened.

At first I took the whole business as a whimsical "divine joke." *How can you take this seriously?* I asked myself. In fact, I very quickly found that I did take a kind of joy in doing these tasks well—and was able to use the mindless routine as yet another meditation.

That afternoon, however, I had barely begun on the first room—moving slowly to keep the cloths and cleaning supplies straight in my mind—when Shanti breezed back in to see how I was progressing. After a few minutes of watching me mix things up, she announced, "Oh, pack all of this up and put it away. I want to go and play." I started to argue that I wasn't finished yet, but she waved my objections away. That showed attachment to the job and resistance to the spontaneity that was constantly replacing one set of rules and systems with others—usually with no warning at all. Life in the Ashram was volatile: People were constantly being rotated in jobs; new jobs and ventures were always being created; and the system you had been rigidly following for weeks might be tossed out and replaced with a whole new set of procedures and a new chain of command.

In short, you never took anything for granted. Initially, I found this merely erratic and frustrating; when I'd been there a little while, I began to appreciate how this kept us alert, attentive, and always eager as a child is eager to see what new surprises a department head, the office staff, or Bhagwan himself might spring on the community.

When the cleaning supplies had been stored away, Shanti took my hand, and we went for a long walk around Koregaon Park. The grounds looked even more beautiful in the late afternoon, when the sunlight had begun to thicken, and the air seemed cooler. Shanti chattered on about anything that came to mind; I didn't understand more than a fraction of her rambling, but I enjoyed every minute of her company.

We wound up at the back gates of the Ashram, where we sat and smoked *beedee*s, Indian cigarettes, while Shanti explained that these gates were for "sneaky *beedee*s" or taking an unauthorized break. The main gates were for taking an official time out.

*Beedee*s were a little part of the whole new world I rediscovered every time I went into Poona. *Beedee*s are like cheroots. They are different kinds of seeds wrapped in a cone of *bodhi* (*pipal*) leaf and tied off with a bit of pink cotton. They have all sorts of different names—*Ganesh, 201s, 501s*, and so forth—depending on the mix of seeds or herbs that give distinctive flavor when you smoke one. These are sold in packets of about twenty-five, and come in brightly colored wrappers.

Sometimes the wonders of Poona were purely Indian; sometimes they were a mix of Western and Eastern that is so much a part of the

Indian scene. For example, a certain type of older, extravagantly designed American car—usually from the 1950s—was favored by the inhabitants of Poona and treasured for its elaborate grillwork, excessive chrome trim, and fins, such as those found on classic Plymouths or Chevrolets. There was one old Jain, Dorabjee, who owned the local grocery-cum-hardware store, whose pride and joy was a burgundy red 1957 Mercury that he kept immaculate in spite of cows, dust, and the countless hazards of the local road. Having never seen an American car—let alone one of this vintage—it only added to my feeling of having stepped into another world, where past, present, and future coexisted in a most appealing way.

In addition to these cars and the rickshaws, there were hundreds of bicycles, with their bells going, on all sides. Nobody in India stays on the proper side of the road, though there are mercifully few accidents. Everybody floors the gas pedal, and only swerves at the last possible moment. From the first, this struck me as the epitome of silent, chaotic communication. No one signals his or her intentions, but they somehow keep from bumping into each other. I felt the scene from Bombay to Poona being reenacted from moment to moment.

Pedestrians shouting after near-misses, dogs barking, pigs squealing, chickens squawking and flapping out of the way added to the general Poona afternoon chorus. Goats and broad-horned cows and dark gray water buffalo plodding along added other notes to this symphony—mainly a double bass in a sure, low tone.

Dotted along the road are little kiosks made of hammered strips of tin or actual cans. About three feet off the ground, they form an alcove—for all the world like a Punch-and-Judy stall—in which sits cross-legged a person who sleeps and eats there. He sells cigarettes, betel nuts for chewing, and *beedees*.

The *beedee* sellers sit from about six in the morning until ten at night. Then they roll down a flap and go to sleep right there. The walls of the kiosks are a riot of colors, what with the *beedee* packets and all the brands of cigarettes. *Paises* and Western cigarettes were kept together in a tin box.

Behind the seller would also be bright red betel nuts on a broad *bodhi* leaf. These are chewed all day long by many Indians, who continually spit out excess juice which stains their teeth and the streets a blood red. The *beedee wallah* would also prepare *pan*, which begins with a green *bodhi* leaf, in the center of which is placed a particular kind of mashed betel nut. The merchant them selects a paste from one of numerous pots near him, smears it on the leaf with a finger, tops it with a few seeds, and folds it into a square. The person buying it puts it in his cheek, like a wad of chewing tobacco. It's said to have speed in it, which gives the user a slightly glazed look and, after an initial burst of energy, a sluggishness and a swaying walk.

Over the years it amused me that many freshly arrived Westerners would refer to the "meditative" look on the Indians they saw, when, in reality, what they were seeing more often than not was the result of chewing this narcotic. These street vendors could often supply a little hashish or other drugs as well.

Along with the *wallah*s were what I later came to refer to as the wheeler-dealers or con men. They were bright-eyed, ready for action, always out to make a quick deal on anything. If they overheard you saying, "I'd really like a cane juice," they'd be off and back with same in an instant. Then you pay them for the goods, plus a little extra for the service.

Around the *beedee* kiosk women would have spread out a selection of wares: secondhand *sari*s, dresses, or knicknacks that very often had come from a garbage dump, but had been cleaned up to make them look nice. In India nothing goes to waste. If you drop a cigarette carton someone will pick it up and turn it into *something*. The people are very creative in that way. A bit of tin, a matchstick, anything will be snatched up. One frequently sees Indian women, with a cluster of children, walking along picking up any kind of discards and tucking them away into a cloth strapped to their back. At the end of the day the sack will be emptied out in the family hut, when all the family members and relatives will sort through the trove. Sooner or later each item will be cleaned up, or combined with something else, to turn up in the marketplace alongside the *sari*s.

One of the things that struck me about India—and which was also very much a part of the life inside the Ashram—was that each group had its own rhythm, and this never disturbed any other group. In the West the encounter between persons moving at very different tempos is going to create impatience and friction. Not so in India. The shouters and hurriers, the dreamers and lackadaisical, somehow blend together in this collective melee. The work eventually gets done, or it doesn't; but it just doesn't seem to *matter*.

The whole of Poona seemed built on advertisements. Since everything eventually gets recycled, even the walls of buildings are composed of odds and ends—a piece of cigarette wrapper, a flattened olive oil can, a sardine tin lid—anything that can be used as a patch. It all has a patina from years of monsoon rains and grime.

Adding to the mosaic of color and texture are the remains of huge movie posters that are painted each week. The face of the star—always a man—leaps out at you with immense eyes under jet-black hair smoothed back. To one side will be a woman, in *sari* and jewels, swooning. Each week these are painted over or simply pulled down to make room for announcements of incoming features. The discarded posters immediately become part of a wall, so you see years of cinema billboards visible now as only a bit of elaborate headdress or a single eye staring out. In later years Greenwich Village in New York reminded me somewhat of all this.

I quickly became one of the cleaners who would prepare Buddha Hall each morning before Bhagwan's lecture. There couldn't be a speck of dust in the auditorium when he was speaking—and making sure the place was spotless was the cleaning department's most important task. This became, for me, one of the most beautiful meditations of my day.

Buddha Hall was barely a third of the size it became before the move to the United States. The flooring was slab concrete with a glossy seal over it. The basic implement for cleaning was a wide broom base without bristles over which was fitted a big mop cloth. Each of these squares of toweling had a perfectly round hole in the center, which was circled with fine stitching. The edges had been hemmed to prevent shredding, and the corners were perfect right angles. A huge bucket accompanied each mop that was issued.

In the morning six of us would line up with our mops behind a row of six cleaners armed with brooms. At a signal the sweepers would move across the floor in formation, moving their brooms in a looping, forward motion. It always reminded me of the choreography in a Broadway show.

When the sweepers had completed a section we would wet and wring out our mops, then attack the floors. Moppers had their own special rhythm: The mop would be thrust forward, lifted high, pulled back, and reapplied to the concrete. As we followed the sweepers, another six people would follow *us*, advancing the buckets along. We would go over the floors twice to be sure that everything was totally clean. All the time taped music would be played to keep us moving in rhythm.

To be sure that there was no dust around Bhagwan, while we were cleaning inside Buddha Hall the gardeners would be wetting down the paths and gardens outside.

By the time this was underway I had already been up for several hours. My day began at 5:30 A.M. with what was called dynamic meditation, which was held in Buddha Hall prior to our cleaning. All the people doing groups would be required to participate; the rest of us were expected to do so. This lasted for an hour, and was accompanied by music. It had five phases, each with a different type of music being played. The first was very chaotic—which certainly helped wake us up—then it evolved through a more hectic climax, before descending through increasingly soothing passages until the final phase, which was a soft flute.

As the flute came on the gardeners would begin their morning watering. The sun coming up mingled with the rising scent of moisture and fragrance from the flower beds, while the gardeners moved in their own kind of silent, stately dance, hosing things down in perfect sweeping arcs. In this way the whole morning became an animated work of art.

Early arrivals for the lecture would gather at the gates of Lao Tzu House or get a cup of coffee at what was then a small restaurant named Vrindavan. This was not a communal mess hall like the cafeteria in Jesus House, but a pay-as-you-go restaurant where you could get everything from a cup of *chai* and slices of home-baked brown bread with peanut butter or honey to a full meal. At the time it was basically a cluster of round tables under a roof of rush matting.

Once the cleaners left, the woman assigned to distribute meditation mats would enter. Working from a list prepared by the office the night before, she would set out the mats—each with a person's name embroidered on it—in the specified spot in the first four rows. Any place not reserved by such a mat was up for grabs when the doors were opened to the crowd outside.

By 6:45 A.M. the "general admittance" group was let into Buddha Hall. By 7:15 A.M. the noise of later arrivals—many of them coming in rickshaws—was becoming very pronounced. There would be a growing sense of anticipation all around. Those of us assigned seats would usually arrive about 7:30. Then everyone would wait for Bhagwan's arrival at 7:45.

Just before he arrived, an unspoken signal would run through the crowd, silencing it. Outside the front gates the guards would walk well beyond the boundaries of the Ashram to stop the rickshaws from arrival and extend the zone of silence. The first sound that would break the silence was the noise of Bhagwan's tires crunching over the gravel as he was driven some 300 meters from the door of Lao Tzu House to the door of Buddha Hall. Lectures routinely ran an hour and a half to two hours.

For all my involvement in the day-to-day life of the Ashram, and my fascination with Bhagwan as a figure of power and mystery, I found the lectures very boring and frequently fell asleep. Early on I decided to skip these sessions. You could stay away without any comment being made—as long as you didn't walk anywhere near Buddha Hall, where you might make noise while he was speaking.

I would either linger in Jesus House or go into Poona proper to a place called The Coffee House, and get a proper breakfast and a good cup of coffee. There would often be a group of other such "rebels" dining together.

From the outset I and a few others (many of whom became my best friends and who came out from under the Oregon debacle in the best shape) formed this morning "coffee klatch." During evening *darshan* we often went to a watering hole called the Blue Diamond and drank beer. I came to value lecture and *darshan* as the only breaks in a day that otherwise was filled with work and meditation every waking hour.

I think some of my ease at finding a balance between obsessive devotion to Bhagwan and indifference came from my early training period in the Krishna House. Office people didn't seem to have the same trip about Bhagwan that other people did—and both Laxmi and, later, Sheela, encouraged this. There was a sense in the office that you didn't have to be near Bhagwan physically, you didn't have to hear him in person—whatever he was to you was something between you and him and it wasn't necessary to be at his feet all the time.

Even so, there was just enough collective paranoia among our rebel group so that we would always return just before lecture finished, and wait outside the back gates until these were opened. At that point, you could mingle with people leaving lecture hall, and look for all the world as though you had been there all morning—and, truly, no one was likely to think that you wouldn't want to be there. Sometimes it would be surprising (and amusing) to see who had chosen breakfast over lecture; but no trouble ever came of these defections. In fact most of us agreed that they helped save our collective sanity, when the long hours and endless rules at the Ashram began to get on our nerves.

CHAPTER 8

Umibushi Plums and Leaving *Darshan*

Kamul and I continued living together for several weeks, but we were also growing further apart. The relationship had changed profoundly. It had been a two-way relationship; our energies would meet in a shared center. Now he was doing this group and moving with other people. I realized, *I still love him; I can't help loving him; this is who I am.* Since we no longer wanted each other to the same degree—I no longer had an exclusive claim on him—I began to rethink a relationship to mean the desire to relate to somebody. Instead of looking for reinforcement from the outside—a man reassuring me that he loved me to the same degree I loved him—I let my increasingly one-sided need for him be enough.

It was all part of that endless process in the Ashram: Turning back on ourselves; constantly reexamining any emotional or intellectual position we took; learning that we had to be complete enough inside—trust ourselves—to create our own reality, our own happiness—exclusive of external things. I became like someone in a "Twilight Zone" episode who moves through her world unnoticed by anyone else and uncaring, because her world is the only world that existed.

The Ashram was a great playground for simply being who you were. As long as you performed "the needful" tasks, no one imposed judgments on the world you created inside and the way it colored your perceptions and interactions. The watchword at Koregaon Park was "Be who you are." But it wasn't totally idyllic. "You are your own responsibility"; "you create your own reality"; "any negativity you feel is your own resistance to personal growth"—all these catchphrases made up the basic language of the Ashram. While some Ashramites undoubtedly were able to believe they felt good, I found that I began not to feel at all—though there were moments when something would touch me, and I would feel things with the intensity I hadn't felt since childhood.

My days were somewhat unusual compared to those of most other people at the Ashram. They would do everything they could to be at a job *before* time—not merely *on* time. Work was a time of trying continually to "drop the self."

I, on the other hand, spent all my energy trying to find ways to get out of what I'd been told to do. It became a joke that you could never find me, but that I'd always have the best alibi. I perfected this talent greatly as time went on—most notably when I became one of Sheela's secretaries. If discovered, the chances were that I was smoking a *beedee* inside the Ashram, where no one was supposed to smoke *at all*. I sometimes wondered if I wasn't kept on as the "devil" any "paradise" requires—in my case, "the kid who never grew up."

I would get up as late as I possibly could. My enthusiasm for the "cleaning ballet" in the mornings at Buddha Hall evaporated early on. I did everything I could to get off that rota—either switching tasks with someone on a later cleaning shift, or simply not showing up and inventing some plausible reason to cover my absence.

My main cleaning duties were in the dormitory called Vipassana. I was responsible for thirteen rooms downstairs. I would always take my bucket along—a bucket left at the cleaning station was a signal that someone hadn't shown up for work. I'd set it in some corner of Vipassana, and go for a quick smoke and chat with whoever else was taking a break at the back gates. These were largely the kitchen staff, because they worked during lecture preparing meals, and were given their official break afterwards.

Then I'd run back to Vipassana and do my own "abbreviated" form of room-cleaning. At first I'd been quite careful to do things *exactly* as I'd been instructed. Every day I would pick up each item and dust it; every piece of clothing would be taken out and refolded; the bed was turned; the screens were taken off and washed.

I learned very fast that all you had to do was change things a little bit, and people would assume that it was clean. Most of the time we were cleaning an already spotless room anyhow.

I had first become fascinated with the idea of surrendering myself, but I was now growing bored with the endless rounds of work, the same clothes, the same routine. So I'd go into a room, move a tee-shirt from the top to the bottom of a stack, fluff things up a bit, and go quickly on to the next room. I'd do three of these in short order, using only a fraction of the hour or so it would normally have taken for deep cleaning. With the free time that gave me, I'd go off to amuse myself.

If I had no money I wouldn't hesitate to go to someone and ask them for it; people would do the same thing to me often enough. If you wanted to, you did—and people usually did, if they had anything to give. I never had to make up an elaborate story: I could simply say, "I want to go into town for an ice cream." This would sometimes come up in regard to groups: They were expensive, and people who had been told by Bhagwan to take this or that group might have to ask for the money to pay for it.

I became notorious for my rickshaw rides. There were always a number of them hovering outside the front gates of Koregaon Place. I'd give a driver five or ten rupees and tell him, "Go anywhere." I'd insist that they drive as fast as they could, while I just sat in the back and to- tally relaxed. When they brought me back I'd smoke a quick *beedee*, run in, then rearrange a few more rooms.

This was the pattern of my days. But several occurrences changed their tenor.

One day, while I was cleaning a room in lower Vipassana, I became obsessed with a jar of Japanese *umibushi* plums that Abiyana, the room's owner, kept on his shelf. These were sour plums in a jar of saltwater; Abiyana, who was trained as an acupuncturist, had acquired a taste for these plums, which are considered quite a delicacy. I had been familiar with them in Singapore.

Each time I went through the motions of cleaning his room, I found my mouth watering for one of the plums. But it was the strictest rule of the Ashram that you *never* took anything from anyone.

Each day I would lift the jar of *umibushi* plums, wipe it off, dust un- der it, and replace it on the shelf. The more I stared at them, the more I wanted one. I began to wonder if he had counted them, if he took one after each meal (which was the way they were traditionally eaten), if he knew exactly how many meals he would be able to follow with a plum.

The idea of taking one from the jar grew in my mind to something on the magnitude of Arthur drawing the sword Excalibur from the stone. This illustrated just how ingrown life in the Ashram could be- come, making us see things all out of proportion to their actual importance.

For about ten days I thought more and more frequently about the plums, and got closer and closer actually to taking one. Finally, one day I lifted down the jar and sat on the end of the bed, holding it. I was frightened that someone would see me, since everything was open around the Ashram. I felt like I was committing a big crime; I got a real adrenaline rush. Underneath everything was the sense—drummed into us day in and day out—that doing anything like this was *stealing from Bhagwan*.

Giving rein to my criminal instincts, however, I unscrewed the top of the jar with the finesse of a burglar attempting to open a safe. The marinated plums themselves had been packed under a layer of seaweed; I nudged this carefully aside to retrieve a plum. Feeling tenser than ever, I popped one in my mouth and quickly resealed the jar.

Then I worried if I had left it *exactly* how I had found it. I could hardly taste the plum because of the *guilt* I was feeling. I must have touched the jar fifteen times, trying to be sure that it was precisely as I had found it on the shelf. In the end I made myself so nervous that I had to go outside for a smoke. My fear that somebody was going to find out what I had done kept me on edge all the rest of the day.

I was so caught up in the mystique of Bhagwan that I began to wonder if he would be able to *know* what I had done. The idea that somehow, in his room in Lao Tzu House, he had *known* what was going on at the very moment I had unscrewed the cap began to obsess me the way the plums had earlier. The longer I stayed in the Ashram, the more I thought the man was capable of. I thought of him as a child might think of an all-seeing God. This idea intensified after I had stolen that lone plum.

After that I could never clean Abiyana's room without suffering guilt to the point of feeling sick. Just recently, while visiting in California, I ran into Abiyana, and we had a good giggle about this little story. (By the way, he *doesn't* count them!)

Much later I had another criminal lapse. I had been reassigned to rooms in Eckhart House in one of the routine job rotations that were the order of the day. It happened in a room that belonged to a woman named Susheila, who kept her shelves jammed with foods: coffee, tea, honey, curry powders, mints. This was very much not in keeping with the usual spareness maintained in the Ashram. But then, Susheila wasn't exactly the typical Ashramite.

What caught my fancy there was a jar of Nutella—a chocolate-and-nut confection that spreads like a cream. This intrigued me the same way as the jar of plums had. I recalled having eaten it only once before, when I was growing up in Singapore. I remembered poking my finger into the jar then, and found I wanted to dip my finger into the batch on Susheila's shelves.

That vivid childhood memory swept aside the more recent guilty incident of the *umibushi* plums. The potential for trouble, however, was even greater with Nutella. While the sourness of the plums meant you would only want one at a time, the chocolate invited you to go on and on. One fingerful led to another; I couldn't stop. I would keep replacing the jar, then lifting it down for one more taste. I would even leave and work on another room, only to be drawn back to the sweet. I'd been without a taste of real chocolate for months, since the real thing was scarce in India.

This crime became even more complicated to cover up, because Nutella is packed like peanut butter, and shows the trace of a spreading knife or finger on top. Susheila always used a knife; I only had my finger. After each foray I'd have to smooth the surface so that it never looked like a finger had been dipping into it.

All along, I wondered how closely Susheila studied the jar. Since luxuries like this were in short supply, people *did* tend to notice things much more sharply. Still, for all my worries, I continued to raid the Nutella jar over the next several days. Eventually, I knew that I had taken so much that I wasn't going to get away with it, so I decided to get rid of the whole jar.

But I couldn't take it home to Music House huts with me, because it had now become a source of worry and guilt. I hated the stuff and never wanted to taste it again. I hid it in my skirt, took it as far from Eckhart House as I could, and hid it under a trash heap.

This was how obsessional even the tiniest things could become in the Ashram; I felt people would zero in on me if the jar ever came to light. And I never did anything like that again in the Ashram.

This story points out how aware we would become of everything around us. It was perfectly reasonable to think that someone *would* know if a plum or a dollop of Nutella had been taken. We were trained to be aware of everything from moment to moment: If someone had used a few squirts of my liquid soap from one round of cleaning to the next I would know it, without consciously studying the container. Working in the office I might have a stack of fifty letters on my desk; from a single run through I could tell you exactly what order they had been in, or if someone had replaced a single item in another order.

We were taught to live every moment in its totality; we learned to notice absolutely everything, without consciously having to think about it. I was reacting to my own sense that even a change as small as a single plum being removed was something *I* would have noticed. I was always surprised that no one raised the issue of my pilfering on either occasion.

I never took my noon meals with other people in the canteen. I couldn't get used to dining in a crowd. I would take my *thali* tray and go off to Jesus House gardens or some other quiet spot to eat. After lunch, I'd finish my cleaning chores. We worked twelve hours a day, seven days a week.

The day would be punctuated by the music of different meditations. In addition to the morning meditations, at 4 P.M., we would have *nada-brama*. This was very quiet, though it did involve some movement. At 5:15 we had *kundalini*, which included more rapid movements—something closer to dancing.

Much of the life of the Ashram was built around groups—which, as we've already seen, would break you down and reeducate you. I didn't do any groups because I had started to work right away in the office. But I absorbed a lot of the attitude and awareness that a person would normally pick up from doing such groups. Nevertheless, I think the fact that I never formally attended group sessions helps explain why I was always able to observe the life around me with an objectivity that I might have lost in formal group training.

The Ashram only paid board for the Ashramites. Everyone else paid for their food—often at one of the Ashram's restaurants—and bought books, videos, clothing, and other items through the Ashram. On occasion, non-Ashramites would conduct groups, but they would have to support themselves outside. They might be given a food pass and a place to sleep, but this was not usual.

By 6 P.M. people would be gathering for *darshan*. Bhagwan would come out between 6:45 and 7. At first only the people directly involved would go; later the whole Ashram (except Music Group) stopped for *darshan*.

My cleaning chores would end about 5:30, when I'd take my supplies back to the cleaning hut. I'd linger over dinner until about 7:15, when I'd go back to the cleaning hut. There would always be some sewing, or planing wood for brooms, or something else to be done. This would last until about 9 or 10, when I'd go to bed. Occasionally, I would be put on a shift that began as early as 4 A.M., with some time off scattered through the day. Since there was never a day off, I felt I was always running in twenty-four-hour segments, in which sleep was merely a break in the endless routine—not a real separation between one day and the next.

Equally important was the fact that, from the moment I saw Bhagwan, I was very much in love with the man. My spontaneous words at our first meeting—"I can't wait for day I can leave you"—acknowledged the fact that I was a novice. I instinctively knew I had found the master I had been seeking all my life, and I was looking ahead to the day when I would have learned all I could from him.

Now that I had been around him some time, however, I found that a desire to leave Bhagwan was the furthest thing from my mind. Though I might find his formal lectures tedious, I was utterly captivated by him.

That was the amazing thing about Bhagwan: Each *sannyasin* would fall in love with him in his or her own way. Some wanted to be his lover; some wanted to be *baktis*, devotees. Each was there for him for a particular reason. I loved him a little as a child might love a wise and kind teacher. I valued him as a master who not only tells you a story, but lets you live it. I relished being a part of this magical kingdom he had brought into being.

I felt the possibility of a depth of understanding that was never possible with my father, because there was so much about the work he was involved in that he would never share. The Ashram was not something I studied about: I *lived* it each day, and learned from the experience.

Bhagwan let us create our whole illusion; I was living in my own fairyland. Where some might identify Bhagwan with a face or body, to me he was an essence that I *felt* in me; and at the same time I felt I was a part of *him*. Although each *sannyasin* was seeing him as part of a particular illusion, you could see a belief that reinforced your own reflected in each pair of eyes.

Sometimes people would say, "I could really *feel* Bhagwan today," and I'd realize I didn't know what they meant. Then my skeptical mind might start questioning how much of what I chose to see was *real*. But I'd shut it up right away, because it felt so much better to go on believing in things as I wanted them to be.

But the skeptical child always remained at the back of my mind, attentive and never fully denied. I could look at that little devil in me and smile at it: I realized I could live simultaneously with doubt and belief. This was just one more paradox to live with in an environment that was infinitely paradoxical: At the most basic level we lived with almost obsessional regimentation and absolute freedom.

Within the Ashram we were creating literally hundreds of realities—as many as there were *sannyasin*s. The more I opened myself to paradox, the less sure I became of what was "illusion" or "reality." The more I seemed to grasp for something, the more it would disappear. The safety valve, the one thing I felt certain of, was this: Even if you weren't, *he* was. Though, if I pushed it further, I realized that his *being* did not necessarily mean *in body*.

I truly believed there was something to be had from being near the Bhagwan—even if that didn't include sitting through each two- or three-hour lecture. I always felt his presence *right there*, no matter what I was doing.

I had Kamul *and* Bhagwan. I felt I could put up with *anything* to keep these two men in my life.

Moreover, I had all these beautiful women around me, who accepted my adolescent self as an equal. The Ashram never acknowledged any difference in age; we were there for enlightenment, and concerns over calendar years or physical differences simply didn't apply.

Sometimes, for all my speaking and acting as I thought a grown woman *should* act, I would find myself desperately wondering, How in the hell do I get from here to there? They were self-assured, able to look each other in the eye candidly; they could hug each other with an easy warmth. They were sensitive and sensual, able to move and dance with grace—all the things I wanted for myself. The Ashram was a tiny town, complete in itself; these women were a community within the larger one—a community in which, for all their reassurances, I felt like an imposter.

All the time we would be told, Whatsoever you want—enlightenment or anything else—is right here and now. That's a sentence we would hear over and over. This reinforced the idea in me that being near these people was the surest way to know and develop self.

On purely aesthetic and sensual levels, the Ashram was a beautiful place to be. The gardens, the little pathways, the smells, the clean air, the warmth, the clothes—loose and flowing with never a tight waistband or pair of jeans—no shoes again. Nobody cut their hair; we wore it long and free; we didn't fuss with makeup; we didn't wrestle with the idea that the body beautiful was hard and thin—now the ideal was softness, roundness.

Yet, at the same time, we kept our hands soft and well-manicured. We learned to enjoy and nurture "the body." We went toward soft fabrics and comfortable clothes that lent themselves to a graceful appearance.

Very quickly, I learned to appreciate in other women and teach myself a way of moving without sudden, jerky movements. The women of Koregaon park walked with grace, smoothly and lightly; even a turn of the head would be done slowly, elegantly. But this was not done consciously—that would have made any awkwardness even more pronounced.

This lightness was a reflection of Bhagwan. He walked as if he was barely touching the ground; when he turned to *namaste* the audience in Buddha Hall, it was one fluid movement; sitting and crossing his legs would be another perfectly executed maneuver. Seeing this grace in him and being aware that everyone around me was doing even the simplest tasks with grace, I was encouraged to learn to do the same. And it *is* a good feeling—almost like doing *tai chi* twenty-four hours a day.

In this way we made every waking minute of our day a kind of meditation, "To become just one, then disappear."

One morning, about five or six months after we'd arrived at the Ashram, Kamul told me that he didn't want to be with me any more.

I was very upset. Hurt and angry, I said, "That's just not possible." Until I was no longer in love, I had to be in love all the way. I tried to make him see this. "I have to be with you," I pleaded. Then I threatened, "I'll follow you wherever you go."

My passionate outburst unnerved Kamul. By this time I was very much involved in the Ashram and, as far as anyone could see, with its standards and beliefs. I'd waltzed in, been immediately accepted by Bhagwan and the office staff, and—barring some backsliding over the *tantra* group—apparently had far less problem with the idea of surrender than many other *sannyasins*.

He called retreat, telling me he was going to go back to the West "to be rid of me." I had become, for him, a stumbling block on his personal road to enlightenment.

"Well, I'll follow you, just like I said I would," I told him.

"You can't," he said, getting angry himself for the first time. "You *live* here." Once again I glimpsed that unspoken gulf between Ashramites who were privileged insiders and those *sannyasins* who lived outside the walls and only shared in Ashram life to a very limited degree. Though I lived in the Music House huts, I did so by choice; and I had been told that I could move back into the Ashram whenever I chose. I worked in the Ashram every day, had a food pass for meals in Jesus House, and could have a place reserved in Buddha Hall if I desired it. In the circumscribed world of the Ashram and its environs, I was one of the "elect." I hadn't sought it, did not place a great deal of value on it. This, perhaps as much as any other factor, led to our inevitable split. It was as close as anything came to class consciousness and conflict in Koregaon Place.

Kamul went ahead with his plans and booked a "leaving *darshan*" with Bhagwan—the official acknowledgment of a *sannyasin*'s departure for the West. At this event it was traditional for Bhagwan to give a small gift to take with you. Usually, this was a little box with some of his hair or something that belonged to him. Called a meditation box, it was thought to be a protective charm or meditation device—though it pretty much could be whatever you wanted it to be. They were quite beautiful, made of inlaid wood in the *mala* shop on the Ashram grounds.

I asked for a joint leaving *darshan*, but I had no intention of leaving—and no intention of letting *him* leave. My *darshan*s with Bhagwan always tended to be animated affairs—and this promised more of the same.

Buddha Hall was crowded as always that evening. Every night the ceremony would call up those who were taking *sannyas*, professing themselves formally as students of Bhagwan. Next would come the formalities of leaving, then arriving. Last would be a chance to ask questions directly.

At the appropriate moment, Kamul and I were called forward and sat down at Bhagwan's feet.

"Anything to say?" was Bhagwan's ritual opening.

Kamul said, "Yes."

"Well, what is it?" Bhagwan asked.

"I have a problem."

"And what is your problem?"

"*Her!*" said Kamul.

At this the entire crowd broke into laughter. I sat there feeling my face going red, but determined not to back down from my position.

Bhagwan began chuckling himself, which signaled everyone to enjoy the joke to the fullest. Laughter was very much a part of *darshan*s and lectures—encouraged by Bhagwan, who would pepper his discourses with jokes, often of the bawdiest sort.

When the merriment had run its course, Bhagwan asked Kamul, "How is she a problem for you?"

To which Kamul answered, "I want to be rid of her, and I *can't*. I want to go back to the West, but she says she'll even follow me *there*. And *you* told her that this was her home, and that she was to stay, but *now* she says she's going to go back to the West."

Bhagwan looked at Kamul for a few moments, then turned to me. I made a movement of my hands, palms up, and shrugged, indicating, *I can't say anything else: That's the way it is.*

Bhagwan turned back to Kamul, and said, "Every fear that you have with this woman is true. You feel that she's going to swallow you up;

you feel that she's going to devour you. *And she is.* You're absolutely
right to see this as a problem." But then he added, "Who is it who's so
afraid? Why can't you feel clear in yourself that someone could be in
their trip? Why do you allow so much to affect you? She's in her own
game, and she's playing it *totally.* She's totally in her own number, and
she's going for it. And, for some reason, you're letting this bug you.
She gave you her love. Why can't you just leave that alone? Why can't
you be inside of yourself and not let it bother you?"

Kamul had thought—and a lot of other people in the Ashram had
agreed—that the fact that I had said I was going to follow him would
prompt an, "Oh *no!* No attachment" response from Bhagwan. Instead,
he characteristically did the unexpected, drawing attention to Kamul's
unsettled inner self. He would go back and forth, reminding his followers that we were fooling ourselves if we believed we could anticipate him.

The situation between Kamul and myself also served as a reminder
that Bhagwan never tried to interfere with people who were really
"clear." You don't try to stop such people, because they are in a state of
"grace"—absolutely certain of themselves and their path. The ones
who needed guidance were the ones who were unsure of themselves,
who were still trying to make out their path.

When he had finished with Kamul Bhagwan turned his attention
back to me. "You know, you really *don't* have to go. This is your home."

I just sat there and argued, "Well, why can't you just tell him to
stay? It would be a lot easier."

Bhagwan laughed again, and said, "I can't tell him to stay."

But I knew there *were* certain people that he *would* ask to stay. And
no *sannyasin* in my experience up to that point would have denied him,
if he made such a request. Looking back, I sometimes wonder if Kamul
hadn't forced the issue in the hope that Bhagwan *would* ask him to stay.

My only response was, "Then, I have to go."

"All right," he said, still smiling, "And when it's finished, you can
come home."

That was the end of our *darshan.* Kamul was upset; the matter had
been closed, and things were just where they had been before. I was
determined to go back with him, and even *less* likely than before to
give it up.

A few days later we left together for England.

As it turned out, our last meeting with Bhagwan seemed to have
(not unexpectedly) thrown his previous decision to separate into
doubt. Bhagwan had *not* suggested Kamul stay; he had implied an

"open door policy" where I was concerned. In Kamul's eyes, I think, my status had risen, and my clarity and strong will had been endorsed by Bhagwan—the most important figure in Kamul's life. In the wake of this, Kamul rethought our relationship and decided to continue it, since Bhagwan had implied that *I*, rather than Kamul, was further advanced along the spiritual path.

Whatever the cause I was delighted, since being with Kamul was the most important thing to me at that time.

CHAPTER 9

The Commune Again

So we returned to England—and to another homecoming, of sorts. The weather was cold—a real shock after eight months in the heat of Poona—and I shivered in spite of the layers of clothing I was wearing as I climbed down from the bus behind Kamul. Everybody at the commune was warm and welcoming as we trudged down the path to the front door, weary from our flight and the long bus ride to the outskirts of Oxford.

But, for all the surprised, pleasant greetings, I felt something was different. There was an electricity in the air—not directed in any particular direction, but arcing from Sangeeta's eyes to Anu's a split second before they waved us inside; evident in Rajive's hesitant, nervous greeting; charging everyone who came out onto the porch or met us in the hall at the foot of the staircase.

Even Kamul seemed to be responding to this, shifting uncomfortably from foot to foot while he gave a vague, hasty explanation for our sudden return. He kept glancing at me as if to reassure himself I was still there, and approved his account.

I decided that my discomfort was the result of jet lag, the sudden time/space displacement after fourteen hours traveling from East to West. My Ashram training was solidly in place: The last thing I trusted were my own impressions. Until I could examine matters without the fuzziness that air travel gives rise to, I refused to let the sense of hovering tension color my heartfelt pleasure at being back on the farm.

I gave Kamul's hand a squeeze, and that seemed to break the momentary spell. Seema said, "You can have the room at the end of the hall upstairs," and we automatically began climbing the staircase. *Tomorrow*, I assured myself, *everything will look right again*. For the moment I wanted nothing more than to sleep.

In the morning everything seemed the way I had remembered it.

The commune was a family, and an extension of the Ashram. In those days people were more comfortable with the idea that you could go on working in the world, not necessarily live in a commune, maybe visit a center occasionally, and still be very much an extension of Bhagwan and his work. But, already, people felt compelled to be as physically close to him as possible. The judgment was that unless you lived in the commune or, ideally, the Ashram, you were cutting yourself off from Bhagwan. There was a steady movement of people from England to India—almost everyone from the commune became an important part of the Ashram over the years. It was unusual for a center to produce so many key players—but, then, the commune was unique in many ways.

The cast of characters included Vipul, who owned the place; Sangeeta, his girlfriend; Anu and her husband, Rajive, who had two young daughters; Vijay and his lady Sunita; Seema, her boyfriend; Shikha, with her little boy, Mukul, whose uncle lived in town and seemed rather amused that his nephew had taken *sannyas*; and Atul, the son of a lord, whose father was the chairman of a well-known auction house and owned a large estate.

A good number of them were nurses at the rehabilitation hospital. Vipul was the charge nurse, a position of some importance; other nurses included Rajive, Vijay, Sunita, Mukul, Atul, and, of course, Kamul. I hadn't known at the time, but my visiting on weekends, as a patient of the hospital, had put all of their jobs in jeopardy. To this day I'm not clear on why they were willing to put themselves in such a compromised position—but I'm glad they did.

Sangeeta took care of the house and coordinated the groups that were the main source of income for the commune; Anu did housecleaning in the village—since everyone was required to be self-supporting and contribute to the commune; Seema also worked as a cleaner; Seema's boyfriend was a pharmacist in the nearby town of Wallingford; Shikha was both a cleaner and a painter, who was a helper in the local school her son attended. Eric the dog did not work, but he supplied emotional support where needed.

I didn't find a job right away, but spent several days just letting myself get reacquainted with the commune and the immediate countryside. I never seemed able to get warm enough, and I still felt somewhat out-of-place—though there was no obvious reason for my feelings.

The groups the commune ran were still not enough to make it self-supporting—in spite of having turned out major group leaders. Several, in fact, went to the Netherlands and opened (with the support of the Dutch government) a drug rehabilitation center similar to ones al-

ready established in New York and London. Dutch and British group
leaders would often visit the commune in England to conduct groups.
They would rent the barn, which had been soundproofed and made
into a group room.

After about a week I decided to get a job. I wound up working at the
Government Employment Centre. I had originally gone there to check
the job listings and sign on for social security; as it turned out, they
hired me the day I walked in. I had just turned sixteen, the minimum
age for such employment.

All day long I met with people who were looking for jobs but who
were really looking for a therapist, because of the difficulty of job-
hunting. I would sit with people, listen to them, and match them with
a potential employer—the exact sort of work I later did in the Ashram.

The job was bearable enough, but evenings at the commune were
becoming something of a problem. Everyone was expected to eat together at the large communal dinner. In the Ashram I never ate in
groups; although I liked the people in the commune a lot, I didn't want
to eat with them. They couldn't understand this, and felt a little put out
by my standoffishness. For the first time I really got the feeling that,
for all the protestations of wanting each other to be individuals, the
atmosphere actually discouraged that. If you were too much an individual, it was considered a negative thing.

All of the people in the house were either therapists or had taken a
number of groups. In those groups they'd had a lot knocked out of
them—and had a lot of programming put back in its place. I've seen a
lot of this thing happen in therapy: You break people down emotionally; then, while they're in that vulnerable state, you tell them how they
should be living. I think there can be many positive sides to this sort of
thing, but the down side is the fact that a few strong people in a group
who have resisted programming and hung onto their own ideas often
are the ones who sway the group the most.

No matter how good a group leader is, these people can very often
pull other group members into their own quarter. Basically, they are
looking for reinforcement for the way they live, and gaining the support of more pliable participants is the way they get such approval.
They get people to lean their way by having the best-sounding argument or, simply, the loudest mouth. You can really see this happen in
twenty-four-hour marathon sessions; there, without sleep or food, with
very high group energy, a person's resistance is quickly worn down
and you can begin suggesting paths to him or her.

Each person in the commune believed that groups were *the* way to grow. A lot of that may have been the times. The world was just discovering groups, and Esalen, est, Arica, and lots of other communities were popping up everywhere.

There I sat: I didn't want to eat with people, and I hadn't done any groups. Everybody decided there was something wrong with me: I must need a group. I have to admit that I was young and not so strong in myself that I could stand up against fourteen or so people and say, "I'm right."

Instead, I began to wonder why I couldn't eat with the others; I tried to force myself to eat at the table, but would end up becoming ill. (When I did return to the Ashram, I went back to my old pattern of dining alone—often outside the Ashram itself—and this may have actually been a blessing later on, since rumors about the food being drugged persist to this day.)

In spite of this bone of contention, we were generally getting on fine together. But, periodically, one member of the commune would be singled out as a scapegoat (a pattern I later saw repeated at the Ashram) and become the dumping ground for the group's frustrations and hostilities.

These outbursts were never caused by a person doing something really crazy; instead, over a week or ten days, you would find yourself caught up in a kind of negative collective consciousness that made the victim-to-be the focus of everyone's attention. You'd start to notice things about that person, and begin to pick on him.

The clearest instance was the case of Rajive. The whole matter blew up because Sangeeta thought Anu, Rajive's lady, should be sleeping with other men in order for her "to grow." Anu had never been with anyone else but Rajive in her life.

Sangeeta, who was a very powerful, very strong-willed woman, had a habit of deciding that if she saw something she felt needed changing, then she was right and the other person has nothing to do but go along with her. The whole situation was complex. Even I, who was still pretty naive in terms of relationships, could see that part of Sangeeta's game was to create a situation for Anu that would set an example for the commune and thus let *her*, Sangeeta, open up her relationship with Vipul and be with other people. Her manipulations of Anu and Rajive were really to bring about a change in the commune that would benefit her.

If Rajive scolded his daughter, Sangeeta would say to me, "I think he's being awfully harsh on her, I wonder what his anger's really about?" Soon, you'd notice that *everybody* was watching and raising

questions about the most trivial actions on Rajive's part. I found myself
doing it. We would all respond to the sense of building pressure—like
a volcano getting ready to explode.

Inevitably, the focus of so much negative attention became para-
noid and defensive, which only heightened the friction. I could see, on
one level, what was going on; but I went along with the game anyway.
The last thing I wanted was for the energy to be transferred to me, because it was very scary. To be walking around your own home, feeling
this angry energy building up against you is terrifying. It was easier for
me to play the game than challenge it, and possibly be lumped in with
the victim.

Things reached a climax one night during a "family meeting,"
which all members of the commune were expected to attend. Whenever someone used the phrase "family meeting," you *knew* some issue
was going to be raised or someone was about to get nailed.

At the time this was going on, India—and, by extension, all the Rajneesh centers around the world—had discovered the no-limit group.
Whatever self-expression happened in group was okay. So we felt pretty
free to attack Rajive that night.

We met in the living room on the appointed evening. There was a
lot of nervous chatter, a few giggles that also betrayed a great deal of
nervousness, and the tension of a group waiting for someone to toss a
firecracker into its midst. Everyone knew there was going to be un-
pleasantness of some sort—it was just a matter of *when* it was going to
erupt.

The living room was small and gave the feeling of a pressure cooker, with everyone crowded in and waiting, waiting. . . . Most of the
people were bunched onto the old sofas facing the huge, old fieldstone
fireplace. Eric the dog was there, his head anxiously swiveling from
one person to the next. He sensed a storm brewing but was uncertain
from which quarter trouble was going to come.

Rajive was sitting on an old armchair; Anu had drawn up a wooden
chair next to him. Her eyes flashed between Sangeeta and her husband—clearly she knew what was going to happen, and just as clearly
she had no idea what the final outcome was going to be. She was visibly shaking. Later I got Anu's number: She was one of those people
who will help push to one of these confrontations, then sit and wring
her hands and deny any responsibility in the matter.

Sangeeta, to give her her due, would create the situation and stick
by her decision right down the line. She was standing near the fireplace that evening, watching each person come in, like a teacher faced
with a potentially unruly class.

There were a few general remarks about commune business, then Sangeeta fired the opening salvo. "I've noticed, Rajive, that you're really negative."

He shifted uncomfortably in his seat. "Well, *I* don't feel negative."

Then someone else piped up, "Well, *exactly:* that's what we mean. You see, you can't even look at yourself. Your answer comes immediately."

"Look at the way you're sitting," someone else called out, "Your body language says it all."

Then it became a round-robin, everyone adding their two cents' worth—always more forcefully.

I sat there, able to feel the anger in the air. It was totally out of proportion to the situation.

Rajive was an easy target. He had twinkly blue eyes, was always up to mischief, and spoke with a heavy cockney accent. He had a slew of jokes to tell, was warm and loving, and hated confrontations of any kind. I often felt he was one of the wisest members of the commune, because he could take life in stride and laugh at its vagaries.

Watching him from my corner near the fireplace, I saw him begin to tremble, and that made me even more scared—clearly, he knew that things were about to get out of control. He tried to defuse the situation by saying, "Look, you guys. If you feel this way, you feel this way—but you're not being specific about what the problem is."

He and Anu were sitting behind a table that had a big tray with a pot of tea, which was always served at these gatherings. Suddenly, Anu snatched up the bottle of milk from the tray, cracked Rajive across the side of the head, and started to scream and scream.

Rajive leapt up; fortunately, the bottle had shattered without apparently cutting him or doing any serious damage, though milk had splattered everywhere. The chair behind him went over with a *thump.* Anu grabbed at him and started pummeling him. Sangeeta and some of the others also started beating on him. Seema crossed to me, shaking, and hugged me. All the while, Anu kept yelling, "You never let go! You're so uptight! You're not in touch with your feelings!"

Everyone was in hysterics. The dog, who was very fond of Rajive, had gone crazy, barking and snapping at no one in particular. I was in shock and afraid, because I identified with Rajive. He wasn't the sort of person to go off screaming and shouting and wailing in tears every time he felt an emotion. He could work with those emotions, learn from them, and simultaneously get on with the business of life.

Sitting on the floor, I realized this could easily be me: I'd already trod thin ice by not eating with people. Meanwhile, calmer heads were prevailing. Anu was still slapping at Rajive; but Vipul, with Kamul's help, had pulled Sangeeta out of the fight. Vijay was dragging Sunita away. With the exception of Seema, who was holding onto me, and Shikha, who stood to one side shouting, "Stop it! Stop it!" most of the other women in the room were still flailing away at Rajive.

The mayhem stopped as suddenly as it had begun. Rajive just sat down and started to cry. In short order *everybody* was crying, with the exception of myself. (I wasn't able to cry until years later, after I had left the Ashram.) If I had been in Rajive's place I would have said to the others, "You just don't understand me." So I was surprised to hear Rajive, through his tears, saying, "You're right. You're right." My initial response was to wonder, *What on earth is the matter with you?* Then, almost as quickly, I began to wonder what was the matter with *me* that I couldn't get how all these people could physically beat up on someone—and have him say they were right.

Everyone began to hug and kiss Rajive, then hug and kiss each other. I felt increasingly alienated from the whole scene. Seema was still holding me, but I was hardly aware of her. I felt the confusion of someone who's walked into the middle of a complex movie and is trying to sort out the plot. The others had worked through this process, accused and abused Rajive, *he* had accused *himself*, and now everyone was forgiving and embracing.

I didn't get it.

Later, I understood what was going on. We would say to each other that Bhagwan's essence was in each of us—meaning it was *our* essence too. If we had a button someone could push, we were taught not to identify with the person doing the pushing, but to identify with the fact that your button was being pushed. In a confrontational situation everything was turned back on the self—it has nothing to do with the other person, but with me and the way I'm taking it on. For me to sit in the room shaking was *my* problem: It had nothing to do with the fact that everyone else in the place had momentarily gone looney-tunes.

I began to examine my reactions, asking, Why have those feelings been created? Who are you in the midst of those feelings? Who are you now that you've looked at that feeling? Who are you now that you've dropped that feeling?

We would go totally into the feeling, into the experience of that feeling, and beyond. But we learned to recognize patterns in ourselves that let us bypass a lot of the working-out of emotions. We would be able to say, "I know where that's leading me"—and move immediately to the end, from which we would strive to move forward another step.

Most people endlessly replay the same emotional patterns; we lived so intensely in the Ashram and the commune that we were always trying to break those patterns and discover new information about ourselves. The everyday concerns that kept people outside the Ashram grounded in their world had very little to do with us. We were always trying to free ourselves from such "anchors."

Also, the majority of people in the house were therapists—not just through the Bhagwan connection (which already gave them tremendous authority from my point of view), but in Britain's eyes. As far as I knew they were absolutely right in whatever they were talking about or doing. I've since found it's very often the case that people will trust a therapist before they'll trust their own feelings. I know that, at the commune, I accepted the fact that they knew better than I did how to deal with life. To a lesser extent I felt there were important lessons I could learn only by staying on.

But, from that moment, I began to learn what it was like to live in a communal situation in total tension and fear—while grabbing hold of every positive experience that I could. And there *were* some very positive things for me at the commune, for all the problems.

Perhaps the most important was the sudden realization, as I sat in my corner of the living room, that the fear might be my problem *but I could change it*. I no longer had to be at the whim of fate. It gave me an unexpected feeling of calm. I felt I could deal with whatever came along. It was like a door opening on another part of my being, and I intended to explore who lay beyond.

The immediate result of this outburst was Rajive's admission that he wanted to change partners, just as Anu did. The confrontation had cleared the air, and the tension subsided as we all went about our business.

About a month later I quit my job. I'd gotten on well enough with the people there: I'd frequently worn orange clothes and my *mala* (though, to avoid problems with employers, this wasn't required of commune members). If anyone asked me, I explained how I'd met Bhagwan, and felt he had something to teach me. I didn't try to "convert" anyone.

What I was involved with then *wasn't* a religion; Bhagwan didn't claim to be a god of any sort. He offered a series of teachings on Jesus, Lao Tzu, Buddha, Mohammed, many of the masters. It was interesting to see the people I met move from an initial fear of the "orange people" to realization that we weren't a threat, that we were just regular people.

We very quickly fit into the life around us. It was a tiny village with two pubs, one of which we regularly patronized. All the people got on with us. We'd play darts, cribbage, and eat steak with them—we weren't strict vegetarians. Most of our parents lived in the area—most had spent their lives thereabouts.

For two years running the commune was used as the fairground for the town fair. Anu did babysitting for the locals. We weren't seen as some weird cult; we were accepted as a group of people who had chosen to live together and who wore orange clothes.

Nor did we have much of a problem with the local puritans. However, when we had more and more groups, some of the people who came were real lunatics. Fortunately, the incidents turned out to be bizarre or amusing, never dangerous.

Twice a guy who called himself "Black Eagle," and who wore black leather clothes, created problems in the sleepy, very proper little village. One evening Black Eagle put on a black motorbike helmet, forgot to put any trousers on, and went knocking on various doors to share some incomprehensible message with the world at large.

Our neighbors took it quite well. No one was upset; they just guided him back to the commune. Since it had happened in the late evening, no children had been around to see; we were simply asked to keep a better eye on Black Eagle in the hopes that this wouldn't happen again.

Once we did a *vipassana* group, similar to ones conducted in the Ashram. One of the exercises required people to wear blindfolds for two weeks, and sit and meditate in the barn. But they'd come out for walks, with a companion, around the garden. The neighbors would just smile and say, "See you've got a group on." If people wandered off, the locals would just say, "Aren't you supposed to be in group?" and steer them back to the commune.

I had contacted my parents when I returned, and things were quite amiable. They didn't come down to the commune, though, because parents were not encouraged to visit. It was too disruptive for everybody to put on a "company face" on those occasions. We *did* have a few parents come, and that always sent everyone off into a frenzy of cleaning, even though we routinely kept the place quite tidy. But things are never as clean as your mother would like.

Our days were always open to any villagers who might want to drop by for tea and have a look-around. But very few did. They kept a polite distance, and that suited us fine.

I visited my parents several times, and often met them for dinner about twenty miles away, in Didcot, where they lived. I think my father was disappointed that I had joined a group; now, years later, I can see more clearly the reasons for this. At the time I just thought he was being a little selfish, possessive, or didn't want me to grow on my own.

My mother thought the whole thing was a bit "off the wall"—odd, but apparently not dangerous. When I told them some time later that I was going back to Poona, she called me and said she'd just purchased two tickets to the Canary Islands and urged me to go with her for a visit. Clearly, she thought that if I were just given something else to do, I'd forget all about India. I thanked her, but declined.

Suzzane came to visit several times. She picked up *immediately* on the tension in the house, even though it was supposed to be hidden from the outside world. There was also an attitude among commune members that people who were not dedicated to the kind of self-exploration required of *sannyasins* were not worth bothering about. I continued my friendship with a number of people in Oxford and elsewhere. This attitude never sat well with me, and pointed up one more area of friction.

Kamul and I seemed to be drifting apart, not for any clear-cut reason, though the pressures of communal living certainly played their part. There were more and more occasions when I didn't want to sit in the living room at the commune and play darts or go in a group to the pub. I wanted to spend a lot of my time alone—or, at most, with one other person. Mukul was a bit like this. He had a motorbike, and we would go off for rides just to get away from things. But that was seen as taking away from the community, not being in the commune, and not being part of the family.

Most of all, I wanted more time to be alone with Kamul—but, that, too, was seen as not being a part of the community. We were expected to be all together all the time—which probably was a major reason the pressure cooker would build up to a "family meeting."

Still, it was an experimental time—particularly in groups. Groups were coming into being all over the place, and the more advanced were pushing the limits of what groups could achieve. At the commune we were saying that people should form one-to-one relationships out of freedom and choice, not old conditioning.

We were constantly working to make the commune self-sufficient, so that people wouldn't have to look outside to earn a living. As the groups started to take off, Sangeeta took over publicity. Seema, Anu, and Shikha would make sure the group room was ready and that the group leader's room was together. I handled all the secretarial work for the groups—and some of the bookkeeping (Sunita would do the final accounting and budgeting). I've always had a natural talent for organization, and an ability to pull together the threads of a project; I wound up in an administrative function at the commune in England, at the Ashram, and at various Rajneesh centers throughout the world.

Each weekend two people could earn money cooking for the groups, which numbered forty to sixty people. They would get paid two pounds per person per group, which added up to a good income.

I didn't have much talent for cooking, but everyone was expected to take a turn cooking meals for the commune. Kamul and I would cook together, which gave us some all-too-rare time together—though chopping carrots and washing lettuce hardly seemed the most romantic pastime.

About two months after our return to England, a forty-eight-hour marathon was scheduled. A well-known swami was to lead it. He had set up drug rehabilitation centers in London, the Netherlands, and New York. He was flying over from the Netherlands.

Sangeeta was to be an assistant group leader for him. Because of the nature of the group, quite a number of assistants were required. There were forty people in the group, which meant about twelve assistants or "trainees," as they were called. He brought four with him, and several came down from London. From the house Sangeeta, Vipul, Atul, and Kamul were also scheduled to be assistants.

As the time for this group drew nearer, it was suggested that I do this group. I kept saying that I didn't want to do a group. This back-and-forth culminated in one of the "sitting room nights," as I called them. The energy bubbling all around was coming from one source: my refusal to do a group.

Finally, without any broken milk bottles, I was given an ultimatum: Either I did the marathon group, or I had to leave the commune. Sangeeta was the ringleader, but everybody agreed with her. They tried to sweeten things by telling me I wouldn't have to pay, and that I'd really get a lot out of it. I just kept repeating that I really didn't want to do it.

Kamul had bought into the trip also. He came to me and said, "Why are you resisting? What are you afraid of?" All the same old lines I was too familiar with already.

I was adamant on this score. "I just don't want to do it," I told him.

But, about three days before the group was to begin, I broke down. I was caught between the ultimatum on the one hand, and my friends' assurances: "Oh, we'll support you in this . . . we're giving you energy for it."

The truth of the matter was I was scared. My final line of defense (to myself) had been, "Bhagwan never gave me any groups, so why do I have to do them now?"

By the night of the group I had resolved to keep my fears in check and get through whatever was going to happen as quickly and painlessly as possible. People had begun arriving early in the evening, and had been directed to the group room. I was lingering in the kitchen, helping with cleanup after dinner, when Kamul came in. "Okay," he said, "it's time for you to go into the group room."

I started to shake, saying, "I really, really don't want to do this." By this point my fear was completely irrational—and nearly overwhelming.

Reluctantly, I set down my dish towel and untied my apron. Kamul escorted me into the group room in the barn.

I walked like a condemned person toward the barn. I knew that once I was inside I would be a member of the group, and my part in the marathon was beginning. In the barn I sat with the others, waiting for the Swami.

The Swami came in, along with several unfamiliar faces, and I felt my heart sink. Everything seemed strange to me; even the people from the commune who were there looked like soldiers getting ready for the kill. Because we were only allowed to wear our underwear, I felt naked and vulnerable. I was utterly miserable.

The Swami started a "chalk talk" at the blackboard about the connections of love and fear and growth—much of which went right by me because of my worries over what was to happen next.

And it was just as bad as I had been dreading. The Swami said, "Now, in this next exercise, I'm going to introduce you to terror. You may think you've been afraid in this life—" (all the time I sat there thinking, *I'm already terrified: what more do you want?*) "—you think you've confronted fear, but I'm going to show you *true terror.*"

By the time he was finished, I had reached the snapping point. Things didn't improve when he made us remove the last of our clothing, so we were all—some forty-five of us—standing around stark naked in the refurbished barn, which was long and fairly wide.

Then he said, "You're going to go to the other end of the room, you're going to put blindfolds on, and when I say, 'Run,' you are all going to run as fast as you can to the other end of the room. And when you get there, or to someone who will touch you or move you, you're going to turn around and run the other way. And you'll continue doing that until I tell you to stop."

All we knew is that we were to *trust* and run as hard as we could.

We arranged ourselves in about three rows, because there wasn't enough room to form a single line across the end of the barn. Waiting, blindfolded, for everyone to get in position, felt like an eternity to me. Suddenly, the Swami shouted, "Run!"

I hadn't gotten three steps before people were running into me from behind. We went down in a tangle of arms and legs. Our instructions were not to touch our blindfolds, but to get up and begin running again.

I was buried under several people, who were screaming with the wild sort of energy these exercises dredge up. I had chipped a tooth in the fall. I got up, ran a few more steps, then ripped off my blindfold and fled the room. The words that formed in my mind were, *Fuck this shit!* No threats of any kind were worth the misery of the marathon. In the instant of snatching away the blindfold I saw that the walls were lined with people holding mattresses, so that anyone who wasn't steered properly wouldn't hurt himself even if he ran right toward a wall. But this had been arranged *after* our blindfolds were in place; as far as we knew there was only solid brick to connect with at a wrong turn.

I grabbed my clothes and fled into the night, scrambling into them in the chill night air. I didn't care about anything except getting away from the nightmare in the barn, even if it meant leaving the commune.

I stood there catching my breath, and trying to sort out my thoughts. Suddenly, I heard a giggle. I turned and there was the Swami, sitting in his car, smoking a joint. "What are you doing?" he wanted to know.

"I'm *not* going back in *that room*," I told him. Then I began to call him all sorts of names. "Look at you," I yelled, "those people in there are screaming and shouting and falling down. I nearly got killed—and my tooth's broken—and you're sitting here smoking a joint."

"Yeah," he said. "And you're out here too." Then he smiled and added, "Do you think I'm crazy enough to be *in there* with *all that*?"

I just looked at him, and then I got it. I began to laugh. "Get in, have a joint."

I did. And we hit it off. I told him about the ultimatum, and my on-the-spot decision to give up the commune rather than go through any more of the marathon.

"I'll tell you what," he said finally. "They'll never argue with me in there. I'll make you an assistant, and you can help run the groups. So no one can say you're not connected with a group—and no one can kick you out."

That was the start of our friendship, which has continued to this day.

Needless to say, this caused a lot more friction between me and other members of the commune. The Swami had chosen me as an assistant, which was different from being one of the house delegates. Sangeeta, in particular, had a lot of resentment—but she wouldn't object aloud, because she respected the Swami very much. The others were also irked by the fact that I had been given a special kind of status, even though I'd never taken a group in my life. I was breaking all the rules *and getting away with it.*

I had told the Swami that Bhagwan had said I didn't need to take any groups. He said, "Then there's no need for you to take them."

The added tensions in the house were outweighed by the advantages of being a group leader—not the least of which was the "bonus" of dope and booze that went with the position. While he was at the commune the Swami took all of us trainees out to dinner several times. He was quite wealthy, having made a lot of money off the groups.

After he left, however, the jealousy that had grown up around me signaled the beginning of the end. I was told that I was not going to be allowed to "get away" with going my own way now that the Swami was gone. "You're going to *have* to do a group sometime," I was told, "You're going to have to work on yourself at some point."

Finally, I said, "Look, I'll tell you what. I'll write to Bhagwan and ask him. If he says that I should do groups, I'll do them. And I'll even ask him what groups I should do. Then we can finish this whole argument."

Everyone agreed to this; and I felt quite certain that I would be given groups to do. I wrote the letter, and we posted it together.

The reply that came back surprised all of us. "No need for you to do groups," Bhagwan wrote. "Don't do groups. If you have to do groups, you can lead groups. Train to be a rebirther."

Bhagwan's answer blew the whole house away. This little punk, who Kamul had picked out of a drug rehabilitation center, had gone to Poona and wound up working in the office; had followed a man (which meant possessiveness and jealousy) and was now a group leader, even though she had walked out of her only group.

By this time the only really positive thing for me at the commune was Kamul, whom I still loved very much. When I could get him away from the crowd there, we really had some good times together. And we did have good friends in Seema, Shikha, Mukul, and Atul.

One night near the end of October, I got violently sick. Vipul called for the doctor. He came, diagnosed appendicitis, and had me moved immediately to the hospital for surgery.

Only Vipul and Kamul came to see me in the hospital. I was pretty much on the outs with the women in the house, who resented my ability to always land on my feet, no matter what.

Within a few days I was in misery, feeling worse than I'd felt immediately after the surgery. But, since I had never had surgery before, I assumed this was all a natural part of the process. I only wanted to go home.

When I got back to the commune the first night, they forgot to bring me anything to eat. I was confined to my second-floor bedroom and felt too weak to go downstairs. Kamul didn't come up until it was time for bed; somehow it never occurred to him to come up and visit. He made up for this the next day by bringing me my lunch *and* dinner. But he was almost the only person who would come up to visit me, though Vijay and Vipul would pop in from time to time.

Two nights later I *knew* something was really wrong. But, in a houseful of nurses, I couldn't seem to make anyone believe I was suffering from anything but routine aftereffects of my surgery. I was in terrible pain and half-delirious when Kamul came to bed. But he just said something soothing, and I either passed out or fell asleep.

In the morning I woke up to find my stitches had burst in a pool of pus and blood. The incision had become infected and had abscessed. Kamul had already left for work, and I had barely enough strength to whisper, "Help me, somebody." But no one could hear, though I could hear people rattling around downstairs.

Somehow, I managed to get out of bed and get dressed. Hanging onto the bannister like a drunkard, I got downstairs. All the time I was moving in a fog.

Anu was in the kitchen, cleaning up after breakfast.

I said, "You've got to help me get to the hospital."

She just looked at me for a minute, then said, "There's a bus in five minutes. You can take that."

I was too dazed to react. But I felt fear and sadness, like a child who's just been punished for something she didn't do.

So I rode the bus to the medical center. The doctor on duty there stitched me up again, then said, "I've got to put you in the hospital. If those people would let you take a bus in your condition, you can't stay with them while you're sick."

But I said, "No, no, no: it was my fault: I didn't communicate my problem properly." My programming had taken over in my still-foggy state.

He drove me home and took me inside. He got me into bed then chewed out Sangeeta and Anu, who were the two people close at hand. At that point there were three children in the commune—Anu's daughters, and the son of a recently arrived woman. When the doctor said that a health visitor would come every day to check my dressings, he added that she "would also check the children to be sure they're well taken care of."

After he left Anu went into an uproar, feeling threatened through her children. I felt rejected because this business—not my illness—was a real cause for concern. And I certainly didn't think having a health visitor look over the children was a bad thing.

But this began the final split.

Kamul was working extra shifts at the hospital, so I hardly saw him during those days. He had been bringing me up my meals; now Anu and Sangeeta conveniently forgot about me, so I had nothing to eat for twenty-four hours, being too ill and mind-fogged to come downstairs.

The next day I was sitting in the bed, feeling very sorry for myself, and making up my mind that I was going to leave the commune the moment I could make an exit on my own two feet. Suddenly, I heard singing begin in the hall outside. A moment later Sangeeta and Anu came into the room, holding a cake they had baked. It had candles all over it, and a big "We Love You, Avibha" in frosting across the top. Most of the other members of the commune were standing behind them, singing.

They put the cake down on the nightstand. I looked at it for a second, then picked it up and threw it against the wall.

The horror on their faces was incredible: They seemed to have no idea at all where my anger had come from.

"How could you leave me alone all this time," I demanded, "Then you bake me this cake to make it okay? Well, nothing's okay!" All the time I was crying and feeling completely neglected. I blurted out that I was going to leave.

Anu and Sangeeta started crying too, and saying, "Please stay."

Finally, I said, "I will stay, because I love you. But I don't understand this way of being with people at all. I'm really quite confused by the group thing and everything." And I began harping on about everything that had been going on.

We made a peace, but it wasn't a lasting one. Things began brewing again in very short order.

The crux of the problem this time around was that Anu wanted to start "experimenting" with other people. How this was to affect me became clear a few nights later at another "family meeting." There Anu went through her shaking and hesitation and several false starts before she got to the point, saying, "Well, I'm really scared, but I'm ready to move out of this relationship now and try being with somebody else. I want to move in with somebody else."

Then Sangeeta said, "Who do you feel that you'd feel safe with, and protected by?"

"Kamul," was Anu's unhesitating answer.

I nearly fell through the floor. "Absolutely not," I said, "No way."

So Anu started shouting, "Oh, you're so possessive, and you won't let him go, and you won't let me grow! And he's the only one I feel I could do this with. And it's a very big thing for me."

And I just said, "Find your own man. Don't pick on mine."

Kamul just looked shocked by the whole thing.

Then Sangeeta pointed her finger at me and said, "You're just too possessive, and you can't drop this trip, and you came all the way from India just to be with him."

"Yes," I agreed, "And when it's finished, I'll go. But, it's not; and *no*, he's not going to be with you, unless *he* says that he doesn't want to be with me any longer."

To Kamul, I said, "Well?" putting the ball in his court.

"No, I still want to be with you," he said, "although I wouldn't mind, just this one time . . . "

"The ultimatum I'm giving you," I said, "is that either you be with me, or you say you want to be with Anu. And I don't care if it's for half an hour and you're never with her again. This is who I am."

Everyone started in on me at once, saying that I'd never done a *tantra* group, so I didn't know what it was to be free and open in this society.

I heard them out, then said, "That may be true. But I don't feel it; and if I said that it was okay"—this last was directed to Kamul—"I could never be with you again. Because that's the way I am."

So Kamul said, "I want to be with you."

Then Anu started wailing again about how we were keeping her from growing. Sangeeta took up the chorus. Suddenly, Vipul asked Sangeeta, "Why do you have such an investment in Anu being with someone else?"

Sangeeta said, "Well, I want to be with someone else."

"That's a little better," said Vipul, "Who do you want to be with?"

"Vijay," she answered. At which point, Sunita got hysterical.

After that, the commune was in an uproar for the better part of an hour. Later that night people decided to try the new "program." Sangeeta was with Rajive; Mukul was with Anu—and the energy that night was incredible.

From that night, however, I realized Kamul had pulled away even further. I think the depth of my feeling for him was too much for him to handle.

And then, one morning in November, I told Kamul, "My goodness, it's finished. I woke up this morning, and all I want is to be back in India. I just want to go 'home.'"

We talked a little bit, then I said, "I'm going into Oxford and walk around." We agreed not to tell anyone else at the commune yet.

In Oxford I met an old friend, Nick, and caught up on the news about my friends outside the Ashram. He suggested that I stay in Oxford for several days. At that point I didn't feel that I could simply "disappear"—I owed some explanation to Kamul, at least.

I went back to the commune to pack my bag. While I was in my room Anu wandered in, picked up some of the undergarments I was packing, and said, "Are you going to make love to this person?" The fact that he was a non-*sannyasin* was especially distasteful to her.

I said, "No, it's an old friend, and I'm just going for a visit to the town I used to live in."

"You'll get back into drugs," she said.

"You're coming at this all from the wrong direction," I countered. At the moment I felt trapped—so closed in by her questions and the atmosphere at the commune that I could hardly breathe.

Then Kamul came in. When I told him my plans he was really quite nice about it. We had already agreed we were going our separate ways. The few other people I saw around the house that afternoon seemed cool to me. But I was looking forward to my weekend and my new freedom.

I went dancing and to concerts and discovered something of the world I had almost forgotten. But underneath it all was the certainty that I only wanted to go "home" to India.

I decided to take a job in Oxford to earn the airfare. Nick said I could use the spare room in his flat to save on rent.

I returned to the commune on Sunday afternoon. I felt very happy, my life was falling together in the right way. I went up to my room and began unpacking my overnight case, because I didn't plan to leave the commune for good right away. I planned to spend a few days making my good-byes and getting my things in order.

I went downstairs to wait for Kamul, and met Anu at the foot of the stairs. She immediately began her whole shaking trip, which I now recognized meant she'd done something or was up to something. She said, "How are you?"

"Fine," I said, "I had a really great weekend. How about you?"

"Oh, no."

"Why not? What happened?"

"I went to bed with Kamul."

"I guess that was in the cards," I said, "You've wanted to for a long time. Why wasn't it any good? I always thought it was." I was a little sarcastic at this point.

She said, "Don't you feel anything? Don't you want to *shout* at me?"

"No, I really don't," I told her, "I had a good weekend. I wish you would have enjoyed yours, since you've wanted this for so long."

Then she began screaming at me; a moment later Sangeeta came downstairs, and *she* began screaming at me.

I just stood there. It was such a contrast to the weekend I'd just had. I started for the stairs.

"What are you going to do?" they wanted to know.

"I'm leaving," I said.

They both went silent. Several other people had come running in to see what the shouting was about, since the three of us were standing just inside the front door.

I went upstairs, threw my things back in the bag, and went downstairs again. I was sorry that Kamul hadn't returned. But I was determined to go into the kitchen and make a real good-bye of it: I didn't want them thinking I had run away only because Anu had gone to bed with Kamul.

Carrying my suitcase, I walked into the kitchen. "I just wanted to say good-bye," I began. To Anu, I added, "And I just wanted to let you know it's *not* because you went to bed with Kamul."

At this, she went berserk, and began yelling at me, "You're not real! You're really pissed off at me! You're really pissed off at Kamul! You're really hurt!"

"I *am* really hurt," I agreed, "because I just don't understand what's going on. But I'm also very happy, because I had a really good weekend, and I'm going to earn enough money to go back to India. And I certainly don't want to be here."

Anu walked over and stood directly in front of me, her hands on her hips, in a typical encounter posture. She continued to shout in my face.

I could feel the atmosphere in the kitchen nearing the exploding point.

Now Sangeeta was screaming at me, "You can't even get in touch with your feelings! You can't even wait for Kamul to get back!"

"I don't want to stay here another minute," I said, "You can tell Kamul I'll call him as soon as I get to Oxford."

At this point Sangeeta hauled off and hit me across the face. That moment was the longest one of my life, because I was waiting for the next blow. It came from Anu. In a minute they were both pounding at me, with Sunita adding a few licks for good measure, while Rajive tried to pull them away.

I dropped my suitcase and ran. My nose and ears were bleeding. Behind me I could hear Sangeeta and Anu still screaming.

Once I was outside I knew they wouldn't bother me. They would never let that kind of violence show outside the house.

When I got outside the gates Vipul stood there staring at me. But he didn't know what to say, so he said nothing.

I just shrugged and turned my back on the commune and never returned to the house, though I did see some of the people over the years.

CHAPTER 10

Laxmi and Sheela

I saw Kamul once, while I was staying in Oxford in Nick's apartment. He came into town to meet me, and we had a long visit. There were no guilt trips for either of us, just a pleasant afternoon strolling through the city and talking, assuring each other that things had worked out for the best, and parting as friends—and we've continued as friends to this day.

I still felt very much a *sannyasin*, though I enjoyed my month of "being in the world" to the fullest. During this time I paid several visits to Seema and her boyfriend, who had moved to London. I also saw my friend Shradda, who was en route back to India. Our talks only made me all the more eager to return to Poona. Mukul would drop by when he was in town; I saw Vijay several times. I had blocked out what had happened those last two weeks at the commune: I separated this completely from Bhagwan's experiment.

The time in Oxford refreshed me; I selected my friends—*sannyasin* and non-*sannyasin*—very carefully. All the creature comforts in the apartment made me feel slightly decadent after the monastic simplicity of life in the Ashram and at the commune. I enjoyed them all the more because I knew it would only be a short time before I returned to India to pick up the threads of my life there.

Nick was a history student and like a brother. We were always good friends, but never romantically involved. He studied most of the time, while I worked several jobs, squirreling away money for the plane fare to Bombay.

Then, one evening in December, I went over to Oriel College (one of the medical schools within Oxford University) with Nick and some other friends. At a gathering in a student garret I met Martin, who was studying to be a medical student. He was very handsome, with blond hair and blue eyes. He had a great sense of humor and an enthusiasm for life that I found irresistible. He wasn't just doing traditional medicine—he was interested in acupuncture, Chinese medicinal herbs, and other alternative means of treatment.

Gradually, the others drifted away and left the two of us sitting on the floor talking. It was three in the morning. We'd had some wine and were feeling a bit giddy.

"So, what are you going to do?" he asked, referring to the fact that the university was on holiday, and most people were leaving for Christmas vacation.

"I want to go to India," I answered automatically.

"Well, I'd love to go to the Orient," he said. "Why don't we go to India?"

"Now?" I said, surprised and excited by the idea.

"Sure," he said, warming up to the idea. "I've got four weeks off. Why don't we just take off?"

"Why not?" I agreed heartily. So we got out the map and began plotting our route. In my excitement I could experience each step of our journey as we talked about traveling through Europe to Greece, then on across the Middle East to India.

I spent the night with him. In the morning, on a whim, we drove to London for three days. The plans for India were momentarily forgotten at the start of our crazy-wonderful affair. As soon as we got back to Oxford we got caught up in a whirl of Oxford Balls (at which I appeared in Annabelinda gowns) and spent several days partying with Martin's friends. But this palled soon enough, and we agreed that the idea of a trip to India was still very much alive in both of us. So we decided to leave there and then.

We gave ourselves one day to get ready, and left the following morning. Since neither of us had the money for a plane ticket, we hitchhiked to Felixstow, took the ferry across to Rotterdam, then continued hitchhiking our way across Holland, Germany, Austria, and Yugoslavia.

Our sudden decision to travel wasn't nearly as outrageous as my traveling outfit. I was wearing red lurex stretch tights, gold stiletto-heeled shoes, and a long oversized yellow tee-shirt knotted at the side. Martin's bluejeans and workshirt seemed pretty dull next to me. I'm sure we made a lasting impression on everyone who gave us a ride.

Four days after leaving England we got to Greece, where the weather was really quite pleasant. But, by the time we reached Athens, we'd spent all our money; so we found a cheap place where I did cleaning in return for room and board and a couple of hundred *drachma* a day.

After my chores in the morning we were able to sit on the beach and enjoy the sun and blue skies.

After a short time, however, Martin decided to go off and pick grapes to earn enough money to start traveling again. By now I was really feeling the pull of India, and was eager to get back. So I went back to the hotel manager and asked him what I could do to earn plane fare.

He suggested I go down to Piraeus, the harbor in Athens, where sailors were arriving all the time with plenty of money from having been *months* on a boat. He said my story about just wanting to get back to India to be with my master would probably strike a sympathetic chord with some of them, since *he* had found it appealing and had already given me some extra money.

So, for two evenings, I went down to the harbor and followed this plan. A friend of Martin's who had also turned up at the hotel went with me, to be sure nothing happened. We would stand outside the bars, and tell anyone who could understand English my story. In no time I had enough money to buy a plane ticket and some to spare.

I bought myself a good-looking, practical red dress and new shoes. Then I got on a direct flight to Bombay, arriving in India the last week of December 1977. Martin had left a week before, as he had limited time to travel. We had agreed to meet in Poona.

I arrived in town too late to go into the Ashram, so I went to the Cafe Bund, a hotel I knew, and suggested that Martin and I might meet there.

Martin stayed at the Cafe Bund about six weeks, though he did go up to Kashmir for a week or so during that time. While he was in Poona he would come into the Ashram each day to visit, and took a number of groups. When we had been in Oxford and en route, he had often said to me that he couldn't understand how I could have gotten involved with "a cult." I'd just answered it was "my trip," and we let the matter drop.

Martin's original intention had been to stay a few days in Poona, then travel around visiting leper colonies and other tropical disease centers related to his medical studies. Within a few days of our arrival, however, he took *sannyas*—which surprised me, since he had always made such a point about how *he* would *never* let himself get involved with such a group. However, on his return to England, he reverted to using his original name, not wanting to advertise his experience or appear to be clinging to a master.

I'd had an arriving *darshan* almost immediately upon my return. At first I went back into the office, which had noticeably more workers than when I had left. Several major changes were also underway on the grounds. A new building, Bodhidharma, had gone up. It was an elaborate hut structure; one side, called "the press office," was filled with desks to handle press releases and so forth. It also handled translated transcripts of Bhagwan's teachings, since he would alternate speaking English one month and Hindi the next, and the latter would have to be translated for the vast majority of *sannyasins* who didn't speak the language.

The other section held a battery of typists. Some of them worked for Arup in Krishna House, the rest worked for Vidya. Arup worked with Ashramites and people living outside the Ashram, including overseas contacts unknown to the Ashram, who would write to Bhagwan with a problem or a question. For people within the Ashram, there were two boxes in Krishna House: one for letters to be read in discourse, one for personal replies. Arup's department handled all of this.

Vidya was also taking care of the problems of people who lived within and outside the Ashram.

From the start there was a strict division between the people who worked for each of these key women. Laxmi was diplomatic, and managed to give the impression of unity; as Sheela took more and more charge she encouraged the separation. She discouraged "her people" from talking with "Arup's people" or "Vidya's people."

Laxmi, for all her skill at not making the separations seem *too* obvious, nevertheless kept things from overlapping. It was Ashram policy that no one was ever to have a complete picture of what was going on. The compartmentalization of duties was the best way to ensure this. Laxmi was answerable only to Bhagwan, so this separation was generally assumed to be a reflection of his wishes.

No one's mind was encouraged to work too much. If people working for Arup got interested in what Vidya's lot was doing, minds start thinking. Assigning the same task over and over kept workers from seeing where their job might fit into the larger picture. Contrary to Western industry, which rotates people on assembly lines to keep them from the kind of mindlessness that leads to production problems, the Ashram encouraged this to bring about a desirable loss of ego while aiding internal security.

Arup was the person *sannyasins* would see to schedule either an arriving or a leaving *darshan*. She would also meet with people who had written a letter to Bhagwan and to whom a reply was to be given verbally—not one that was to be written down. This became especially common during the time of the sterilizations that were strongly suggested to Ashramites.

But the range of things covered was infinite. If, for example, someone had written to Bhagwan about suicidal thoughts, he would be asked to see Arup so that she could get a firsthand impression of where the person was coming from. Though this person would think he was being interviewed only by Arup, in fact, Laxmi and Sheela were also assessing him. Final decisions would always consider the spiritual side of the issues raised first and foremost.

Letters would come into the office all the time, but the boxes were routinely cleared at three o'clock each afternoon. About five-thirty, when everyone was getting ready for *darshan*, the key administrators in Krishna House would gather in a back office and go over the day's letters. The content of the letter was noted in a person's record before any decision was made on how best to respond.

Careful records were maintained on *everyone* in the Ashram, as well as those living outside the walls. A person who applied to take *sannyas* would be required to fill out a form that included space for a passport-size photograph and lines for legal name, *sannyas* name (to be filled in when bestowed by Bhagwan in *darshan*), birthdate, place of birth, occupation, hobbies, domicile (both in India and at home), and parents' names (or next of kin).

Vidya's typists would deal with these forms; two photographs would have to accompany it, or the form would not be processed. Even if you didn't take *sannyas*, but were asking to pick up mail at the Ashram or going to use "17 Koregaon Park" as a mailing address, you would be required to fill out one of these forms.

These same typists would transfer the information to 6- × 8-inch cards. If the person was a *sannyasin*, the card would have orange lines to type on; a non-*sannyasin*'s card would have blue lines. One photograph would be glued to the card, the other photograph would be attached with a paper clip.

If the person, for any reason, seemed "whacko," on top of their card was the code "PC" ("potential cuckoo"). This person would be carefully watched. He or she might have done something to draw unfavorable attention, or have a problem with drugs, or seem a bit unbalanced. Arup's staff actually worked from a manual of guidelines for dealing with potential troublemakers, which was also used to encode the type of problem and seriousness on the card.

Arup would also deal with consular people if someone's problem became so severe they had to be deported. They would come up to the Ashram, and she would arrange for the interview and do what she could to facilitate the person's departure. However, the Ashram never paid a return fare for anybody; they left those arrangements to the consul. If someone got into trouble outside the Ashram walls, Arup would also be the person to deal with the local police and, if necessary, alert the consular authorities that one of their people was in prison. The Ashram would never take responsibility for anybody.

There were certain hard-and-fast rules in the Ashram, "no smoking" being one of the most obvious. A more general rule of "discretion" governed things like use of drugs. For example if a woman with obvious needle marks up and down her arms was muddling her work in the office, she would immediately be brought in to Arup or Sheela or Vidya and confronted on the matter. But if she wasn't "losing it," and was able to function, she might be asked, "What's going on?"—but she wouldn't necessarily be told to stop, although she might be advised to stop work for a while.

On the back of the card was a permanent record of letters that the person wrote, even after they had returned to the West. They recorded the date the letter was received in the Ashram, whether it was a letter going to Bhagwan, whether it was personal or for lecture, and whether it was coming from abroad. The date the letter was written was also noted, as well as the date any reply was sent.

A lot of the time, when people thought Bhagwan was looking at a letter, he wasn't. In the office we had a huge file of standard quotes from Bhagwan arranged by topics: *birthday, newborn, marriage, suicide, general "up," general "down"*—all sorts of subheadings. When such a response (which theoretically came directly from Bhagwan) was sent out from the office, we noted the first two or three words of the quote and its reference number—to prevent anyone from getting a repeat of previous advice. Since the letters themselves wouldn't be kept too long, this system provided an ongoing record should a problem recur one in subsequent letters, or if the person visited the Ashram in person.

If a question was responded to in lecture this would also be noted on the back of the card, with a number cross-referencing the tape of the lecture. All of Bhagwan's lectures were recorded, taped, and transcribed. These formed the basis for numerous books issued by the Ashram and later by the Ranch in Oregon.

Answers to questions generated from within the Ashram rarely ran to more than about three lines. Usually, these would run in the vein of, "This, too, shall pass . . . " or "Surrender, and go with the flow. . . . "

Sometimes, the answer would simply be, "See Arup," which meant the problem required some delicacy of handling, or that more information was needed by the office staff before suggesting an answer.

The questions came from a box that was always kept in the reception area. It had a stack of paper beside it on which you wrote your query, and indicated whether it was a "lecture" question or "personal." If it was personal, you would get the answer the next day, typed on a little piece of paper and delivered through the mail room. If you had submitted a lecture question it *might* be read aloud and answered in the general sessions.

At this point I still believed that, if you asked a personal question, Bhagwan saw it and at least dictated an individual answer. Later, I found that most of the answers were generated by the inner circle of the office staff.

Initial breakdown of incoming letters happened at the mail room in Krishna House. A woman called Padma would open every letter, glance over it, and forward it on to Arup, Vidya, or (in rare instances) Laxmi. These last would be letters that came from someone who had been close to Laxmi or Bhagwan during their stay at Koregaon Park. A well-established hierarchy was already reflected in how the letters were routed.

When Padma first sorted the letters she would code each in pencil with routing instructions (like "AR" for Arup), assign it a number, and log it in, including destination. Before a letter reached Arup or Vidya or Laxmi, it went to "Irish" Mukta, who pulled the person's file card and clipped it to the letter. She was brought these letters by runners, usually the younger children around the Ashram, who also brought the log book. Each letter would be signed for next to its assigned number.

When she was finished she would cross out her initials, which had been penciled in by Padma, and return the letter and card to Padma. At this point the letter would be forwarded along to Arup or whomever. A letter could never go astray; it could be traced each step of its route.

Sometimes a letter would go to multiple destinations. One that came from abroad, for example, addressed to Bhagwan but indicating the person wanted to purchase a book and tape, would be routed to the book and tape mail order departments. All such purchases were also noted on the file card.

If the letter came from a *sannyasin* who had lived in the Ashram at one time, and was now overseas, it would routinely be sent to Sheela and Laxmi. They maintained close connections with former Ashramites who had returned to the West. It was rare that any correspondence went in to Bhagwan; if it did, it was retyped and placed between clear plastic sheets before it was submitted to him.

By the time it reached Arup, the final destination, all the necessary information was annotated on the card, which was still clipped to the original of the letter. When she dictated a reply to Geeta, her right-hand assistant, three copies were made. Any correspondence from the Ashram required backups in triplicate.

If the reply was an "original" piece rather than a stock reply, this would be noted and the substance of the message would be recorded on the card. Then the original letter and first copy would go into Arup's file, arranged by date. (This was while Laxmi was still in power; when Sheela took charge a whole new system was incorporated, including her "S" files, to which only she and a few select assistants had access.)

Orders for goods and the like going *out* of the Ashram were channeled through Vidya. If, for example, the *mala* shop needed new cutting blades, something that had to be ordered other than through a *sannyasin* contact, she would review the request and then have someone from the *mala* department come in to justify the need. This held for all departments, for everything from a printing press to paper clips. She would operate on intuition, refusing a request if she thought people were being greedy or lazy.

All mail in and out went through the Krishna House station. Personal letters for *sannyasins* were not screened, but simply passed along; only letters to Bhagwan or to the office were routinely opened by Padma. From time to time, she would pull out letters that seemed to need an answer right away, and these would be given "priority" attention—often Padma would hand-carry it directly in to Sheela or Arup the moment she had logged it in.

People returning from the West who were known in the office would be greeted personally when they went to arrange their arriving *darshan*. They would be asked if they had any news about other *sannyasins* in the West they might have come in contact with. Office staff were especially alert for reports of *sannyasins*, or events connected with various centers, that might be "not good" for the Ashram. Such indiscretions might first filter back as gossip, but this would also be noted. If the person in question wrote a letter, Padma would immediately treat it as a priority item and take it directly to one of her superiors.

Anyone applying for *darshan* had to set up an appointment with Arup through the receptionist the day before. The receptionist kept a list of people scheduled for appointments, and pulled the cards for each. Arup would review these in the evening before meeting with the people; she would make a note of what was going to happen to them in *darshan*.

This formed the basis of a second list prepared the day of the *darshan*. On it were the names of those doing arriving *darshan*, leaving *darshan*, people with questions, and groups. Every group would go for a beginning *darshan* to "get energy"; here the group leader would be asked by Bhagwan about the group or be given guidelines for conducting it. If a group was running for a longer time—say two or three weeks—it would have a second *darshan*, in silence, where the group leader might come forward and speak with Bhagwan. This would often happen if someone in the group had become a real problem, *had* a real problem, or the group leader was uncertain where to go with this person in group. The person in question might be brought up with the group leader to sit at Bhagwan's feet, while Bhagwan advised them how to proceed.

Anyone who worked anywhere in the Ashram participated regularly in workers' *darshan*; these happened every two weeks at first—less frequently as the Ashram staff grew. People who were living outside the Ashram proper could sign up for a *darshan* once a month. They were also included on the *darshan* list drawn up the day of the gathering.

The average *sannyasin* had no idea that such a list existed—let alone how thorough it was. This list indicated where each person was to sit in the auditorium: If a workers' department was attending, for example, they would be assigned a cluster of seats together. One or two members of the group, however, would be singled out for seats in the first four rows. Such people would be selected because a department head would come to Geeta, who drew up the list (subject to final approval by Laxmi and Sheela), and request an up-front seat because a person had done outstanding work or was going through a particularly trying time or whatever. Conversely, people who had been assigned such seats might be pulled back for a variety of reasons.

The arriving *darshan*s all sat in one area; likewise, those in leaving *darshan*. Again, an exception could be made. The Ashram was always concerned with the balance between form and special cases. This helped people believe in the "magic" of the place; the apparently spontaneous mention of someone or some group by Bhagwan reinforced the idea that he knew everything that was happening every minute. So much that seemed to happen on the spur of the moment, however, was actually carefully choreographed in advance.

A star beside a person's name meant they were to be singled out for some particular reason. It might indicate someone who had previously lived in the Ashram had returned (though this, in itself, was no guarantee of an up-front seat or any special notice). It could as easily mean the person simply looked great that evening and must have a front seat.

Although the list was technically completed in the afternoon, I or someone else from the office would be standing at the gate as people filed in for *darshan* and could, on rare occasions, make last-minute changes. Inside the auditorium Shiva, Bhagwan's personal bodyguard, could indicate people were to reseat themselves in the front for no apparent reason—though, in fact, *nothing* was done without a reason. He might simply be doing it because he wanted to go to bed with someone—or had enjoyed them the night before. It could as well be that he'd been told to do so by Bhagwan for the latter's own reasons. But all of this contributed to the magic atmosphere; and it caused people to gravitate towards people like Sheela or Shiva, who were able to make things happen.

This list could also be used in a very different way. A person who had met with Arup, and been routinely scheduled for *darshan* on such-and-such a day, might have a note put by his name—for whatever reason—that would prevent him from getting into the hall. It was a way of keeping the group off balance. Nothing was ever to be taken for granted.

Such a person would have gotten washed and changed, only to have a "sniffer" say, "You smell of perfume" or "smoke." As a result of being turned away at the gates to Lao Tzu House, a *sannyasin* would reverse this disappointment onto himself rather than challenge the decision. He would feel there was something wrong with him, that he wasn't surrendered enough, that he wasn't clean enough. The trip that people laid on themselves and each other was, "You really don't love him *that* much, if you allowed yourself to come here and smell."

Such guilt trips were always internal processes; nobody would actually reprimand you. The "sniffer" would smile and say, "It's all right; you can arrange another *darshan*." But the disappointment would be crushing. If the smell of shampoo was causing the problem, the people at the gate would say something like, "Oh, go and try with a scarf." Then your hope would come up, and you'd tie up your hair with a scarf. At this point you might be let in—or you would just as likely be turned away a second time.

It would always be noted on the *darshan* list *in advance* whether you were going to play this trip or that with a person. Probably no more than a handful of people in the Ashram were aware that such a list existed and how it was used. This kind of manipulation made people twice as grateful to get inside, and helped keep the larger community in line.

The official reason for the existence of "sniffers" was the fact that Bhagwan was allergic to perfume, scented shampoos, cigarette smoke, and anything with a strong fragrance. Also, there was a practical reason for discouraging any smell that might become overpowering in the warm and crowded auditorium. But the main importance, I think, was that it provided an ideal tool for manipulation. Once the *darshan* list left Geeta it would pass by Sheela, Laxmi, Shradda, Asha, and myself for any final stars or comments.

Some people who were working in the Ashram (though they were not Ashramites at this point) wrote to Bhagwan (via the boxes in Krishna House) saying they'd run out of money. At this point they would have already borrowed what they could from other people living and working in the Ashram. Usually they would be told to go back to the West, make enough money to support themselves, then write and wait to be told to return.

People working outside the Ashram might apply to Vidya (who handled all work details inside the Ashram) for a job, since this would eventually get them a pass to eat at the canteen—and would put them a step closer to being invited to live in the Ashram. Vidya would ask them how much money they had left, then tell them either, "Yes, you can go to work in the Ashram" or "Write to Bhagwan."

More often Vidya would take it upon herself to reschedule an appointment for the following day. Later she would consult with Sheela or Laxmi, and they would make a final decision. The characteristic response to an applicant upon his return would run, "No, it's not possible for you to work in the Ashram at this time. The suggestion is that you go back to the West, establish yourself there, make money, learn how it is to be in the West, apply all that you've learned here, and then write when you feel ready to return." No guarantees of any kind would be given at this point.

So two types of people were going in: one who already worked in the Ashram, and one who wanted to. In both cases they were being advised to return to the West. Their cards were pulled and a careful study was made to answer such questions as: Who is this person? What is their specialty: What have they done in the past? How have they been in the Ashram? Often this would include discreet inquiries (great care was taken not to let the person know they were being checked out) with several different people to get a clear idea of the person.

Favorable results of this investigation would lead to a special mark on the list when the person attended leaving *darshan*. The usual departure time was within three days of *darshan*. During the assembly Bhagwan would give them words of farewell and the token gift.

As soon as the person left *darshan*—at which point he'd be feeling higher than a kite—or within the next three days, he'd be approached by one of three people who did *not* live or work in the Ashram. These three had money, were highly visible about the Ashram, and clearly had some sort of status. Though they lived outside the Ashram, "the commune" had bestowed on them food passes and other clear signs of favor, including gifts.

These three were obviously special in some undefined way. When they approached someone who was about to return to the West, they brought with them an implied approval. They would say something like, "How would you feel about taking a suitcase of mine along with you when you return? Just take it through to London"—or Paris or wherever the person's final destination was—"and you'll be contacted in one way or another. Just hand over the suitcase and you'll get two thousand dollars"—or some such sum—"for the trip. Then you can return here."

That was a dope run. A lot of the people were naive enough *not* to know what was going on. Sometimes there would be set-ups—people would be singled out ahead of time to be busted, so the dealers could get another lot through while all the attention was focused on the one "pigeon."

Money would sometimes come in from donations from wealthy people who took *sannyas*. A person who donated any amount of money—as little as a thousand dollars in those days—would have a better chance of getting a room in the Ashram at an earlier date. Such "bonus" monies from a run could be applied to such a "room reservation"—and this provided added incentive.

Even people who knew full well what they were involved in had the idea that somehow they were being protected by Bhagwan. If he said, "Everything's going to be all right. Go back to the West and make money. It's going to be a good time for you," the person making the run was apt to feel "invisible." He would feel that nothing could happen to him, because he had such complete belief in Bhagwan. This lack of fear was what often kept these people from being caught by customs officials who were looking for telltale signs of fear.

The runners would know that they were not to travel in their orange clothes. The paranoia that would blossom later was already in existence, and was by no means limited to those doing dope runs—people wearing the characteristic *sannyasin* colors and *mala* were likely to attract undesirable attention or even hostility. So runners would travel under their legal names.

People doing a dope run understood that if they got caught they weren't to bring Bhagwan's name into it, because that could hurt him and the Ashram. And the most important thing was that the Ashram continue to exist. It was presumed that anyone who got busted would not say anything to implicate anyone connected with the Ashram. The threat was not that someone would kill you, but that you could hurt Bhagwan and put his whole experiment in jeopardy. This kind of emotional blackmail proved remarkably effective.

The emphasis on making money quickly to assure a quick return to India led people to take any kind of job—since the nature of the work was unimportant and the higher goal of making money and returning to Bhagwan was everything. For example, a large number of strippers working from London's SoHo to San Francisco's North Beach were *sannyasins*. Later, when the Ranch was established in Oregon, such *sannyasins* "in the world" would send a part of their wages to support the work.

In those days, women might be told before they left that when they returned to, say, London, they should report to Kalptaru Center there. This was the main center in England. Upon arrival information about strip houses, prostitution rings, and other quick ways to make money would be made available to them, unofficially, of course. Through Ashram programs of "assessment" and "programming," such women would not only be assured of feeling no guilt about what they were involved in—they could actually feel like a *devadasi*, one of the traditional Indian temple prostitutes, dedicated to the service of a god (usually Siva) and regarded as teachers in the art of love.

Constant screening through the Ashram offices indicated who was best suited for runs or likely to accept and thrive in fast-payoff operations not necessarily condoned by society. But even potentially bad judgment in selecting a likely person was unlikely to cause major problems, because the "us" and "them" conditioning reinforced that no one would ever, *ever* jeopardize Bhagwan. Even if a person was approached who was only concerned with spiritual enlightenment (whatever other evaluations might indicate), and refused to do the job suggested, he or she would *never* blow the whistle.

So the people who came to take *sannyas* were known by the Ashram to be dope dealers. They were assisted by the Ashram, inasmuch as the *darshan* list would be available to them, and it had information on who was leaving and who would be a good one to contact. Some dealers set up operations in Poona primarily because these were prime "mules"— and there was a whole group that was there not for Bhagwan, but solely to make money.

As with so many aspects of Ashram life, the key was often the groups. When you went to one of these groups you were in a room with forty or fifty people, from all walks of life. That might include a housewife who had a very rigid sense of morality; it could just as easily include prostitutes or junkies coming off whatever stuff they were hooked on. People got out of it what their potential was. Some people went in as junkies and came out of it and never touched junk again— but became artists or corporate executives or whatever.

Some people went the other way. They came in as so-called pure spirits and came out ready to poison people. You went into groups with all different types of people. In that closed situation, for a week or two, you learned to disregard what people were in the past. You also dropped your own past—just as you were instructed upon entering the gates to "drop your shoes and mind."

You were no longer in the world; you no longer had society and all the different moral systems to check yourself against. It was all gone. You were immersed in an environment that was amoral, and changing constantly, which eliminated both boredom *and* the chance to think clearly.

One of the key guidelines I formed from all this was, "I wouldn't do that, but it's *your karma*." I would hear myself saying this a lot. Other people would say the same thing: "The choice is up to you, and it's not anyone's place to pass judgment." This was another point that was reinforced in the Ashram: What you're doing is your business; what someone else is doing is their affair; problems would only arise when this distinction was ignored.

People were also assessed as to whether they could be used to smuggle goods into the Ashram. If someone wrote and said he'd be arriving in, say, a month, the office might write to him and ask him to bring in an Olympia Report Deluxe typewriter. Bringing such materials into India was illegal in those days, but such objections were overridden by laying stress on the fact that this was "for the Ashram and for Bhagwan."

The initial letter would ask whether it was possible for the person to bring the typewriter. If the person agreed, he would get back a photocopied form letter that indicated where to buy the item and a complete description of it. It would also advise nicking it and dabbing on white-out to make the item look secondhand. Secondhand items came under less scrutiny. Anything that *was* stamped on the passport had to be accounted for when you departed.

Almost no one refused such a request—if they did, it was simply because they did not have the money to make the initial purchase. The initial contact letter would also suggest that, if the person couldn't bring in a typewriter, he might be able to bring in a supply of typewriter ribbons, or something else less costly. When the letter was returned indicating whatever goods would be provided, the office would advise how these alternative goods could be brought through customs.

Even people who might otherwise never dream of smuggling could be encouraged to do these favors for Bhagwan. And this was done on a *massive* scale—coordinated by Sheela's group, which included me. We oversaw everything, but attended to our own special enterprises that very few others knew anything about.

During this time I had begun living with a man named Parijat. Occasionally, that Bhagwan would send a message that this person and this person should be together. Which is what happened to Parijat and myself.

I continued my duties in the cleaning department for a time, and was quite happy. I remained friendly with Martin, but he was increasingly involved with his own travels and medical research.

Outside the office I was caught up in the sphere of Deeksha, who had her own kingdom inside the Ashram. She ran Vrindavan, the restaurant. Over the years she expanded her empire to include a much-enlarged version of the restaurant, which became a prime money-making operation for the Ashram. She also bought up land around the Ashram to put up her own Ashramite housing.

Deeksha and I met in an extraordinary way. She always had a certain number of people who worked for her whom she supported in one way or another. She manipulated them first with money; if that didn't work, she'd play the office game of guilt.

One day I was standing on the steps of Krishna House. I was wearing my then-favorite dress. Suddenly, this big, fat woman with the most beautiful face swept down on me. "Oh, you have something on the bottom of your dress," she said. With that, she leaned down to the hem of my dress and ripped it from bottom to top along a seam.

I was stunned. When I could speak again, I said, "Well, I hope you're going to get me a new one."

She laughed and said something like, "Of course, of course. Let's get you some new clothes."

Before I could say anything more, she took me by the hand and led me to the small boutique on the Ashram grounds. All the time we were being followed by the entourage that accompanied her everywhere.

Into the boutique we went. She said, "Try this one. Now this . . . " Almost every dress I tried on, she decided to buy. I had very little say in the matter, though I must admit I was enjoying every minute of it. Then she said, "We need towels for you, and Almay scentless shampoo"—this was hypoallergenic, and only available from the West. Deeksha had all this stuff stockpiled: European cigarettes, brandies, whiskies, gins, shampoos, soaps, deodorants, Western nail clippers— anything that might be needed.

She made me a gift of everything. Then she asked, "Do you have any money?"

"No," I replied, because I'd pretty well run through the funds I'd brought with me from Athens.

"Okay," she said, and straightaway made sure this aspect was taken care of.

"Where do you live?" she wanted to know.

"With Parijat, in Vipassana," I explained.

"That's okay," she decided, "but let's go over to the room and check everything."

So we all marched over to my living quarters. At the time there were four of us living there: Parijat and myself, and two men named Arpitam and Tarpan. They all worked for Deeksha at the time.

She walked into the room with her entourage and announced, "All right, this room is going to be redone!" Then she took all the sheets, bedclothes, all the things from the shelves—*everything*—and replaced it with new and better—plus extras, like bars of chocolate!

By the time my roommates got home the whole place had been redone. This was a typical Deeksha technique; she could just as easily take it all away and leave rags in the room. She was very Gurdjieffian.

Before she swept out, she asked me, "Where are you working?"

"In the cleaning department," I replied.

"Oh . . . do you have a food pass?"

"Yes, but I don't like the food very much."

"Then you'll eat in Vrindavan," she said, as if it were the most obvious thing in the world. And, with that, she left.

So I began eating occasionally at her banquets, which were renowned throughout the Ashram. She'd have the finest cheeses and wines flown in from everywhere for these feasts, which happened every night.

She continued, off and on, to take care of me for most of my stay at the Ashram.

One day not long after this I was strolling near the front gates, when a man rode up on a motorcycle. One look at him, and it was love at first sight. I later found out his name was Shantam.

All this time Parijat and I had been faithful to each other. While I wasn't about to toss this aside, I was captivated by this man climbing off his motorcycle. I told myself, *I'll just ask this person if we can go for a drink this evening. That will get it out of my system.*

So I went up to this absolutely gorgeous person, and said, "Would you go out with me this evening for a drink?" We looked at each other for a moment, then he said, "Yes."

I had no idea who he was or what his capacity in the Ashram was. It didn't matter; I was flustered and fascinated. So I went to the boutique and bought a gorgeous new dress. Then I went to Parijat and, though I'd never lied to him before, I said, "I won't be around at *darshan* tonight: I'm going for a walk."

We went to the Oasis, which was a restaurant downtown. As it turned out, *neither* of us wanted to be seen—though I thought it was only *me* who didn't want to attract attention. All the time I kept fooling myself that he was going to show me some side of himself that I wouldn't like, and this would get him out of my system. On the contrary: The more I was with him, the more I *wanted* to be with him.

When we left the Oasis he suggested we go for a ride in the mountains. Although it was very late by then, I felt that time had vanished.

As we drove his motorbike out and parked to look at the stars, I felt completely at peace.

When we were ready to come back, I asked Shantam if I could drive the bike part of the way back (although I had never driven one before).

He agreed, so I climbed on and off we went. The night, my feeling of excitement, *everything* set me off; I kept going faster and faster. Suddenly, a car came up alongside us. In silent communication we decided to race into Poona. I felt like nothing could touch me. Time stopped, and I was totally caught up in the moment.

Abruptly, dead ahead, the road spilled into a concrete roundabout.

"Do you know where the brake is?" Shantam shouted at me.

"Yes." I was so intoxicated with the night, I called back, "But I'm not going to use it."

"*Then I'm getting off!*" he shouted, and jumped.

"Okay," I answered.

A moment later I went straight into the abutment ahead. I remember watching every second of what happened in absolute clarity: hitting the wall and being thrown back, landing in the street and the bike landing back on top of me.

An instant later Shantam pulled the bike off me. I no longer felt I was in my body. My consciousness had become a liquid floating above the scene of my accident. I knew that my body was hurting me. Then, like silvery, shimmery mercury, I began to pour myself back into my body. But I was blocked from filling my left arm and leg. I put all my energy into finding tiny channels to begin reclaiming these limbs a bit at a time.

I knew I was back in my body; and I was aware of some pain—but nothing unbearable. By this time we were surrounded by hundreds of Indians, all running around and shouting. Over the babble I said to Shantam, "Lie on top of me. I need some weight on top of me to stay here." I felt that my consciousness was going to float out of my body again; and that this time, I would float away forever.

So he did—giving who knows *what* impression to the audience we had gathered. After a moment I said, "I'm okay; I'll be fine in a minute."

Just then a Dutch doctor named Megha drove up on his motorbike with his boyfriend Naranjan, to see what help he could give. Our friendship had already been formed before this. He took one look at me and said, "You've got to go to the hospital!"

"No," I said, "I *have* to spend tonight with Shantam. I'll go into the hospital tomorrow if I have to."

So they scraped me off the road and carried me to Megha's apartment, which was nearby. They laid me on the bed; I was euphoric, feeling no pain at all. I was in love and that was *everything*. I had no idea of the extent of the damage I had suffered, and I was giving Megha no help on that front.

I just kept protesting that I *had* to be with Shantam that one night, whatever happened in the morning. So Megha dosed me up with pain killers, and they put me in a taxi.

At the Ashram Shantam lifted me out of the cab and carried me through the gates—for all the world like Clark Gable carrying Vivien Leigh in *Gone With The Wind*. If any of the guards had seen us and dis-

covered that I had been in an accident, I would have been made to go
to the hospital.

For reasons that were never totally clear to me—though Sheela once
attributed it to my "elf-like qualities"—I had come under the protective wings of the most important people in the Ashram, outside Bhagwan himself. For someone like me, who would "hang out" with the
powers-that-be, an accident would have raised a major uproar. I wanted
no part of that kind of drama: I was playing out my own drama that
night.

One night guard did spot us, but only commented, "Oh, how
romantic!"

Shantam took me up to his room, and we spent a marvelous night
together. The next morning he insisted I had to go to the hospital. But I
argued him out of it and managed to stall for three days, lingering in
his room. We had to go through some complicated maneuvers to keep
the cleaners out of his apartment; things were further complicated by
the fact that I hadn't told anyone where I was going.

He would bring me food from Miriam Cafe. I ignored my pain and
concentrated on happiness. But, at the end of three days, Shantam
brought Amrit, the main doctor in the Ashram. He took one look at me
and said, "You've got to go to the hospital." He wasn't about to listen to
any of my arguments.

So I was loaded again in the back of a taxi and taken to the health
center, which was the Ashram hospital. Amrit's lady, Makima, ran the
center, so they were able to sneak me into a bed away from everybody.
Because no X-rays were taken, it wasn't until tests were run in Italy that
three cracked vertebrae in my neck were discovered.

In short order I was swathed in plaster and hung on pulleys. Still, I
was able to remain comfortably hidden for another eighteen hours,
during which time Shantam was my only visitor. For all that we had
been through together, we still knew very little about each other. But
we both knew that if the office found out what had happened, all hell
would break loose.

Then another of Deeksha's proteges wound up in the bed next to
mine; he had been beaten up in his apartment by some Indians. Five
minutes after he arrived, in walked Deeksha, Shantam, and Parijat.

For a few minutes they gave all their attention to my roommate.
Then Deeksha wandered over to look at the poor creature wrapped in
plaster. The moment she recognized me, she went into hysterics. "My
god! What's happened?" she screamed, then went running out to get a

full account from Makima. She came back a few seconds later with Makima in tow, demanding, "How come she's here and nobody knows? What's happened?"

At this Shantam had gone white-faced; I still hadn't figured out what *he* was doing there. Parijat gave one look at me and nearly fainted. Shantam and I just kept looking at each other, while Deeksha turned the moment into grand opera. She could create drama out of nothing; with something to work from, she turned the medical center upside down.

It was complete pandemonium. I felt she was genuinely upset, because she hated for anyone she had feeling for to have any pain at all. And in this case there were two of us.

When things had calmed down somewhat, Deeksha asked me what had happened. Then Shantam, whose name means "Divine Silence," cleared his throat and said words to the effect of, "I forgot to tell you, Deeksha, that we wrote off your motorbike when this happened." Because he always kept so much to himself, and rarely spoke to anyone, Deeksha didn't seem to find his reticence in this matter so unusual.

"What?" she cried; then she said to me, "I thought you were with Parijat."

"Well, yes, but this was just for one evening."

"So you were driving the motorbike when this happened?"

"Yes," I said.

"Then," she decided, turning to Shantam, "As soon as she's up from this bed, you teach her properly how to ride it."

There was still the unresolved question of Parijat, with whom I had been put together by the express wish of Bhagwan, and whom I did love in a brotherly kind of way. As it turned out, both Parijat *and* Shantam were Deeksha's right-hand men. They worked together all the time, taking turns visiting me in the hospital, and not showing any resentment over our peculiar circumstances.

When I got out of the hospital the question was who I was going to stay with. I loved them both; both of them loved me. We decided it would be easier for me to be in Shantam's room because there were no stairs, while my old room with Parijat was up one flight.

Shantam would carry me out to the back gate for *beedee*s. Parijat would come to visit, and we agreed that things were simply turning out differently than either of us could have imagined. Finally, I wrote to Bhagwan, saying, "You put me with Parijat, and I really do love him— but I've met Shantam, and I really love *him*. What to do? Which one?"

And Bhagwan wrote back, "It doesn't matter which one, as long as it's only one. Be with just one."

I chose to be with Shantam from that time, though Parijat continued to be a friend, and remains so to this day.

CHAPTER 11

Sterilizations and Veggie Villas

While I was with Parijat, and before I met Shantam, I had gotten pregnant. I lived with Parijat because Bhagwan had said we should be together. When my pregnancy was confirmed I remember wondering if it was "divine," because of the special circumstances of our relationship.

In those days the routine response would have been to have an abortion, because Bhagwan didn't encourage having children. But this situation felt extraordinary enough to warrant asking Bhagwan. My letter said, "I've become pregnant: what to do?"

The little note I got back advised me to "See Arup." Once I knew that the answer wouldn't be written down for me to hold onto, I could already guess what it was. Arup asked me, "Why did you feel that you should write about this matter?"

I answered, "Since I'd been put with Parijat, I thought it was something I should ask about."

She said, "The suggestion is—" I should note that anything prefaced with those words was presumed to have come directly from Bhagwan "—to have an abortion and, at the same time, get sterilized. But, before you do that, wait just a little while—a week or two. Get used to the idea of being pregnant: get to know the being, speak to it, be friends with it, *explain* to it what's happening: that although it's there, it's going to have to move on this time. And then check in at the clinic."

I agreed, and went my way. I felt *blissful*. On the most basic level I was relieved to have the decision made for me. All along, I had told myself I would never have children. I knew the kind of person I was— I liked to be free—and was fully aware that taking on a child was taking on a tremendous responsibility and a commitment. This was a step I wasn't ready to take.

But for a short time I had the luxury of being pregnant, of walking around with a very different way of looking at things. Wandering the Ashram grounds, aware of this other being that was with me, showing it trees and sunsets, sharing the elephant ears and the *parijat* blossoms and all the other flowers in Rada gardens and around the Ashram— this became a beautiful time for me.

I would get into my silent language, smelling the rising damp from the just-watered flower beds or feeling the mist from a fountain, and try to transfer all that I was seeing and feeling into this being. I was very much aware that this being was going to move on, and would explain that to it as I strolled or sat.

After about two and a half weeks I realized it was time for us to part. Up to this point, while I had been doing this meditation with that other being, I had felt a warmth and glow inside. Then it just stopped; it wasn't there anymore. So I booked an appointment and went in to have the two operations.

I went to a *sannyasin* Indian doctor, Adjit Saraswati, who had his own clinic in Poona. The place looked like any number of houses in Koregaon Park. Parijat went with me. We took a rickshaw to the clinic. Because he had to get back to Vrindavan, he left me at the entrance. I remember saying to him, "Don't stay, just let me be." Outside the doors were two little benches, one on either side; I sat on one of these while waiting for my call.

I brought with me the box Bhagwan had given me months before at my leaving *darshan*. My understanding had been that, whenever I needed to check into myself, I could hold this box on my third eye, or if I was in pain, I could put it on the pain and meditate on it. There was no promise it would make the ache go away, but it would help me experience the pain as a learning experience—something positive. Now I held it cupped in the palm of my right hand, and began to cry.

After a short while a nurse came out and took me to reception. I paid the hundred-rupee fee, which was nothing, and filled out some routine forms. All the time I kept on crying tears of exhaustion and relief. But I just couldn't stop the weeping and wailing. A little Indian woman in a *sari* helped me undress, did some pre-op work, then walked me into the operating room, which was just a small room with an operating table in the center. She settled me down and put a cloth that looked like a dish towel on my chest.

All around me were bottles and jars of different colored liquids and powders, which made the place look like an apothecary shop. My clearest impression was of everybody wearing green gloves—not surgical gloves, but the kind of gloves I would use for cleaning at the Ashram. I was staring up at a battered, intravenous drip arrangement. The funky quality to it all helped me relax a bit—it wasn't nearly as intimidating as a Western medical office.

I was given a general anesthetic and told to count to ten, which I began to do. . . .

The next thing I was conscious of was going off into a field of yellow daffodils. I was skipping along, feeling lighter and younger than I was physically. I put my hand out, and somebody took hold of it. But I couldn't turn to look at the person, though I had this incredible sense of trust. The sky overhead was bright, bright blue, and the yellow fields of flowers stretched out endlessly. I wanted to go on running through them forever.

I next recall waking up in Parijat's bed up in Vipassana. The doctor, Megha, was there taking my pulse. Then he gave me an injection.

"Megha, what are you *doing* here?" I asked him groggily. "How did *I* get here?"

"You've been back four days," he answered matter-of-factly.

"No," I said, confused, "I was just in this field. . . ."

"Something's wrong," he told me, "You have a very, very high fever."

"But I feel *fine*," I protested, drifting in my half-awake state.

"That's because I just gave you something. We've got to get you straight to the hospital."

He and Parijat bundled me off to Ruby Hall, the Indian hospital in Poona. There they put me to bed while Megha and other doctors ran tests. I had peritonitis; apparently the physician had accidentally punctured the intestine when he had performed the surgery on me.

Though I could remember *none* of it, it seemed that after the operation I had taken myself out of the clinic, gotten into a rickshaw, and come back to the Ashram. I had strolled the grounds, keeping to myself, just wandering.

At that time you got seven days off when you had the sterilization, so no one questioned why I wasn't working. This seven-day "holiday" was a part of the reason people were so willing to get sterilized. The normal work schedule in the Ashram was twelve hours a day, seven days a week. If you worked in the office, you worked *eighteen* hours a day. To have a full week off was *incredible*. (This recuperation period was considerably shortened as time went on.)

Also, the sterilizations were strongly encouraged—we were even given printed handouts on the subject—because children were "a distraction from the path of meditation" and "very few people had the *karma* to have children in this lifetime." If you were here with Bhagwan, why be distracted from that and go off on a different tack? the reasoning went. The better choice would be to be with him *totally*.

Most people had already decided on their own not to have children. So when the question of sterilizations came up, with the added bonus of a holiday, people were quick to go along with the idea.

I later heard that everyone who saw me wandering about after my own operation thought I looked extraordinarily *blissful*. The reality was somewhat closer to *really stoned*. Unlike a Western hospital, where you might well be kept overnight for observation, we would be roused after the operation and sent on our way as soon as we could walk.

I talked with some people that afternoon and sat in Rada gardens. No one noticed anything seriously wrong. It wasn't until the next day or so that Parijat realized that it was more than just some aftereffect of the drugs—that I was slipping into fever and delirium.

In the hospital they quickly found that the puncture was a small one. The only real treatment was to put me on antibiotics and see that I got plenty of rest. I would just lie in bed, feeling *wonderful* in that dreamy-drifting state, while the medication took effect.

This was also my first brush with the sleep therapies used in the Ashram. To keep me still and speed up the healing process, they kept me heavily drugged—which felt *fine* to me. I think the drug was *phenadrin*, an opiate often given to women when they're going into labor.

My stay in the medical center lasted several weeks. Most of that time is a blur. I would wake for a short time, then fall asleep again. The environment at the medical center was very nurturing. In the afternoon a nurse would come and give me a foot-rub. The room was airy, with big windows and fans overhead. Special care was taken with the food, which was always very fresh, light, and inviting.

But, although the break in the routine was certainly welcome, I was aware that if you were sick too often—and "too often" varied from person to person—you could be told to go back to the West.

Parijat came to see me as often as he could get away from his duties at Vrindavan. He was supportive throughout, agreeing fully with the decision to have the operation. During the weeks before the abortion, he began talking to the little spirit. I think we became closest during those weeks that followed.

In the closed world of the Ashram things quickly became very "esoteric." This is what happened with the sterilizations, as they became increasingly common. The seven days off never meant "seven days off from the Ashram." During that time people stayed on the grounds and *meditated*. It gave us a chance to enjoy the beautiful gardens and interesting bypaths, visit friends, and do all that we were too busy most of the time to do.

The sterilizations really brought home just how little time we had to ourselves. We reveled in these interludes, when we could enjoy the *other* rhythm of the Ashram: quiet, space, and beauty.

As far as we knew there was never an official policy on sterilization; things of this sort would just filter into the collective consciousness. Later, when I worked in the office, I understood how such ideas were put into circulation—it was all a bit like *Animal Farm*.

The sterilizations were first regarded as a "special" time. We would talk about how the whole process made you "feel like a woman." (At this time men weren't being sterilized.) We would have time to sit and *be*. We felt more centered, grounded—perhaps this was some effect of the operation on our bodies, but we reinforced it in each other.

A strong bonding between women happened at this time: Some of the most lasting friendships I made were sealed then. On one level it's extremely traumatic, but we never acknowledged that. It wasn't a conscious suppression, because at the time I could honestly say I was *blissful* that it had happened—long after I had recovered from the peritonitis.

During those seven days there was no need to rush around. Time slowed to a delicious crawl. If I were to describe me at that time, I'd say I felt *round* and *glowing* and as if my eyes were opened to *so much more* than I'd ever seen before. It made me a little melancholy, too—but not depressed.

This was a very silent time. I would often walk slowly along the path to Jesus House gardens, pausing to look at a blossom or leaf, feeling in awe of it and one with it at the same time. If I met a friend we would just hold hands and walk along together, without ever saying a word. Somehow, we were able to transform what had happened to us into something else for a while.

That "while" lasted during the time the Ashram was coming to its peak. In those days, even something like sterilizations or a death could be changed into a positive experience. One time I was sitting on Jesus House lawn, looking at the grass, and just being *delighted* that the grass was on the planet with me. Realizing how the grass couldn't exist without the soil or the water or the air, I felt the links that tied it all together. I realized I couldn't have appreciated that moment in that way, if it hadn't been for everything that had happened to me to give me this richer way of seeing and the time to use my new eyes.

On the larger scale, we had no outside influences at this time. During the nearly two years I had been associated with the place, there had been a refinement of the people living and working at 17 Koregaon Park. They were now of a similar kind—though they may not have come in that way. We had built a new environment and were now living in it completely. We no longer had information coming through to us from the outside world, except what was filtered through the office or brought in by newly arrived *sannyasins*; we were no longer judging things by outside standards, whatever our particular backgrounds had been.

When I left this hothouse world years later, I went through a time of anger over the sterilization business. But the fact remains that, at the time I did it, I was *very clear* from my perspective that it was the best decision I could have made. At the very least it gave me time to experience the Ashram without worrying over "should I? shouldn't I?" or "Am I? Am I not?" Now I will try to have the process reversed. If everything works out the way I trust it will, then I'll still have children—and be the better mother to them, for having had to make a very conscious choice.

Of course, there were children in the Ashram. People came with children, who grew up there. There were always children around; and we could take responsibility for those children to a certain extent. From that experience I realize I could be happy adopting a child, rather than having my own.

My feeling that my decision was the *only* one I could have made at the time was strengthened by the fact that the suggestion came directly from Bhagwan.

Later, the sterilizations became a routine fact of life—for men as well as women. The women had been done first because the doctor at the clinic was a gynecologist, and only able to perform tubal ligations. When the Ashram medical staff was enlarged, the men had their turn. The office had a harder job of selling vasectomy wholesale to the men, but eventually, most agreed to it.

The drugs, which let us spend so much of the recuperation time just lying on a bed or lawn and spacing out, helped ease the process. Because we had to be *there* so much of the time, it was better than a vacation to simply let your mind slip its moorings and drift. I think it's similar to the use of recreational drugs among high-pressure business types. For us, a bout with hepatitis or some other illness was often the only way to give our minds a vacation from the intensity with which we were expected to live and work every minute.

We were all like children in this as in so many things. Joining the "club" and comparing scars became a kind of game with us. When the men walked around all taped up, we would giggle—just like children discovering the differences between boys and girls for the first time. It all seemed familiar and "normal" because that was the world we had built and were living in every minute of our lives. I thought it was all very playful and great to be included in this sisterhood where I could compare scars and stories of how it happened.

Because of my age, this was the world I was growing into; nothing seemed unusual. Now I sometimes find myself wondering how an adult, who had lived for years in the outside world, could have walked into this place and joined it. That's a question I couldn't answer for anybody. But they did, and always more and more of them.

Sickness, like the sterilizations, was often valued as a chance to get out of work and get back in touch with some part of ourselves that had to be ignored in the everyday routine. Hepatitis was known as a "negative" sickness: if you got it, they said you were getting your anger out, because this was a liver disease, and the liver was the seat of negative emotion. On the other hand, a fever might just mean you wanted a rest.

Nobody took any of this very seriously. Even when people got typhoid it was taken as a spiritual thing. Whatever life dealt you was your *karma*. So you'd take it in stride. If someone you knew got sick, you'd visit her and do what you could to make her feel better, but you'd end up more often than not in an esoteric discussion about what the disease "meant."

People would let an illness run its course as much as possible. Afterward, for as long as you needed to, you could just *be*. You could use this time to go inside, without any pressure on you. During this time you would be taken care of, your room kept clean, food brought to you. Ashramites never had to worry about paying bills or filing insurance forms or anything of that sort. Your basic needs were taken care of: Your only obligation was to draw out of the experience whatever lessons you could. In that way it was very healing, and people never seemed to suffer the long-term damage such illnesses often produce.

If you weren't an Ashramite, however, the chances were a serious illness would get you sent home as soon as you were able to travel. If you were a *sannyasin* who lived outside the Ashram, the Ashram wouldn't take any official responsibility for you. Still, if someone came down with hepatitis, and a friend brought word to the office that there was no money to hire anyone to help out, there would be a run of people who worked in the canteen who would take "tiffins" of special foods to the victim, since foods that weren't spiced or fried were hard to find in India. Anyone who didn't live near a "tiffin run" could have a friend pick one up from the canteen.

The response to sickness was low-key, but the question of crimes near the Ashram was a matter of critical concern. For example, if a person who wasn't officially attached to the Ashram, but lived in a hut near the back gates, got beaten or raped, the Ashram guards would go into action. They'd do everything they could to find out who was responsible, because they didn't want anything to happen to anyone directly connected with the Ashram.

They put a lot of energy into protecting people, which often resulted in very harsh treatment of Indians. In those days the guard staff was already extensive, supplying guards for the whole 17 Koregaon Park complex, the health center, the Music House outside the Ashram, and various private houses in town where numbers of *sannyasins* lived. When such a place had a significant number of people in it who worked in the Ashram, the office would note this and the recommendation would be made that a guard or guards be posted there. By this time the Ashram also maintained a dormitory complex at 8 Koregaon Park, that was divided between Ashramites and those who paid to stay there. It also had guards.

A special set of guards, the elite *samurai*, guarded Lao Tzu House. They were responsible for Bhagwan's personal safety.

In addition to guards stationed at various locations, others had Ashram motorbikes and would drive around the area, checking with various guards to be sure everything was okay. Since the Ashram guards didn't have walkie-talkies, these "floaters" would monitor everything on a regular basis. The guards would also drive around Poona, keeping an eye on things and making sure no *sannyasin* was having a problem.

Most of the Indians around the Ashram seemed frightened of Westerners. Although they might shout, especially if they were a little whacko, it was rare that they would touch you—they'd be afraid that something would happen or they'd be accused of something.

Very, very few Ashramites were native Indians: I would guess no more than three or four percent. More came as visitors from around India—and though the numbers grew as the Ashram did, I'd estimate they never amounted to more than fifteen or eighteen percent, compared to Westerners (the term "Westerners," for some reason, also applied to people from the Orient).

Ironically, Bhagwan was very rude about Indians; Sheela and

Laxmi, both Indians, didn't like them at all. They weren't welcome—save a very select few. We had to *deal* with Indians all the time—the police, the immigration authorities, most merchants—but even the ones we dealt with in these ways were selected. These, especially the businessmen, had to prove themselves; if anything ever seemed the least shady, they'd be cut.

Relations with the government of India were often strained. In 1978 Moslem demonstrators protested some of Bhagwan's comments about Mohammed during his Sufi lecture series—in much the same way that his often outrageous comments or jokes about such persons as Mother Teresa or groups such as Jews would provoke hostile reactions. Bhagwan always claimed that his irreverent remarks were merely part of a teaching method designed to shock people out of preconceived and unexamined ideas and open new doors to awareness.

Shortly after this incident the Indian government imposed a ban prohibiting any foreign news media from filming the Ashram or its activities. At the same time travel restrictions were temporarily imposed on *sannyasins* attempting to reach Poona. Also, an application for establishing a small commune in Gujarat was held up indefinitely (and was ultimately refused).

Such difficulties prompted Bhagwan to denounce the government in New Delhi as being "utterly sexually frustrated, repressed people"; to refer to politics as "a kind of neurosis"; and to comment,

Just by preventing the BBC, the Spanish TV unit, the Australian TV unit, the German TV unit, and journalists from reaching here, do you think you will be able to prevent me from reaching people? . . . We have 200,000 *sannyasins* all over the world. Nobody else can claim that. And we have almost a million lay followers, lay disciples . . . 3,000 *sannyasins* are almost always present here. Every year about 25,000 people visit from all the countries all over the world. No other place can claim this. (from a 1978 lecture reprinted in *The Secret of Secrets*)

Nor were such outspoken comments necessarily limited only to the Indian government. "Indian culture," he suggested (*The Goose Is Out*), "is the most rotten culture that has evolved in the world. . . . It is so rotten that it has forgotten how to die. To die one needs to be a little bit alive, and unless you know how to die, you simply vegetate, you stagnate."

This uneasy relationship foreshadowed some of the problems which many claim helped turn Bhagwan away from India and to the West.

If an Indian was caught trying something like climbing over the walls at night, he'd be *really* beaten. (It's important to remember this is how any wealthy Indian living in Koregaon Park would treat an intruder.) But incidents like this only happened about three times that I can recall. Once word got around, very few were likely to run the risk of such a beating.

The people of Poona regarded the Ashram and its steady stream of visitors as a great source of income. Dealing with Indians was a frustrating affair, in large part because they would always tell you exactly what they thought you'd want to hear. For example, if you went to a dressmaker with cloth and a skirt you wanted copied, and asked, "Can you have it ready by tomorrow?" He'd reply, "Yes, yes, yes."

"Are you sure?"

"Yes, yes, yes."

"I don't want to come clear across town if it's not."

"It will be ready. Yes, yes, yes."

Of course, when you'd get there the next day to pick it up, you'd be told, "Oh, sorry, sorry, the dressmaker is not here." This was where the screaming game came into play. This rarely involved any real anger, and it seemed to satisfy some deep-seated desire for drama on the part of Indians. Once a successful bout of shouting was past, they'd find the dressmaker pretty quickly and he'd stitch up the skirt on the spot.

This type of thing went on everywhere. If you'd say to a rickshaw driver at the gates of Koregaon Park that you wanted to go to Laxmi Road, he'd immediately try to take you the longest way around. You couldn't simply tell them not to go that way. You'd have to yell, "Hey, *baba!*"—"Hey!"—"No, no."

His immediate response was likely to be, "No speak English."

At that point all you can do is slap him lightly on the side of the head. Then he'd turn around and take you the right way, because he'd know you're not going to put up with it. And then he'd try to overcharge you at the end of the ride. In fact, *anything* you tried to buy, they'd try to overcharge you for.

I never begrudged them their games; most of the time I even enjoyed them. I'd go through the required screaming with a woman selling *saris*, we'd come to our agreement, then I'd often sit and have a cup of *chai* with her—and maybe watch her children for a while while she ran an errand.

Beggars were another caste unto themselves. You couldn't walk out of the Ashram without twenty beggars crowding around you shouting, "Hey, *baba!*" and touching you and pulling on your clothes. "*Paise, paise, paise!*" New people would try to give them money; but it was hopeless, because more and more would always come out of nowhere. I found the best way was to locate one that you were particularly drawn to. A lot of India seemed to work that way. Somehow, you were able to make the individual contact in the midst of the endless press of people and demands. Once it was established that you'd chosen one to sponsor, they'd leave you alone.

I think the Ashram only existed as long as it did *because* it was in India. Although the Ashram was only five acres, when you stepped outside *it wasn't the Western world*. It was a colorful and magical place— an extension of the magical kingdom inside. It was a world that let you be in your own environment. Strolling through the slums or the *sari* market or past the *beedee wallah*, you were in a fascinating world, but not *of* it.

The cacophony of cows, pigs, chickens, rickshaw horns, and bicycle bells; the shouting matches with a taxi driver or dressmaker—these were all background noise. If it got too loud, or you felt too tired to haggle over the price of a dress, you could simply retreat to the quiet and calm of the Ashram. The world outside the gates was there to enjoy, to delight in—but it could never make any *demand* on you. We were in India, but we were always in our own world first and foremost.

Trying to do the same thing in the West *just wasn't possible*, as we later found out. Since the majority of *sannyasins* came from the West, putting them in a situation where the sights and sounds they had grown up with were right outside the gates made the world inside seem out-of-place. Part of the reason it worked so well was that we weren't flooded with *things*. The story of the *umibushi* plums or the Nutella would be meaningless in a world that had a Seven-Eleven twenty feet away. We found value in *not* having a ready supply of *stuff* at hand.

So much energy went into justifying our position, *reassuring* ourselves, maintaining our identity in the West—it was very different from the easy acceptance that Poona gave us. There, our obvious success and growing wealth were something positive; in the West these increasingly became reasons for suspicion and resentment.

The core of Bhagwan's teachings was steeped in Buddhism and Hinduism—traditions that Indians were used to, and which much of the West has yet to discover. India has a long history of *gurus*, whom it values as pools of wisdom. So often in the West, however, one "teacher" can only ascend if he can discredit the teachings of those who have gone before him, or who are sharing their message at the same time.

In my opinion the majority of those who complained about India probably wouldn't have changed it for the world. Even those who wouldn't admit to this at the time surely felt it when things rapidly fell apart after the move to the United States.

Before that, when Sheela would visit the West twice a year to pick things up, we were thrilled when she'd bring back big boxes of sheets and trinkets. Even a plastic Mickey Mouse key ring was something precious, because you couldn't get that quality locally.

In the West such things are meaningless, because we're literally *flooded* with goods. In India it wasn't having first-quality Western fabric to make into a dress that was precious: *you* felt precious. Each one of us felt individual, like a jewel. I loved the exotic blooms all around, but my favorite blossoms were marigolds because the seeds for them had to come from the West. To me, the longer I was in the Ashram, the more the West became like a magical place.

In India or the West the Ashram was "a world of its own," but this concept meant very different things in the two settings. This was most clearly seen in our appreciation of things and people around us. In India we could hold things a little apart from ourselves and savor them. In the West something else would cry for attention the minute we tried to experience one thing. There wasn't a single television set in the Ashram, which also helped us maintain a balanced perspective on material goods. Unfortunately, it also proved to aid us in losing our perspective on the outside world.

But, for all that, the Ashram was up to date on the latest technical innovations. Bhagwan's lectures were videotaped; the video center would duplicate these for shipment to centers throughout the world. They could also be bought by individuals or groups, and this became yet another substantial form of income for the Ashram.

A lot of effort in those formative days went into keeping up the image of the Ashram as an idyllic place.

Staged events kept the illusion of magic at full tilt. One of the more memorable was the marriage of Swami Rakesh and Big Prem. It was all like something out of a romantic fantasy. They had fallen in love, and had been together for a while, and now wanted to make the commitment to marry.

Big Prem came to the ceremony on an elephant draped in flowers. Everybody had flowers and long dresses and followed along behind, singing and dancing. She climbed down into Rakesh's arms, and they were married in the afternoon under a perfect blue sky, with almost the whole of the Ashram attending. Afterwards, they rode back to their room on the elephant.

This sort of image was played up, and helped attract a lot of people to the Ashram. But we all shared in it. It was like a Hollywood fantasy—only it was real, it was happening to people we knew, and *we* had created it. Even when things began to tighten up, and such things didn't happen so much, the *memories* were very much there.

A person who just arrived and looked in the eyes of people who had been there for a while would see joy in them. Even when Bhagwan stopped taking such a personal part in things, and everything was changing, it wasn't apparent for a long time, because people were still delighting in their memories.

People would come in on these stories, fascinated by the fact that this was not only a "spiritual mystery school," but a place where these crazy theatrics would happen. Clearly, it was no boring monastery, but an alive, vibrant, ongoing celebration.

Around this time Deeksha's lover, Krishna Bharti—"K.B.," as he was nicknamed—contracted hepatitis, and went into the hospital. As a result Deeksha was left pretty much on her own. Since she and I and Shantam were friends, we started going out together to places like the Blue Diamond.

Shantam had always been quiet and a bit aloof. Now Deeksha conspired to draw him out more. Since I wanted him to enjoy the things I enjoyed so much, I encouraged Deeksha as she gave more and more effort to the business of drawing him out of his shell.

Things began unraveling one day when Shantam, who had some kind of a stomach upset, had stayed at home in bed. I took some time off from work and went to look in on him. When I came to the room, Deeksha was sitting there. For the first time I felt a "vibe" from Deeksha that I wasn't wanted. She was enjoying "doing" for him, and she wasn't happy that I had come in.

She left rather hurriedly. I felt a little strange, wondering if she was no longer going to be satisfied with the fact that Shantam and I had a relationship, while she was only a friend to us both. But I quickly passed it off.

At the time Shantam and I were living in the Ashram, in a building nicknamed "Veggie Villas" (because the vegetable gardens were right out in front of it), which backed onto Lao Tzu gardens. At this time they had just begun the practice of extinguishing the lights throughout the Ashram halfway through *darshan*; and the rule of silence during *darshan* was now much more strictly enforced. Shantam and I didn't have that much time to be together, so this was one of the times we took to be alone. We had two male roommates at Veggie Villas, so time to ourselves was always at a premium. Rather than running off to the Blue Diamond at such times, I had taken a hut outside of the Ashram, around the corner, at a place called 60 Koregaon Park. I did the place over to our liking, and made it into a home for us. It became our retreat whenever we wanted privacy, though Shantam also kept his room in Veggie Villas.

Things were becoming more complicated on other fronts.

K.B. was recovering, but he had become very close with Yashu, the woman who was his nurse. He was still very devoted to Deeksha—as she was to him. He had come out of the hospital and returned to his rooms with Deeksha above Vrindavan. But Yashu would bring him his food or walk with him when he wanted to take a stroll during the afternoon, because Deeksha had her ever-expanding "empire" to oversee.

In the hothouse of the Ashram gossip tended to become self-fulfilling prophecy. Talk about K.B. and Yashu probably lent itself to the power of suggestion as they heard rumors about themselves. At the same time I tried to ignore the fact that Deeksha was "looking more into Shantam's light." More and more she would keep him after work to talk about K.B. or himself.

One night I was lying awake in Veggie Villas, waiting for Shantam. Deeksha frequently started up the kitchens at Vrindavan after *darshan*, and Shantam would be involved because he was one of the main overseers.

As it got later and later, I began to imagine that something was going on between Shantam and Deeksha. I laid on the bed going through total hell, telling myself, *Oh, God, don't be so attached*. A minute later, I'd think, *It's not attachment: It's sneaky. Why couldn't they be honest with me?*

Finally, I worked myself up into a total rage—mostly directed at Deeksha. Although we were friends, I felt she had abused me. I felt that she had taken advantage of my inexperience. I also knew that she was a powerful person in the Ashram. She could pull a lot of strings—or create hell for me, if she wanted to.

What angered me the most was the realization that here *I* was, lying in bed, beating myself up inside, telling myself, *Oh, be more surrendered. Oh, don't be so attached*—using all the language I had learned in the Ashram.

At the same time the little devil I carried around in me all the time kept saying, *Yeah, but she's had a hell of a lot longer time at this. She should be better at being upfront with this, and straight about things. Why's she sneaking around?*

Then I'd haul myself back to the other side and say, *But this is part of the game; this is how you win somebody.*

And then: *But she should know better: what we're trying to do here is get beyond playing these games anymore. And what's his part in all this?*

In the end I convinced myself that lying in bed, not confronting the situation, was dishonest. I was also angry at them because they had forced me into the position of going to where they were, which meant marching out of Veggie Villas and past Lao Tzu House at nearly one o'clock in the morning. I would be putting a lot on the line, because Deeksha was a major player; and, in this situation, I could very well be left standing alone if it came to a real showdown.

Imagining climbing the stairs to her room, knocking on the door, the moment of confrontation—it reduced me to tears. I knew that everybody who saw what was going on would savor the drama—and have it spread all around the Ashram by the next day. Since Deeksha was involved, I felt it would get back to the Bhagwan, and the whole thing would probably be brought up in lecture—my worst nightmare.

But by not raising the issue I felt I was living a lie—something I did to myself a lot in the Ashram: in whatever position I found myself uncertain, I would think, *Look, are you here to fool around and play this half-heartedly? Or are you in this all the way?* Since I had always had the feeling that this was my "last time around," I was attempting to play for the ultimate.

I decided I had to "go for it"—whatever the immediate consequences. I would be confronting myself in those other people, and living up to what I felt was my commitment to take every situation in the Ashram to the limit, without turning tail and running.

I got "dressed to kill" in my newest gown. Then I charged out, storming past Eckhart House, past Buddha Hall, unobserved by anyone except for some small animals I heard in the shrubs.

My luck ran out when I reached the doors to Lao Tzu House, just beyond the gates. I had my hand on the bannister to go upstairs when Hamid, one of Bhagwan's *samurai* and a handsome Arab, said, "Wait, Avibha! Where are you going?"

I just turned around and walked to the gate. He opened it for me. By now I was shaking, and all I could get out was, "I'm going to kill her! I'm going to *kill* her!"

Startled, he said, "Oh, okay." To this day I felt that what got me past was being *so clear* that people wouldn't dream of stopping me.

I turned out of the gate and hurried up the stairs as fast as I could. I saw that the lights were on in Deeksha's room. I hesitated a moment, then I rapped sharply a couple of times, and, without waiting, walked on in.

They were just sitting on the bed, talking.

When I had gotten over my shock at *not* being shocked, I laid into them. "What are you doing? Why aren't you in bed together? All night I've been lying in bed with this idea of what you were doing—and you're *not!* It's there: It's in your mind. Why can't you just cop to it?" I must have looked and sounded ridiculous.

Deeksha, mercifully, didn't use the classic office response of defusing the situation by saying, "Well, that's totally your trip." I think I would have gone through the roof if she had. She had the decency to go white, because, whatever the actual circumstances at the moment, all three of us knew this was exactly what was in their minds.

Then she started crying, I started crying, and Shantam just sat there, caught between the two of us. In that moment all questions of power and Ashram principles and everything just fell by the wayside: Deeksha and I were two women who I thought had been good friends who were suddenly caught in a painful situation.

We just stood there for the longest time, sorting through emotions, trying to get a fix on where each of us was in that moment. Finally, she said, "I'm sorry."

"I'm sorry, too," I said.

Then I sat down beside her on the bed and we hugged each other, crying and feeling loving at the same time. Then Shantam said, "But the truth is, I don't *want* to be here." I guessed that was what they had been talking about when I had come in. "I want to be with you."

So we went back to Veggie Villas together.

As we walked hand-in-hand I thought about the hunger I had seen in Deeksha's eyes. And, feeling Shantam's hand in mine, I thought about what we often said in the Ashram, That if you feel that something can be taken away from you, then the "I" is still there. In which case you're not very far along. *And look at yourself in that.*

In spite of the mildness of the night, I had begun to shiver. Shantam put his arm around my shoulders. Everything felt topsy-turvy. I felt chilled, and my skin felt uncomfortably hot under his arm.

"I could see in her eyes that she *really* loves you," I said to him when we were back in our room.

He shrugged.

I was walking around the room, feeling stifled. My head was swimming. Deeksha had clearly, surely fallen in love with the same man I was in love with. What was I to do? It's hard to play old games when it seems the other players are as much victims as yourself. All I could do was stand there, feeling naked in the moment, because there was nothing I could put up to keep me from seeing how she loved him.

"How could I ever be with her?" Shantam said suddenly. "She's so *fat*." He had brought the whole business right back to earth.

I resented that remark for two reasons: although Deeksha was fat, she was in no way ugly; in fact, facially, she was quite beautiful. Secondly I resented this because of what I'd seen in her eyes. I was rubbing my arms because I was *freezing*, but I wouldn't let myself climb into bed just yet. I felt things had not resolved themselves. I felt as if I was holding back something.

That need to resolve something continued over the next few days. I would observe Deeksha. She would look at me with sadness, and at Shantam with that desperate need. But she couldn't play any of the flirting, dishonest games that would have been open to her in the outside world. Shantam worked for her; she could have done a lot to manipulate him, but she didn't to my knowledge. She was completely honest. Everything was there to read in her face, and that hurt me the most. I also felt physically out-of-sorts.

Then, one night not long after, while Shantam and I were in our hut at 60 Koregaon Park, I said to him, "Shantam, you have to go to her. Just go and *be* with her."

"No, I don't want to," he said.

"In a way you *do*," I answered, "If you would just forget her body. She's beautiful and you know it."

"No."

"You *have* to," I said finally.

Finally, he agreed, "All right, I'll go. But I won't sleep with her."

"That's all right," I said, "Whatever. *Just be with* her."

He got dressed; I was lying down on the bed. When he bent over to kiss me, I only said, "I'm so *cold*." I was shivering, like a person with a bad case of shock. My teeth were chattering, and you *never* get that cold in India. He began piling blankets on me. "*Just go*," I begged him.

I knew that I loved the two of them completely. I trusted that I had done the best by all three of us.

For a long time I lay there under the mounded blankets, still shivering.

Shantam didn't come back.

Finally, feeling that I'd never been colder in my life, I fell asleep.

CHAPTER 12

The Inner Circle

The next thing I knew I was *hot* with fever—and when you're sick in India, it seems far worse, because while you're burning up on the inside, the heat of the day is smothering you. I was lying on the floor of my hut; I didn't know if I had collapsed there or simply lain down there because it was cooler than the bed.

Sylvia, a beautiful Frenchwoman who had once been a Christian Dior model, was holding my head. As I stared up at her face she looked to me very much like an angel with long, long blond hair.

I remember her saying, "It's okay, it's *okay*. An ambulance is coming now. They'll take you to the hospital."

The next four hours were pretty confused. I knew I was sick. But I was also certain that I was feeling *shock* from what had happened between Shantam and me—though I had felt very strong at the time I had told him to go to Deeksha.

It was the result of living twenty-four hours a day at peak awareness. There was never a time I could simply go home and shut off my mind. The intensity was so great that even *looking* at somebody, I would know exactly where he or she was at. I was no longer outside that person: I *became* that person.

Things were further complicated by the fact that the affair of Shantam and Avibha certainly was noticed around the Ashram: two people who really loved each other without much drama, any shouting or screaming at each other was not usual. Bhagwan would single out affairs such as ours and talk about them, as if it was the ultimate of two people relating to each other without putting each other in cages. He once likened us to two birds that flew together in the sky, as if they had been together all their lives. I was fortunate, at that age, to have found a relationship of that type. Friends nicknamed us the "White Knight" and the "Princess."

When I said to him, "Go," I blew myself away. In the aftermath, I kept checking back with myself, asking, *How do you really feel about that? What is this really?*

Lying in the hospital bed I felt like I was flying and flying and flying, free, free, free. I didn't feel like I'd been trapped: I felt like I had taken one flight more, beyond any I'd ever taken. For me, the idea of "bodies" had dropped away, and our "spirits" had joined in some essential way. Even if we died in the next moment, I felt our spirits would remain together. I could feel other realities, because that was so much a part of our Ashram training. We lived with these ideas every minute. We lived these fluid ideas, no longer accepting *anything* as reality, but questioned everything.

I could never say to myself, *I know this is a book or a pen*, because a whole stream of questions would challenge me on what I could know or how I knew. That sort of questioning, I believed, was what would bring me to enlightenment, to the "ultimate." So you could never rest, never take for granted even the smallest details of life, because the minor things as well as the major could help move you further along.

Letting Shantam go brought into focus the idea of surrendering something of myself as an individual to more important concerns. We were there for ourselves and whatever our relationship was to Bhagwan. Now, however, I was giving up myself—*my* idea of what *my* path was—and directing somebody else into a third person's "movie." This was a reflection of what was beginning to happen throughout the Ashram: a movement away from doing things solely for yourself, doing things for the *commune*.

The first part of the time I was in the medical center in Poona I was put fast asleep to heal me, because I was really sick with fever. I'd come out of it from time to time, taking in things in bits and pieces.

Deeksha and Shantam came to see me once. I was aching and aching for him in my drugged state. But we all just murmured things to each other that I've since forgotten.

Sheela was there at one point. Vidya was sitting on the bed. Parijat came, but he didn't know what was happening, and I didn't want to show my pain at Deeksha's and Shantam's desertion. As in a dream, I couldn't hear what they were saying, though I felt I understood what they wanted me to know.

When I finally came around, and they stopped drugging me so much, neither Deeksha nor Shantam dropped by to see how I was doing. All my holier-than-thou feelings about giving Shantam up for one night dissolved into resentment.

Sheela visited frequently. The nurses were putting a lot of energy into taking care of me; and I knew, in the Ashram, that this indicated someone highly placed had put the word out that I was to be given this extra attention.

For three days I was in hell, wondering where Shantam was. I had given him up for one night—not *forever*. I couldn't understand where those two people were.

At last I got word that I would be returning to the Ashram in a day or so. That relaxed me a bit. I decided that there had been so much work that he hadn't been able to come to me. I was trying desperately to write off what had happened.

I was walking shakily down the path towards Veggie Villas, when I saw Shantam: He wandered straight past me as if I didn't exist. He looked me right in the eye, but he didn't *see* me. I went into shock again.

When I'd gotten my composure back, I went to the office. From the moment I stepped through the door I sensed something in the air, some expectancy. I knew that Bhagwan would play games with people to get them to drop their attachments, but I wasn't in the mood for games. I felt very uptight.

So I marched over to Vidya, who was seated at her desk, and said, "Look, I can't be in the Ashram anymore. I have to go back to the West." I must have sounded hysterical, but I felt very clear inside. "I have to go within the next twenty-four hours, and you've *got* to give me a ticket! Then, I'll just leave, because I can't be here with Shantam here and not be with him." All the time I'm watching myself carrying on this way, thinking, Oh, my God! You're going to get slaughtered for this one. People simply *did not* present themselves and demand a plane ticket—or anything else—from the office.

But Vidya merely smiled slightly, stood up, and said, "Just wait a minute." Then she disappeared through a small door at the far side of the office. After a moment, she stepped through the doorway and said, "Come with me."

I followed her into a small, comfortably furnished room. This was the inner sanctum of the office. Laxmi was there, seated on a couch beside Asha. Sheela was sitting on the floor near their feet. Vidya hovered near the door, which she closed silently behind her.

"Sit down," Sheela invited. Laxmi was giving her more rein. How very different this dark, intense, self-assured woman was from the first time I had seen her. She had been the receptionist when I had first arrived at the Ashram, and had seemed hardly distinguishable from the other women working in reception. Now she had moved so quickly and surely into her new position of authority that the transition had seemed effortless. Looking back, there was hardly a ripple at all, because her move felt like the most natural thing at the time. But now, when she spoke, it was with full awareness of her growing power. She rarely had to raise her voice to get results; but people moved quickly to do what she wanted done.

Most people assumed she had moved into this position "overnight." A few of us were aware of certain steps, but we didn't grasp the whole situation until she was in her new place. From later conversations with Sheela and others close to her I got a picture of her total calculation. It had begun even before she set foot in the Ashram, and it carried her along in carefully planned steps to a position where she became the motivating force behind Bhagwan's move to the United States and the unwitting engineer of the collapse of his American-based experiment.

I sat in one of the padded chairs facing the others. Though we had been friends, I was uncertain how to gauge the present situation—especially since I had come in and *demanded* something.

"What is it you want?" Sheela asked.

"I just have to leave. I can't be here in the Ashram with this thing going on. But I don't have the money. Just give me the ticket." The words were tumbling out.

She said, "Look, you have two options. One is that you can stay, move in here, and work for me personally. I feel for you as I would a daughter. And I will train you in everything that I know and everything I've learned. But I have to warn you of one thing: I'm the biggest bitch you've ever, ever met—or will meet. I'm totally ruthless. My offer is that you can work with me, you can learn from me, and you become exclusively mine.

"Or," she continued, "you can leave your *mala* on the table there, and I will give you a ticket so you can leave today."

She was offering me a chance to come into the inner circle of the office. Anything that came out of the office was coming directly from Bhagwan: This was constantly repeated in lecture. So, while she was giving me this talk, I understood exactly the opportunity she was offering me—and she knew that I had gotten the whole picture in those few sentences.

She was basically asking me *for total surrender to her*. Bhagwan continually stressed that the greatest thing was unconditional surrender, to give up the ego. It appealed to me as a way of putting things back into balance in my life.

Sheela continued talking, but I hardly heard what she was saying. I was swimming in a kind of euphoria mixed with excitement. It was thrilling to be right at the pulse of Bhagwan's experiment.

I knew I had to make my decision right there; in the Ashram you never have a moment to go and think about something. But the instant I heard her offer I knew what my answer was going to be: "Yes," I said. But I know, as far as she was concerned, I had already sealed the bargain with the excitement in my eyes.

"Great," said Vidya, coming forward to give me a big hug. Laxmi and Asha also expressed their delight with my decision. Then someone signaled to one of the clerks outside, who brought in chocolates and whatever anybody wanted to drink.

Now I belong to Sheela, I told myself. I glanced over at her, where she was talking to Laxmi, and she looked back at me and gave me a little smile. *This is what I've wanted all along*, I realized. Also, while I was accepting the offer, at the back of my mind was the thought that, *Maybe, in this position, I'm more likely to see Shantam*. If Bhagwan was going to intervene in our situation before this, he would probably have intervened on Deeksha's behalf. Now I felt the cards could be dealt either way.

Ironically, Shantam and I had *never* related to each other on this kind of level before; but, with that one conversation, my mind had switched to the beginning of calculation.

Laxmi's desk was the first thing you saw on entering the office. On one side was Sheela's chair, which was really just a chair for anyone taking dictation from Laxmi. On the other side was Arup's chair. Laxmi's chair was behind the desk on a dais, because she was a petite woman—a shade under five feet. She had graceful hands and big, big eyes that seemed to swallow you up when you were talking with her.

For all her forcefulness of character, Laxmi had a childlike quality. She made decisions, and could read through a contract and instantly spot anything that needed changing. This was all the more amazing since much of this was intuitive—her reading knowledge of English was imperfect. In spite of this, she would sometimes pause in a discussion to show you a trick toy she'd just acquired.

She had a beautiful hardwood desk, and the top two drawers were filled chock-a-block with tiny windup toys, trick pencils, invisible ink. With some callers she would appear very hard and firm; yet she might just as easily go to shake a visiting Indian's hand with a "joy-buzzer" hidden in her palm. She'd get people to laugh, and while they were laughing she'd get them to agree to something. She was an incredible businesswoman.

She always wore a red head-scarf in those days. She had three absolutely identical red dresses, cut very severely; over her dress she would wear a little top. She wore little red slippers everywhere.

Although she was tiny, she projected such presence and charisma—especially when she was sitting on her chair, looking over her desk. When she'd fix you with those eyes and give you a direction, you'd snap to it, with never a thought of answering back. It wasn't only *sannyasins* who bought into this: even Indian merchants, who could be overbearing toward women, would never dream of pulling that on Laxmi.

Indira Gandhi was a close friend of hers, from the time the two of them had been very young girls. But when Mrs. Gandhi withdrew her favor from the Ashram, Laxmi never waivered in her support of Bhagwan's experiment.

She was Indian herself. Her father had been a banker or a merchant-banker. Somehow she heard of Rajneesh Chandra Mohan when he was a philosophy teacher (he taught at Jabalpur University from 1957 to 1966), and went to one of his university lectures in Bombay. She was charmed, captivated—and deeply impressed with what she saw and heard. At that moment her life rearranged itself with Rajneesh at its center.

At the time they met, he was teaching full time—though he did give occasional lectures throughout India. He was, as yet, hardly known to Westerners. She went to him and told him he should be lecturing all the time; he agreed to this and she began arranging tours for him across the length and breadth of India, and handling all the secretarial duties. She made a vow of celibacy, devoting herself completely to the work of sharing his teachings with the world. In a way she began his whole guru trip, because she made him one in her own mind and heart.

According to his autobiographical discourses and writings, Bhagwan was born on December 11, 1931, in the little village of Kuchwara, Madhya Pradesh, Central India. His parents were *Jaina*, a religion that stresses asceticism. One of five sisters and six brothers, he was raised by his maternal grandparents until he was seven, when his grandfather died. He then moved to his parents' home at Gadawara. A bright, lively, even at times mischievous child, he was forever questioning things (and often experiencing unexpected alterations of his awareness).

He achieved his first *satori* at age fourteen in the ruins of a temple on the outskirts of Gadawara. Later he described it thus: "If you accept death, a distance is created; life moves far away with all its worries, irritation—everything. I died in a way, but I came to know that something deathless is there." In 1952 he had a second *satori*, while meditating in a tree in Jabalpur. In his own words, he came to "my realization of the spirit that is within every human body." Shortly after that he began experimenting with out-of-body experiences.

He attended Jabalpur University, where he wrote for Hindi newspapers and later began lecturing. He was enlightened at 2 A.M., on March 21, 1953, while sitting on a bench beneath a *maulshree* tree in a garden at Bhanvortal, Jabalpur. He described it as "an explosion of consciousness," commenting, "In that explosion, the old man of yesteryear died. This new man is absolutely new. The man who was walking on the path is dead and is no more. What is, is a new man altogether."

He graduated from the university in 1956, and accepted a position as lecturer at Raipur Sanskrit College the following year. He became a professor of philosophy at the University of Jabalpur in 1960. During this period he conducted his first meditation camp at Rajasthan in 1964. He was known as "the Acharya," "the Teacher" (a name he dropped in 1968 when he assumed the title "Bhagwan," which means "The Blessed One" and "He who has recognized himself").

In 1966 he resigned from the university to devote all his time to traveling, lecturing, and counseling his growing numbers of disciples. In 1969 Laxmi helped him establish a base in Bombay, in an apartment called Woodland Hills. He began to assign Indian names to his disciples, and had them wear orange outfits and *malas*. He also continued conducting meditation camps. He spoke on a range of subjects related to the spiritual quest and the search for the highest state of human consciousness—enlightenment—touching on everything from alchemy to Zen, and drawing on the insights of great spiritual teachers from Western and Eastern traditions. Drawing also upon his background training in religion and psychology, he offered a unique blend of mysticism and therapies and techniques from the human potential movement.

Bhagwan soon attracted more and more followers, many of whom came from the West. In the fall of 1970 he initiated his first neo-*sannyasins*, and the trickle soon became a torrent of visitors seeking the new "Master." With Laxmi's help he moved to Poona in the spring of 1974, and established the Ashram.

By the time he entered *satsang*, silent communion, on April 11, 1981 (before to the move to America), he had delivered more than 2,500 discourses and *darshans*—teachings totalling over 33 million words and reflected in worldwide sales in excess of 2 million books.

Bhagwan remained the focus of Laxmi's devotion for some twenty years; she was always his self-styled handmaiden. She would deny herself things in the service of *him*. Even when there was plenty of food she would almost be starving, because she wouldn't want to presume to take anything that might be for *him*.

She talked of what was happening as "*his* work." She referred to herself in the third person, as "Laxmi." When she spoke of Bhagwan it was always as "*he*" or "*him*." A lot of people thought of her as "enlightened." As Bhagwan retreated more and more into silence and retreat, people focused more and more on one of the matriarchs to become "the channel." And Laxmi was a natural focus for this sort of worshipful attention.

Even through the ascension of Sheela and her own fall into "disgrace" in Oregon, she remained loyal. And Bhagwan always had a soft spot in his heart for her—though, at one point, he did let Sheela force her off the Ranch. (Since she had nothing, she was supported by *sannyasins* living around the United States—until Sheela relented enough to allow her, under severe restrictions, to return to Rajneeshpuram. Through it all, she maintained that it was all Sheela's fault; *he* could never say or do anything wrong. During the decline and fall of the American adventure, after Sheela was gone, Laxmi protested that Bhagwan had had no idea of what was going on; he was still *wonderful*.)

There is a bizarre footnote to the whole incredible chain of events that led to the United States debacle and Bhagwan's abrupt departure. It has been reported that, while Bhagwan and his entourage were encamped at a hotel in India, after he left Oregon and before he fled India following the threat of prosecution, they ran up a staggering hotel bill. Laxmi, who had gone back with him, was sent to raise the money to settle the accounts. According to the rumors she took what money she had, and left for parts unknown. In many ways that absurd apocryphal story is the epitome of what happened at the end.

But, in those early days in India, I could only marvel at the intensity of her devotion. Truth to be told, however, long before the Ashram disbanded, our awe of her single-mindedness began to wear a bit thin. For all of our own "high-mindedness," I and others wearied of the fact that she never, never stepped out of the handmaidenly role and related to people on a merely human level.

I worked for Laxmi briefly, before I began working full time for Sheela, and we became quite good friends. Once I was working for Sheela, however, a distance grew between us. This was due in part to the fact that when you worked for someone in the Ashram, you worked exclusively for that person. I would never betray something Laxmi had said to Sheela; nor would I ever break confidence with Sheela in the other direction. You might use an item to your own advantage, but you would never play off one superior against another.

Years later, during the frantic, final days in Oregon, when Sheela had left the United States and Laxmi was again living on the Ranch, I had been dragooned back at Bhagwan's request into service to try and help sort out the mass of documents, accounts, and so forth that were in total disarray. While I was there a friend told me that, when Laxmi heard I had come back to help, she had freaked out. I had always thought we had been on good terms, so it startled me to hear that Laxmi had begun ranting, "Oh, she's terrible! She's a snake! She's just like Sheela! Sheela trained her, and she's *awful!* She shouldn't be allowed in! If she's here, then everything will go wrong!" And so on.

She was afraid I would become "the new Sheela." I was very upset to hear all this. I went to Hasiya, who was then serving as secretary, and suggested, "Look, we'd better ask Bhagwan about this, because something weird is going on." I explained that I felt hurt, and very funny about working at the Ranch if she felt this way.

Hasiya took my message in to Bhagwan, and returned with his reply: "Who do you think trained Sheela?"

Then I was able to put the incident in perspective. Laxmi had trained Sheela as surely as Sheela had trained me. She saw me as the "third generation"—and she knew what sort of a businessperson and game player she had helped create via Sheela. She had seen her own ambitions and skills mirrored in Sheela, and she simply presumed I would be a reflection of Sheela. Had we remained in India, had a lot of things not changed—who could say? But Laxmi's fears had no basis in fact by the time things fell apart.

Laxmi was the one who asked Bhagwan about different issues that had come up. When she was running the show, her devotion was such that she wouldn't make a real decision without getting a "Yes" from *him.* She would never take the initiative that way. So I think it's fair to say that during her time as "mediator," Bhagwan knew *everything* that was going on. Certainly, he knew everything that was going on with the Ashramites. If she observed something or heard one of us saying that such-and-such was going on, she'd tell him. If an Ashramite wrote, she would tell him. Ashramites could be sure of being dealt with directly by Bhagwan.

Laxmi was secretary to the whole commune at this time. Sheela was still dealing primarily with Indian *sannyasin*s or Indians the Ashram came in contact with in a business or political way. Laxmi oversaw absolutely *everything*. She was the eyes and ears of Bhagwan; whatever information reached him was filtered through her.

In her position as secretary to Laxmi, Sheela was privy to almost everything that was going on. She would report everything to Laxmi because she knew that, if she didn't, somebody on *her* way up would try to push Sheela out of the way by reporting an oversight to Laxmi and making Laxmi wary of Sheela. So she was *meticulous* about telling Laxmi every detail. As time went on Sheela *flooded* Laxmi with so much detail that the latter finally began to say, "Oh, there's no need to hear that." Then Sheela began taking it upon herself not to say certain things. If she was called on this, she would always have an out: "But you said not to bother you with that."

At this point one did not see Bhagwan outside of *darshan*. You would only see Laxmi, his intermediary. Bhagwan said of her, "Laxmi never does anything on her own. She is a perfect vehicle. This is why she is chosen for this work. Laxmi has no ideas of what is right and what is wrong. Whatsoever is said, she does" (*The Sound of Running Water*).

Bhagwan lived with Vivek, the "mystery woman" who was his bedmate, and a few other intimates who resided in Lao Tzu House. Vivek, an Englishwoman whose real name is reportedly Christine Wolf, saw herself as more than just a "companion"—and so did everyone else in the Ashram. Bhagwan spoke of her as the reincarnation of a girlfriend of his who had died in 1947. Eventually, she had some other boyfriends and things changed between her and Bhagwan; but she remained devoted to him—and the only one with unlimited access to him.

Even Ma Asta, who cleaned his rooms, never saw him, because he would be out when she went about her tasks. But she must have heard something because Asta and her boyfriend fled Oregon in the middle of the night shortly before the end came.

Vivek and certain other members of the "Lao Tzu crew" were outside of the office; they were exclusively involved with Bhagwan—although, like the rest of us, they might not see him. In a way, Vivek was to Lao Tzu what Sheela was to the Ashram as a whole. But she would *never* interfere with one of Sheela or Laxmi's people, because that would be going over their heads. The office people wouldn't steer clear of her, but she would make a point of avoiding us. Ultimately, Laxmi wielded power over everyone *except* those who lived in Lao Tzu House. Messages to them from Bhagwan would always come through Vivek.

Bhagwan was becoming more remote, more of an enigma all the time. When I first went to the Ashram he was much more available. You could go up and sit and talk to him or ask questions in *darshan*. The first major indicator of the change was this business of putting questions in the boxes in Krishna House. You no longer went to *darshan* to ask questions—except on special occasions. You learned from this *not* to ask questions; it reinforced the idea that you were supposed to look inside *yourself* for the answers.

Still, for all that he distanced himself from the community at large, Bhagwan was becoming more outspoken in lecture. People would write letters to say, "I wrote to the office to ask about such-and-such, and they gave me this reply, and it just doesn't feel right." In response, he would stress again and again, "*Whatever* comes from the office is coming *directly* from me. Everything that happens in the Ashram is known to me."

Or someone might write and say, "I saw one of the guards mistreating one of the Indians. I went to the office to complain, and I was told it wasn't my business." He would simply repeat that whatever happened he was aware of and he was very happy with the way the office was running things.

In effect, by retreating he gave the office more and more power. But the *darshan* lectures served to remind everyone that the ultimate authority came from *him*.

Another thing that assumed more importance as Bhagwan pulled back was the habit of being called in to be given a "Bhagwan gift." These could be anything, including his own (freshly laundered) sheets, a gold *Mont Blanc* pen, or cufflinks—and people could read into each gift whatever they wanted to.

You'd be called into Lao Tzu, and Vivek would give you the gift with a big smile, as though it had some tremendous significance. The impression was always that Bhagwan had singled *you* out for *this particular gift*. Since you were unlikely to get to talk to him directly, this seemed to be his way of acknowledging you. If you happened to be going through a hard time, and got a "Bhagwan gift," it would reinforce the idea that he was still aware of what was happening in your life. This was all the more impressive if you hadn't written to him or said anything about anything that was happening to you.

Then you were apt to make all sorts of connections for yourself about the meaning of the gift. If you were having a problem with a relationship and were given a set of double sheets, you'd probably think the gift "sanctioned" your relationship, and so decide on the spot to put more energy into working out the problems in this area. For me, this sort of thing always seemed a little bizarre—especially the way some really outrageous interpretations were given to a pen-and-pencil set or a pair of cufflinks. But we were still at that point in time where people could go off on these tangents, and you'd just think, *Oh, God, that's their trip*. Since each of us was at the Ashram for *our own trip*, we didn't question what someone else believed.

Whatever was given—a ring or a *Cartier* pen—was always exquisite, and usually expensive. Although we weren't supposed to become attached to wealth and *things*, the fact that the item might well be made of gold added to the feeling of its importance—and to the idea of our own importance in Bhagwan's eyes.

I tended to think of this, somewhat cynically, as a bit of skillful P.R. While some people would think of these gifts as something directly between themselves and Bhagwan, with only Vivek as intermediary, the fact was that in the back room of the office we were busily typing up lists, keeping an eye on what was happening in the Ashram, and deciding who would get what. We'd know that people were reading "this" into watches and "that" into the gift of a ring, so we'd match people and gifts accordingly.

But even those of us in the office who understood the way things were going down were told it didn't matter that we were making these lists. People had already put us on a pedestal because we were working in the office, so the fact that we were making these decisions was only the next logical step. Bhagwan had validated us repeatedly. The most important thing was to watch the effect on people's lives when they were given a gift.

The process was similar to a person who prays for help one night, and wins a lottery the next morning: It's natural to connect the two. And people were making these sorts of connections all the time. It added to the mystique of Bhagwan over and over; he functioned as a combination of "God" and "Dear Abby." And everytime you used your *Cartier* pen or slept on your new sheets, it would make you feel good, like Bhagwan was with you.

This could—and did—become a factor in changing many people's lives in the Ashram. It made you feel you were "in a state of grace" and let you draw off of the collective consciousness and energy of the Ashram. Very often, you'd begin to see yourself in a better light and be able to put your problems in perspective. It's very much the psychological principle that if you *think* things are better, they begin to *be* better.

My own favorite Bhagwan gift was a pair of red slippers that I received somewhat later, on the day I was to begin working in Lao Tzu house.

Being able to come and go in Lao Tzu was like getting the highest security clearance; for me it was a mark of how far I'd advanced in the Ashram. Some people were cleared only to go into one section—the video department, which really wasn't in the house proper, but had been added on alongside the original structure. Others, who had a close friend living in Lao Tzu, were on a "guest list" that permitted them limited access. This was convenient for a person who had a boyfriend or girlfriend living elsewhere: In the case of a falling-out, your ex's name would be removed from the "guest list" and that was that.

But my clearance was for the *whole* house—with the exception of Bhagwan's personal living quarters, which were out-of-bounds for everyone except Vivek and his personal cleaning person. I was allowed to what was called "the green curtain," which screened off the area in which he lived. It made me feel very close to him; sometimes I'd see Vivek bustling in and out with trays of food or whatever. There was generally a meditative silence in the house—but it was a "happy silence," sometimes punctuated with a giggle. Once you walked through the gates, you were aware of entering a sanctuary.

Actually, it *was* a sanctuary for me later. I became friendly with the woman who ran the video department. When I was in the studio no one could get in touch with me, because they were never allowed to call in case they were doing a taping. As soon as I was in there, we'd close the door and hang a "Do not disturb" sign on the door. It was the only place in the Ashram that this could happen, and people *had* to respect it. We'd often brew up coffee, and send a runner out for cakes, and while away a good part of the afternoon.

When I was told by Sheela that I could go to Lao Tzu, the first thing I did was hurry over to Lao Tzu to test it—just like a kid with a new toy.

I waltzed up to the gate in as serene and meditative and ego-less a place as my excitement would allow, and was thrilled to have the guard open the gate the moment my hand touched the bars, without any questions on his part. I went to the place where you left your shoes—because they were never worn inside a building. Just past the door Ma Asta, who lived in the house, came up to me and handed me a pair of beautiful new red slippers. They were red velvet with rope soles.

"These are for you. And he says you're to dance through Lao Tzu when you're here."

I put the slippers on immediately and walked around, testing every area that I could now go into. I felt exactly like a little girl again, when my mother had given me a red coat that I adored. I wouldn't take it off, even to go to sleep. When the time came to leave I decided that Bhagwan hadn't said that I *couldn't* wear them anywhere else—just that I *should* wear them in Lao Tzu.

I was so proud of my red slippers that I didn't take them off until they wore out. A lot of people had a judgment on that. "How could you abuse his gift?" they demanded. I kept telling them, "He told me to dance, and so I'm dancing." Just walking in them was wonderful: They were the most comfortable shoes I had ever owned. When they finally *did* wear out, I threw them away; and *this* really horrified people.

"They're only a pair of shoes," I said. "I know he gave them to me, and I loved them while they lasted. But, since they've worn out, why keep them?"

But some people had begun to lose sight of the fact that we were here to work on ourselves. If they felt that I wasn't surrendered or didn't love Bhagwan, because I threw my shoes away, that was their trip. I felt it was ridiculous.

So I had I moved into the "inner circle." From that moment on, no other world existed for me outside the office, the Ashram, and scattered Rajneesh centers around the globe.

I wound up working for Sheela because I was the right person at the right time. She had made up her mind to begin training an assistant, and I literally thrust myself onto her attention by charging into the office on that day. (Though I'm sure that, all along, I had been under consideration. I was precocious; she later explained that she saw herself in me.)

I had already demonstrated an ability to think clearly and speak well, and I had evident business sense. I had the right potential—but I was young enough so that I hadn't been filled up with a lot of ideas about how things ought to be done or, on another level, about what I could and couldn't do. I was coming like an empty page just ready to be filled.

I was also totally vulnerable because of our relationship: she was giving me so much and demanded so much in return that it was far more involving than even a love affair. I was dedicated to her twenty-four hours a day. She was offering me the opportunity to make the most of what I felt was my "last time around." For a long time the certainty had been growing in me that this was my final cycle in the chain of rebirths that had been allotted to me. I believed that each time around, you took a certain amount of awareness with you, always building to that point where you no longer have to be born at the whim of fate, but become the master of your own destiny, through birth *and* death.

The last time around meant the last time being born willy-nilly in time. It might mean simply reaching the point where you have an element of choice in the next go-around—or it might mean leaving this plane of existence altogether. If I had to define it more exactly, I'd refer to it as the "last time around for unconsciousness."

I can't say exactly when this idea came to me, but it was clearly fixed in my mind by the time I started working for Sheela. Being given this chance to participate in the game as one of the key Ashram players felt like *karma*.

Though I had worked in the office, and for Sheela, on previous occasions, this was the first time I had worked there exclusively.

Before I was invited in, however, I was already playing in the lion's den, since I was so close to Deeksha who was already building her empire. That relationship was unusual in that I wasn't working for her; when I was asked if I wanted to work for her, I said "No." I didn't want to let employee status cut into my very happy access to all the love and drama she would shower me with in her grand, *Italian* way. I didn't want to run the risk of becoming browbeaten, as so many of her workers were. However, until our falling-out over Shantam, she remained my patron.

At the time I was sixteen, and Sheela was twenty-nine or thirty. She was married to a man named Chinmaya, who had Hodgkin's disease. They lived on the upper floor of Krishna House, and Sheela was completely devoted to him. After he died, his birthday would always be the one day of the year when she was *totally* vulnerable. When he died the changes began in Sheela.

Even though she had planned so much of her rise in advance, she wasn't ruthless in an evil way. I think, in those days, she believed that for the good of Bhagwan, she would be able to run the place the best way. And, I think she really thought it would be best for him to be in America.

In a way Chinmaya was her conscience, her moral consciousness.

When he died that went out the window.

One of the conditions of my taking on the job at the office was that, for the next few years, I did not get to see or talk to Deeksha or Shantam *at all*. At first, I went crazy around this. Poor Chinmaya, confined to his bed as he was, became the only person I could go to and talk about how unhappy I was on this particular issue. He had a wonderful sense of humor, and could always cheer me up. We became fast friends up until the time he died. He would sit there and laugh and tease me, saying, "This is awful. I'm sitting here dying of Hodgkin's, and I can't get away from you complaining about Shantam." Then we'd both laugh. He had an incredible capacity to love.

He helped me adjust to my life without Shantam, and to my feeling of *incompleteness*. Things had been left hanging between us from the moment I said to him, "Go and be with her."

And, indeed, I didn't speak to Deeksha or Shantam for some years, though we were all living in the Ashram. I would only see his *feet*, never his face; because, once I started working in the office, I worked in strict silence, celibate, and was required to keep my eyes on the floor unless I had an official reason for talking with someone. I would hear his voice near my desk, recognize his leather boots or shoes, but would *never* look up from my papers. And he would never speak to me: I think he too had been instructed as to the rules of the game.

Long before the last days, however, events were becoming increasingly strange as Sheela began working out her convoluted, long-range plans for Bhagwan and the Ashram.

CHAPTER 13

Office Politics

Although Laxmi was officially in charge, it was really Sheela who recruited me. The next day, when I began working in the office at my new job, I discovered to my delight that Shraddha, my friend from London, was also working in the office. We gave each other support over the next several months, and even shared a giggle or two.

What had happened to me caused ripples in the Ashram—but of a positive nature. It stimulated people. It didn't matter that it had happened to me: a lot of people rode on that energy of seeming to have been plucked out of nowhere and moved into a position of authority. More of the Ashram "magic" at work. In those days we reaffirmed each other; if one person was upgraded it would lift the spirits of the whole commune.

Perhaps the story that best illustrates this shared energy is the story of Nandan.

While I was still in the cleaning department, I became friendly with Nandan, a German woman. She was a lovely, softspoken woman with dark brown, very expressive eyes. She was quite large and had a motherly feeling about her. Her eyes always seemed to have pools and pools of laughter in them; when she smiled she only had to lift the corners of her mouth the littlest bit to beam. She lived in a hut outside the Ashram, with no Ashram extras. She was simply a worker. She had a daughter called Disha, who was just as warm as her mother.

Nandan stitched the toweling squares for cleaning Buddha Hall and did incidental mending, such as aprons for the kitchen staff. When work garments or curtains wore out she would sew new ones.

At the same time there was a man living in Lao Tzu called Christ Chaitanya. He was a delightful Jewish man from New York. He was a riot himself, and supplied most of the jokes with which Bhagwan peppered his lectures. Whenever you stopped him on the path he would have a good joke to tell you. Somehow he managed never to repeat a joke to the same person. He also led all the meditations—dynamic in the morning, *nadabrama* in the afternoon, *kundalini* in the evening, and any other in between.

For all his sense of humor he was never a loud person. He would walk around in his *lungi* and nothing else. His eyes were always dancing, which was a mark of how fully involved with the life of the Ashram he had become.

One day he noticed Nandan. Things would often happen in this way. You could be around each other for years, but you'd suddenly *notice* each other. There was no hurry to date and be with each other in the Ashram. There was time.

So he would just drop by now and again to visit her. Though nothing had happened, those of us who knew her noticed a warm glow about her when he had been by. We felt the energies dancing in a certain way.

Then, one evening, she went to *darshan*. Bhagwan had started calling people up at arriving or leaving *darshan* and would put his finger on their third eye. Sometimes he would pick Vivek or someone else who lived in Lao Tzu to sit behind the person, because sometimes the person he touched would fall backwards in a state of total relaxation or ecstasy. We all wanted front-row seats, because then he would simply point and call you up—often out of nowhere—and you'd have one of these exchanges.

This particular evening Nandan wound up in a front-row seat. Three times she was picked to steady people Bhagwan had selected to touch. When she came out of the auditorium she was *radiant*—as though Bhagwan had actually touched her. And it turned out that was the night Christ Chaitanya had gotten permission for her to stay overnight with him in Lao Tzu.

Nandan's good luck and happiness were picked up by the whole Ashram. It was as if what had happened to her was happening to all of us. While you might feel it more intensely if you knew the person directly, you'd still feel it very strongly even if the person was a total stranger. It always rippled through the collective consciousness.

The next morning, in lecture, Bhagwan started talking about Nandan, telling us that she would be moving permanently into Lao Tzu. He spoke about how beautiful she was, how totally surrendered, and how beautiful her soul was. Everybody in lecture—and there were now almost two thousand people in Buddha Hall—immediately started looking for her, because being singled out this way always gave a person terrific energy. And everyone who knew her or saw her would also get a surge. A part of that energy was the idea that if it could happen to her, it could happen to anyone.

But no one could spot her. After lecture she was found down at the coffee house, having breakfast. She had to come to the office to get formal word that yes indeed, everything had been arranged *on the spot;* space was made for her in Lao Tzu and her things were moved in that same day. She was immediately issued a food pass; from now on, she would be taken care of completely. Her daughter, Disha, was moved into Veggie Villas.

For a while, though she was living in Lao Tzu, Nandan continued with her sewing duties for the cleaning department. After a few weeks the message came that she was to begin working in the library. Bhagwan had an extensive library inside Lao Tzu. If books came in that were too scented, they would be rebound and put out in the auditorium for a time to air. Previously, this had only been done by Lalita, an Italian woman.

But Bhagwan didn't just talk about Nandan that one day. Every few days he talked about how beautiful she was, and how surrendered. The whole commune would get a rush out of this. And the more he talked about her in that way, the more lovely she became. If you were picked out in a personal way like that, you *did* glow and glow. And Nandan grew more relaxed, silent. She stayed on through the American adventure, but returned to Italy when the whole thing folded.

Bhagwan often spoke of what he called the "secret transmission" that happened between a master and a disciple, or a teacher and a friend, or whomever. This was a time when you simply "got" the message, and would then carry on the work. Nandan was a prime example, because it never occurred to her that she had been deserted when Bhagwan left America. For her, that was his way, and she continued her own life quite contentedly. Moving from being completely taken care of to suddenly being on her own in the world was no big worry to her: She had internalized Bhagwan's teachings about allowing what happens to happen, without anxiety about the future.

I later had my own example of this when I sat with my father so many years after under Arthur's Stone. Then, in an instant, I "got" insight into him, myself, and the world. In the Ashram we lived for these intense moments, when we felt our awareness suddenly jump to a higher plane.

In those early days Bhagwan would talk about himself as a "candle with a flame." When a student came near the master he could "get" something, in much the same way that an unlit candle, held close to a lit one, will suddenly itself catch fire when a flame jumps the distance between the candles. The candles never actually have to touch. That was the way he said it would happen to *sannyasins*: Nothing would actually be *taken away* from the master; nor is anything *given* to the disciple. The disciple suddenly becomes, in an instant, aware.

It can also be as simple as discussing something, and the other person suddenly "gets it." And yet, if you actually traced the words back, you wouldn't be able to see in their substance what triggered that response: the *words* themselves don't give you the knowing. The space *in between* somehow gives you that understanding. This is what Bhagwan meant by a "secret transmission"—I think it's what Gurdjieff or any of the other great teachers meant, for all that they may have had different words for it. The word that comes to mind is *satori*, a *glimpse:* Some of the greatest masters throughout time have been able to give a disciple a moment of, as one phrased it, "the master's eyes." Yet, in the moment that you're seeing it, it isn't the master's eyes: *you* are seeing it for *yourself.*

Bhagwan said that as people "got" from him more and more, experienced their own "blazing into the flame of awareness," such "jumping" would happen not from the master to disciple—that distinction wouldn't exist any more—but from one to another. And I realized that as Bhagwan became less available, people began to look on Nandan or Laxmi or others (for the most part, in Lao Tzu) who embodied this higher level of awareness. And you could touch it simply by looking in their eyes. You only have to think of how the eyes are used in hypnosis to get some idea of this tremendous power.

Now, when I see friends following various teachers—Tibetan Buddhists and others—I see mini-Ashrams again and again. I've noticed that the type of people who move into this search don't even *need* to be programmed to take this beginning step: It's a natural thing that we do. The basis for programming in the Ashram (which is why it was so subtle) simply built on this side of human nature. *And we manipulated it in each other.*

You can see this, in the example of Nandan. Bhagwan had given her all this "juice," so that when you looked into her you saw Bhagwan's energy going through her. She'd believe that; *I'd* believe that, seeing her or talking with her. I guess we believed what we wanted to believe.

In a similar way a person can get a rush off simply running into a movie star at a restaurant or a celebrity in the supermarket. And the chain reaction will be passed along through friends. We had agreed, when we walked through the gates, that *Bhagwan was the first one:* he was all our celebrities and movie stars or whatever rolled into one. Instead of nearly as many "idols" as there were people in the Ashram, we had one single focus for such hero worship. Bhagwan touched that responsive chord *in everyone.*

But it never sank to the level of name-dropping. It depended on the eye-contact. And each person was ultimately seen as a facet of Bhagwan. Whether you singled out Nandan or Laxmi or Vivek or someone else, what made them special was their role as a mirror of Bhagwan, a reflection of his "light."

Sannyasins split in their interpretation of this phenomenon. Some people believed *Bhagwan* had some secret key to the medicine chest, that he could give you enlightenment. Another group, just as large, felt that he was able to open your own door. If he were absent or dead you would feel no loss, because you had yourself; and ultimately it was *you* who was going to unlock the door to *yourself.*

There have always been two types of seekers: those who always need to be validated by someone else, and those who can go off into the Himalayas and sit in a cave and don't need to look in others' eyes to find the answers. I've sat in those caves in Nepal, and the fact is you *can* find yourself that way. The trigger becomes—as in *tantra*—the rocks, the air, what you see in your dreams. These can open you to the divine glimpsed in and through nature, provide a momentary vision of "the otherwise invisible countenance of the Goddess Mother whose play (*leela*) is the universe of her own beauty" (Zimmer, *Philosophies of India*).

Bhagwan set himself up as "The *Tantra* Master"—though his version of *tantra* was too physical for anyone who has studied the subject in any depth. We were supposed to be able, finally, to *look through* him to reach a new awareness. At the same time he was to be the channel through which energy flowed into a person like Nandan, in her good fortune, or myself, dancing through Lao Tzu House in my red slippers. And all the people we came in contact with got energy off of us. The same thing would happen each time a gift was given out.

This was the Ashram: Bhagwan was a certain glow. Vivek behind that. And then, of course, there were all the different departments that would attract all the different types; all the different centers throughout the world. The lines of energy ran from Lao Tzu House and Buddha Hall halfway around the world. *And it all capitalized on human nature* . . . on that widespread need to find something—a god, a guru, a philosophy, a political movement—that defines you, energizes you, lets you feel you can "jump" to something more than you think you are.

The moment you walked through the gates it was like approaching an intense fire. When you walked *away* from it it got cooler and cooler. But in the heat of that flame, of feeling close to the *center*, you'd get caught up in the process wholeheartedly. When you left you could see things more clearly. Recently, several people have gone to court over the sterilizations. But the first thing they're asked is, "Did you choose to do it?" And anyone who's honest has to say, "Yes, *but* why do I feel I was drugged?"

The Ashram functioned as a kind of "tesseract," an idea that I remember from a book called *A Wrinkle in Time* by Madeleine L'Engle. A tesseract is a place where space and time fold in on themselves, and you can instantaneously cross light-years. In the Ashram if you emptied yourself of ego, and just opened yourself to experiencing, you could enter a "wrinkle in time" and use it to jump to another level of consciousness. With another person you could make the leap to a higher level of shared awareness. It's not an experience of mind; in that moment, you are not the body, not the senses. You have to surrender all those to have this instant "outside" of the limits of time and the everyday world.

You're not aware when the journey begins, but you become aware of yourself *in* it. It's a little like an out-of-body experience, but you're not so detached: You feel like you're *right there*. And everybody—*sannyasin* or not, seeker or not—has had something of this experience. It can come when you walk away from a conversation thinking, *That was a really incredible talk*. But it wasn't necessarily what you talked about: It was a feeling that was transmitted. Coming back into the body after this kind of sharing, you feel drained.

The more we moved into the Ashram—or, as we said, "into Bhagwan"—we would become *lighter*. Sometimes you'd feel as if your feet were only barely touching the ground.

This lightness was especially noticeable when people would come out of "energy" *darshans*. Bhagwan had begun experimenting with these late in 1978. They included music, the introduction of mediums, and "blackouts." All Ashram activities ceased while *sannyasins* meditated with the lights out (though in Buddha Hall the music group would continue playing, and people would go on dancing in the dark). It was like living on a psychic level, while bringing some qualities of it into the world to function.

We could also transfer that positive energy: Later, when a politician or an immigration officer or a redneck would come to look at the Ranch in Oregon and bring all their preconceived ideas, they would often go away thinking, *Those people are really nice; they're really easy-going.* We'd get carloads of people driving into Antelope to look at the Ranch and the "orange people," as though it was Disneyland; they'd be allowed as far as the town center, so they'd get a good look. We'd give them guided tours if they wanted them. Even people who made it clear they planned to hang onto their notions come hell or high-water would sometimes find their attitudes changing.

Some people might cry, "Mass hypnosis!" Others might say, "Brainwashing!" If any label might be put on it at all, I'd call it "mass self-hypnosis." But this suggests "mass hysteria," in which a group experiences a single, shared perception. In fact, while we shared and helped sustain the same heightened awareness in each other, we were all getting different "reports" or perceptions, depending on our individual personalities and tasks. Yet, at times, we could use this altered state of consciousness in a very practical way to transmit or receive information outside "normal" channels of communication. We could "jump" to levels of understanding on our own, or with someone else, by dropping the "personality" and tapping into a zone of undiluted awareness and sensitivity, so that we could understand a person's real nature in a glance or see the solution to a complex problem in a flash.

In the Ashram this kind of stimulation was happening continually. This was why we felt high all the time. When we returned alone to the West we would fall into a depression, almost a withdrawal.

But for all that we moved in and out of higher levels of consciousness and devoted ourselves to the business of becoming enlightened, those of us in the office had to commit ourselves to the very down-to-earth business of running the Ashram and taking care of its increasingly far-flung and complex dealings.

One of the basic things I learned after beginning work as Sheela's secretary was that Bhagwan's name was on no legal documents—*nothing.* (Rajneesh Foundation was the first group set up; then it became Rajneesh Foundation, International, Rajneesh Corporation. Then there was Rajneesh Neo-Sannyasin Commune, which was a different organization altogether.) To the best of my knowledge, on the books, he was not a legal part of Rajneesh Foundation. This was done so that nothing could come back at him.

The big thing was that he never touched any money, never had *any-*

thing to do with any money at all. That was total bullshit, because Deeksha went over to Europe with Sheela on one occasion, and they opened Swiss bank accounts for Bhagwan, Vivek, and Sheela Silverman (Ma Anand Sheela). At least, those were all that I knew of.

So many things were going on simultaneously on so many levels in the office. It wasn't at all unusual to pick up the morning's dictation from Sheela and find she'd have slipped in the directive to, "See Soand-so and tell him that he has to leave the Ashram." Something that could literally change a person's life was sandwiched in between orders for a dozen nuts and bolts and a routine response to a request for videotapes of one of Bhagwan's lectures.

Because we were dealing with so many different items, we lost the ability to distinguish the relative importance of one job compared to another. Everything assumed equal importance. We were expected to throw ourselves as fully into the business of ordering spare parts as into ordering someone to return to the West. How the decision affected the person I was speaking to was not my concern. I would keep myself detached from anything but my role as messenger in letting him know that his letter complaining about his job had been considered by Bhagwan, and the "suggestion" had been passed along that he no longer stay in India.

If I *was* touched in some way—if it was a friend, say, or there was really something distressing in the person's eyes—I'd simply remind myself, *This is between him and Bhagwan; I'm only delivering a message.*

For all the detachment we maintained, because we were constantly striving to be *aware*, to be fully "in the moment," we could sometimes be influenced by a person's response to the message. If they were strong and clear in themselves, they could change the whole decision. The policy was to remain *open*, while performing the job exactly as directed. If, for some reason, this person was able to make me continue being with them after I had delivered the message, they could actually get me to request a change in the decision.

This would happen on all levels, from requesting someone to leave to assigning someone a new job. I would never buy into it if the person was the kind who would argue for argument's sake, or if the response was simply a knee-jerk reaction.

The longer people stayed, however, the *less* they had the ability to challenge any directive—with the exception of the small group we nicknamed "the rebels." They always seemed able to keep the awareness of who they were, and were thus able to produce the response that they wanted. The majority, however, would lose any sense of who they were or what was right for them. Yet, they were the people who seemed to be in the most pain when such decisions were handed down.

We learned to "sit with" emotions and sensations, experiencing them, exploring them, *transforming* them in many cases. Or we might simply shut them off.

The most vivid example of this that comes to mind was a time when I'd been working for Sheela for a little while. Deeksha and Shantam were in her office when I walked in to take dictation. All the old feeling I had for these two people came back in all its intensity—although I had accepted by this time that I wasn't going to be speaking or communicating to them at all.

I walked through the doors and stood there with my bundle of letters. Shantam noticed me at once, but Deeksha was in one of her shouting matches with Sheela (they would often shout at each other—discharging energy, never really angry). Shantam didn't say anything; Deeksha seemed unaware that anyone else was in the room. It had been easier for me never seeing them; the last thing I wanted was to run into them face-to-face.

I turned to go immediately, but Sheela gave me a look that said, *Stay.* So I sat down and waited, while this whole thing played itself out. When it was done Deeksha and Shantam walked out. Shantam gave me a quick glance, nothing more; Deeksha marched past me as if I were nothing more than a piece of furniture.

As soon as they were gone I sat down to begin taking dictation, but I could feel myself on the verge of tears. Suddenly, Sheela said, "If you let one tear fall, you can put your *mala* on the table and leave the Ashram."

"If you just let me go for a minute," I said, "I'll be back and I'll be fine."

"No. You stay here and we do this."

And we did. It took a tremendous amount of energy to shut off the whole of that feeling and get on with what I was doing. What she was instructing me to do—and what I was doing—was *be here and now.* "Put this emotion aside," she was telling me. "Right now you're here to take dictation, *be totally that.*"

From that day on I just *functioned.* I immersed myself in the work of the office. Even if I felt a little down, or somewhere in the back of my mind a little warning bell would go off saying, *Something's not quite right here,* I'd remind myself, *You chose to follow this path of meditation.* And I'd pat myself on the back for not wavering. I was proud that I *could* put this emotion to one side. For all the energy it took, I felt that I had overcome some *weakness* in myself by being able to stop a flow of tears and get on with what I was doing.

In a sense we did on an emotional level what a *fakir* was able to do with physical pain. We would channel it into another direction, making it a *positive* part of our lives. Much later, before I left the Ashram, I got thrombosis. I had a whole day of walking up and down flights of stairs with my leg swollen up from a blood clot, but I didn't even *look* at it. I was detached from my body and from anything apart from my single-mindedness about what I was to be doing at that moment. I focused completely on the task at hand.

After I had (or hadn't) gone to lecture, I would begin my work day by taking dictation in the office. I'd go in to Sheela with a file of correspondence; then she would dictate the response to each letter, which I'd take down in shorthand. Afterward, she'd give me filing and other work that had accumulated on her desk.

For all the systems-on-top-of-systems, things were done largely off the cuff. There was no formal training: We were told the essentials, but we just seemed to intuit most procedures—from routine secretarial matters to dealing with people in crisis situations. Yet it all seemed to work. Within a week or ten days I knew exactly the answer Sheela would give to almost any letter routed to her.

The office situation also increased my ability to remain focused on my immediate task, while remaining aware of what was going on around me every minute. The common space was shared by Sheela, Laxmi, and Arup, each of whom had a steady stream in and out of assistants, visitors, and runners from other departments. Even while my total energy was with the dictation or whatever Sheela and I were working on, I could also tell you every single conversation that was going on in that room.

I think a lot of people do this to some extent unconsciously—you sit in a bus or restaurant, having a one-to-one conversation with someone, yet picking up bits and pieces of conversations around you. Consciously, you might not be able to recall any of those other discussions coherently—though under hypnosis you might very well be able to give the substance of them quite clearly. In the Ashram, if you worked in the office you trained yourself to note and be able to recall *everything*. The office was a *unique* place to work. This skill wasn't required or encouraged of people outside the office.

From the moment I started working for Sheela I felt in awe of her. She had phenomenal skills. When I'd take dictation, for example, I'd make the inevitable mistake from time to time of *thinking* I'd heard what she was saying, but having in fact misunderstood. When she'd ask me to read it back she could tell if the slightest word wasn't exactly as she had said it: She had total recall. Through working for her I developed similar abilities. If somebody came to me with a message from Sheela, I could tell if they were delivering it to me verbatim or if they were improvising. Once I knew it wasn't exactly right I would say to the runner, "But you must remember this word for word. Empty yourself. Become the message. Why do you allow your mind to come in and feel you have to interpret in any way? If you allow your mind to become completely empty, you can just deliver back the message as you heard it."

None of this could be called "brainwashing": that suggests there was still a brain to be washed. This meant becoming a totally empty vessel. A messenger, for example, would be filled with this information until the moment when he passed it along. Once it was out of his mouth he would have forgotten it.

This is the way we would all work. If you speak to many former *sannyasins*—whether they worked in the office or elsewhere—you'll find that they have little (if any) recall at all of what happened. They were *perfect vessels*, filled with the business at hand, forgetting things once they were completed. The past would disappear from one moment to the next, unless it was necesssary to performing a specific task.

On those occasions when my mind was distracted, I'd substitute a word or phrase when typing up my dictation notes. Sheela would always catch this when she read over the letters at the end of the day, before signing them. Sometimes she would make me go back and retype the mistakes; sometimes she would just point it out and let it go.

But even if she let it go, I would still feel this incredible inferiority. I would beat myself mentally harder than anyone could. When I was first there, I would vow, "I'm going to do better." But if you've really got the "empty vessel" idea, you know that setting out a program for self-improvement is counterproductive, because it involves too much *conscious* effort; as soon as the mind is involved, you're bound to mess up. So I would work harder to go into a "*no*-mind mode."

I wanted to be the best I could for Sheela. I adored her from the moment she said, "I'm the biggest bitch." Something in those words really hit me. Even though, at the point where she offered me the job, she wasn't running the show, I *knew* in an instant that she was going to be far more than Laxmi's assistant. Somewhere in me I already saw her directing the Ashram's affairs.

It wasn't the fact of *what* I felt she was going to become that so in-

trigued me, it was *her*—the energy, the power, the *charisma* I sensed
there. I wanted to imbibe it *so desperately*. She seemed so clear, so centered, so graceful—I sensed this in everything from her hand movements to her laughter.

You wouldn't get caught on her words, but you'd pick up a vibe
that went with them.

Again and again, I came back to the picture of her sitting on the
floor of the inner office, when she offered me the office job. As she was
talking her black, black Indian eyes would lock on mine. The words
were abrupt, abrasive, self-mocking, but the *feeling* I was getting from
them was, *If you stay in the Ashram, you'll have a chance to walk through
some new doors.*

From the moment she began speaking, there was no doubt in my
mind that I would stay. It was as if, looking in her eyes, listening to the
tone of her voice, and watching her hands move, she was speaking to
me in a private language.

Later, when I failed to do anything *perfectly*, I would feel I had really missed some rare opportunity. I would constantly urge myself, *Get
out of your own way.* If I let a mistake creep into my work, it was because
I was too much there: My ego was holding me back from being the best
worker that I could be. So I gave myself over as fully as I could to the
intense training of seemingly contradictory states: *totally losing myself*
and *totally being there.* I was learning to use different senses than the
ones we usually practiced in the world.

Sheela was extraordinarily beautiful, with long, thick, thick black
hair. She had graceful hands—within the Ashram hands were important. We would *consciously* evaluate people the way most people in the
outside world would do it subconsciously; we were always probing beyond a person's words or most obvious mannerisms to *get* who they
really were.

I always thought of Sheela as "the high priestess." That impression
first came to me clearly on the day I met with her, Laxmi, Arup, Vidya,
and Asha in the little room adjoining the main office—the room I nicknamed "the crystal cave." It had a huge plate-glass window on the side,
and you could see everybody who walked around Jesus House past
Buddha Hall and up past Lao Tzu gate. The rest of the room was faced
in marble. Two settees, very soft and covered in thick, cream linen
cloth, were built into the wall.

Much of the magic of the Ashram began in the crystal cave. I always
felt clean and cool there. That first day, however, it was merely a back-

drop: Sheela instantly became the focus of my attention. She was sitting curled in a corner of one couch, with one arm on the sofa back and her legs folded under her. She reminded me of a mermaid.

In those days her eyes were *clear*. They had intense black pupils and very, very dark brown corneas, which contrasted dramatically with the whites. They seemed huge and piercing; yet just as often they would give you a feeling of warmth and sympathy. Afloat in them, I would feel serene and grounded, yet have the impression that I was playing on the edge of multidimensional space.

When we first met I was standing up and she was seated; but, looking into her eyes, I felt she was meeting me as an equal, with no sense of superior and inferior roles. I thought of two priestesses meeting, even as she motioned me to take a seat. In that moment I felt I was encountering Sheela for the first time—as though I had never seen her before. In seeing her, I saw myself for the first time as a *woman*; I no longer felt shy or at odds with myself, as I had felt around Paras and Shanti. Then I had still reacted like an awkward adolescent; now, for a few minutes, I could see my full potential.

Meeting Sheela, I felt I had tapped into some *unlimited power* in myself—though I could not have said exactly what the nature of that power was. I had a curious double-vision of her: Something about her suggested death, the grim reaper; and yet she embodied the ultimate in life. It was almost as if she could only live life to the fullest on the edge of death.

I "got" all of this while she explained to me some routine things about my duties and office procedures. I felt we were both playing on several levels.

Even later, when she was involved in horrible dealings, I would see the high priestess: Whatever sword she was wielding, she was totally behind it. She commanded respect, even from people who found themselves on the receiving end of that sword.

And I saw myself in her. It was thrilling to look at her and recognize her as a major player; to see that she had given herself permission to "go for it," to take the game to the limit; and to realize, seeing myself mirrored in her, that *I* was standing on the threshold of a crucial new phase of my own involvement in the game. In that room at that time, I felt that I was being given the key to the door.

All of this happened in those first moments of that meeting with Sheela—and those impressions have always remained clear in my mind. They became a kind of touchstone against which I was always checking myself, charting my own evolution as a player.

She would brook no argument from anybody, but this never made you want to *react* to her. You *wanted* to do for her; you wanted to do as she requested of you, because you got higher carrying out her wishes.

There was a softness about Sheela, and a gracefulness that gave her an almost *regal* air. There was a nicety about her actions that gave you the impression that every movement or gesture was carefully considered before she made it. She had a weakness for chocolate-covered cherries, but even these were served on a small silver tray.

An ambience of incredible wealth pervaded the whole Ashram, but was particularly noticeable in the office. If you worked in the office, whether you were a typist or a department head, you wore beautiful dresses and always had carefully manicured hands. All the women and men there seemed separate from everything—even the bottoms of their feet never seemed to get dirty the way those of anyone working anywhere else in the Ashram would. They always looked carefully pedicured and soft—which was unusual in India, where the heat tended to dry out your skin very quickly. The air-conditioning in the office helped, and the marble floors were always kept spotlessly clean.

The reception area gave the impression of so many nymphs or angels wandering around to the clattering of the typewriters, in the steady, cool breezes from the air-conditioning. In the crystal cave, everything was quiet, but through the huge windows you could see a constant hustle and bustle of people on the street. Everything was immaculate; *chai* was served in cups of beautiful, translucent porcelain.

The whole place gave off an aura of wealth. But it wasn't wealth in a financial sense; it was a wealth of *self*. It was the feeling you get from people who have become so rich they no longer seem to touch money; it becomes a part of them, so that they create an expensive impression without any effort on their part. It just *happens:* Jeeves comes in with a tea service, their clothes never have a wrinkle, the best of everything is always at hand when they need it.

This was the illusion the office created. The closer you worked to the people in power, the more stress that was placed on how you looked. Many people who joined the Ashram followed a "California creed," stressing healthy diet, untrimmed beards and hair, unshaved legs or underarms, that kind of thing. Outside the office that was perfectly accepted as the right and natural way to live.

The office, however, was a very different matter. About two weeks after I'd started working there I got a message to go in and see Sheela. As soon as she saw me she said, "Go upstairs. The women are here from the Blue Diamond"—the only place in Poona considered a true hotel.

"Oh," I said, "what for?"

She grinned and said, "Well, you need to have a manicure, a pedi-cure, your legs waxed, your eyebrows arched, the whole thing."

So off I went to put myself into the hands of two little Indian ladies who had set up shop in one of the rooms upstairs. They had their little potboiler with a can of wax on the burner already going, and several other office staff were there.

In short order they had trimmed my hair, ripped my eyebrows and legs into form, shaped and buffed my nails, and pumiced my feet. By the time they were done, I felt like a new me. I felt like layers of my old self had been peeled away; my skin tingled so that I felt it was glowing. When I left I felt lighter and more graceful—as if I had liter-ally shed my old skin.

This signaled a change in me from funky-casual style to low-key elegance and careful attention to my appearance. I still had a healthy naturalness about me, but it was the difference between someone who drinks any old bottled springwater, and someone who insists on *Evian*. Now I can smile a bit looking back and wonder if we weren't in danger of becoming "yuppie spiritual seekers." But, the fact is, these outward changes made you feel that inwardly you must have moved into a dif-ferent zone to be attracting these changes.

Of course if you lost your food pass the next day you would also think, *I'm attracting this,* and you'd knock yourself for having done something wrong, even though you had no clear idea of what that might be.

When I first saw Sheela she looked radiant. Her dresses, though simple, were always of the finest material and cut. She was like one of those women you spot in the finer restaurants, whose hair is perfectly in place without a hint of lacquer; whose nails are unpolished but obvi-ously perfectly manicured; who dine with such effortless grace you're hardly aware of them eating at all. They seem to have emerged from the chrysalis as a perfect butterfly, and to have been granted the ability to maintain it without a wrinkle or a spot or a hair out of place *ever*. You'd never see them touch the bill, but it would somehow be paid.

This was the illusion created in the office. Sheela was its clearest ex-ample but *all* of us took part in it. And I realized that, somewhere in me, this was how I always expected the world to be. After all, I *am* a Leo, with seven planets in the house when I was born; and, traditional-ly, Leo the lion rules all the other beasts. I'm one of those people who loves the idea of royalty as something that you *are*—not something you acquire. The office produced that feeling, even while making you feel like a "Sufi nun." There was always that paradox.

This paradox permeates Eastern spirituality. Even high in the Himalayas the Tibetan monks keep their hands and robes in incredible condition. They go off trekking and on pilgrimages through some of the muddiest mires imaginable, yet somehow it doesn't seem to get above their feet. Even when they're finished walking through the mud, it's just a momentary tap and their feet are clean again. We visitors would have the dirt clinging—almost mocking us—in spite of our best efforts. So you begin to judge this as something that comes from within.

When Sheela first met me she described me as "a diamond in the rough." Working under her was like going into the grinder, polishing me to my full potential.

When I thought about the Ashram, a story I once heard ran through my mind a lot: "When you walk the spiritual path, when you take the first steps, mountains are mountains, and valleys are valleys. But as you walk along for a little while, and you begin to become a part of this path, mountains are no longer mountains, and valleys are no longer valleys." The scenery hasn't changed, but your perception of it does. You no longer know what you once knew; you move beyond the old assurances that this is a valley and that is a mountain. Everything is uncertain.

Then you walk a little further and mountains become mountains again, and valleys become valleys. But *not* in the same way that you knew them before. It *feels* the same, but there's been an intrinsic change.

This change in perception happened all the time to people arriving at the Ashram. I think of Sylvia, who had been a high fashion model before she came to India. When she first arrived she was *exquisite*, with gorgeous eyes, hair, clothes. But she went through a hard time, you could see she was going through some struggle inside. Like everyone else she had come into the Ashram with all her "baggage" from however many years she had been on the earth. Once inside the Ashram you begin to shed that "baggage." You'd have to take a hard look at who you were and what you'd done and where you wanted to get to. At the same time you were living a new life, and trying to fit all the pieces—old and new—together. It was very much the process that nuns go through during novitiate, where prayer or working in the garden becomes both an entry into a new life and a way of shedding the old.

You could see all this in Sylvia. She would look drained or stressed when things came up from the past for her to deal with. There was no way to avoid this kind of self-examination: Every doubt, every holding back was magnified in the Ashram. And when you walked through the gates you made the commitment to yourself that you were going for enlightenment and were going to do *everything* to move toward that.

Sylvia passed through the difficult transitional phase and emerged both filled with grace and graceful. It was as if the gracefulness that she had brought to the Ashram had been a role she had taken on; when she had shed that role, a natural grace came out. It was no longer an artificial or cultivated quality, it was spontaneous now, something from within. It was the same sort of quality Sheela manifested so dramatically.

Many of the women who were close to Sheela and Laxmi had this grace. When they moved they created no ripples, no disturbance; they were almost ethereal. I could watch Laxmi cross from Krishna House to Lao Tzu and, no matter how hard I looked, I could never see if her feet actually touched the ground. She seemed to float. The eyes of all the office workers were totally alive. They seemed to gaze in even while they were looking out; and they would hold all the different feelings in them: laughter and deep sadness and a thousand other emotions.

This was a part of the metamorphosis everyone went through. Then you would go beyond that to an almost translucent beauty. You'd look the same as you did before, dress the same as you always had, but now there would be a difference shining from within. When you saw that or got near to that in somebody, you wanted to share in it yourself. Meryl Streep, the actress, is a good example of this quality: her features might not be classically beautiful, yet people look at her and say, "She's beautiful," because she manifests something *inside* that makes people respond in this way.

This transformation could happen to anyone. Walking through those gates turned around our old ideas that people come into the world a certain way and have to accept their lot.

In the Ashram *nothing* seemed impossible. When, for example, Bhagwan picked Nandan out of nowhere, she became a kind of *princess.* Simultaneously, people began to notice her and something began to happen *in* her. That collective consciousness filled the Ashram. An individual could draw off of the group's positive attentions, at the same time that the group could be energized by what was happening to one of its own.

Being selected and groomed by Sheela involved me more fully in this process than ever before. We all believed that just being near someone who had this translucent, incredibly centered energy would spark something similar in you. It was like Bhagwan's teaching about how the flame can leap from a lit candle to an unlit one. In my case Sheela became a mirror I could use to change certain things in myself.

You never felt like the *change* came from outside; only the opportunity to change. It felt all along like *you* were doing it. If things turned out positively, you took credit for it; if you attracted negative things to yourself afterward, you blamed yourself. The responsibility was always *yours*.

CHAPTER 14

Life with Sheela

When I was friends with Deeksha she took total care of me. She gave me a food pass and a place to live—things that most people would have to work for over a longer period of time. This saved me from many of the games in the Ashram, such as trying to gauge when you were "surrendered" enough to risk asking for a food pass. This required tremendous energy. On one level it's a very primal thing to ask to be fed. On another level, if the office said "No" you would go through all kinds of trips about not being surrendered enough. You would worry that concern about where the next meal is coming from would keep you from moving toward enlightenment, and *then* you would knock yourself because that kind of worry meant you weren't surrendered enough—and so on, through a vicious cycle that could leave you wishing you'd never opened your mouth in the first place.

Ironically, I didn't really like to eat in Miriam Canteen that much: I preferred eating in town, where I could get the real spicy Indian food. Miriam served much blander items. But it *was* always available if I wanted it. And that was a privilege a lot of people would have given their eyeteeth for.

After two weeks of working in the office, however, Sheela told me that I couldn't speak to Deeksha or Shantam. She called me upstairs to her room one morning. She was lying on her bed, and she told me to sit down. I was tense because this sort of deviation from routine could mean *anything*. We didn't often go to each other's rooms; these were private places—individual sanctuaries, in a way. I was worried that I had done something very wrong. I perched on the edge of the bed, looking for a clue in her face.

"How are you doing?" she asked. A caring quality in her voice relaxed me. When she wanted to, she could make you feel totally cared for, without ever coddling you.

"Fine," I said. "I feel like things are really going well."

Though I was much less tense, I was still wary. I knew her well enough to sense that something was about to go down. She—the "panther"—was in the attack stance.

"And you're getting along with everyone all right?"

"Oh, yes," I said, *waiting.*

But we just chatted for a few minutes about this and that. I was beginning to wonder if I had misread her when she abruptly asked, "Have you gotten over Shantam yet?"

This off-the-wall question caught me by surprise. "Yes," I said quickly, "I mean, I'm working with it."

"So, put your whole energy into the work," she said. "Now you're here with me, so be here completely. All you have to concentrate on is being here with Bhagwan and doing his work." She paused a moment, and I remember thinking, *This is it.*

"I don't want you to accept anything more from Deeksha," she continued. "And anything that you still have from her, you must give away or get rid of, so that you have nothing left."

I said, "Everything that I have was given to me by Deeksha." It's hard to express the intensity of feeling I had just admitting that I was so beholden to that other person. On the one hand I was warning myself, *Drop it, drop it, drop all the feeling that comes with these things.* In the same moment I was overwhelmed by the love that I still felt for Deeksha. And here was Sheela telling me to get rid of even the smallest reminder of that. She was telling me to drop it all, and surrender totally to Bhagwan.

Sheela would never say, "Surrender to me": It was always "to *him.*" Throughout the whole Ashram nothing was ever done for the person who was giving you the directions: That person would always make it clear that this was "for Bhagwan," or "for *you* with Bhagwan."

"But Sheela," I said, "then I don't have anywhere to stay." Even as I was saying this, I could feel the panic coming into my voice. "Where will I sleep? How will I eat?" I stopped suddenly, when I saw how she was looking at me. That instant I *got* it. *Drop all of it,* her eyes were saying.

I just sat there in silence, feeling dangerously close to tears—and Sheela couldn't *stand* anyone crying. Then she said, "It's time for you now to surrender totally. You think that you've surrendered, but, really, you haven't at all." The first half of our talk was all leading up to this, the "zen knock," as I call it—when the Zen master strikes the disciple to get his attention. "You've just been drifting through up until

now. You haven't really meditated in yourself. You're just full of yourself, full of your ego. You need to learn a little humility. And so you're
not to tell anyone about this. Don't tell anyone you have no money or
nowhere to sleep or whatever. I just want you to *trust* and to go with
the flow. Just be in that mode."

She was dealing with me the same way she would have dealt with
anyone who had gone in to her for direction. She was telling me to
give up the idea that anyone owed me anything.

"Will you at least give me a food pass?" I asked.

"That's your whole trip," she snapped, "You want people to give it
to you, and what makes you feel you have any right to be given
anything?"

If I had been totally clear in that moment, I could have been given a
food pass and a room in the Ashram. But I wobbled. I was saying, "But
. . . but . . . but. . . ." I was coming from an insecure, I-don't-deserve-it
position. I was putting out all that negative energy about being a nothing and a nobody.

Sheela finally said, "So, just go, put your total energy into the work,
but you mustn't tell anyone about this meeting."

Feeling utterly at odds with myself, I left. And, for ten days, I went
on working and working and putting aside the whole idea of eating or
sleeping. I would curl up in Rada gardens at night. Since I wasn't an
Ashramite anymore, I wasn't supposed to be on the grounds after sunset, so I would hide in the bushes as soon as it began to grow dark and
sleep under a hedge. In the morning I'd get up at first light and run to
the public showers near Vrindavan and clean up. There was a charge of
one rupee per shower. Since Sheela had forbidden me to ask for anything from anyone, I would even have to sneak in there. But I did,
since I couldn't continue working in the office if I was dirty: I wouldn't
fit the immaculate image, and I would have felt like a grub to myself.

It wasn't the same as working in an office in the West, where you
always want to be crisp and you get obsessed with always looking like
you just stepped out of a bandbox. Here it was a question of mastering
the art of being translucent and pure without any effort. The longer
things went on, the further I felt from that goal; I felt crazy, running
from under the hedge to steal a shower to give the impression that I fit
right into the office.

My eating was catch-as-catch-can. Sometimes I'd be near the back
gate and an Indian would come by with a trolley of *somosas*, Indian
snacks, or fruit, and someone sneaking a *beedee* might say, "Hey, would
you like to try one?" Or in the office someone might say, "Let me buy

you a dessert," because Vrindavan used to make wonderful desserts in the afternoon.

After ten days of living like this, Vidya came in and said, "I have something for you." Then she proceeded to make this whole production of giving me a half-pass for food, which was good for one meal a day.

I just stared at her. I was furious: All my old dislike of her came to a head at that moment. I shoved it back at her and said, "I don't want this from you!" Finally, I let go of my anger. Then I went in to Sheela, feeling very much in control of myself and the situation, and said, "Please, never *ever* have Vidya give me anything. I prefer not to eat, not to sleep, than to be given to by this woman. She made such a huge *performance*, like she was giving me the gift of the gods."

I felt very clear in that moment; I knew exactly what was important to me and what was demeaning. "I don't need this," I told her. "If you want to give me a food pass, then give me a food pass. I don't want a half-pass. When you feel ready to give me all that I need, great! But, until then, I'm just fine!"

There was a little smile in Sheela's eyes, but she didn't say anything more. I went back to my desk and got on with my work. Ten minutes later she called me back into her office and said, "Well, your room's ready." Having a room in the Ashram meant automatically you had everything you need.

At that point I moved into another room in Dormitory no. 8. It was all created from my being centered.

Adjusting to my separation from Deeksha and Shantam was a tremendous energy drain on me; at the same time, I was trying to put myself totally into my new job. Also, my office "make-over" and my status as an Ashramite gave me the feeling that my changed outward self was a sign of inner changes, and that I really was "on the path."

My new duties included writing a lot of letters to the United States. The grammar and spellings and idioms are very different from British usage, so I would often spend an hour or so each afternoon with Chinmaya, who would help me polish up the correspondence.

Those times with Chinmaya were incredibly good for me. He taught me, but I could also talk with him about how I felt, and he could help me sort things out and put them back in balance.

We didn't talk much about our lives before we came into the Ashram. When you came into the Ashram, and took a new name, your past was gone. All I knew about Sheela's background was that she was an

Indian, and she was married to Chinmaya, who was an American Jew from New York City.

Within a few days of working with Sheela I discovered that she was only just learning to write in English, though she spoke it fluently (and, as I've already mentioned, she could spot the most minor change when I was reading back to her from my notes). When I gave her the stack of letters to sign at the end of the day, she could scan through them and pick out any mistake. But when it came to fine points of the English language, she arranged to have Chinmaya "tutor" me—though our relationship was always one of friends, never pupil-teacher.

Sheela came from a town called Baroda, northwest of Poona. She was part of a large family; her brothers and parents would come to visit her fairly often. Though they never really took *sannyas*, they became very involved with the business dealings of the Ashram—especially after the move to the United States.

Not knowing much about a person's past added to the magic and mystery of people in the Ashram. She was the "priestess" to me in that moment—and that's what she had been forever, as far as I was concerned. And we really *did* enjoy the illusions we would create; they added to the "magic kingdom" idea we were living. I was never much interested in where Sheela—or anyone else, for that matter—had come from. We seldom discussed whether we'd been a housewife or a professor before we had come to Koregaon Park; you never knew whether a man you were talking to was single, married, or had kids.

I think that's why we could fly off in so many different ways: if we had started talking to each other on that level, it would have brought things down to earth very quickly. It may have been part of the programming, since our sense of that kind of reality vanished once we walked through the Ashram gates.

For example, where Sheela had met Chinmaya, an American, was not important: to this day, I don't know. I know they lived in India for a while, traveled to America, then returned to India, where they heard about Bhagwan and met him formally in 1972. Even in those early days Chinmaya knew that he had Hodgkin's Disease. Bhagwan told Chinmaya he could live as long as he needed to.

The hours I spent with Chinmaya were precious. His hair was a rich reddish-blond color that always seemed to catch whatever bit of light was in the room; I thought it was like a halo. He had the patience of a saint: I never saw him show any pain from his disease—or any annoyance when I brought him an extra amount of problem letters or talked longer than I should about my own problems. And he had a sense of humor that never quit.

Sheela—despite the fact that she issued hard instructions and always had answers at her fingertips—would always become soft around her husband and defer to him. She was extremely protective of Chinmaya. And, at the time, she depended upon him to tell her what she should do or if she was doing right or how he felt about how she was being. She was very devoted to him.

Seeing that side of her made it easier for me to cope with those times when she was being hard on me. I knew that she wasn't hard through-and-through, so I was much more ready to believe that any tension between us was the result of some failing on my part. And I had seen her when she was sitting at the feet of Bhagwan. Those two men were people *she* would become totally surrendered to.

Chinmaya was completely bedridden when I met him. He and Sheela had then been together about seven years. At the time Sheela— with Chinmaya's full knowledge and agreement—was going out with a man named Veetrag, who worked in the *mala* shop. He had been a pilot in South Africa. He was a short, stocky guy, very muscular, with long black hair and a bushy black beard—his nickname was "Caveman." For all his rugged looks he was gentle and kind.

For all of Sheela's grace and strength, she had a childlike quality. Especially around Veetrag, she was like a little kid. It was delightful to see this vulnerable side of her. It seemed to manifest itself most often around men. She was very, very insecure; but this came out in an appealing, refreshingly childlike way—never in a "wimpy" way. When she was in her office mode she would override this: Whether it was a man or woman she was dealing with, she was solidly in control. She never let personal emotions enter into her decision-making.

But when it came to Veetrag it was altogether another matter—and wonderful to see. I remember softening to her completely one evening when I was in the *mala* shop talking with Veetrag, who was also a friend of mine. He was finishing up some of the little gift boxes Bhagwan would hand out during leaving *darshan*. He was at the lathe, and I was running on about Shantam, which was still, in spite of my best efforts, an unsettled corner of my heart. I knew he could be trusted not to talk to Sheela about what I told him.

He made a joke about something, and we were both laughing when Sheela came in. She had her hair down, and she was wearing a long dress; something about her reminded me of a little girl. In her hand she had a small bowl of strawberries that she was bringing Veetrag. The look on her face was the look of a teenager with a crush on somebody: overwhelmed by love and incredibly shy at the same time. You could see that she desperately wanted to give him her gift but was so charged with her emotions she could hardly speak.

She just stood there in the doorway with her bowl of strawberries looking like she might cry, because it was so much. I could feel how much she envied Veetrag's and my easy laughter, which came of our having nothing between us except friendship. She was completely caught up in the childlike love they had for one another.

I added the vision of her standing there, flooded with love, to the images of her sitting with Chinmaya and holding his hand, or of her sitting fully surrendered at the feet of Bhagwan—and these acted as a buffer when I got a heavy dose of her harsher side. I never could hate Sheela, because I knew her too well.

Chinmaya had formed an attachment with a woman named Gopa. Sheela, who was extremely possessive, never liked her. She liked her men to be completely faithful. But, along with the intensity she felt, she struck me as being *scared* of love—both receiving it and giving it. She had to feel she was in control of the situation before she would let herself love or be loved. She would become embarrassed or shy if you became emotional toward her in loving her. Yet, you could see that, at some level, she liked the attention—even when it threw her off balance.

One day Puja, who had been a nurse, came to work in Krishna House. She decided that Sheela needed vitamins. I was sitting in the room when Puja lectured her on the subject. Finally, Sheela said off-handedly, "Oh, I'll never remember to take them."

"I'll make sure that you get them," I said. Turning to Puja, I added, "Just tell me what time she's to have them."

So I would regularly bring her the vitamins and a little glass of water. And I could see that she really liked being taken care of, even in this small way—though she might talk of the pills as an annoyance more than anything else.

A lot of us took care of each other, because you wouldn't think to take care of yourself. For example, it was easy for me to get caught up in the work and forget to eat or sleep. Often my friend Shraddha or someone else would—without making an issue of it—pick up a tiffin of food and bring it to me, or simply remind me how late it was getting. Often, I'd have no idea who'd brought the tray of food: it would simply be there.

We tended to be careless of ourselves because it would be too egotistical to pay attention to such needs. In every way we worked to submerge our egos into an idea of Bhagwan, the Ashram, and our work.

Laxmi was the prime example of this: She would never eat. She was always working. She didn't like to eat in the office, because she felt it wasn't right to eat in front of other people. She was constantly deferring to the other person as more important.

On reflection, I can see it now as a very subtle game: By saying "I'm not important," you're actually putting the responsibility on others to take over for you and assure you that you are important. It's a way of begging the compliment, of getting ego-support in an environment where ego exists only to be denied. In the office we would view people like Laxmi and Sheela as little fragments of Bhagwan; to allow Laxmi to go hungry would, by extension, be allowing Bhagwan himself to go hungry. To let someone who was putting as much energy as Laxmi into the well-being of the commune starve was to hurt the whole group, including yourself.

So there was the game-playing side of it, but there was also a bliss that came from caring for the key players. One woman's exclusive role was to make special food for Laxmi and make sure she was eating enough. You could see that being so aware of somebody else's needs became a meditation for her; she would immerse herself completely in Laxmi's needs—never imposing herself or her ideas on the other, but becoming the "empty vessel"; identifying so fully with her that she really functioned as part of Laxmi. She was fulfilled in this. At the same time, by indirection, we were putting Laxmi and Sheela on pedestals—even though such hero worship was officially discouraged.

The living arrangements on the upper floor of Krishna House were peculiar. Sheela and Chinmaya had their bedroom above the office. If you went into Sheela's room, her bed was against one wall and Chinmaya's against the other; these were separated by a partition. The room opened onto a wide sunporch that looked out over Rada gardens.

A second door near the foot of Chinmaya's bed connected with an adjoining room, which is where Veetrag lived. When Sheela spent the night with Veetrag, they would share that second room, though she kept her own space in the main room at all times.

What was so special about Veetrag—and, I think, a big part of the reason Sheela loved him—was the fact that he was one of the "rebels." He was following his own agenda; he had no ambitions outside of the *mala* shop; the game-playing that was becoming so prevalent in the office meant nothing to him. He—as were so many—was very aware and creative, but he directed this inwardly and was concerned only with his personal spiritual journey. In this way, he was an escape from the pressures of the office and the links with the outside world—particularly the United States—that Sheela was forging in a variety of discreet ways.

These rebels set their own course of action. They were single-minded in their goal of enlightenment—they kept themselves apart from the political and business concerns of the Ashram, and rejected what they saw as regimentation. They were clever enough to duck in and out of *darshan* and other gatherings; but they were very much a part of the community, never consciously setting themselves apart enough to cause friction. They had devised their own "divine dance" to let them skirt all of this, without coming off their own path.

Other men who might be attracted to Sheela were "yes men," for whom she would be the boss all the time, in bed or in the office. She liked Veetrag's independent streak; it lent spice to their relationship.

Even while Chinmaya was dying, she was desperately looking for someone who loved her in the same way he did. Chinmaya loved the Sheela whom he had first met when she was quite young—the girl who, in later years, seemed to disappear. She reappeared in flashes— I'd see that person in the shy woman holding strawberries at the door of the *mala* shop or when Chinmaya had pain and she'd break down and cry, because she would feel it so acutely.

Being around Chinmaya so much, I was able to see Sheela through his eyes. When you saw what a good and beautiful man he was, you thought that if he could love her there must be something in her that made her worthy of such a deep love. Chinmaya touched my life in a wonderful way I'll never forget, and he and Sheela will always be together in my mind.

The fact that Veetrag could love her was also a positive note in her favor. He would laugh and say, "She's the biggest bitch I've ever met, but she's also beautiful." On one of my last visits to the Ranch in Oregon Veetrag said, "She went off her rocker, but she's still beautiful." Then he sighed and said, "We saw a Sheela that most people never saw."

Most people, in fact, saw the strong side of Sheela. Very few people could play on her level. Even though she had some other strong people around her, very few were ruthless enough to want to play at her level. And she knew it. Sometimes I'd see her sitting in the crystal cave, staring through the window, and I'd imagine she was calling for a playmate—someone she could match wits and skills with, someone she could use to sharpen her awareness.

She was always a great "zen stick" for other people; whether they were being struck or stroked by her, they were getting something out of the encounter. You could see she hungered for the same sort of teacher for herself. The only one who could really take on that role was Bhagwan, but she hadn't yet found her rhythm with him so that she could begin to play the match on that front. There was simply no one else in the Ashram that she could volley with. Vidya and others simply rubber-stamped her; they didn't offer much of a challenge.

You had to admire Sheela: She would commit herself completely to a course of action, and follow it without any holding back—where the rest of us might keep at least one eye on the door for cutting and running. There was never any middle ground for her. All or nothing were the only stakes she played for.

Even at this moment, when she's in jail, I have to admit—whatever my feelings about *what* she may have done—that she put her ass on the line in playing the game she chose to play. She was always a player, while most others sat on the sidelines, waiting to run up and share in the victory if she won, or wanting nothing more to do with her when she lost. This was nowhere clearer than in the collapse of Rajneeshpuram and what followed. So many who had been close to her were the first to turn around and denounce her when things fell apart.

She could be ruthless. No one could deny that. Each of us, when we walked through those Ashram gates, knew that whatever we wanted we could manifest. Sheela went for something and she got it. In the office she could take and take and take, until she bled you dry; yet, at the same time, she could rejuvenate you. She would work all the hours God sent without a break; she'd be at her desk before you got in, and she'd still be there when you were leaving at the end of the day.

She remembered everything, even comments made in passing. And she would always follow up on what seemed, at the time, like casual suggestions to be sure they'd been carried out. She could say things spontaneously and remember all the details exactly. People would often say something to Sheela in passing and be stunned when, months and months later, she would say, "But you said such-and-such to me that day." She seemed to be constantly sifting through your words for items of solid information she might later use for you, or against you, depending on the circumstances.

She would store up information from all sources, and was constantly making connections: A person visiting a certain city should be put in touch with another *sannyasin* living there; some item the Ashram needed could be supplied by someone who had written to the office months before. Her thought processes were more global than linear; and, with her total recall, she acted as a kind of one-person clearinghouse of information for the Ashram. I had something of this same facility, which is why we got on so well from the start. She was forever pushing me to sharpen my abilities in this area. This became increasingly important the more I became involved with the Ashram's expanding business network.

Sheela was fascinating in that way. Though she had no formal education, she was a brilliant woman. I don't know that she had ever worked in her life before she met Chinmaya. He was a very bright, very bookish person, and taught her a lot. It was just one of the many ways they complemented each other. Sheela sometimes looked at him the way a devotee would gaze at a god.

She had amazing self-confidence. She never pretended to the office staff that she had a degree or a better education. She accepted the fact that she had the ability to acquire whatever knowledge or skills she needed, and that was enough. Even though she was lacking in her ability to read and write English, when it came time for her to come to the United States for the Ashram and to develop major business connections, we simply made up things that she had done—*and she carried these charades off without a hitch.*

She could be charming, and she had the gift of gab. She would say, "Once people have done business with you for a while, they'll realize they're happy doing business with you. But if you walk in the door and say, 'Look, I'm an illiterate Indian from Baroda,' they're not going to want to do business with you. So, what you do is make up all these references, make up all this stuff." Which is what we would do. Once she had her "background" in hand, she could play the part to perfection, opening whatever doors she needed to. One time we gave her the persona of an interior designer who was supposed to have an income of $150,000 a year. On another occasion she was an investment consultant. But she preferred to appear as an "artsy" kind of person.

I learned from her just how completely you can take on these roles—which is both a plus and a minus, because sometimes you lose track of where illusion ends and reality begins. Sheela could slip right into any role, and give the impression that she had been doing this all her life. She could elaborate endlessly on her fictitious past, *and remember every detail.* Once she had begun a story you wouldn't find any discrepancies even a year later, if she needed to take on that role again. She would *be* that person.

I learned so much by watching her become "Sheila Silverman, graphic designer, graduated from Such-and-Such College, owned own interior design shop for these many years, earned this amount of money yearly." She would sit there with her portfolio, and when someone would ask, "Who are your clients?" she would rattle off the names of very wealthy people in the Ashram—who, of course, would never contradict her. She would even be generous with the details of how she'd done the home, and the color scheme she used.

She was so good that even those of us who had helped create the new persona would believe. People on the outside would be taken in, would do business with her, and would straightaway find that she was as sharp in dealing with them as she must have been in her "interior design business."

The results were astonishing. At a large New York department store she had an enormous line of credit—*from absolutely nothing*. In one sense this was a tribute to the power of illusion; on another level, however, she would take on the persona so completely that it *wouldn't* be something separate from her. It was as if she had been that all of her life. It wasn't something outside of her, the way an actor puts on—then discards—a stage role. It was as if she had been that person.

When I started looking at this business of creating personas backed by whole packets of false references, a part of me questioned, *Is this right?* raising the inevitable ethical questions. But this all collapsed when I realized that there was a point where "truth" and "the sustained illusion" became indistinguishable from one another.

The fact is that if someone had said to Sheela, "Okay, you're such a hot-shot designer, go and decorate my apartment," she could have done it. It's sort of like an understudy who says, "I can do that," then has to go on for the star and triumphs. But, in the Ashram, we had to take on *multiple* roles. Most people, for whatever reason, get channeled in one direction, have one dream; we were able to create a variety of incredible characters and carry them all off.

Years later I became involved with the purchase and sale of Lear Jets—even though I knew *nothing* about airplanes. But there I was, sitting and *selling* airplanes. My total experience was one hour of being walked through a Lear Jet. I had actually fast-talked my way into the position by saying I had a number of nonexistent jets, and had been around them all my life. It was all a grand charade that let me get from company representatives precisely the information I needed to give back to them in order to let me convince them that I knew what I was talking about.

It was yet another case of realizing, inside, *Yes, I've never done it; but I can do it.* The ability to recognize this—and act on it—was something I learned from Sheela. Both she and Laxmi were incredible at this. The commune was small when I first joined, but it grew rapidly. We were always finding ourselves in new situations, and creating the personas we felt each situation demanded. At first it was simply a matter of expediency: We didn't want to look as though we didn't know what was going on or how best to deal with it. The last thing we wanted to do was give the impression that we were a load of novices setting up this commune without any idea of what we were doing. We were simultaneously dealing with the Indian authorities, who were suspicious of our having all these Westerners over here—and we were putting on a show for the *sannyasins* themselves.

One thing that was required of everyone coming into the Ashram was *intelligence:* We were creating a Disneyland of the mind. The universe inside the gates was so refined, there were *so many* different levels, it could attract all sorts of people. And this became a virtue, because you were able to look around and say, "I'm living with so many different kinds of people that I would *never* associate with in normal society." An invigorating collective energy grew out of the idea that so many diverse people had been gathered in a single enterprise: the building of the new commune.

If you probed below the surface, however, you found that the Ashram meant different things to different people. The Ashram never really jumbled people together under a single dogma; it was so well put together that each individual could create his or her own space inside it. Truth was a chameleon in Koregaon Park: It would take on the coloring of a person's background—a different "truth" for each person who had come to the Ashram.

All the time, each one of us was being subtly manipulated, though we wouldn't realize it. I know for a fact that even people who said, "I could never join a cult," would walk in as if on a dare and emerge no different from a person who had entered as an eager seeker. Even journalists who would come to write exposés on the doings at Antelope would come out feeling, *The place is really a nice place, those people are really fine people.*

And the truth is that the Ashram, both in India and in America, *did* create a nice place. People did find it appealing. The community was certainly warmer than even the coziest home town anywhere else in the world. For a start, people *really* knew each other and *respected* each other. People in small towns in the outside world might know each other's business, but they will always be poised to pick each other apart. In the Ashram this was never an item of interest: if today you were an adulteress, that was *your* business; if you felt the need for forgiveness you didn't look for it from the community, you looked for it from *yourself*. Bhagwan's appealing message was, "I am not here to create any guilt in you. My whole effort is to help you get rid of all guilt" (*The Goose Is Out*).

In the office we were creating the "truth" that was necessary to get the licenses to run things, to give the impression of a smoothly run, highly efficient organization. At the same time we were creating a certain impression for new *sannyasins* coming in. We were representatives of Bhagwan: how we ran the office was seen as a reflection on him; how the place appeared was a reflection on him.

At every moment we had to "have our shit together." Even if a problem came up that I'd never dealt with before, I couldn't let my face drop or say, "Well, I don't know." I could never stand in front of anyone who wasn't part of the inner circle and admit, "I don't know." At the very worst it would be "Well, come back tomorrow and I'll have an answer for you."

The illusion was so complete that the person—*sannyasin* or outside business contact—never got the idea that Laxmi or Sheela or I had no idea what we were talking about. We left them with the impression that we were going to meditate on the reply or discuss it with other powers-that-be.

We became masters at weaving these webs. This ability to immerse ourselves so completely in a role that we actually could *become* what the situation demanded was increasingly important to the Ashram's expansion. If there was any danger in this, it was the increasing effort needed to distinguish what was truth from what was illusion. In the last analysis we would wonder, *If you become this thing to your fullest capacity, is it an illusion any longer?* None of us could foresee that this facility for merging illusion with reality so completely that a role became a very real extension of the self would, at a much later date, let some people assimilate the role of "murderer" as completely as we would become an interior designer or whatever.

We all came into the Ashram with different information, and we would grow by building upon that. In actual fact most people grow very little, relative to the amount of information they have taken in. They may claim that their "life book" shows a great degree of evolution; but a hard look reveals there's been very little fundamental change from the original persona they built for themselves. Most often they equate a change in lifestyle with a change in themselves.

In the Ashram, whether we were changing in each instance or not, we were certainly much more able to move into realms people would never normally put themselves into—realms that would *force* growth upon us. There was no way you could play the game at more and more intense levels, and slip comfortably back to the old, unchallenging levels.

Some remnants of the old Ashram language catch the essence of what we were going through once we passed through the gates: "Whatever happens, happens. Whatever is, is." It all comes down to giving yourself permission to dance in whatever realm you chose to pass through.

When Sheela and Bhagwan left the Ranch in Oregon, many people felt that everything had fallen apart. No one knew anything except that, while Sheela was there, things worked—for all that people felt she was terrible. They had lost that creative energy that had made the Ashram work; they had let a single way of looking at things—Sheela's—erase their own integrity as independent seekers after enlightenment.

In a sense they "lost their original face," an oriental expression. A Zen master will say to you, "Show me your face before you were born," which means the essence you are with or without the body. It somehow embodies your past lives, present life, and future lives. But a lot of people in the Ashram got thrown off their path by identifying with several powerful beings rather than coming back into themselves.

Still, you can't really judge them on this basis, since that was their *karma*, to come off the path that way. We never felt it was our place to stop anyone from following a certain course, since that would inhibit their experiencing and learning something for themselves.

At the same time we each had a responsibility to follow our own paths, the way Sheela, Laxmi, and, ultimately, Bhagwan, followed—and continued to pursue—their particular paths. In the end, there should have been countless *sannyasins* forging as many different paths toward enlightenment. In fact, by the time things reached a crisis point, too many were blindly following Sheela along the path she was marking out, and precious few were building on the vast potential the Ashram had once held out to all.

CHAPTER 15

Circles within Circles

As the Ashram grew, new problems were created, and changes came about faster and faster.

During lecture on May 22, 1980, an Indian who was apparently a member of an extreme Hindu organization got up and threw a dagger at Bhagwan. The man was turned over to authorities and later reports mentioned that three other men were also arrested in connection with a Poona-based conspiracy. Bhagwan remained seated calmly through the incident, offering the comment that a true religion does not need to be protected by assassins.

Actually, his ability to sit without flinching through a potentially fatal attack came from the fact that *he knew it was a set-up*. The guy was paid to do it. He was beaten by the Ashram guards only to convince the Poona police that this was the real thing. The incident served to increase fear for Bhagwan's safety and devotion to him.

Within twenty-four hours metal detectors were being shipped from the United States: one of the walk-through variety; several hand-held models. Although this sort of material was not supposed to be brought into India, the office had located the equipment, arranged for payment, and made arrangements for its delivery in less than a day. That sort of efficiency characterized the whole of the Ashram.

Sheela had simply said, "We need a metal detector." The role of her staff was not to ask, "How do we get one?" From the moment she made the announcement, her part was over. It was up to us to manifest the equipment. You could almost hear all the little wheels grinding away in our heads as we sifted through thousands of bits of stored information until we found those connections—people, materials, transportation—that could be put together to get things accomplished almost overnight.

Sheela prized people who had these computer-like minds. I've been told that when I'm playing the stock market or working on some business problem, my whole face goes blank; inside, I *become* a machine. I can absorb a battery of information almost instantaneously, but this isn't done from *conscious* mind—it's almost subliminal. I didn't have to sift through categories in my mind; instead I had a mental image of a huge screen containing all thoughts and data, and in a flash I'd locate the bit of information I needed. This "floating mind" was something I discovered in myself from working with Sheela.

Everything was done in a subtle fashion. Once I'd been told to obtain a metal detector I couldn't simply go to the P.A. system and request, "Anybody who has any information on how ... " Things were never done in an obvious way. It was up to me to acquire what was needed without making waves or even ripples. You hardly even raised the issue with your coworkers, unless they were expressly involved in the project.

This all comes back to the illusion of magic in the Ashram. Since only a handful of people even knew that the metal detectors were on order, you can imagine the uproar the next day when everyone going to lecture suddenly found themselves caught up in a whole new routine, which ran as smoothly as though the screening process had been going on for months.

Overnight, all the guards had been brought together and briefed on the new security procedures; the equipment was put into place; bowls were set up to hold keys and other personal items while a person walked through the scanner; and a thousand other minor details were taken care of, including alerting the kitchen staff in Vrindavan that they would have to wake up earlier to compensate for the fact that the altered routine would mean a delay in getting people into lecture. While most of the Ashramites were sleeping, a whole little army was running around to make sure there would be no awkwardness the next day—that the new system would be fully and flawlessly operational before the cleaners arrived at Buddha Hall.

By the time the *sannyasins* woke up, they would begin to understand that things had changed. But everything had been done without a ripple; the new equipment and procedures seemed to have sprung up by *magic*. I used to think of most *sannyasins* as "the children" who slept on Christmas Eve, while the office "parents" trimmed the tree and put out gifts to give the illusion that Santa Claus had been and gone.

If there had been the least fumble, the tiniest detail that needed to be ironed out, you can be sure the person responsible would be working in the kitchen the next day. Money couldn't buy this type of devoted efficiency. Doing the best job imaginable grew out of the certainty that this would move you further along your path toward enlightenment. When you ran into a problem, you looked to your own resources, your own awareness to solve it—not to a consultant or a bigger staff. To look for answers outside yourself was to miss a chance to test yourself and gain new self-awareness.

If the solution wasn't immediately obvious, you worked to "clean the inner windows" and change your perceptions until you *did* see the answer. This sense of self-commitment was the intrinsic difference between the way we worked in the Ashram and the way people worked in the world outside.

The type of magic that could change the Ashram's routine overnight was a constant part of life in Koregaon Park. The best example of this was Deeksha, who, even though she had her empire in Vrindavan, ran the handyman department—though ultimately everything was under the control of Laxmi and Sheela. Deeksha could put 250 men to work and a building would go up overnight. You'd walk to lecture the next day, and there'd be a whole new dormitory.

The energy of the Ashram could be seen in the way it was constantly changing. It was exciting—but, as with so many things, we internalized the excitement. If a building were tossed up overnight in a city neighborhood, there'd be a lot of chatter about it the next morning. In the Ashram it would simply be accepted as part of the atmosphere of magic that everyone felt.

"Nothing is what it seems to be" was the watchword of the Ashram. By not talking about it we kept the excitement at a higher pitch, because the more you talk about something the more you dissipate the energy. What was fresh and new soon becomes old hat.

Everything was charged, changing, growing. The Ashram really began to bloom. Although it was a slow rhythm, a slow unfolding, it was becoming richer and richer—the elephant ears were getting bigger and bigger, the poinsettia plants were was getting taller and taller and redder and redder. More and more people were living in the Ashram, and this meant more and more jobs to keep them supplied with food, clothes, and all the other necessities.

By the time I'd been working for Sheela for a few months, Buddha Hall had a roof on it, Rada gardens were completed, the boutique was really coming alive. People were no longer wearing the funky Indian *lungis*; there were now two people sewing clothes full time. You rarely saw anyone in shabby clothes anymore; most people had good clothes. And they looked healthier too, as more and more ate in the canteen where the food, for all that it struck me as bland, was undeniably nutritious.

The changes all around us connected with the dreams we had when we walked through the gates: we felt positive changes happening in us. I know that I felt more centered than I ever had in my life. Before, I had always had tremendous amounts of energy—but it was *undirected*. The Ashram gave me the direction I needed to channel that energy for my own growth. In a very real sense I saw my own inner maturation reflected in the growth of the Ashram.

After I'd been with Sheela for a full six months I felt like I'd taken a deep breath, exhaled all the old doubts and distractions, and inhaled the energy to take myself to the highest levels of the game. All my life I had seen a lot of different possibilities for what I wanted to do with my life, but they pulled me in as many different directions. Now, in the Ashram, I found the centered, single-minded energy to pick and choose among my dreams, find the ones that worked for me, and to go for these. I no longer wobbled from one track to another; I learned to be very much *here* and *now*. I could draw on everything I had known and bring it into this moment. Sometimes I'd talk with others about what I felt happening in me. And we all seemed to be sharing in that same sense of collective energy and purpose. Outwardly, everybody looked beautiful. It was almost as if each of us as an individual was spinning on her own axis; at the same time the office and various departments were all turning on *their* axes; all this happening simultaneously would create a rhythm for the Ashram.

You became so much a part of the life of the Ashram from minute to minute that distinctions between yourself and the commune would actually blur. As you went through something personal, you felt the whole Ashram was going through a change at the same moment. I know that's where we got the strength to work the way that we worked. Unless you felt that, you could never work eighteen hours a day, seven days a week, in the unimaginable *heat*. We were constantly plagued by problems like amoebic dysentery; but we trained ourselves not to focus on such things even when they hit us. They seemed to be happening on another, much less significant, level. Unless you were absolutely floored by an illness, you kept on functioning.

The office maintained the highest energy level of all. There was the constant murmur of voices, movement, clatter of typewriters—to the point where I'd sometimes stand in the door and think, *Oh, my God! This place is in total chaos.* But there was always an underlying clarity; everything that needed doing got done.

One of the ways of raising the Ashram-wide energy level was the idea of "celebration days." These would always be turned into incredible festivals that everyone participated in. We knew where each event fell in the calendar; but no one seemed to begin preparing for them until about four days beforehand. This was typical of the way the Ashram ran. You'd never plan for something months in advance: It was always done a few days—or the day—before. A festival never had a set form; it would be made up on the spot: "Let's do it this way," or "Let's try that."

It was up to the office to choreograph this sort of thing. If Lao Tzu was the heart of the Ashram, the office was its mind. Everything that originated with Bhagwan was filtered through us; we mediated between him, the *sannyasin* world, and the world beyond the gates. The office was the hub: like a circus performer keeping more and more plates spinning on sticks, we kept the ever-expanding Ashram departments and enterprises spinning along.

Every now and then a department would get a breather, because the office wasn't focusing on it. The workers would go along at their own pace for a while; then you'd see people "looking over their shoulders," bracing for the next "energizing" swoop by the office.

This could take any form. The *mala* shop, for example, had its own rhythm, being required to turn out a certain number of *mala*s and Bhagwan's boxes. The workmanship was exquisite, but the level of production was always low-key. At the same time the Ashram boutique was still pretty small-scale and funky, plodding along. Both had been largely ignored by the office, because we were working on other projects.

Suddenly, Sheela remembered the *mala* shop and announced, "It's time we put some energy into it. They can start making things to sell in the boutique." Immediately, a message went to the people in the *mala* shop: "You have to make twenty-four lampshades, thirty-six meditation stools, and increase your production of boxes, because we're going to sell ones like Bhagwan gives out—but now we want them inlaid with silver and ivory."

The place was transformed in record time from a small operation to a much larger one. The department head (one of the few men who headed departments in the Ashram) was expected to acquire—practically instantaneously—more wood, silver, ivory, more people to work in the *mala* shop, additional tools, more plant space to absorb the new people and supplies.

The sort of expansion that, in the normal business world, would require weeks of board meetings beforehand and months afterward to make it happen, was expected to happen *in the moment* the decision was reached. You could feel the energy going into play right away to make the office "suggestion" a reality.

But the *mala* shop wasn't sitting out there on its own in a desert somewhere: Changes in one department had a ripple effect on the whole Ashram. There were no isolated events. In the case of the *mala* shop, for example, people were excited by its sudden and complete transformation. What had been just a minor part of the commune had suddenly become the focus of tremendous energy and growth—as though Bhagwan had personally touched it with his holy wand and said, "Divine *mala* shop, here you are! Produce, come forth in abundance!"

There would be a chain-reaction on other departments and projects. People would tune into the energy and see where else it could be applied. Not long after this, for example, it was decided that a new roof was needed for Buddha Hall. The word went out that this was to happen overnight, and, indeed, it did.

Today, looking at the people who came out of the Ashram, I can see that some sank, and others jumped to a higher level. These last are able to say, "My God! Whatever that was that I just went through, it was one hell of an initiation for being in the world." The ones who can only say, "I was ripped off and disillusioned," clearly never took in the most basic lesson of the Ashram: however good or bad your experience, it has something of ultimate value for you, whether that means jumping to a higher level of consciousness or simply building up your inner resources to tough out the worst that life can throw your way.

If the Ashram was a training ground for spiritual disciplines, the office was also an intensive course in matters practical and much more worldly.

When we started opening bank accounts in different places under different names, we had to learn quickly the rules under which each bank operated, and the relevant laws of the country in which it was situated. The idea of "legal" or "illegal" was kind of like the idea that ran in the Ashram of "time" and "no-time." As I was involved in setting up these accounts I never thought, *Oh, my God! I'm doing something illegal, so I must make sure that I do it in such a way that I won't get caught.* It was more abstract—like throwing a rock into the water and allowing the water to close over it, without making waves.

This is the position that we operated from: We come into the world, and there's a set society with a set of rules that the collective consciousness has agreed upon. We recognized that *most* people buy into this trip, but they're forever trying to wriggle around the boundaries. It's as though, having endorsed them, they spend the rest of their lives finding ways to dive in and out of them, so that they don't feel the constraints too much.

We, however, *didn't* buy into the idea that we were part and parcel of a social order that was cast in concrete, though we interacted with it continuously, through necessity or choice. Paradoxically, it *did* provide some kind of form for us to become formless around; we found we *could* use such a structured society as our gameboard for playing in a variety of different realms.

We saw ourselves as an alternative society. All our energies were directed toward surviving and *blossoming* and becoming something to be examined, whether or not others would ultimately decide to join us. We wanted people to become aware that an order could lie parallel to existing society. And to grow we had to go into that other society, play to a certain extent on that level, and raise ourselves out of it. That, I believe, was the original vision that brought the Ashram into being. We were helping create something so clear, so strong, that it could emerge, stand apart from structures that had evolved over thousands and thousands of years, and offer people a real choice.

The erosion of that vision turned the creative energies into self-destruction. As time went on, while many of us felt comfortable with the idea that the current society and our evolving one could exist side-by-side, at least as many began to believe that the real goal would be achieved only when the established society had been eliminated. Some people wanted to set up the commune as the one-and-only social order. I think this was when the downfall really started: When people began to think they were totally right, and that anyone who didn't agree with them was wrong and needed to be converted.

In my work with the bank accounts, I got a thrill from having done something so perfectly that it was still legal, but we were getting everything we wanted from it. That is the ultimate game as I see it: to put yourself on this planet and to live totally the life you envision and create for yourself, without hurting another. If somebody gets hurt along the way, through their own masochism or whatever, then there's nothing you can do about it.

The ultimate test of gamesmanship for Sheela was to be able to do these things *without being seen*. Certainly, while we were in India, that was the stance we were taking.

We threw ourselves into each phase of the game completely. We were getting a thrill from juggling bank accounts, dancing around all the rules and restrictions: For example, "The bell goes off at $10,000; if you do a deposit of $9,999.99, no flags go up." We'd take equal pleasure in just looking at all the different options for check designs and checkbook folders. We would give as much care to matching these to the various accounts as we'd get from establishing the accounts themselves. There was always a *childlike* quality in our dealings that balanced the clear, calculating mindset that played with questions like, "What name are we going to use here? Which references? How much can safely go into this account? Where will we transfer the money from?"

For Sheela alone we set up accounts under "Ma Anand Sheela," "Sheila Silverman," and "Mark Silverman"—Chinmaya, who was bedridden and never used the funds himself.

Each one was for a different activity. The "Ma Anand Sheela" account developed after Deeksha and Sheela came over to the United States and Sheela established herself as an officer of the Chidvilas Center in New Jersey, when they turned the center into more of a business. "Ma Anand Sheela" would be used to sign checks in this regard. The "Sheila Silverman" account was to do business with people who had no knowledge of—or wanted nothing to do with—the Ashram.

Finally, the "Mark Silverman" account was used to bring certain prohibited materials into India when Sheela would explain to the authorities that Mark—Chinmaya—had Hodgkin's disease, and needed all this equipment. The videos were "because he's a dying man and this is his last wish" and so on. There was one story after another. When the bulletproof Rolls Royce came in—the *only* Rolls Royce that came into India—that was presented as Mark's dying wish that he have a Rolls Royce and be able to tour India in it. And the Indian government bought into all this with surprisingly little challenge.

Some years earlier, Sheela and Chinmaya had lived in New Jersey for a short time to be near his family. At that time Sheela began Chidvilas Center, which was to become instrumental in bringing Bhagwan to America.

At first it was just a small operation. In those days you could write to the office and say, "I want to open a center." When permission was given, a person would open whatever type of place his or her funds would allow. Some centers were simply places that stocked a selection of Bhagwan's books, tapes, and photographs. Other centers, like the commune in England, were more elaborate—*sannyasins* might live together, sponsor groups, provide information, and that sort of thing.

The office would send the centers different information on what was happening in Poona or in other centers around the world. When Sheela and Chinmaya set up Chidvilas, it was very small; but when Sheela became more powerful she put a lot more energy and money into it.

To understand what was going on, we need to look at the situation in the Ashram at that time. Laxmi was installed as the secretary: Nothing was going to get Laxmi ousted, *unless* it was something that Laxmi wouldn't be able to deal with. *This* is where Sheela saw her opening: Laxmi wouldn't be able to function in America. She had the Indian side wrapped up, and could have kept us very comfortably in India for as long as we wanted. Sheela found her strategy in the fact that Laxmi knew nothing about the West.

Chidvilas was Sheela's gambit: a crucial link in the chain of events leading Bhagwan from Poona to Antelope, Oregon. In the office we began to use the center more and more as a base of operations in the United States. It became the primary anchor for the Ashram in the West. Up to this point the Ashram had no responsibility for the other centers; even if you opened one, you had to sign a release stating that anything that happened there, anything that drew publicity—especially if it was bad—would not be identified with the Ashram at all. While they could list themselves as "Rajneesh centers," it was made clear from the outset that they were *not* a representation of Bhagwan and did *not* represent the Ashram in Poona.

Each such center was treated as a wholly independent operation, completely self-supporting. The one advantage that they got was a certain discount on books and tapes bought in bulk quantities. Apart from that they got no assistance from the Ashram.

Chidvilas changed all that. The changes were small at first. For example, if there was a letter to go from Chidvilas to someone in the United States or Europe, it would many times be generated from the office in Poona, on special letterhead indicating Chidvilas as the source. To avoid an Indian postmark packets of such letters would be sent back to the United States with *sannyasins* to be mailed there.

Although Chidvilas seemed to be just a center in Montclair, New Jersey, in 1979 it was actually being run by Sheela from India. But few people realized this.

It was fairly ingenious. At the outset the letters going out from the Ashram under the Chidvilas letterhead were just routine business. The only obvious difference from dozens of other centers was the rate at which Chidvilas was expanding. Two people, Swami Avinash and Ma

Avibasa, were the designated center leaders; but a majority of the center's letters were coming directly from India. A typical one might run, "Thank you for your letter of such-and-such to the Ashram, concerning the fact that you're going to be going back to India. We would like to donate to the Ashram in India four Maxell Sixty-minute Video Tapes, plus an Olympia Report Deluxe. If you would be at all happy . . . "

What had happened was this: We were no longer sending that type of letter from the Ashram, it was now being sent directly from Chidvilas. At this point most people had the impression that this was one little center among many that wanted to donate something to the Ashram. As a matter of fact, it was actually being *financed* by the Ashram.

Two important personalities were involved in this operation: Sheela and Deeksha. Although Sheela was setting up the Chidvilas connection, it was Deeksha's inspiration. Sheela didn't want to be beholden to Laxmi, because she hoped to take over that position herself; but she was listening to Deeksha to find out how to organize such an enterprise and keep it growing.

By this point Deeksha's kingdom within the Ashram had grown considerably. And she had allied herself very closely with Sheela's fortunes.

In 1979 Sheela and Deeksha went to America. En route they stopped off in Switzerland to open bank accounts for Sheela, for Bhagwan, and for Vivek. The rationale for these bank accounts was that, if anything should ever happen (already they were thinking in this light), then there would be money for Vivek and Bhagwan to get their hands on. All along, everybody operated under the idea that Bhagwan, although he was the center of this whole enterprise, wasn't to be *involved* in anything that went wrong. He was *above* any of this . . . though, in fact, he was saying "Yes," to it all. We functioned on the pretext that, although he was playing on this level, he was playing for the good of all. Whatever happened, we believed, he must always be free to get on with his experiment somewhere else.

The account for Sheela was opened because she had started to do business in the United States. When the knife was thrown at Bhagwan, and all the security equipment was brought in, it was trumpeted around that there was no account—no access to large amounts of money in the West—that could be drawn on without asking for donations. So one of the things that came from the incident was the conviction that we had to have some money somewhere outside of the Ashram that could be gotten hold of for whatever reason.

At this point we were trying to cover issues *before they came up*. And we were also looking ahead to a major change. For years Bhagwan had been talking repeatedly of the "new commune" that he wanted. As far as anybody knew, this was going to be in India. He certainly never indicated it was to be anywhere else.

Recently, Laxmi had been sent to look for the location of the "new commune" by the express wish of Bhagwan. She was traveling hither and yon through India, looking for the appropriate site. Meanwhile, Sheela was bringing in more and more typewriters, recording equipment, and videotaping equipment, which emphasized the point that India was inadequate to meet our demands. We now had thousands of people to feed, so we needed electric mixers—but not Indian mixers, which had a habit of throwing *chapatis* all over the walls. We needed good-quality Western merchandise. This became our justification for stronger ties with the West, and with the United States in particular.

A lot of people who came to the Ashram were into health foods. You didn't want to discourage that, but you'd justify a lot of equipment—rice hullers or whatever—by saying, "There are more important things to do." This became the rationale for a lot of things that took the burden of attention to minor details off of us.

And Bhagwan endorsed such corner-cutting. One of his gimmicks was "shortcuts to enlightenment." I doubt there's anyone seeking spiritual enlightenment who hasn't attempted to speed up the process. Someone said to him, "One day you say, 'It's impossible to follow me, you can only get enlightened under your own awareness and experience.' And the next day you say, 'A master is a shortcut to enlightenment, because you don't need to go and write all the textbooks to get the degree: you can simply go to the library and pick them up. Or, if you're in a really good university, you'll have a really good don who will feed you the information.'" Bhagwan was setting himself up as the "don," the one who could be counted on to bring bits of nourishment the way a mother bird brings nourishment to the chicks in her nest.

Some people come into the world and believe you have to work so many years at a nine-to-five job in order to fulfill a certain dream (i.e., accumulate a certain amount of money). The attitude of many people in the Ashram was this: Decide how much money you need, then figure what will bring you that amount in the shortest period of time. If you need $50,000 to secure your place in the "new commune," you have two options: You can go and earn that through the usual means, which might take you ten years or more while living in the world day-to-day.

Or you might decide that some scheme—marginally legal or illegal—is going to bring you money much faster. We had big egos (for all our protestations otherwise), and we believed it was more important that we were in the Ashram meditating than sitting in a routine job earning money the straight way. Bhagwan was always stressing the point that he could leave his body at any moment, and that our time together was very short. Any long-term options were out, so choices were few, and urgent.

We could justify anything, including a dope deal. A typical rationale would run: Here you are at point A, which is, "I have to go back to the West to make money to come back and continue living in the commune." At the same time we have point B—Bhagwan, who is the "Master," is saying to you, "A shortcut to enlightenment is to be here with me," which adds a certain pull. Life in the commune has emphasized that, unless you're with *him*, you get a diluted experience.

At this point you sit with it and ponder the consequences of a dope deal. On the one hand there's the fast return which will let *you* return to Bhagwan quickly and affluently. On the other hand there's the possibility of getting caught, which has to be treated as a very real possibility. But Bhagwan has said—and I can cite chapter and verse from his books—if you meditate in a prison cell, that's as good as meditating in a cave.

This leads you to the decision, point C. Whatever you experience in this world, you bring upon yourself, and there must be a reason for you finding yourself in this position. So if the dope deal works, and you collect the $50,000, and you get to donate it to the Ashram and continue living there, then *that's what was meant to be.*

If you do the dope deal, get caught, and wind up in jail, then *that's* what was meant to be. Strangely, it often seemed more attractive to sit in a jail cell for ten years than to be out earning money for a decade. At the very least, it was argued, you'd be able to *meditate* better. That was one of the delusions we fed ourselves.

In retrospect, I realize that, although my inverted ego was saying, *Oh, to sit in a prison cell for ten years! What a great discipline! What a great enlightening experience! My God! What a meditation! This is certainly beyond what normal people would be able to do!* The truth is it would have been a hell of a lot *harder* for us to deal with a nine-to-five job for ten years than to sit in a five-by-five prison cell. I suspect that's what Sheela is doing in her prison cell at this moment: *What* a meditation—and it's not your fault if you wind up in jail anyhow, because *society* is to blame. This suggests a somewhat naive view of the prison realities; but, the fact is, those few *sannyasins* in my experience who *did* go to prison saw to it that they *benefited* from their incarceration. (However, I do need to add a footnote here to the effect that I've never met a *sannyasin* unfortunate enough to go to a maximum-security prison. Under such circumstances I'm sure this illusion would be knocked right out!)

Two women ended up going to open prisons. One, who was jailed in England, told me she chose to start studying. She now had access to study and on-the-job training that, ironically, she might never have been able to take advantage of had she not been thrown into these circumstances. I sat and listened to her description of what she was doing: *That,* in a way, was what we were trying to do in the Ashram. Create a world where basic needs were taken care of, opportunities for self-growth were made available, and we were removed from the workaday world of cares, pressures, and frustrations.

In conjunction with such questions, Win McCormack, in an article reprinted in *Oregon Magazine/The Rajneesh Files,* reported:

"Bhagwan's disciples are under no pressure from our organization to smuggle drugs," protested Ma Yoga Laxmi . . . in a statement issued by the foundation's press office on February 24, 1980.

Laxmi . . . was reacting to evidence presented at several trials of Rajneesh disciples on drug-smuggling charges in France and England. . . . All four disciples were traveling from Bombay at the time of their arrests.

Defense lawyers for all four argued in court that their clients had been brainwashed at Rajneesh's ashram in Poona . . .

The cumulative testimony at the four trials left it unclear as to whether Rajneesh or his official organization was directly involved in the drug trafficking . . .

An article in the French magazine *L'Express,* commenting on [one] case, said: "It doesn't appear that the ashram directly organizes the traffic, but it hardly matters. The money will get back to them in one way or another, through donations, bequests, offerings or the 'salaries' of [ashram] therapists. Utterly dependent, the disciples are ready to do anything to prevent the umbilical cord that ties them to the Master from being cut. Smuggling, swindling, prostitution: whatever is necessary."

Yet, for all such unresolved questions, there was one thing we all had in common within the Ashram: We weren't interested in dealing with currency, we weren't interested in this perpetual wheel of earning then having it taken away from you so you had to earn more. We were free of the concern with money, which does take up a huge part of people's lives—not to mention the business of using the money to buy food and pay rent and all of the thousand and one things that go with maintaining yourself in the world. As bizarre as it sounds, prison life didn't seem that far removed from Ashram life—or monastery life, for that matter.

For all that we were working eighteen hours a day in the Ashram, we were doing it *free* from all pressures but the single concern with our job. To sit in prison for ten years and meditate was very similar in some ways: nothing was expected of you. If you *do* become creative in prison, and you can fight off the worst that's thrown your way, you're patted on the back for the smallest step forward you take. A person who takes a college degree in prison is certainly acknowledged more than the thousands who take them every year from colleges.

If those people who got busted for doing dope deals had actually gone out to make money in a legal, everyday way, the reasoning ran, they would have cheated themselves of crucial experiences—win or lose. If they scored successfully the credit was theirs. If they blew it the responsibility was equally theirs. You have no one to blame if you can't make it in the game that *you've* chosen to play. In the end the spoils— win or (apparently) lose—went to those who played for the highest stakes.

When I look at the dissolution of the Ashram, I think that ninety-eight percent of the people were totally ignorant of what was going on. Of the two percent who actually *did* know, probably one percent merely looked on and only one percent actively took part in things. Those last are the ones I hold responsible. The majority, who never chose to find out what was going on, are the ones who sit around now and say, "Oh, the Ashram failed, it's all *their* fault." They're the ones who are complaining they've been ripped off. How anyone can go through such an experience and say that it failed, I don't know. It was a vast learning experience for us all, from the days of chasing the high vision to the last days of paranoia and collapse.

Not long afterwards Bhagwan sent Laxmi out to look for a location for the "new commune," since the Ashram at Poona was only a "way station" for gathering personnel and resources to establish the ultimate "mystery school" at some as-yet-undesignated spot. Presumably, this would be in India, since Laxmi's instructions were to travel the length and breadth of the country until she found a site that Bhagwan would agree was predestined for this final phase of his experiment.

Up to this point Sheela had not been seeing Bhagwan personally. She would send a folder in with Vivek, whereas Laxmi had routinely gone in each day to get the feedback directly from Bhagwan.

When Laxmi had been away for a while, Sheela was suddenly told that she was to take in her papers personally. I remember that we had to go over our typing with extra care to make sure things were letter-perfect (as they routinely were, in any case) when Sheela brought them to Bhagwan. She had us put them all inside a clear plastic envelope, because she didn't want to be responsible for taking any germs into his room.

When she came out you could feel the exhilaration in her. Whether she had planned the whole thing from when she had first entered the gates or not, there were definitely moments of great excitement for her in the unfolding of events. You could see it in the way her face would glow. She came out of that first official meeting with Bhagwan like a child, or someone very much in love.

Before she went in she looked like someone with a crush setting out on her first date. She kept asking us for advice on what she should wear, how she should arrange her hair. At the same time she was trying to downplay these concerns, because it could look too much like "ego." And she went over her notes again and again, checking every point over with us. "It's got to be *absolutely* clear," she said, "I don't want to fuck up, and get in there, and he says, 'What is that?' and I don't know. You have to go over *everything* with me."

It was, in a way, like the first time she saw him—certainly, it was the first time she'd interacted with him in this light. Now she had the opportunity to give her impressions directly to Bhagwan, and he was very easy to guide. Intermingled with the upbeat excitement was a nervous excitement arising from the fact that there was *so much* at stake for her. The one thing you knew in the Ashram was that, if you got something wrong the first time, it was a long time before you'd be given a second chance. Sheela couldn't afford missing this opportunity.

By the time she went in to see Bhagwan she had Chidvilas as an iron in the fire. It was still little more than a pipeline for typewriters and tapes and that sort of thing, but my impression was that she already had formed long-range plans around the center. She also knew that she functioned very, very well in the West. She knew how to talk to people, how to walk in with a batch of "references" and become the part she was playing; she could assess people in a moment and play back to them exactly what they wanted—while also getting back what *she* wanted. She knew just how good she was at these games.

Bhagwan and Chinmaya were the only two people that Sheela felt could "see" her. It was a walk-through getting past the people in the West; these two were her real hurdle. Chinmaya, because of his illness, was the lesser challenge in some ways. On reflection, I can see that there was a tremendous amount of concern in her over whether she was going to make it: Could she secure her new status with Bhagwan without overplaying her hand or revealing that there was far more on her mind than simply becoming his secretary?

I think Sheela had a plan right from the beginning, and that each move she made was in line with that; but I also think that she was ready for it to be found out and stopped at any point. She was always keeping her eagerness to "go for it" and her fear of hurting her chances through overeagerness in a state of dynamic tension.

Watching Sheela come back from Lao Tzu, flushed with excitement, feeling secure about her new position, I shared something of that same excitement. It was like watching a knight come back triumphantly from a quest of some sort.

But many other impressions were at work in me simultaneously. At some deep level I sensed that the balance of power had shifted in some subtle, but critical, way. And, fleetingly, I had the idea that, in our magic kingdom of the Ashram, the return of this knight meant the king and queen and others might want to touch their crowns and be sure they were securely in place.

CHAPTER 16

Expansion

Laxmi was concentrating her search for the "new commune" site in the northerly area of Manali. Bhagwan had said that once the Ashram had established itself in Poona for about two years, he would create the "new commune." Up until it begins, he said, "I will still be attracting people from everywhere." But when he felt the circle of *sannyasins* was complete, this select number would abandon the Ashram at Poona and seal themselves off from the world in the "mystery school" that was the end-point of his grand undertaking.

"The new commune is going to be a great experiment in Buddhahood," Bhagwan promised his *sannyasins* in 1977.

Energies have to be made available to you: possibilities have to be made clear to you. You have to be made aware of your potential, and you have to be given a safe place from where you can work; a place where you are not disturbed by the world, a place where you can go on without any disturbance from the crowd, a place where ordinary things, taboos, inhibitions, are put aside: where only one thing is significant—how to become a Buddha. (*The Diamond Sutra*)

This idea arose from Bhagwan's teaching that, hundreds of years ago, he was a teacher with a group of followers. But, before he could enlighten them all, or pass on his teachings fully to them, he had to leave that body. So he made a promise to the faithful that some day he would come back and gather those people to him again from whatever corners of the earth they found themselves in. Though they might have been through the process of rebirth several times in between that appearance of Bhagwan and the current one, he explained, they would know who they were and would come to him.

When this group was regathered the teachings would continue and be completed. The purpose of the Poona enterprise was to let more and more people hear of what was happening; it was P.R. for the specific purpose of gathering the scattered former followers who had all been reborn in this generation.

In connection with this, Bhagwan said, "For in the West, the seed would be planted in England, and the blossoming would happen in America." But he said that some seven and a half years before the moment we're talking about. No one really linked the idea of the "new commune" with America at this time—except (presumably) Sheela and (perhaps) Bhagwan. Certainly, Laxmi didn't: She was tirelessly scouring northern India for the proper location to found the post-Ashram community.

It was generally assumed that Laxmi's discovery of a site that Bhagwan concurred with would coincide with the arrival in Poona of all the reborn followers who were finding their way to India. Then, Bhagwan indicated, we would go into the "new commune" and "close the gates," so that nobody would be able to come in and nobody would be able to go out. This would truly become the ultimate mystery school. All the disciplines, teaching methods, and devices that have ever been—and some that haven't been discovered yet—would be in use in that commune. Such "tools" would include Zen, psychology, controlled use of drugs, anything that would help us free ourselves to achieve higher levels of consciousness and eventual enlightenment.

Bhagwan certainly led everyone to believe it would be founded in India. Years before, just after I had returned to Poona for good, a directive from the office had announced, "We have found the new commune. The train is leaving on Thursday."

We all ran out and bought our train tickets and sat and waited.

Nothing happened.

I have to admit, I bought a ticket. I wasn't, however, one of the ones who went so far as to climb aboard a train. I was with a group that waited near the front gates on the day specified in the announcement and the gossip that was buzzing throughout the Ashram. No one thought it odd that Bhagwan hadn't mentioned the move once during lecture that morning—nor had a single box been packed anywhere. We stood outside the front gate after lecture, wondering when it was going to happen, and how we were physically going to move the Ashram. We were just going to go, and somehow everything would miraculously get packed and taken.

Since that was the way things usually happened, none of this seemed especially bizarre to us. As it happened, years later, when the Ashram *was* moved to the United States, nobody knew. Everyone was happily going about their business, only to be told that Bhagwan had left two days before for New Jersey, that his closest and dearly beloveds were with him, and the Ashram was going to be dismantled. For all intents and purposes the move was already accomplished: all the strategic people had left and been put into position in America. The worker bees were still buzzing along, unaware that the hive had been declared surplus.

We took a perverse joy in all these little instances—and there were many others—that came from the spontaneity. It wasn't that strange for us to move from discovering that a building had been erected overnight to accepting that the whole Ashram was moving.

It never was made clear exactly where the releases had come from announcing the proposed move. We all had the typed-and-copied memos, including train schedules, ticket prices for first-, second-, and third-class accommodations, and destination. But this only gave the end of the train run—it did not indicate where we'd be going beyond the final station. But no one *expected* to get any more information at that point. It seems totally bizarre now; but, at the time, it didn't seem unusual at all. That's the way things worked.

A few years ago Bhagwan came out with a list of people who were enlightened, people who were *bodhisattva*s (which meant that they would either get enlightened in this lifetime, or at the moment of death), and those who were *promised* that they would reach enlightenment after they were dead. And people *believed* this. I was named a *bodhisattva*, and I turned to Sheela and said, "You know I'm going to deny this; you know I'm not!"

People started actually treating you as if you were something special. Overnight, Bhagwan could declare your enlightenment or your *bodhisattva*hood, and people would truly deal with you as such. I was going around saying, "But this isn't true: I'm just the same as I always was!"

And then Sheela would say, "Yeah, and if you deny it, then I'm just going to say, 'That's her way of creating a device for you, because she's going to make it more difficult for you.'"

There was always an explanation for any position anyone wanted to take. At one point Bhagwan declared one of the *sannyasins*—who was in a coma at the time, enlightened at the moment of his death. Everybody fell for it, though some of the more cynical among us said, "That's easy enough to say: you know damn well he's not going to come to and say anything." But it was taken seriously by the majority, who clung to the hope that what could happen to *him* could happen to *them*. Who knows? Maybe he was enlightened. It just doesn't matter. We believed it and attached importance to the saying-so at the time.

On another occasion Bhagwan said someone else was enlightened. Then he added, "But you'll never know that he is, because he'll always deny it." There were all sorts of these little catches, which let you see a "no" as a "yes," "black" as "white," or anything as "meditation."

Although we lived in an environment of self-denial, we lived in very comfortable rooms, and we certainly never wanted for anything. One of the hardest things for people leaving that environment was the rude awakening of realizing that without the collective effort of hundreds of people working to make things happen, it's very hard to make things happen on your own—especially when you're trying to hold down a job to pay for money, food, and rent.

But, for all that we got, there was plenty to take. One little scam that involved the "new commune" came about while Laxmi was still searching for the elusive site. All the time Bhagwan was harping on this idea. Suddenly, this new project began.

To raise money the Ashram started selling houses in the still-nonexistent "new commune," so that people could book their living quarters in advance. This was a whole new wrinkle, because the arrangement before had been that you worked in the Ashram and, after a certain amount of time, you could work your way up to getting room and board. *Now* they were saying you could *buy* your space. A lot of us could hardly believe this was going on. (This project was said to be sanctioned through Laxmi, though she was still on the road, looking for the "new commune." Sheela was really running things at home.)

What they offered fell into several different categories. You could buy a small bungalow for a family that had certain features (the office would spell out the basic design and so forth), and this cost around $50,000. Then you went down on the scale to accommodations around $25,000, which was a cottage shared with a limit of two to three people. For $10,000 you could buy a room, but you were given no information about the type of room or the number of people you might be sharing space with. My impression (though this was never specifically said) was that it was some kind of dormitory situation.

So they merrily sold all these bungalows and rooms in the "new commune." But, because the Ashram was a "nonprofit" organization, and because people trusted that they were dealing with Bhagwan, the money that changed hands was listed as a "donation." Though it was legally donated, it was understood that once the "new commune" was established you would be given space in keeping with your "donation."

This venture was largely directed at the Europeans and the Orientals, who came along and happily gave their money. It never occurred to anybody—particularly with Laxmi busily searching hither and yon through the northern provinces—that the "new commune" would be anywhere *but* India. No one dreamed back then that it would be established in a country they couldn't live in.

People got high on the idea of buying housing, and it was a joyful thing all around. The ability to buy space was particularly appealing to those who were working in the West, and who had certain living standards they hoped to maintain. These people weren't all that happy at the idea of moving into what might be less-than-desirable quarters in the "new commune" after having worked their way up the ladder financially—especially in light of Bhagwan's statement that after the gates were shut that would be it.

Some of my friends who didn't have any money were worried they would be kicked out. But most of us who were already Ashramites assumed we would get to stay.

Of course, when the move to America happened, almost none of these people could live in the States anyhow. Most wound up simply returning to whatever country they had originally come from, though they had given away what would have at least served as a down payment on a house in their native country.

Logically, one could say that only an idiot would have gone to India and signed a paper stating that "this is a donation" in return for which, as a "devotee," you would be guaranteed a space in a hypothetical "new commune" to be established at some unspecified time and place. As it turned out there were *lots* of rooms in the "new commune," but none of these people could live in them. I guess most people had come to the Ashram to get away from the corruption in the outside world; they weren't about to acknowledge it also existed here. They assumed that this was the one place it *wouldn't* happen.

If you *were* the kind of person who *did* sit there and say, "Well, where is it going to be? I want it more legally tied up," You'd hear, "Where's your surrender? There *are* no guarantees in this life. Trust that, with Bhagwan, whatever happens will be right." And if you did begin to pipe up, after you'd made your donation, you'd get assurances that Laxmi was getting closer and closer to finding the promised location. And most of us believed that. At one point, she even sent photographs of a site they were thinking of purchasing. Through all this poor Laxmi was running around in good faith, honestly believing the place she selected would be the ultimate "commune."

But Sheela knew (though even I didn't know at the time) that

America was the place she wanted for the "new commune." By bringing Bhagwan there she would be in control. In India Bhagwan was
very much in his element; he knew the Indian people and politics the
way only a native can.

For example, he could lecture on the politician Shri Morarji Ranch-
hodji Desai, who was the prime minister at one time when we were
there, and be totally negative about the man. He'd go off on a tangent
and make fun of Desai. If he tried that in America he'd have been
slaughtered; the lawsuits alone would have been incredible. Desai, on
his part, might publically denounce Bhagwan as a "charlatan"; but he
certainly wouldn't bother getting into lawsuits. America was a whole
different ballgame. And, once they got to America, Sheela's plan was
effective. It seems Bhagwan *did* defer to her for everything.

As the Ashram grew a variety of new projects were being undertak-
en on every side. In 1978 the Ashram presented the first of a series of
arts and crafts shows held in Bombay—which drew favorable attention
from the press and visitors.

One such venture was the creation of a Shakespearian theater
group. Quite a few members of the Ashram were English Stratford actors and actresses, many of them very famous. One woman living in
the Ashram was a well-known clothing designer, who created spectacular costumes. It was great P.R. as far as India—and the world—was
concerned.

The Ashram had early on learned the value of good media coverage.
In 1978 the German press arrived at the Ashram to report on the accu-
sation of a German film actress who claimed to have been assaulted
during an Ashram encounter group. Her story was quickly revealed to
be a publicity stunt, but Bhagwan said of the hoax, "All that bad publicity is going to help my work. . . . My *sannyasins* will be enough to answer that bad publicity" (*Hallelujah!*).

In fact the German reporters did find a much more interesting story
in Bhagwan and the Ashram. Their detailed coverage spread Bhagwan's name throughout Germany and most of Europe, resulting in an
increased number of travelers from the West.

That same year the British Broadcasting Corporation filmed the
March 21 Enlightenment Day Celebration. This program proved pivot-
al in attracting worldwide attention. Later, in June 1978, a television
crew arrived to film Ashram life and Bhagwan in lecture and *darshan*.
Since the Indian government was still imposing restrictions on foreign
filming, non-Indian reporters hired film crews of Indians to get around

the ban. This was added to by documentary films and videotapes produced by *sannyasins* in the Ashram. As interest worldwide continued to grow, even *darshans* grew to as many as two hundred attendees when groups were present.

In April of the following year Bhagwan participated in an internationally televised conference on the future of humanity. This was the subject of a full-length feature film, *Bhagwan*, which was widely distributed in Europe and America.

All this was tremendously exciting for *sannyasins*. It was most exciting to see these lavish productions of *A Midsummer Night's Dream, Twelfth Night*, and other plays.

The acting, the costumes, the sets—everything was absolutely first-rate. The Ashram never did anything by halves. The costumes were out of this world: The most beautiful pure silk chiffons were dyed all sorts of colors and made up in patchworks. Some of the costumes were photographed and featured in major European magazines.

India had never seen anything like this. The British dramatist Peter Beresford, who worked with Dudley Moore and Peter Cook, caught a performance of *A Midsummer Night's Dream* in Bombay and later told me, "It was incredible . . . not just because it was in India, but it was incredible by theatrical standards anywhere in the world."

The Rajneesh Theatre Group toured India and eventually traveled to England, where it also did quite well. Laxmi had known Indira Gandhi for many years, and she arranged several performances in New Delhi expressly for the prime minister. This gives a pretty clear picture of just how successful and professional the Ashram was.

The company put on a few shows at the Ashram, then began touring in earnest. This fed tremendous amounts of new energy into everyone; we felt high because they were doing such a fine job, and outshining almost anything similar that had been attempted before. And the Ashram made the most of the good press and photographs of people like Indira Gandhi shaking hands with the performers and so on. Anyone who would be approached to sell land for the "new commune," we felt, couldn't help but be impressed by this group that was making such a splash.

The tours never turned a profit, because of the expense of mounting such extravaganzas; but the favorable public relations fallout was incalculable. And this was a joy, too. We knew already that we were living in paradise, with buildings of beautiful marble, furniture handcrafted in rosewood or teak, exquisitely inlaid; the clothes we wore were attractively made in the finest fabrics; *now* we even were able to produce a theater group that was being applauded all over India and in Europe. Fittingly enough, we were stepping out for the first time with fantasy on the grand scale, and people *loved* it.

As this was going on a woman named Tanmayo, a photographer friend of Greek Mukta and the actor Terrence Stamp, came over from England and took photographs in the Ashram. Her series on Bhagwan was used in one of the books the Ashram published. But she also did photographs of Ashramites like Vimalkirti, the Prince of Hanover, his wife, the Princess, and their little daughter; Asheesh, the man who ran the *mala* shop; and others.

Life magazine picked these up and did a *ten-page* photo spread. And, while the magazine went for her photographs primarily, it's also a fact that every single subject of her photos was a player in the Ashram. So we were getting reinforcement from outside—the beginning of what I call "pulsing," sending out energy from the Ashram and getting it bounced back stronger from the world beyond the gates. Later the Rajneesh Theatre Group produced a musical comedy called *Hollywood Musical Night* and formed the Rajneesh Junior Theatre Group, which performed *Peter Pan*. Things were on a roll, and we could all feel it.

Things were expanding on other fronts all the while. Deeksha and Sheela went to America and set up modest bank accounts in the neighborhood of $10,000 to $15,000 each. Sheela also employed the services of a New York accounting firm to handle Ashram business in the United States. And, while they were there, they visited Chidvilas and reorganized the center's finances. Deeksha took Avibasha aside and suggested a whole new way for the center to make money. She proposed to design and produce clothes in India, which could be shipped to Chidvilas for sale.

When she returned to the Ashram Deeksha used this to expand her enterprises even further. At the time the Ashram included the office, the *mala* shop, Buddha Hall, the boutique, book publishing and video production facilities, the kitchen, Miriam Canteen, and living accommodations. Deeksha, meanwhile, had her restaurant, Vrindavan; her own private restaurant for select people; her own clothes designing studio and fabric mills; her own jewelry department (another offshoot of the Chidvilas connection); her own *mala* shop for the special *malas* she sold in the Ashram and elsewhere; and other shops that produced elaborate boxes of all sizes, lampshades, and a variety of other goods.

Things grew so rapidly that she built her own dormitories to house and feed her own workers. For a long time Bhagwan just kept giving her more and more juice. He recognized she was a first-rate businessperson. She could be ruthless (I suppose that's fitting in someone said to be Mussolini's granddaughter), charismatic, and had a real saving grace in her wonderful sense of humor. And the money kept rolling in through all her enterprises.

In a very short time we had come up from virtually nothing to a point where we were feeling pretty rich and pretty stable inside ourselves. Now we were beginning to take our first solid steps out into the world. And the standard we set for ourselves in meeting the world was to be *the best*. The game had already been set in play a long time before, but now we were ready to raise the stakes dramatically. And we were the most efficient organization imaginable; what we promised, we delivered—or there was hell to pay.

We threw ourselves into this wholeheartedly, because this wasn't being done merely for some corporate board of directors just to keep a job; everything we did, we did *for Bhagwan*. By extension, of course, that meant we were doing it *for ourselves*. Failing to get anything done was failing in yourself.

I believed that Sheela would be the ideal teacher as I began my part in this game. My particular vow to myself was to be absolutely clear and do everything right that I was given to do. To do it any less meant I was playing the game halfheartedly. And it was made clear that if you did mess up, you were out—there were no second chances in this game. You had to be totally certain at all times that you were playing the game to the utmost of your commitment and ability. When anything went wrong, you blamed yourself—it would never occur to anyone in the office to blame Sheela, or someone else in charge.

So I studied Sheela and played the game to the degree that was appropriate. This became my "meditation."

In July 1979 the United Nations Commission on Human Rights announced that it would investigate the charge that the Indian government was discriminating against the Ashram and *sannyasins*. Things continued on a rocky course between Bhagwan and the government in New Delhi.

But for all the "harassment," as it was termed, the Ashram continued to thrive. In August Rajneesh International Meditation University was created. Courses included psychology, religion, philosophy, agriculture, ecology, fine arts, medicine, and healing arts. It offered Bachelor, Master, and Doctor of Meditation degrees.

I saw Laxmi rarely during this time—perhaps twice. She was calling in instructions to Sheela. The Chidvilas situation was solidifying, though it was still just financial arrangements and a guaranteed steady supply for the Ashram of needed American-made items. A move to the United States was inconceivable at this point.

Mass sterilizations began around the same time. Before, it had been a matter of a few people here and there. Now, lists of employees who were to be sterilized on a given day would be posted, and they'd do it with almost no argument. Women always had to be handled at the hospital in town, but the men could be treated as outpatients and only needed a local anesthetic. The men's operation was being done by one of the European-trained doctors in the Ashram's own health center.

Most Ashramites got free sterilization—others had to pay a nominal fee. But the clinic charged little; and the Ashram had a longstanding arrangement with the doctor at the hospital, who performed the surgery on women for a very small fee. Inevitably, it was placed in a positive light: Everything from a vasectomy to dysentery would be turned into a spiritual experience.

I could see evident tension between Laxmi and Sheela on those increasingly rare instances when Laxmi would return to the Ashram. I had always sensed friction between them; but it had appeared to me to be a creative tension, growing out of Sheela's impatience at being Laxmi's pupil and her recognition that Laxmi had a lot to teach her. Although everyone was too well-behaved and graceful to sink to the level of rudeness, I began to notice new tones creeping into Sheela's conversations with Laxmi: "There's no need, Laxmi," she would say. "I understand that. We went over that before."

As Laxmi came back from the "new commune" search, the tension grew. Sheela hadn't completely gotten through the door yet; many people were intensely devoted to Laxmi. I think that most people who knew of Sheela were wary of her from the first. It was clear that she was coming from a very different direction than Laxmi, though no one guessed her long-range plans or the extent of her ambitions. And I could sense a subtle role reversal. I remember reading somewhere, What of the king stag, when the young stag is grown?" We had a situation where two queens were quietly vying for a single throne.

I know others were seeing this too, because several expressed the hope each time that Laxmi returned that she would stay and resolve the question. Clearly, Sheela was gathering more power and not simply "looking after the shop."

In my opinion Laxmi was as ruthless as Sheela, if not more so. She was very good at giving the impression of the little lady devoted to

Bhagwan; people would become devoted to her through that. Yet, in private, she was like a precocious little child: She wouldn't eat, or would forget to eat, then she would only eat her special diet. I often would stand there and think, "Well, if you're really so devoted, and you're really so disappeared from yourself, why is it such a hassle to keep you alive?"

Laxmi was able to gather much more sympathy than Sheela ever could. She was also quick to respect the fact that Sheela was doing an excellent job of running the Ashram in her absence. This was a blessing for her, since she would no sooner arrive for a visit before Bhagwan would send her back out to keep up the search for the "new commune." I don't think Bhagwan had grasped the whole of Sheela's plan yet. Even when Sheela knew the "new commune" would be overseas—and the property was purchased *long* before we ever moved—she kept Bhagwan from knowing until everything had fallen into place.

When the move to America did happen, there was almost no protest—or much surprise, even. Because of the way things were always done in the Ashram, it didn't seem at all bizarre to wake up one morning, hear that the Master is now half a world away, and that anyone who wants to join him will have to make their own way to where he is. We would have found it boring to have someone who was always predictable: And, by keeping things up in the air so much of the time, he kept us from taking too close a look at our situation.

I also think this played a part in how Sheela got to where she did. Laxmi, at this point, had already been with Bhagwan about ten years. When he met her she certainly had the enthusiasm, the learning, and the ability to pull together all the strings of this huge experiment. And, I imagine, there was tremendous excitement in the day-by-day discovery of what worked, what didn't, and how to keep the enterprise expanding.

But now her systems were set up and highly effective; she had become master. Here was Sheela: young, very beautiful, very clever. She could easily grasp the existing structures, but also represented a whole new realm of ideas and possibilities. I think Bhagwan found Sheela more and more stimulating as time went on, as she quite literally opened a whole new world to him. In a way it was an application of that old saying, "A change is as good as a rest."

And he could see that Sheela was making things happen all the time. She could reach into the West the way Laxmi never would: She would have kept us in India, using Indian products, always tied to the Indian political and cultural scene. But Sheela was careful to make those Western connections more and more important as time went on. And Deeksha continued to be her ally and mentor while, as the poet says, "Westward the course of empire takes its way."

The money to fund these new adventures came from many different sources. It came first from groups, which accounted for some very large amounts, since many groups were going on continually; and it was rare that anyone visiting the Ashram wasn't directed immediately to several of them, to be paid for out of his or her own pocket. Books and tapes generated a lot of funds. The Introduction to *The Rajneesh Bible, Volume I*, comments, "In India, during the Bombay and Poona years, Bhagwan's talks in English and Hindi filled a staggering 350 volumes, most . . . published by Rajneesh Foundation International."

Vrindavan provided meals for almost all *sannyasins* who lived outside the Ashram walls—mostly in the local hotels—but worked or took groups at 17 Koregaon Park; and the food in Vrindavan wasn't cheap. In India at that time you could get a really good meal for a couple of *rupees*. In Vrindavan you'd pay ten *rupees* for a bowl of soup; ten *rupees* for a fresh fruit salad; another five *rupees* for cream on that (we were all pretty "decadent").

Another major source of income were the "celebration days." In the old days, we would have mass celebrations on Bhagwan's birthday (December 11), his Enlightenment Day (commemorating his enlightenment on March 21, 1953), and *Guru Poornima*, honoring the enlightenment of all gurus past, all gurus present, and all future gurus. This celebration is held by all Eastern religions on the first day of the full moon in July, commemorating Buddha, Jesus, Lao Tzu—everybody—and the master/disciple relationship.

Any celebration day would cost about fifteen *rupees* to attend. The main evening event would be dancing in Buddha Hall, while Bhagwan presided over things from his chair. Cost: fifteen *rupees* a head. Even people who didn't live in the Ashram would plan their holidays around these festivals, and travel to the Ashram for the occasion. In addition to set fees to get on the grounds and into Buddha Hall, all these visitors—as many as four or five thousand—were eating in Vrindavan. The vast majority of these people would buy at least two Bhagwan books (every celebration day at least five new books were available); there were special commemorative portraits of Bhagwan prepared for each event; the boutique would display whole new lines of clothes, gift boxes, and jewelry. People always did a mad amount of shopping at these times: It was like Christmas three times a year.

A number of extra groups would also be opened to such visitors. Already, at any one time, there were something like fifty-five ongoing groups, each with something like forty participants, who were paying at the very least something like $100 per person. It added up quite rapidly, because the Ashram was not even paying the group leaders.

The Ashram had no overhead for all this, beyond taking care of the Ashramites themselves. And while we were taken care of very well, it really wasn't that expensive. Miriam Canteen, where the Ashramites ate, was big on soya products like tofu, tempe, soya curd, and soya milk. The whole rooftop was given over to growing soybeans.

But the Ashram was intensely creative on many fronts. Before America had really gone into the idea of energy from wind turbines, these were being designed and set up at Saswad—a parcel of land to the north of Poona, which was, as we shall see, the site of the abortive Indian "new commune."

All the time the Ashram was growing on its own—as well as through Sheela's best efforts. The medical facilities alone had to be tremendously expanded to accommodate the needs of the steadily increasing population. But the majority of new people flocking to Poona were coming because of Bhagwan—certainly not because of Sheela's regime. At best, they put up with her.

Another tremendously successful project we went into was hydroponics. It was introduced for the Ashram itself, but the *sannyasin* who developed our systems was invited to lecture all over the world, and was even flown to Israel to study work on the *kibbutzes* in desert situations. In the Ashram we grew all the vegetables hydroponically. This immediately cut down the disease risk of buying from outside sources, and the nutrients could be varied for the highest yield. The systems that were in use were based on solid nutrients with a very small amount of water to sustain a huge field of hydroponics. The channels for the water were at carefully calculated angles that let the water trickle down at a predetermined pace. At the end of each row it would be gathered and pumped back to the start, so the fields got maximum use of limited supplies of water.

The water in use was constantly filtered, which reduced the danger of amoebas and other parasites. Almost anything you touched in India could run you the risk of some infection. The hydroponic systems not only grew nutritionally better vegetables, but also cut down on illness because of the way they were grown, harvested, and washed with filtered water. The water filter itself was later patented and became another source of revenue for the Ashram. It is still widely used throughout India and the Orient.

One of the doctors who is still with Bhagwan was directed by the office to put all his energy into the study of amoebas and parasites. He developed a number of sterile procedures for use in bathrooms and kitchens and so forth that disrupted the disease cycle and cut way down on incidents of infestation. Papers that he published appeared regularly in *Lancet*, the journal of the British Medical Association.

Disease control was always a minor, but persistent, theme in the Ashram. Much later, when things were established in Oregon, the AIDS crisis prompted Bhagwan to speak out and order all the people living at the Ranch to follow "safe sex" procedures. Recently, a health counselor in San Francisco commented, "The one incredible thing that no one's really acknowledged the group for is the AIDS thing. Because, even though people were laughing at them for what they were doing, *everything was procedurally absolutely correct.* If you could only get everybody to do the same, you'd go a long way toward controlling this epidemic."

But, at the time, I have to admit I was one of the many who thought this was only a further warning of just how crazy things were getting at Rajneeshpuram—just one more symptom of "Sheela's paranoia." But, as the counselor went on to point out, *only* in a controlled situation like the Ranch could you get *everybody* to practice "safe sex," because there the belief is stronger than any resistance. The fact that so much stress was placed on "doing for the other" as opposed to "doing for oneself" also made people more responsible for their behavior.

In the Ashram we could indulge our creativity to the fullest, because we didn't have the normal limits. We didn't have to worry about budgets, as long as the office thought a project was worth pursuing. Our energies weren't channeled in certain directions, the way they would be in a corporation or family; we were governed by a single directive: to be *the best* in everything we touched.

And so, from disease control to ornamental gardening, the Ashramites would try to develop the best systems they could or create the most beautiful landscape imaginable. There would be a lot of money to explore these things—though people would look for creative solutions to keep from taking money away from the "new commune." Still, if the gardeners decided certain plants from outside India were just what was needed to give a final touch to Rada gardens, these would be flown in at any cost.

Ma Savita, a young Englishwoman, was an accountant for the Ashram. Until Sheela became really powerful, Savita took care of the money things. Laxmi identified herself with Bhagwan in overtly giving no real importance to money, though she was very watchful on how it would be spent. So Savita was always the one who kept running tabs on how much we had, would project how much was needed for a given project, and how much would be coming during a specified period. An entire department, some ten or twelve people backed her up—but she had her finger on the economic pulse of the Ashram.

Laxmi had to sign all the checks. However, each department would have small "cash floats" to cover routine expenses; Savita could sign checks in these instances, as could Vidya. But when Sheela set up her new bank accounts Savita had nothing to do with them. The checks would be typed up by myself or someone else working for Sheela, so Savita never even had the checkbooks in her hand. The accounting office arranged for the initial transfer of funds to these accounts, and was then out of the picture.

All the Chidvilas mail was coming to Sheela directly, unopened by the mail department. Any money that the center was making through mail order, any donations from there, were being fed directly into Sheela's accounts without being filtered back through Savita.

Things were further complicated by the fact that Deeksha had her own bank accounts within the Ashram—as well as accounts that had nothing to do with the Ashram. She had come aboard as a reported multimillionaire and donated heavily to Bhagwan—but she always retained control of the bulk of her funds. Later on, this began to irritate Sheela, who had control over the financial purse strings of every department *except* Deeksha's. Deeksha could have a dormitory built or buy pounds of gold for her jewelry shop on a whim.

Money generated by Deeksha's enterprises was supposed to be channeled right back into her empire as operating or development capital—or into the Ashram, if there was a surplus.

If she got any flack from the office about how much was being spent on something, Deeksha would simply use her own money and proceed. There was no stopping her when her mind was made up; she would simply blow through any office attempt to block her. For all the complaints that were raised about her empire, the fact is that she took better care of her workers than the Ashram did of the rest of us.

Greek Mukta, who is connected with the Onassis family, is a very wealthy woman who reportedly gave millions to the Ashram. She ran the gardening department and operated independently of the office at times. If one of her people needed help, she would give them cash or whatever to tide them over, and never consult Savita or Sheela.

However, every department that did not have Deeksha or Sheela in charge was accountable for every single *paise*. The most trivial discrepancy was regarded as a failure; the "meditation" had broken down. Vrindavan and Sheela's discretionary accounts were really the only exception to this ironclad system of bookkeeping.

One of the largest enterprises they oversaw was the book department, which ultimately produced some five hundred titles in India and the United States—with only fifty produced by outside publishers. That's an impressive list for an independent publishing house. It involved full photographic and design facilities, and translation of those books originally in Hindi into English. It also handled extensive mail order requests from individuals as well as shipments to Rajneesh centers and bookstores worldwide.

The Ashram was also supporting a full medical center, with all the research facilities attached; a dental clinic; the "groups" department; the boutique, including the mills that produced the material in the accepted spectrum of shades of red, yellow, orange; the theater company; the jewelry department (separate from Deeksha's); the hydroponic farm; and numerous other undertakings. An entire department was responsible for looking after Bhagwan and maintaining Lao Tzu house, including people to rebind all books for his library or—if not actually rebinding them—making sure they were kept outside for ten days, being fanned constantly, so no trace of odor would linger. Just keeping the Ashram proper running smoothly employed about 1,500 people— which seems understaffed, when you realize the amount of work they were doing.

Donations tended to be in larger amounts—$10,000 was considered "modest"—from people who could afford it. No one I knew donated, say, a few hundred dollars, because they felt that was too small to be worthy of being called a "donation." No one would *say* that to you, it was just an impression people picked up on. On the scale of things, $50,000 was a more "reasonable" donation—but a large number of people actually donated *a million or more*.

Since there was never a financial statement issued, only a handful of people were privy to anything like the Ashram's full financial picture. And even this would be incomplete, because of certain "reserve" amounts known only to one individual. Savita would have known the most. Laxmi could always take a look at the books or ask for a full accounting, but she never did, since that was distasteful to her. At this point Sheela would get such information by suggesting to Laxmi that they ought to look at the books for some reason that she would make up. However, with Laxmi away so much, Sheela had a much freer hand to say, simply, "I want to look at the books."

One time a dope dealer brought in over a million dollars in cash in a suitcase, and they had to sit and count it. Sheela said, "We're not going to say anything about this, because we don't want to spotlight so-and-so." This "donor" had been brought in to work in one of the departments as just another *sannyasin*, since he was going undercover for a time.

It was around this time that Sheela began instilling paranoia, emphasizing the idea that you could be ripped off in the outside world, but never in the Ashram. She began to talk of threats to the Ashram from inside the walls. Soon everyone became suspicious of everyone else, and no one compared notes: the ideal setup for corruption. Not saying anything about the suitcase full of money was to protect a friend of the Ashram, because *"they* were after him." Even within the circle at the top, Sheela suggested, you might not know who could be trusted. Though they might be loyal at present, you could never know who might "wobble" at some later date and put themselves in league with the shadowy *"them"* outside the Ashram.

So the cash went into the fund for buying things—especially those things best paid for with cash-up-front. *Sannyasins* running errands to the West could also be supplied with the "ready." The intrigue, the fact that nobody knew what we were doing, certainly made it more exciting to play the game.

The "suitcase man" went to work in one department; his wife went to work in another. No one thought anything about this. But then a "miracle" happened: they were suddenly moved into Krishna House after a week. The handful of office insiders knew why they'd been moved; but everybody else decided they had been singled out because there was something extra-specially "meditative" about them. It was generally presumed that Bhagwan had recognized in them some of his former followers from that time so many hundreds of years before.

Other people would give less dubious amounts of cash. When Americans wanted to donate cash, they were encouraged to do it through Chidvilas center. They might never know that the funds were going to stay in America in a Chidvilas account, since they would get an official letter of thanks from India signed by "Ma Anand Sheela."

This was the sort of correspondence that Sheela kept in her "S" or "Sheela" files. The original of the letter above, for example, would go to the person in America, and the copy would go into the "S" file. If a letter accompanying a donation requested a book or tape, only a *copy* of

our acknowledgment for a donation and the assurance that the requested materials would be sent "under separate cover" would be forwarded
to the mail-order department with that part circled. Once again, the
original donation letter and a copy of our response donation letter
would go into the "S" file.

There were different sections of this file. While the "S" file had a
copy of every single letter that had been typed for Sheela, the "S-2"
held all original letters for which only this one copy existed. Any correspondence encoded "S" was never to go outside the office.

The "S" file would be used for Sheela's notes recording things that
had happened or comments on certain people and what they were up
to. It also held all the typewritten notes that Sheela had taken in to
Bhagwan.

When she fled the Ranch in Oregon, she managed to take all these
files with her, at least as far as anyone can determine. These records include all Bhagwan's written directives to her—including some that
show, contrary to his protestations that he knew nothing about what
was going on, that he knew *everything*. In these notes she tells him
clearly what's happening, what they're up to, and asks him specifically
for direction. My guess is that these are in Germany somewhere. I've
also heard that she has fourteen videotapes of her private sessions with
him, since at one point they stopped writing down everything and she
would just videotape the meetings.

Looking back over this mosaic of events and impressions, it's easy to
trace how surely and steadily Sheela was beginning to steer the rapidly
growing Ashram towards America and eventual collapse.

But at the time we still saw her in a golden light, for all that she
seemed ruthless or devious. She believed that she was working for a
cause—something outside of herself that sanctioned anything and everything she did in the name of that cause. Later, this changed. But, for
now, she saw her every move as calculated to further Bhagwan's message. Like the rest of us, she was watching herself grow; we were working for this greater cause, Bhagwan, because we really did believe he
had something important to give to the world. It was important for
people to at least *hear* what he had to say, whatever their final decision
about it might be.

CHAPTER 17

Growing Pains, Pleasures— and Paranoia

Laxmi, Deeksha, and Sheela formed a sort of steering triumvirate at this time. Laxmi was looking for the "new commune"; Deeksha was expanding her empire; and Sheela was taking more and more charge of the day-to-day functioning of the Ashram. She was taking it upon herself to answer routine correspondence, handle requisitions from various departments—things that would normally have come to Laxmi—except that Laxmi was so overloaded at this time that she welcomed the redistribution of responsibilities. At the same time, this helped consolidate power in Sheela's hands.

These were exciting times for us all—watching the Ashram grow in quantum leaps and mega-bounds. This was dramatically shown in the growth of Buddha Hall: By early 1980 the cloth roof had been replaced with a very smart, white, permanent roof.

The ritual aspects surrounding Bhagwan's lectures also increased. Now, about ten minutes before he arrived, one of his chairs (which were specially made by Asheesh, who ran the *mala* shop) would be positioned on stage. It would have a cover on it that would be taken off and folded to be used immediately after the lecture, when the chair would be taken back to Lao Tzu House. Where Bhagwan entered Buddha Hall, there was now an elegant podium of white Carrara marble. Even the pathway he walked from his car to the auditorium was inlaid marble. And Buddha Hall itself was surrounded by huge flower beds bursting with brightly colored flowers and lots of greenery—all shaded by tall, graceful trees. One of the gardening department's duties was to see to it that *every leaf* was picked out of the gardens *by hand*. No dead matter was to remain on the soil between plants or on the lawns around the flower beds.

A Japanese landscape architect came to visit and created a special bamboo garden, with plants almost a foot in diameter that had the deep, deep green of malachite. Everywhere we turned we enjoyed beauty. There wasn't a corner of the grounds or a building that wasn't in some way idyllic. Even a simple cleaning hut where a few buckets were stored was made of fine woods, and handsomely finished off.

This was all stage dressing, but it seemed very appropriate. Our feelings about this were best expressed some years later, when Sheela first asked Bhagwan about getting him a Rolls Royce. Her reasoning was, "He has *nothing*, but he gives us *so much* of his being. A Rolls Royce means nothing to him; but at least we can give him the best car in the world." He was our Master, and we wanted to give him things to show our love for him. The impression was never that he expected or demanded such things; they were *bestowed* on him by the *sannyasins*. It was our own "neurosis" that made us want to give these things to him. And the luxurious new additions felt like they belonged to all of us—those living in, or at least working in, the Ashram.

At the same time this tied into the idea that Bhagwan was a "mirror" for each of us. We saw all this display as an outward sign of Bhagwan's own enlightenment—and it was a reminder of what could happen to us when we became enlightened. Though the paradox is that, when you become enlightened, such things don't matter.

In between Jesus House and Eckhart there was a vegetable garden. Here the Ashram gardeners gathered for tea every afternoon at 3 P.M. Tea would be served in immense tea urns, which required two people to lift them, using bamboo poles. Every department stopped work and took *chai* in their meeting place. These gatherings were an opportunity to chat, but they could also be used for meetings between department heads or general discussions or putting forward new ideas. The general rule of speaking only "the needful" was relaxed—though this directive applied far more to other departments in the Ashram than to office personnel. They were always worried that we would talk about what we were doing. By the end of 1979 it was being stressed more and more that we talk less and less to other people.

In general, all the departments met with their supervisors after lecture. Over this morning tea, assignments for the day would be delegated. You would never know ahead of time what you were going to be doing each day. Even if it seemed that you'd been doing the same job forever, you would still have to check each morning to be sure that was the task you would still be performing. You could never get settled into a routine—no matter how much it might seem like one, you were trained to question things every day.

Early on the gardening department built a small tea house for itself in the vegetable garden—just large enough to accommodate its own people. Later, they built a huge tea house out of bamboo and woven rushes behind Buddha Hall. The general office staff met informally on the terrace outside of Krishna House; individual departments met in their own offices. Those of us in the inner circle held our meetings in the crystal cave.

Sheela kept a low profile as she orchestrated much of the explosive growth of the Ashram, but Deeksha was a highly visible force behind the rapid expansion of many of the commune's key operations.

When she took over Vrindavan was only a small kitchen with a few small round tables with stools. Above the kitchen she built an addition where she put a bedroom for herself and a guest bedroom, with a balcony outside. This is where she began making the clothes for her staff. Before she had used items from the boutique, or had sent her shoppers around to buy necessary items from Indian retailers on Mahatma Gandhi Road or a shop on Center Street that had only items in orange fabric. In short order she had four seamstresses working Vrindavan, producing a set style that became known as "Deeksha" dresses!

Deeksha set the trends, particularly in clothing. In addition to her own staff she had special clothes made for, and took care of, certain other people whom she had taken under her wing on impulse. Shortly after Laxmi had gone off in search of the "new commune," Deeksha decided it was time to make Sheela a whole new wardrobe. Sheela had always dressed quite well, but now she was suddenly outfitted in "very Deeksha" fashions.

They had always been friends; but Deeksha had always run things her own way, free of any interference from the office. Bhagwan had stressed that she was to be let alone to do things whatever way she wanted to. It was typical of Deeksha to focus suddenly on someone (as she had done with me), have all their clothes given away, and outfit them in new things from head to toe.

Though Sheela complained about "not being able to wear my funky old things," she was clearly delighted with the results. She suddenly looked very smart, and loved being the center of Deeksha's attention for this brief time.

Deeksha moved on impulse—and, characteristically, never did things halfway. One day she stripped out the whole of Vrindavan.

Originally, only part of it—where the kitchen was located—was covered; the unroofed portion was for seating. Suddenly, Deeksha had all the freestanding tables and chairs hauled outside, ripped out the built-ins, and put in brand-new tables inside and all through the garden outside. She expanded the kitchen area and increased the entire food service.

A few months after that she built a mezzanine overlooking the garden. Everything was white, built along very simple lines, and decorated with gorgeous paintings, some brought in from outside, some the handiwork of Ashramites—as well as a striking selection of photographs of Bhagwan.

The restaurant was self-service; the food was all Indian but very Westernized and mild. Then Deeksha decided to redo the menu so it included tofu and tempe burgers, minestrone soup, and delicious desserts—a whole range of healthy, Westernized food that was an immediate hit with everybody in the Ashram.

She didn't confine her efforts to Vrindavan. Not long after revamping the restaurant, she got a bee in her bonnet and trundled all her right-hand people over to Miriam Canteen, which she had decided to take over. She simply ousted Sagar, the German manager of the place, started moving people around, and announced, "This food is terrible: we're going to redo it all." She arranged to have huge batches of food cooking in Vrindavan, and would send portions of this over to Miriam.

Sagar seemed happy enough to give over control of the place. It *was* hard to run; he'd gotten into a rut with the limited Indian menu they served. He continued to work as a supervisor, but Deeksha's hand-picked people were actually managing the place. But there was no resentment: When Deeksha began such a project, it was always "high energy," and people rode on that. Before Deeksha took an interest in running it, Miriam was pretty laid-back: It got the job done, that was all. When her people were in, nobody could get away with long breaks at the back gate and so forth. Everyone had to give full attention to their work. If there was one thing she was an ace at, it was going to a situation that was total chaos and sorting it out. She might create a whole new chaos for a time, but she got the job done—and the results were always solid.

Once Miriam was functioning to her liking, she decided it should do more than simply *sell* soy products: It should grow the beans and prepare the tofu and tempe in the kitchens. So, above Miriam, she set up rooftop gardens to grow the soybeans.

Things didn't stop there.

Behind Vipassana-Go-Down, the dormitory, she built twelve beauti-ful single rooms. This was unusual, because it was almost impossible to get a room to yourself in the Ashram; each normally housed three peo-ple. But no one challenged her on the design since she was using her own money to finance it. She managed the "handyman" department, so she used her own workers to construct it. Everybody else was ex-pected to go to the office for initial assignments, but people could also bypass the office and go directly to Deeksha and ask for work.

When the new rooms were under construction, there was a lot of in-terest in who was going to be assigned to them. Were they to bring in more people to live inside the Ashram? Or were they going to be por-tioned out to those of us who were already Ashramites? The latter would still create additional space for newcomers.

Deeksha moved her right-hand people into five of the new rooms. She had gotten permission to build it by promising the office that the Ashram could have seven for its own use. But, since these went to peo-ple who had given large donations, it really didn't free up much space for the average Ashramite.

Things were happening all over the Ashram—and outside the im-mediate walls. The medical center, which had previously been located at 120 Koregaon Park, now bought the building at 70, immediately be-hind and adjoining the Ashram proper, at 17. The new property was a huge, two-story house, with immense gardens. They turned the down-stairs into the medical facility, and kept the upper floor residential. There were also a number of smaller huts on one side of the property, where they made scentless soaps and shampoos. On the far side of the house they built a bakery to supply all the breads and desserts for the two restaurants, which had really started taking off.

Technically, the office governed all this; but Makima, who ran the medical center, oversaw the other enterprises at 70. By 1972 there were also some huts where Ashramites were living. Just behind the medical center they built a huge concrete platform, roofed it over, and turned it into a discotheque. Nearby they added a sauna and rooms where you could pay to get a massage. They also built a huge hut as a communal house for the Ashram's children—some fourteen kids. This took the pressure off living situations where kids would be sharing a room with their parents and someone else. The children were delighted, and the parents raised no objections.

Number 70 was rented from some sort of maharishi, who would come down once a year to inspect the property. Everybody would have to take all his furniture—these incredible antiques, worth a fortune—

out of storage and replace it, because the property had been rented furnished. Number 80 was rented from a private individual. Number 17, the Ashram itself, had been purchased outright years before.

The boutique was expanded at this time; the gardens were finished off. The hydroponic planting was in full swing near a house at 80 Koregaon Park. The cleaning department got a separate "cleaning booth" on the corner of Buddha Hall, on the way to Jesus House. There was now a plumbing and electrical department, which was moved out of Rada Hall into Lao Tzu. They even opened up a dental office at this time.

The whole place was really buzzing. They put a screen-printing studio on top of Jesus House, which is where Deeksha established her "launderette." It had washers and dryers and ironers unlike anything existing in India at the time. The *mala* shop was expanded, as was the "group" department, which had more and more groups all over the place—wherever there was a house rented.

Where we once "left our shoes and mind at the gate," and went about our business peacefully enough, *now*, after the assassination attempt on Bhagwan, we were required to walk through metal detectors for every lecture. It became the cleaning department's responsibility to build a structure where you would check in your bags, purses, shoes, all those things—hundreds and hundreds of people at a time. This also helped solve the problem of sorting through several hundred pairs of shoes after lecture—and the growing headache of items "disappearing."

The attempt on Bhagwan's life woke us up to the idea that he might die. People got panicky that if they weren't "surrendered" enough, he would leave his body. So, along with the good feeling that things were really coming together, was the growing fear that Bhagwan, who had set this whole experiment in motion, might just as easily decide to abandon it. As always, we were never allowed to get *too* complacent.

At the end of 1979 a restaurant was opened at 70 for non-Ashramites. It was open for lunch and dinner. At first it was used by those non-*sannyasins* who worked at 70, or by *sannyasins* who weren't working. It was designed as a proper restaurant, with full menus for everything from salads to ice cream desserts. Unlike Miriam or Vrindavan, it had table service. The whole of 70, plus all the expanded or new services at 17, added up to a small, self-supporting town.

Up to this point Bhagwan's books were either being published in the West, or being printed in Bombay from manuscripts prepared in the Ashram. But, in 1980, they brought printing presses and bookbinding equipment into the Ashram and built a bindery behind Buddha Hall. They did beautiful first editions, and also rebound books for Bhagwan's personal library in red silk with gold embossing—a picture of Bhagwan with a circle around it saying *Thou art that*.

Between Buddha Hall and Krishna House they pulled up the gardens and erected another office building. On the lower floor, in one section, were typists who would use Bhagwan's "quotation book" for answering letters; the other main section had batteries of typists handling routine typing, transcripts of Bhagwan's lectures, translations of those discourses given in Hindi, and so forth. On the floor above were the art, design, and photographic studios used by the publishing department to prepare the books for press. There was also some accounting done on this level.

The guards who were stationed at the front and back gates of the Ashram, at 70, and at Music House no longer simply sat on chairs: they now had proper guard booths made of bamboo, three-sided and roofed. This was typical of the overall change: We were moving from funky to a level of real professionalism.

More and more people attending more and more groups meant a dramatic increase in workers. The pay restaurant at 70 began to make basic lunches that were provided to the workers there who had food passes, since Miriam Canteen could no longer handle everyone. By the end of 1980 a restaurant was created at Music House—which, with the dormitory huts in use there, was now called Somji Estates, to accommodate the Ashramites living there.

By this time no more space was available on the Ashram grounds to house people. Additional apartments were rented near Somji Estates, and later all around town, to absorb the overflow of bodies. There were probably 300 people living and working in 70. Somji Estates was another 350. The additional people scattered around town added about another 1,000 Ashramites to the 1,500 already living and working at 17 Koregaon Park.

The next major innovation was the installation of two *samadhi* flotation tanks in yet another acquired property, 120 Koregaon Park. It was used for group training in use of the tanks, as well as other sessions in massage and so forth.

The Ashram expanded steadily—not by acquiring properties and then filling these with Ashramites; but by purchasing or renting well-maintained houses where groups of *sannyasins* were already living.

The town of Poona was changing in response to the Ashram's dramatic growth. By the end of 1979 the Blue Diamond Hotel, which catered to wealthy *sannyasins*, was enlarged to include Western-style amenities, including a pool, a menu reflecting Ashram tastes—even the hotel boutique shifted from traditional Indian souvenirs to orange clothing and Indian replicas of materials being produced in the Ashram. Many items duplicating Ashram designs were now being shipped routinely to the West by Indian manufacturers.

It was no longer necessary to travel to Bombay or bring in betterquality fabrics from abroad. Now a walk down Mahatma Gandhi Road revealed that most of the goods displayed in the clothing stores were orange, and much improved in quality. Almost all the fabric on sale was confined to the red spectrum. Even the shoes, underwear, and handkerchiefs on sale were orange.

The Ashram was visibly contributing to Poona's economic growth. It still had the beggars, the dogs, the *beedee wallahs*—so the exotic flavor of the place was still there for us. But more and more apparent was the "orange" influence: new buildings were going up; much more merchandise filled the stores. While we Ashramites had very few possessions, the *sannyasins* visiting from the West for celebration days and such were passionate consumers. They would go into town and shop, shop, *shop*.

Inside 17 Koregaon Park, the boutique expanded again, and more kinds of items were offered for sale. In time visitors from the West were buying almost exclusively from the Ashram. From people producing souvenir boxes in the *mala* shops to the seamstresses producing dresses to workers preparing food for sale in the restaurants—*everybody* felt the wealth flowing in. We appreciated it as an indicator of just how successful our efforts were, and how the Ashram was blossoming.

None of us ever felt we were entitled to a share of all the money the Ashram was making: We felt we were already getting the benefit of it, as it was clearly being pumped back into the Ashram. For some eighteen months, while the commune functioned at its peak, it was very exciting to watch the marble podium go up in Buddha Hall or the buildings expand with a Western solidity, rather than the cloth-and-bamboo Indian-style additions we had been so familiar with.

An interesting note: Though the structures had a "permanent" feel to them, they were all *collapsible*. They could all be dismantled at any time and moved on. This *again* reinforced the idea that the "new commune" would be inside India; the prefabricated buildings were beautifully designed to look good—yet they could be knocked down in twenty-four hours and loaded on an ox cart for immediate transport. So that, even while we were aware of change and expansion within the Ashram, the portable nature of the additions kept reminding us that the "new commune" was drawing nearer.

The changes were also upgrading our Ashramite lifestyle. Before, along with living space and food passes, we had been supplied with clothing—but most of this was secondhand, often patched-up. As Deeksha began to make more and more clothes for her shop and her own people, she would more frequently single out other Ashramites— paying special attention to people in the office or Lao Tzu—and start clothing them. As more money filtered down to divisions like the cleaning department, they would begin making arrangements to clothe their own workers.

Pretty soon Sheela began giving her staff certificates to the boutique. This program was later expanded so that all department heads were allocated a certain number of certificates per month to use at their discretion to provide for people in their departments. So, although the boutique was primarily a money-making venture, it also became a kind of clothes warehouse for other divisions. In the beginning, people would simply draw off the boutique stock. Later, Deeksha started making clothes in bulk in her sewing shop and *selling* these to the boutique—things like basic handyman or cleaning outfits. In return she got cash back that went to her discretionary funds, or credit for items she might need that would have to be produced by a department not directly under her control.

Also thriving with all the growth was the Ashram's jewelry department. It was formed quite by accident. Bhagwan gave out a series of cufflinks to people as gifts—some fourteen pairs. One woman took one of these to a friend who worked in the *mala* shop, a man who was doing woodworking but had been a jeweler. She asked him to turn the cufflink into a ring, which she would pay him for as a side job. So he did, making the gold-and-ruby cufflink the centerpiece.

When Sheela saw the results she wanted a ring made for Chinmaya. Then somebody else wanted the same, and so it went. Pretty soon the Ashram decided to form a separate jewelry department. It was typical that whenever the office saw an opportunity for a commercial venture, it would move on it right away . . . though the prime mover in all this rapid growth was really Deeksha. Sheela *loved* being around Deeksha and drawing energy from her.

Deeksha would have extravagant banquets in the evening, with fine china and all the extras. She would use these to try out new dishes that would ultimately find their way onto the menu at Vrindavan or the pay restaurant at 70. These dinners were always very cliquish, with special attention given to people in the office. They underscored the fact that, though we were all meant to be "equal," the office workers separated themselves off. People on the outside would look at us as though there was something "special" about us.

Deeksha seemed to get a perverse joy out of spotlighting this fact, and would orchestrate her banquets to stress this by inviting all the so-called leaders. Those excluded would say, "This is awful: It's just a 'superior' trip." To which Deeksha would say, "Yes, it is. But what's *your* trip that you're reacting to it this way?"—the stock Ashram reply to any kind of anger or resentment. She could be counted on to enliven the proceedings by stirring up things with a kind of malicious amusement.

Sheela, on the other hand, loved to be exclusive in this way. I think we all thought we were "above corruption," having denied ourselves so many things for so many years, having worked so many hours each day, seven days a week. In a way, too, I think we needed to reinstall some kind of "reward system" to keep people channeling their energies away from the Ashram's very real need for increased output and higher efficiency. Invitations to these feasts, the sudden gift of a new wardrobe, these brought people into the richness of it all, the "game" of it all.

But some things remained unchanged, including the obsessive attention to detail. The office staff was growing to keep pace with things. Vidya, who took care of immediate Ashram affairs, suddenly got an assistant, who took over as her right-hand person. She was very sweet-tempered: an American who had been living in London for quite a number of years, where she had helped run the big center. She was short and skinny, attractive in a cute sort of way, with an air of innocence about her. When things fell apart she was one of the ones who left with Sheela, so she seemed to have bought into the whole trip by then.

I'm not sure exactly how she got her position with Vidya, presumably it was through knowing someone. Most people were brought into the office because they had a connection there. To that extent we bought into the same kind of patronage system that exists in so many Western businesses and political circles. Vidya and her assistant were quickly making joint decisions on a variety of matters; within three months the assistant's role began to change. While somebody might apply directly to Vidya for a job change, he or she would go to the assistant to get the decision and particular directions.

Even this right-hand person idea started with Deeksha. She would have her chosen handful at her side literally every minute. As she walked around doing her inspection of the kitchen, for instance, she might suddenly decide, "This place is filthy!" Even if they were in the middle of serving meals, she might decide it was time for a deep cleaning. Everything would begin being ripped apart that instant. At this point her entourage would sweep into action to carry out her orders. If anything went wrong, one or the other of these would be held responsible. Most of them were women: Shantam, who headed the handymen, was virtually the only man (except for Asheesh, who ran the *mala* shop) who was in charge of a department—and he would directly defer to Deeksha. If there was any matter he needed addressed directly to the office, it would be delivered by Deeksha.

When Deeksha was on one of her sweeps, everybody simply got out of the way—generally with good grace. If she was in the restaurant, she'd hurry patrons who had already purchased their food outside, then hang the CLOSED sign out before any new customers could come in. The clean-up would have to be done pretty quickly, since Vrindavan especially was used by so many people not only for meals, but for snacks and breaks. Some would actually have to do without lunch or whatever. In cases like this her impulses were a source of real irritation. But she was insulated because Bhagwan had talked about her so much, and had called her an incredible "Zen master." We weren't to argue with anything she did, but simply "go with it." She was looked upon as a kind of living Zen koan—a "meditation in motion," if you will.

Looking at her whims in this light made it easy to defuse whatever resentment you might have. On the other side of the coin, however, people who worked for Deeksha were often very scared of her. I can't pinpoint exactly what the source of that fear was, but the fact was that Deeksha could ruin your whole day if she had a mind to. And she had unlimited power and unlimited *carte blanche* from Bhagwan. You could be sure that you were never going to get the better of any run-in with her. For those who were dependent on her for room and board, her wrath could be even more devastating, since she could turn off the supply of favors as easily as she could put you on the receiving end.

While someone from the outside might question such seemingly erratic behavior, it never occurred to those of us in the Ashram to wonder about it. Bhagwan always reinforced anyone like Deeksha with the message that there was "method in her madness." If you couldn't see this, the implication ran, there was something wrong with *you—never* with Deeksha or her approach.

During this period of very intense growth, when everyone was feeling energized, Bhagwan would actually encourage the more impulsive behavior of people like Deeksha. If anyone suggested that this was actually making *more* work, Bhagwan would repeat, "We are a mystery school. What would sometimes seem the most logical course of action may not be the most constructive view of growth."

There were a million little sayings to support the way we were being. And, though it might *seem* like total chaos, things *were* getting done. The Ashram *was* expanding; people were getting housed, clothed, fed. Amid all this growth the systems *were* operating efficiently. Nor was anything sacrificed in terms of the quality of life: For all the new buildings that went up, new gardens were designed around them. Although it was only five acres, the place always felt extremely spacious.

Still, for all the exciting growth and dreams of soon moving to the "new commune," the one attempt on Bhagwan's life left a lingering undercurrent of fear in the Ashram. We found ourselves looking at visiting Indians suspiciously. If somebody moved in a sudden way during lecture, you'd come alert to that person and watch him or her. The security arrangements changed completely. Once there had been a single guard near Bhagwan; now guards, supervised by Shiva, were dotted throughout the crowds in Buddha Hall. They were very much in evidence, where before they had always tended to blend into the crowd and keep a low profile. During lecture they would continually move their heads to survey the whole auditorium, and were positioned at such angles that everything was under surveillance at all times. But they were taught to move their heads very slowly, so as not to disturb others by frantically bobbing their heads all over the place.

At times trouble from the outside was not so unlikely. The Sikhs were often stirring up things. There were conflicts between Moslems and Hindus—and sometimes this would spill over into Moslem opposition to the Ashram, since it was so firmly rooted in Hindu traditions. It was feared that the trouble in Iran might ripple through the Iranian community in Poona, including the people who ran the restaurant in the Blue Nile Hotel, which was put "off limits" for a time. If trouble seemed to focus on a particular part of town or a particular apartment house where *sannyasins* were staying, the Ashram would move quickly to get people out of potential danger zones.

India was a "guru state," and quite a number of Indians were attracted to Bhagwan: but they really had to push to get inside. Bhagwan had little sympathy for the native-born, by and large, though he did take good care of his family. His mother, father, and three brothers (one of whom was mentally ill) were *Jains* who lived in a separate house in the Ashram.

Bhagwan clearly had a high regard for his father, whom we called Dadaji: When Dadaji died, Bhagwan declared him "enlightened" at *darshan*—the first *samadhi* among people living in the commune. One brother, Surrendra, was a very gentle man, who worked in the legal department; the other was an M.D., working in the clinic, who was abrasive and not very popular—he was on far too much of an ego trip for the general taste. The mother would often come to the office to weep and wail and complain to Sheela because she had no easy access to Lao Tzu House. After her husband's death, however, she was allowed to visit more often. She and the three sons later moved to the Ranch in Oregon.

But, just when we would find it easy to slip into the illusion that things were fine, with guards at the gates and good feelings of peace and achievement everywhere, and a sense of Bhagwan at the heart of things, like the proverbial shepherd keeping watch over his flocks by night—at these moments, we would be thrown off-kilter by Bhagwan's own paranoia.

In lecture one day he announced, "There's no point in guarding me from anyone from the outside, because the person who's going to kill me is going to be one of my disciples. And it will be one of my closest disciples."

Thus he began the road to inward paranoia for everyone. Now, not only were we looking at each other, but many of us began looking at *ourselves*. The immediate intense feeling would be, *Oh, I could never do that.* And then the thought would come up, *I hope I could never do that.* From that point on I began to doubt myself.

In retrospect, I think that inner paranoia was what destroyed us, because we were no longer a secure, trusting, single-minded body. If they hadn't been so harsh on everybody, it might have worked out all right. But it went from paranoia as an intellectual exercise to paranoia as a way of life. In short order you'd find yourself wondering every time people said, "Trust me," what was *really* in their minds—why did they have to stress the need for trust?

Up until that point trusting or not trusting had never been an issue. Raising the possibility suddenly flooded our minds with all sorts of new ideas. We could no longer simply do a job, giving all our attention to that job. Now a part of our awareness was always on the lookout for the potentially dangerous person, for the threat to Bhagwan.

We were less concerned about physical threats to our well-being (after all, we routinely coped with things like dysentery and worse), than about the possiblity of losing our Master. When he first announced the threat I felt an immediate willingness to lay my life on the line to protect *his*. Before this happened, when I'd hear of martyrs or heroes who had given up their lives for a cause, I'd think, *What an incredible person!* Having gone through this in the Ashram, I now think it's much less a selfless act than one of reverse egoism. I view it as being full of ego: Some part of the mind is assuring you you'll be in the *Rajneesh Times* for your "selfless" action.

We had been looking at each other with love, but now we looked with love tinged with suspicion. We had initially been taught that true love is unconditional, is freedom, is completely supportive of who the other person is and what he does. Now we loved unconditionally—but with the mental reservation that we were going to keep an eye out to see that the other person didn't hurt a third party who was also loved.

This conditioned us to *mis*trust and opened us to more direct manipulation from higher-ups. This connected very directly with what we had been taught all along in the office: that whatever you did there was private, and you just didn't talk about it outside. This was understood both by the staff and by people outside the office. It wasn't done to question the office: People seemed to make up their own ideas of what went on in there. And they seemed happy enough to let the office have its own way, provided it performed functions like keeping away the Indians or later, in the United States, keeping away the "feds."

At the end, I think Sheela was getting it from both sides: Bhagwan was telling her, "Whatever you have to do, do it! I just don't want to know what you do." And everybody else was telling her, "No one cares how you do it, just do it!" In the aftermath, no one was about to admit that they urged her to do anything: It was seen as all *her* doing.

In the office we were all being quiet about what was happening—just as what went on at Lao Tzu was kept under wraps. But a steady trickle of stories from Lao Tzu reminded us of the joy that still seemed so much a part of the Ashram—and that kept Bhagwan very human (and very real) to us.

One night, for example, while Bhagwan was in the bath getting ready for *darshan*, and he was all lathered up, the water pump blew. One of the guards, who'd only been in Lao Tzu a very short time, came running out and told us we'd have to get a bucket brigade going to get the soap off Bhagwan. This struck me and many others as a riot, and made him that much more real to us. There was a lot of very happy, good-natured laughing as buckets were run in and out of Lao Tzu House, and it became almost a communal act of love, this rendering unto Bhagwan the rinse that was needed.

However, the guard who had told everybody about the "soap-sudded guru" got dragged into the office and creamed by Vidya, who did Sheela's dirty work. "How can you ridicule the Master?" she demanded, "How could you do that? What is your ego trip that you have to let people know you're working in Lao Tzu?" The fellow was immediately bounced *out* of Lao Tzu for "humiliating" Bhagwan and wound up working at one of the "outer estates" in Poona.

My impression is that this was totally Sheela's attitude: At that time Bhagwan would most likely have laughed the whole thing off as a wonderful irony. When Sheela first rose into power Bhagwan *was* loved. And Laxmi, when she was in control, never worried about Bhagwan that way: It would never occur to her that a silly little incident like that could hurt him. With Laxmi away in search of the "new commune," however, Bhagwan became Sheela's complete responsibility—rather like being left to babysit a precious child: It's easy to become overprotective. Sheela was totally devoted to the Master; she was hurt by even the *idea* that someone could laugh at Bhagwan. I think that if she could have wrapped him up in cotton-wool to be sure nothing happened to him, she would have.

When she was first coming into power, although she had a desire to control, it wasn't coming from a negative place. I think she honestly believed that she could take care of Bhagwan best. It was the same way when she would watch Laxmi's dealings with America and know—because she, Sheela, had been there—how much better a job she could do. If there was a frustration for her about the soap-suds incident, it was a sense of guilt over the fact that he had been entrusted to her care and no one could even keep the water pumps running properly for him. He was staying in his body to enlighten us (and we have to remember at all times that Sheela, Laxmi, and Bhagwan were Indians, with a particular way of looking at the world), and we can't even keep the soap out of his eyes.

Bhagwan was still at the "giggling" phase; but, the more Sheela came into power, the more he would listen to her. He could see her total devotion; he knew how familiar she was with the way the world—especially the Western world—worked. And I think that Sheela believed exactly what she said. More and more she saw America as an opportunity we could really move on; but at the same time some apprehension kept her from moving even more quickly, because she appreciated just how tricky such a move could be in a society so money-oriented.

When she was traveling back and forth to the United States and setting up bank accounts, she seemed to be saying, "We can only play with these people if we play with them on their own level." Although she tried to tell us that we wouldn't get caught up in the money thing if we kept it in perspective, it didn't work out that way. We fooled ourselves into thinking that we were ready to play in this arena, and we weren't. It was the realm of the "hungry ghost," which the Zen masters point out is one of the most dangerous zones the spirit can move through. We felt like living actors in a mystery play, but the script got out of hand.

Fear would be instilled by incidents like the demoted guard: It became clear that the least infraction of the rules (and you often didn't know that there *was* a rule until you'd broken it) could change your entire situation instantaneously and without appeal. At the same time we were being introduced more and more to the idea of hierarchies. If someone who had screwed up in Lao Tzu wound up as guard at Music House, it implied that Music House was a "punishment," and therefore an inferior situation. So a subtle pride of place within the Ashram complex became more and more evident.

It was ironic that, with the expansion, we could be more fluid in terms of placing people—but it also bred a contempt for certain jobs and certain situations and a concern for where you found yourself in the pecking order. It was almost as if the larger canvas of the new improved Ashram highlighted when you were moving "up the ladder" or sliding "down the snake" in terms of the Ashram organization. To be sent to the kitchen was apt to be seen as a punishment, rather than a unique learning position; a job in the office became a "promotion"; working in Lao Tzu meant reaching the highest level, a kind of *satori*.

Of course, none of this was officially approved or made explicit. People assumed this collectively, because in the office particularly we were taught never to use terms like "inferior" or "superior." But there's a way of giving lip service to something that implies something very different: It's easy for the president of the United States to sit in the White House, surrounded by aides and servants, and say, "Everybody is equal." The hierarchy was an unspoken fact of life in the office, for all that it was denied. If I had made that observation, however, I would have been kicked out of the office on the spot.

The fact is that, I *did* feel superior working in Krishna House. And I *did* work hard. I'd often be there counting money or whatever until 11:30 P.M., then stumble off to bed, only to be awakened by some little runner at 3 A.M., with the message "Sheela wants a cup of tea." So I'd fix her one and bring it to her. She might just as easily send word, "I can't sleep: Let's do dictation" or "design the new kitchen" or whatever. But part of me felt a glow at being one she would choose to wake up in the middle of the night to make *chai*.

More than ever it was stressed in the office that we were to keep really quiet about things. You *never* talked about the bank accounts that were being opened overseas, or Sheela's trips to the United States. Four of us worked in different ways for Sheela—and we were all told repeatedly not to speak to each other about what we were doing. We were instructed to cover our work (letters, files, and so on) whenever we left the room—and they were to be put away or taken with us if they were "S" files.

Most people, I suppose, would have let it go at that and done what they were told. For me, as soon as I was told *not* to bother with what other people were doing, that little "imp of the perverse" at the back of my mind would prick up its ears. I'd be going through the "S" files late at night to find out what everybody else had done that day.

The warnings about minding your own business went out to other departments, also. In the cleaning department, for example, people were told not to talk about what they may have seen in a room or overheard. Gossip during breaks was actively discouraged. *Total silence* became the rule for cleaners.

All these instructions made sense spiritually: Reflective silence is a very real way to avoid being distracted from meditation by useless talk or objects. But they also estranged people from one another and fed into the growing paranoia. People were now being constantly moved about, which increased the sense of discontinuity and uncertainty.

At the medical center patients were to have no visitors. The official rationale was, "We aren't a holiday camp. This is a mystery school, a meditation school." Around this time sleep therapy was begun on a fairly wide scale; people would be knocked out for long stretches of time to hurry the healing process. But, because we were still open, because suspicion hadn't really taken hold of our minds at this point, we were still able to view things like "no visitors when you're sick" as a meditation. It would never occur to you that something could be happening to someone there which we ought not to see.

There was a general crackdown on the laid-back approach to rules. When I first came to the Ashram, there was an easy flow of Ashramites and non-Ashramites through the gates. If you had a pass for lecture and decided not to attend, you might just hand it over to someone else. But all this changed as the place grew more efficient.

The main means of enforcing rules was still psychological manipulation. For example, if you were caught giving someone your lecture pass, you wouldn't be reprimanded as such; you would be hit on an emotional level. Humans feel better if they're punished for a misdeed; it evens the score. In the Ashram, however, you'd be interviewed by one of the office heavyweights, who'd stand there giving her best goddess impression and fixing you with characteristic puppy eyes. She would never raise her voice; she would just stand there with the improperly used lecture pass in her hand. With a shake of the head she'd ask sadly, *"Why* did you *do* this?"

You'd get an overwhelming sense that she was filled with love and compassion for this poor person who would stoop so low as to rip off Bhagwan. "Where are you coming from," the argument would run, "that you'd begrudge us this five *rupees* for lecture? The fee helps us all; it helps us keep Bhagwan here. Don't you see that, by doing this, you're not only taking from *Bhagwan"*—which was the same as telling a devout Catholic he'd just taken something away from the Pope—"but you're ripping *yourself* off? It doesn't matter to Bhagwan; you're the one who's being hurt." And so it would go, laying an emotionally charged guilt trip on the person, using the "compassionate" stance to leave them feeling absolutely wretched.

Actually, most of the "crimes" we had to deal with in the office were pretty minor at the beginning. I never heard of one person who stole from the boutique or *mala* shop or anything. But, as guards were brought in to float around and make sure no one *did* steal anything, things changed. It was the old self-fulfilling prophecy: Once you made it clear by posting extra guards that stealing *was* a possibility, it became inevitable.

By February 1980 Sheela was pretty much in full control. Laxmi was seeking the "new commune," and her visits to the Ashram were less and less frequent. The clearest evidence of Sheela's power was her increasingly tight rein on things, though it wasn't until they moved to America that Sheela was put in total control. Prior to that she would always be "acting" spokesperson "because Laxmi was away." Though Bhagwan *did* say in lecture one morning, "Whatever Sheela or the office tells you to do is coming directly from me. Likewise, for anybody working for Deeksha in Vrindavan"—even he had to acknowledge that Deeksha was running a separate empire within the Ashram.

In 1980 the lecture passes, which were simply designed with your name on it, were replaced with much more elaborate cards with your photograph on them, sealed in plastic to prevent tampering. These were first issued on a celebration day as "celebration passes"—but we were then told to keep them as official I.D. within the Ashram. Initially, the accounts department had requested this after they started to do their own foreign exchange for *sannyasins*, rather than send them to banks in Poona. The new cards were now proper identification for such transactions, since they also had our legal name, which was required by law for banking matters, picking up registered letters, and the like.

These were replaced soon after by color-coded cards. Sheela was becoming increasingly nervous that, as the Ashram grew, you no longer knew exactly who was who or who belonged where. Occasionally, a whacko *did* wander onto the grounds and create minor problems. But, given the growing edge of paranoia, it was only a matter of time before security was tightened even more. These color codings took care of a large part of that. The guards would have master maps of the Ashram and *all* the properties it owned, with sections keyed in color, so that they could tell who was to have access to a building or area and during what hours. These codings also indicated whether or not a person was an Ashramite, had a food pass, and so on. With the exception of a handful of us in the office and people in Lao Tzu House, few had total freedom to come and go at all times of the day.

Before, for example, a lot was done on trust: If you went for a meal to Miriam Canteen, it was simply assumed that you *wouldn't* be there *unless* you had a food pass. Suddenly, you had to show your I.D. card every time you went for a meal. This system both added to the prevailing paranoia and dramatically emphasized—in terms of the degree of clearance a person had been granted—just where everyone fit into the hierarchy. Someone with a red code would feel superior to someone with a blue code—though the official line maintained that codes reflected duties, not status; that it was simply to "regulate traffic" in the increasingly crowded Ashram. Again, anyone who would verbalize this idea of "superior/inferior" was accused of having an ego problem.

The dizzying sense of change at this time was capped by the announcement that Laxmi had, at last, found the "new commune."

CHAPTER 18

Saswad

In 1979 word flashed through the Ashram that Laxmi had at last bought the site of the "new commune" at Saswad, some two and a half hours (twenty-five miles) by bus outside of Poona, on a high plateau area. Bhagwan, we were told, had already confirmed it as the long-sought location. It was an old (maybe sixteenth-century) Moghul fortress, 40,000 square feet, with a stable and two wells attached; the two Indian brothers who sold it retained rights to cultivate the adjoining fields—though, according to reports, they later had several run-ins with *sannyasins*.

Laxmi straightaway sent some people out to begin the work of refurbishing the existing structures. To be among the first sent there was thought of as a "gift," and *sannyasins* were delighted to be a part of the "first wave." They worked very hard to get it ready for the proposed move.

Then, one day, Bhagwan announced that we are all going to go the next day and visit Saswad. Bhagwan was always the biggest game-player of them all: His announcement came out of the blue, in the middle of a lecture one morning, without a word of warning to the office. He was talking about moving, *within twenty-four hours,* some 2,500 people working in and around the Ashram. An estimated 1,500 visitors were also to be included in the excursion—plus anyone else who might turn up in the meantime and want to join in the trek. Eventually, some 7,000 made the journey.

We (the office staff) had one day to rent over fifty buses and arrange for more than two hundred private vehicles, including motorbikes, cars, and minibuses. Some were donated by *sannyasins*, others were rented. And then, of course, there was the "etcetera," which always distinguished any Ashram undertaking: It would never be a simple matter of renting a certain number of buses, loading everybody aboard, and driving out to the site for a quick glance. To begin with it was a major event, because most of us rarely left the Ashram. The fact that it was the long-looked-for "new commune" made it even more cause for celebration. Since we were talking about a mass exodus for the day, arrangements had to be made to keep the commune running on a skeleton staff and to rearrange agendas around this unanticipated holiday.

Practical considerations included food for a picnic lunch for the mob at Saswad, and plenty of water for the journey, because it was the hot season. And, since we could never do anything by halves—even though simply supplying "the needful" in such short order was a mind-boggling task—there were plenty of extras to be provided, such as *prasad*, which is considered a "gift for the gods" and a required part of any celebration in India. It consists of a small amount of food, like nuts; flower petals; and some dye which can be presented in a little box—but we were supplied this in little bags, because there were so many of us.

Bhagwan's apparently casual announcement sent the office into turmoil; we worked all night pulling things together. We were doing nothing less than arranging the movement of a whole town for the day. And we did it in style, even renting elephants to give a show as we were motoring along in buses.

The people already at Saswad had been alerted to prepare food so that, when the first travelers arrived, huge trestle tables set out with pots of food were waiting for them. And the fortress itself had been decorated festively—fitting for what was touted as "Rajneeshdham Neo-Sannyas International Commune."

It really was a beautiful site; and the first arrivals had done an impressive job of cleaning and building new rooms. It may have been thrown together on the spur of the moment, but the day went beautifully and everyone had a fine time. We returned home at the end of the day exhausted, but excited to have actually walked through the "new commune" that was, fittingly enough, rising on the foundations of the antique fortress. History was being made. We felt that we were simultaneously a part of history that reached far back through the centuries, beyond the time when the fortress walls were raised, back to the time when Bhagwan walked and taught in his previous incarnation. At the same time we were caught up in the business of creating our futures and the mystery school that was to be the culmination of Bhagwan's grand experiment.

The very next day Laxmi and Sheela began picking people to go and live at Saswad. At first only enough workers had been sent to clean up and prepare for the crowds that would follow. These second-wave transferees were told that they were to "put energy" into the place, as part of the long-range plan for moving into it. The fact that Laxmi had moved out there added to the belief that things were really going to happen there.

But the tone of Saswad changed very quickly: Being "sent to Saswad" began to mean being punished, as in "sent to Siberia"—especially for an Ashramite, who had full privileges in the commune. It also meant being isolated from Bhagwan. People who had journeyed halfway around the world to India just to be near him now found themselves cut off from seeing him at lecture, or *darshan*, or simply knowing he was a few yards away in Lao Tzu. And Bhagwan *never* went to Saswad.

The perception that the "gift" had turned into a "threat" came about in large part because of the pattern of selection. It was not just workers who were being bundled off to Saswad: There was an across-the-board selection of people who were perceived as a threat to Sheela.

Laxmi later returned to the Ashram; but a skeleton crew was left at Saswad during the remainder of the time the Ashram was based in India. With greater and greater frequency Sheela and Deeksha exiled people there as a punishment. Offenders would be sent on "two-week" stints that became indefinite stays. Once there, you simply weren't invited to return. Since few cars were available at the site, travel to and from was a major undertaking involving Indian buses—always an adventure! What's more, there would be no room at 17 Koregaon Park if you took it upon yourself to come back anyway. And Sheela and Deeksha, with Bhagwan's blessing, were answerable to no one for their actions.

Sheela would send people for no apparent reason—but often with malicious glee. On one occasion she invited Big Prem from the press office in to see her. They had a long chat about this and that, then Sheela told Big Prem, "You should write a book—" adding, after a suitably effective pause, "—in Saswad!"

Exit Big Prem.

If anyone had doubts about whether Saswad was, indeed, the "new commune," the slow evolution of the place, the fact that people and supplies trickled out to it rather than gushed, convinced even the true believers within a few months that Saswad was a dead end, not the road to the future.

When Bhagwan left Poona for Antelope a lot of the people at Saswad came back to the Ashram, only to find that they were even more isolated from the Master than they expected, since only those who were United States citizens could even go to Oregon. And few, if any, of them would be invited to the Ranch.

During this period I increasingly became an extension of Sheela. As a result I was granted a number of privileges that underscored my advanced standing in the Ashram. I could carry my shoes into lecture, because I might be called away at any moment to deal with an urgent bit of office business. I ignored the metal detectors. I also had a front-row seat in Buddha Hall whenever I chose to attend lecture or *darshan*. It was assumed that people in the office were "above reproach." This was, in part, why Sheela could do the things she did without anyone questioning her. Much later—long after the time when it could have done any good—Bhagwan said he should change secretaries every six months.

Sheela ordered a Rolls Royce for Bhagwan and had it shipped via Chicago, so that it could be armor-plated. But, with these larger things on her mind, she never lost her acute eye for details. One time, out of curiosity as to just how fine-tuned she was to routine matters in the office, I deliberately set aside several letters that she had dictated, but which I had not typed and mailed.

Two and a half months later, after we had sent out hundreds of similar letters, she casually mentioned that she knew I hadn't sent those particular letters out.

"I was seeing if you'd remember," I said.

"You're really testing me," she said. "You're the only person who's questioned me." She smiled a little and said, "It will be interesting the day you can beat me." Then she repeated, word-for-word, what had been in the "test" letters.

More and more, as Sheela took charge, we moved away from the idea that we were hundreds of individuals seeking enlightenment with only ourselves and our particular goals as the measure of whether we had succeeded or failed. Bhagwan was a teacher and a "mirror" to us of our own potential—but the focus was always *inward*. Now we were being told that we were to measure our own advancing or backsliding in light of how closely (or distantly) our actions and goals mirrored Bhagwan's teachings and how fully they reflected our selfless devotion to the Master. Before, a worker in the cleaning department would never waste a bit of soap because (on the mundane level) the department wasn't rich and (on the spiritual level) the meditation not to be slovenly was a way of disciplining and instructing the inner being.

Now it was all reduced to the idea that such carelessness was "ripping off Bhagwan."

It would be drummed into us how much we owed Bhagwan for lingering on this plane in this body to help us towards enlightenment. He'd be lecturing and showering us with wisdom and love, and we always felt like such "schmucks" compared to him. We saw more and more evidence of material things being bestowed on him, but we felt such things were *nothing* compared to what he gave us. Where once we had felt good about ourselves, we now felt that nothing we were or did was enough.

As the pressure built we began to feel *inferior*—and this ate away at us. Whatever we undertook was sure to come up wanting. Sheela and others were quick to point out failure. When a new room was built, for example, you could count on someone to comment merely, "It's a pity the window isn't completely straight." This was done to keep everyone off balance, though a lot of people didn't wake up to the full depth of the changes until after the move to America.

People who felt uncomfortable with what was happening were reminded that it was all part of the large-scale experiment Bhagwan was conducting—and only he could see the secret pattern in full.

"Status symbols" popped up everywhere. A room in Lao Tzu was better than a room in Jesus House, which was better than one in Krishna. Having a pass to Miriam Canteen was better than one at 70, which was better than one at Somji Estates. Even the *mala*s played their part. The first ones had been an oval of lucite. Later, they had the carved features of Bhagwan. Then came all-wooden *mala*s. Finally, we had thick, chunky ones of lucite again. The style of *mala* you wore indicated how long you had been a follower of Bhagwan—and (presumably) how relatively far along the path to enlightenment you were.

If Sheela, Laxmi, and other office staff were experts in keeping the rest of the Ashram off balance, then Bhagwan still had the privilege and the playful impulse to keep his top people off balance themselves.

When Laxmi returned from Saswad, she took up her old room in Lao Tzu, where she had always lived. However, after Chinmaya's death, Bhagwan moved Sheela in with Laxmi.

There could hardly have been a better study in contrasts than these two. Laxmi was a puritan. She followed her own weird dietary regimen and lived like a little nun in her utter devotion to Bhagwan. Sheela was vivacious, a woman of healthy sexual appetite, and, in her devotion to Bhagwan, like Cardinal Richelieu or Machiavelli.

To say that Sheela was doubtful about the new arrangement was

putting it mildly. She would not go against Bhagwan's express wishes—but clearly she was not at all happy about the new set-up.

Deeksha saved the day. She assured Sheela that things would work
out fine—then set about redecorating Laxmi's room more to Sheela's
taste and rearranging things to give the two women maximum privacy.

For a time Sheela discreetly went to Veetrag's room when she wanted to be with him. But then Bhagwan sent word that Sheela had to
sleep in Lao Tzu House. She and Laxmi came to a working arrangement
over things, but not before it caused a fair amount of friction between
them. I think Bhagwan had sensed that Sheela was following her own
plan—though he probably had no clear idea just how wide-ranging her
plans were—and shuffled things around a bit to clip her wings.

She gave love to Bhagwan and respected him as a teacher, but she
was also afraid of him: She believed he could see multiple flaws in her.
But for all the complex emotional ties she felt to Bhagwan, she never
totally submerged her ego (though her devotion was unwavering).
Once he told her to start wearing a headscarf, which she did—though
it made her look like a frump. She would dutifully wear it every time
she went into Lao Tzu to confer with him, but afterwards, she would
pull it off the moment she was back in the office. She indulged herself
in the very disobedience that she wouldn't tolerate in others. There
was always one set of rules for herself, and another set the rest of the
world was to live by.

Fear grew out of many destabilizing factors—over and above the
deliberately introduced paranoia. It was becoming obvious that two
spheres of influence were operative in the Ashram. Laxmi and her
"new commune" group were still focused on Saswad. Sheela was running back and forth to the United States, steadily cementing relations.
She was continually bringing back new equipment from her visits, as
well as gifts for key personnel: chocolates, alarm clocks, sheets, and
"deckers," the shoes so much desired by people in the Ashram. She assured everyone that the prevailing attitudes in Western Europe and
America were very favorable towards Bhagwan. In point of fact she
had arranged in April 1981 to buy a "castle" in Montclair, New Jersey.

Part of Bhagwan's insistence that Sheela and Laxmi room together
was to make them appear unified, and also to defuse the division that
was threatening to get out of hand in rumor, if not in fact. At first the
plan seemed to backfire because of the tension between the women.
But this gradually faded as stories filtered out of the office about their
ability to get along—even in the strained (though amusing) circum-

stances of having Sheela bring her lover into the same room as the fastidious Laxmi. Bhagwan continued to remind everyone that power resided in the office—but by letting it be known that Sheela and Laxmi were his mouthpieces, he underlined the problem of two queens in a single kingdom.

Another factor that tended to keep things edgy included the steady influx of new people: Our old sense of being a tightly knit group of friends vanished. And the stakes became higher as the money rolled in and Sheela worked to make Rajneesh and his experiment a force to be reckoned with in the Western world. The office staff became something between "parents" and "Big Brother" to the Ashramites.

When Sheela discovered that some Ashramites were playing "guard groupies"—hanging around some of the guards and partying with them while they were supposed to be on duty—she had the guards put on warning. The groupies were summarily kicked out of the Ashram, which meant they lost out on any favors from male Ashramites.

The increasing efficiency and stricter systems weeded out what laxity there still was around the commune. But, at the same time, something of the old spirit of friendliness also fell by the wayside. Anyone who covered for someone else would get chewed out; so people stopped helping each other, and the sense of community broke down. People were very conscious of the new hierarchy, and stepped on each other to advance themselves.

Perfectionism was still the order of the day. If a job was not done *absolutely* correctly, it was a failure. The Ashram rule was that it didn't matter *how* you got it done or *why* you messed it up—the end product was *everything*. There was no such thing as "good enough." At one point I was given responsibility for overseeing the production of gift portfolios in red silk with gold embossing that were to be sent through Laxmi to friends of the Ashram. When the publications department brought in the books I noticed that one inside corner had been pasted down imperfectly on each—it was a fraction crooked. I called in the two people responsible and told them this was *not acceptable* and, to meet the schedule, they would have to repaste the whole order in four hours.

I wasn't about to listen to their complaints that the flaw was so minor and the time so limited that it could be ignored. I knew that if I had okayed things and passed them along to Laxmi, *I* would have been called on the carpet. These portfolios were, in their own way, representing Bhagwan; and so they had to be *perfect*. I lectured the publications people on the need for *caring enough* to do the best possible job.

You never attempted to explain away any shortcomings to your supervisors; and you were never pressured to appear the "nice guy" to those working under you. The results were what counted. If I had a list of five hundred addresses to type up, I was expected to produce a list without a single error or dab of white-out. You earned your place in the office by being able to achieve the required degree of perfectionism—and you kept your place only by maintaining impeccable standards for yourself. If you objected you might be demoted to a job with less responsibility, or you could "go to Saswad." More and more people were being dismissed outright, and sent back to the West or wherever they came from.

We were still guided by the *idea* of the "new commune"—but few of us had any illusions that Saswad was the place. Laxmi still believed this, because Bhagwan had initially agreed to the location. But, wherever it was to be ultimately, we were single-minded in believing it was up to the office to manifest the dream by assembling the people and resources needed to establish and maintain the envisioned mystery school.

We certainly had plenty of evidence of material success. There were now regular allotments of spending money: fifty *rupees* (about three dollars) a month. The Ashram opened its own full-service bank on the grounds. Luxuries included a full-time hairdresser and a steady supply of Western-quality chocolate. The hardships of living in India were easing just as the health risks were being steadily reduced. Everywhere, we were reminded that we were living in "paradise."

But the serpent was always around in the form of mistrust and outright fear. It was easy to look around, see the gardens in flower and the white marble walls shining in the sunshine, and suppress your doubts for a time. But they would never stay buried; and soon enough something dangerous was gliding under the flowers or a cloud was sliding across the sun, and a vague insecurity would take hold of you again.

Sometimes the fear and paranoia threatened to get out of hand, to be disruptive rather than useful, or actually turned against the office as the cause. Then Bhagwan (or Sheela or Laxmi, who were his pipeline to the community at large) would warn people, "If you feel fear, remember: it's coming from you. Only you can dissolve the fear. You're *projecting* it onto the office." So the fear and frustration were turned inward, and people trapped themselves in paranoia. "Point it out to each other," the office said, deftly seeing to it that fingers were directed everywhere but at Krishna House.

New restrictions continued to separate groups and individuals. Now, unless you were a worker with the appropriate I.D., you couldn't go into the restaurant at 70, which was the "in" place to hang out after *darshan*. Next, only Ashramites were allowed to visit dormitory rooms in the commune. Sheela continued to choreograph the divisiveness, while using the general uncertainty and factionalism to increase the authority of the office. Some people looked to us to provide reassurances and stability and welcomed the rules and regulations as a sign of order; others resented them and thought of ways around them, which only added to the overall sense of tension.

One specter that came back to haunt us was Jonestown. News of the massacre on November 18, 1978, had been one of the few events in the outside world that shook us in the Ashram. Without television or radio or regular access to newspapers, we tended to be cut off from a lot of things. But Jonestown struck a responsive nerve. Bhagwan had made a point of reassuring us in lecture, "We're in the business of living: it could never happen here." But now the level of fear and doubt was such that many of us began to wonder . . .

CHAPTER 19

Deaths

My own uncertainties and doubts were brought into sharp relief by a
series of deaths in the Ashram that followed hard upon one another.

Death was not unknown in the Ashram. A worker or even a *sannyasin* who was not an Ashramite would be given a celebration in Buddha
Hall at death. This would not happen in the case of a junkie, or a ques-
tionable death on the grounds—such as the time a man (not an Ashramite) got decapitated by an Indian in one of the huts at the back of 17.
This incident led to tighter security and increased guard patrols at the
Ashram gates.

One worker from the *mala* shop, who had been ill for a long time
with hepatitis and serious complications, passed away. His funeral was
typical. The body was brought into Buddha Hall wrapped in an orange
shroud so that only the face was visible. The corpse was laid out on the
floor, on an orange cloth, just below the podium (which indicated that
he had died short of enlightenment). Then everyone would dance
around the body to music provided by the Music Group, which normally played in Buddha Hall while people were filing in and out of
darshan. They played a variation on Sufi music, featuring guitars and
Western-style drums, and a singer, Anita, or sometimes a man called
Anubhava. During *darshan* itself a second group would play *tablas*, *sitar*,
hakimachi flute, small drums, sticks, and Tibetan brass bowls. When
Bhagwan had finished speaking directly with a person during *darshan*,
and laid his hands upon the person's head, this would be the signal for
a musical interlude.

When the dancing was finished the body would be placed again on
a bamboo stretcher, and taken to be cremated on the burning *ghats*.
These were about two and a half to three miles outside of Koregaon
Park, across fields that lay in the opposite direction to Poona. Stepping

onto the path leading away from the road to the *ghat*s was to enter another world altogether.

A lot of the crazy people in the area lived on the way to the *ghat*s—a phenomenon I've seen elsewhere in Asia. But whether they were crazy to begin with or were driven crazy by their proximity to the *ghat*s is a moot point. It's a widespread belief that, while a body is being burned, the spirit of the person on the pyre and all the spirits that ever surrounded that person hover nearby. Each new burning brings these spirits back, as well as the ones they attracted in death, so that the site of a burning-*ghat* is simply loaded with disembodied spirits who have nowhere to go. But, so the story goes, in the moment of burning or if you stay the night afterward, these spirits can attach themselves to you and drive you crazy. It's a kind of spiritual "catch-22," since you're going to wind up demented in any case.

Some might gravitate to such places because they can live by begging from the mourners or earning a coin by helping clean the *ghat*s between burnings. Such "*ghat*-dwellers" were rarely scavengers; most would be very careful to avoid touching the ashes. Some would sell incense to mourners on their way to the *ghat*s. But the real reason for such people living in a dangerous place surrounded by spirits looking for a way to grab and hold is rooted in religious belief.

In the West people tend to look for "white" religion—not in terms of skin shade, but in terms of "white" magic, goodness, benevolent supernatural beings and powers. These people, however, are Kali worshipers, attracted to the darker side of the universe, nature as devourer as well as creator. They would feel closest to this "black" goddess at such a place of death and negativity.

In many of their faces I would see a certain expression, a way of looking slightly to one side that suggested they were looking inside. Sometimes I saw the kind of lunatic whose eyes seemed to burn with manic energy—the eyes of a tormented beast. But these people would stay just as quiet as the introspective ones—they didn't jump up and down or endlessly move around, which seems typical of this type of mental disorder in the West.

They would squat by the path, their mouths running with blood-red betel-nut juice, staring out with blazing eyes. For the most part, they'd be still; but every once in a while one of them would start leaping around the flames and dancing and shouting.

The road in was lined with their little shanties. Like the beggars in Poona, these people assemble shacks out of refuse: flattened tins or bits of cardboard. Unlike their counterparts nearer town, however, they would avoid the bright collages that made the other hovels look cheerful in spite of the poverty. Everything here was drab; everything was covered in buffalo dung to blacken it.

There were no flowers along the way. The children were hollow-eyed and silent, unlike the bright-eyed urchins who grabbed up a discarded cigarette box or begged a *paise* in town. Death was the keeper of these people: You saw him in their eyes, in their silence, in the dark-colored rags they wore—so different from the rainbow-colored *saris* and patchwork along Mahatma Gandhi Road.

The air near the *ghats* perpetually reeked of incense—not the lighter smells like sandalwood that greeted you in the shops in town, but a cloying, pungent smell that would cling to your skin and clothes long after you'd left the area.

The burning-*ghats* are always located right by a river. And the local river, like almost every stream in India, was supposed to flow into the Ganges, the holy river. Just before you enter the compound you pass the *ghat*-house, which is where the *ghat*-keeper sits. *Ghat*-keepers are always quite strange. Ours looked like the quintessential yogi—his hair long and tangled and filthy, hanging in what look like dreadlocks, wearing only a loincloth.

The *ghat*-house at our local burning-grounds was painted a hideous "government blue," thick and chalky looking. The place was splattered all over with red dye. This stuff—red, orange, and all shades of the red spectrum—is the same kind used for caste-marks, and is always brought to funerals in little pouches. It's thrown on everything when a burning happens. So even if you're in the march to a burning, Indians will come and throw the dye on you. This is supposed to be good luck and protection. They will also put *parijat* flowers around each other for the smell.

The *ghat*-house was on the left near the river. The three *ghats* themselves were further along on the right. One had a high, high corrugated iron roof for burnings during the monsoon season. The other two were open to the sky. They were so close to the shore that someone was *always* doing laundry there—life going on, I guess.

Each *ghat* was a rectangular slab of concrete, with a small grid in the center. Underneath was a slight depression for collecting the ashes. It is very important that, after three days, *all* the ashes be swept up and taken out. Usually, these are then put into an urn which the *ghat*-keeper provides, and this is thrown into the river. The *ghat*-keeper's main job is to watch the ashes during the time between burning and consignment to the river to be sure that none are taken. The belief is that taking any of the deceased's ashes would be like taking an arm or leg from a living person. During this period the *ghat*-keeper sits beside the ashes, day and night, and sings or dances—and probably smokes opium. In the West he'd probably be declared a yogi or guru just because he's so crazy.

Usually, some friends of the person who died will sit alongside the ashes, repeating little *mantras*. The overall effect of the *ghats* is a mix of lunatic and curiously colorful and meditative, with all the singing and chanting going on.

Whenever we went to the burning-*ghats* Bhagwan would insist that every piece of clothing worn there be burnt, and our *malas* were doused in linseed oil, which he said would take away all the negative *karma* from the place. We never took incense with us to the *ghats*, so very little fragrance would cling to us from the burning-grounds; but Bhagwan would insist that we shower and shower to rid ourselves of the "bad vibes" that he said would linger. He would say, "You can't really shower enough after you've been to a burning."

Burnings took a real physical and emotional toll. When I came back from a burning I would be totally exhausted for three days afterward. There was usually a big crowd following the body. The day was very often hot and sticky. We'd sing all the way from the Ashram to the burning-*ghats*, which is a Hindu tradition. By the time you got near the *ghats* there'd be a lot of music, because our singing would mix with the Hindus singing their own dead along to the river. And tradition required that we walk the corpse the whole distance.

Three funerals, however, were dramatically different—not only in the way they were conducted, but because of the impact these deaths had on the Ashram as a whole.

The first was Bhagwan's father, Swami Devateerth Bharti, nicknamed Dadaji. He was a very sweet man who looked a lot like his son, though a bit heavier. They got along quite well; Bhagwan often spoke about his father in lecture—not as a guru but just as a "nice father." Whan Dadaji became ill Bhagwan spent most of one full lecture talking about how beautiful his father was, and telling us stories about him. He painted him as a warm, very colorful character.

After about a week Dadaji was released from the Indian hospital in Poona, and was back walking around the Ashram grounds. Because I had heard Bhagwan talk about him so much in lecture, I began to look at him in a different light. He seemed very happy and serene. And there was something in his face—I don't know quite how to express it—that told me he was going to die. I saw that same *something* in the faces of the other two people who died not long afterwards. It wasn't that they looked sick or anything: These people's faces seemed to *shine* with an intensity that I've never noticed in any other circumstances.

Before his illness Dadaji would stay inside the house that the family had been given. Now he seemed to want to take a little more time with the world—even if that meant no more than sitting in the sunshine in one of the gardens. Sometimes he would sit in Buddha Hall during one of the meditations or just sit on the steps somewhere. People would often sit quietly beside him, just sharing in the tranquility he embodied.

About two weeks after that he got very sick again, and had to go back into the hospital. I reacted very strongly. Because this was Bhagwan's father I felt as if it were my own father. It touched me more deeply than any other death had.

As soon as his father was back in the hospital Bhagwan began talking about him during lecture again. The more he spoke the more I felt his love, and the more I felt I wanted to get to know Dadaji.

One evening I returned from the Blue Diamond, where I'd gone during *darshan*. I was sitting in my room and I suddenly had the impression that Bhagwan wasn't there. No one had said anything about his leaving. In fact Bhagwan had never been outside the Ashram gates. I was staying in Veggie Villas at the time, which is the nearest residential building to Lao Tzu; so I would be one of the ones most likely to know if Bhagwan had left, since my window would give a view of the car coming out through the gate of Lao Tzu.

What was amazing was that *everybody* felt the same thing—Ashram-wide. There was no announcement, but we could walk around and *feel* the absence. The place felt incomplete. Later that night I saw the car returning to Lao Tzu, so I knew he'd been out.

But his brief absence really shook us up. This change in routine, for all that we understood the reason and felt warmly toward Dadaji, affected us because our lives had become so wrapped up in him. For him to go away, even for such a brief time, threatened our sense of inner well-being. If things got too hard, we were constantly told, Bhagwan might simply leave his body; his being away from the Ashram jolted us with the feeling of what it might be like not to have him on the planet.

It brought home to me how much my *own* relationship with Bhagwan had altered. When I had first encountered him I looked on him as a teacher, and I had planned to stay until I had learned all that he could teach me. When his father became sick and he started visiting the hospital, I realized how strong my emotional ties to Bhagwan had become. I was terrified that he might die—just as his own father was dying. It was no longer a matter of losing a teacher who had so much wisdom to share: Now I felt that there was something alive between Bhagwan and myself, just as there was between him and the whole of the commune. I wasn't ready to lose him; I needed the level of emotional support he represented.

At this time I recognized to what extent I had become a *devotee* of Bhagwan—far beyond being a student or even a disciple. This perception also colored my relationship with Sheela, bringing home the impermanency of things and intensifying my desire to get—*right now*— all that I could from our teacher-student relationship in the office.

Somehow, all of us in the Ashram had collectively assumed that Bhagwan would never leave—in spite of the warnings to the contrary. Those few brief hours he *was* away woke us up to the possibility that, if he was able to leave for a few hours, then *anything* was possible.

He went to visit his father twice that week. Each morning he would talk about his father as he had been in the past or as he was in the present. He was quite open about the fact that his father was going to die.

On September 8, 1978, in lecture—curiously, the other two deaths we're going to talk about also happened during lectures—the message was sent in that Bhagwan's father had died. Bhagwan just sat there and smiled; then he said, "And he died *enlightened*." This came as a wonderful revelation at the time—one which we accepted with delight. (However, when the next death was also declared "enlightened," I have to admit a cynical thought crept in: *It's easy to say they're enlightened when they're dead. Why doesn't anyone get enlightened while they're alive?*)

What happened then throughout the Ashram was amazing: There was a mixture of tears from the people who knew Dadaji well and had lost a good friend, and tremendous joy in the fact that Bhagwan had said he was now enlightened. Then Bhagwan announced that the body would be brought to Buddha Hall in twenty minutes, that he was going to leave, but he would return when the body arrived.

As he left the Music Group came in and played, while everybody began singing. Usually, those of us in the first six rows would sit and sway and sing, while those behind us would get up and dance as well as sing. The musicians would begin with slow, rhythmic themes that would gradually build up to tremendous crescendos and bring us to a peak where the dancing was really crazy and the singing was taking us away. Then they'd gradually bring us down again to the slower, more subdued expressions.

Dadaji's body was carried in by *sannyasins*, including Shantam and Shiva, Bhagwan's personal bodyguard and the head of the security division; and the sense of celebration flared again. This was the first time there'd ever been a "do" like this, because this was the first time someone in our midst had achieved enlightenment. Bhagwan's mother, weeping and howling, followed the body in. The body was wrapped in an orange shroud, since Bhagwan's parents and his brothers were all *sannyasins*.

Dadaji was laid out on the marble podium—something else that had never happened before. It shook us to see Bhagwan's father lying there, dead, because he looked more like Bhagwan than ever before. Flowers were massed around him and covered the whole body, except for the face. Bhagwan's mother, Ma Amrit Saraswati Jain—called Mamaji—sat beside him, weeping and just staring at him; the brothers had places of honor in the front row.

Everybody else was singing and dancing because, before Bhagwan left, he had said, "Dance and sing and just enjoy this man. He died enlightened, and you should be celebrating that." Much later, when I studied *The American Book of the Dead*, it said the same thing: If you cling to somebody in tears and woe, it's harder for them to leave. Even if there are tears, at least be singing and letting go in some way. This is what everybody was doing. So the energy was getting higher and higher, and the music was getting louder and louder, and the dancing was getting crazier and crazier. The whole of Buddha Hall would have matched any Holy Roller meeting anytime.

Just at that moment we could see Bhagwan's car coming around to the entrance. The energy in the place took off to a phenomenal degree—just the way it did, to a lesser extent, every time he would drive around to begin lecture or *darshan*. We'd be uplifted like at the best revival meetings. The dancing and singing went through the roof, while everyone immediately around the podium turned toward the car in a *namaste*.

Bhagwan got out of the car, walked across the podium to his father, and looked down at the body. Looking at him, I was projecting how I would feel in the same situation—sad, but also happy that Dadaji was getting such a send-off. I also realized I was still feeling a little surprised by the fact that Bhagwan was coming out for someone—even his father. He always seemed so self-contained, so aloof from emotional display, that this was not something I ever had expected to see.

After a moment Bhagwan knelt down beside Dadaji. This tiny thing again caused ripples of surprise, because no one had ever seen him do more than climb out of the car, walk slowly to his chair with his hands folded in *namaste*, sit down exactly the same way day in and day out, cross one leg over the other—and never move a jot for two hours, until he reversed the procedure getting up and leaving. We'd certainly never seen him *kneel*—I know there was a part of me that wasn't even certain his knees bent that way.

People went crazy for this, shouting and clapping—you could *feel* the raw energy, the way you sometimes can at a rock concert.

Bhagwan put one hand on his father's head, and one hand on his father's "third eye." At that instant I felt I had gotten a burst of energy. When I talked about this with others afterwards, I realized *everyone* had felt the same thing. Call it what you will, it was an incredible experience. He blessed his father; then he stood up and put his hand on his still-distraught mother's head and blessed her. Finally, he began clapping out the time to encourage the celebration—another gesture none of us had ever seen before. Then he descended from the podium, walked back to his car, and left.

This celebration, of course, was *not* proceeding in a vacuum. There were very practical matters to be dealt with. For example, there were no piles of wood down by the burning-*ghats*, ready for the next cremation. All sorts of arrangements had to be made—and these had begun the moment Bhagwan announced his father had died.

Deeksha and the Vrindavan crew were running around looking for wood to hustle to the burning-*ghats*, flowers for *everybody*—masses of them. When the funeral pyre is built the body (especially the body of Bhagwan's father) is covered with flowers, and blossoms are layered throughout the pyre. Funerals in India are always very colorful and beautiful in this way. Also, *prasad* had to be given out—so this meant people were out at nine o'clock in the morning, trying to find *prasad* for two thousand.

The majority of *sannyasins* who were there celebrated this enlightenment totally oblivious to what was going on behind the scenes. Everyone working in the office or Vrindavan was going mad trying to pull together all the details: Is there enough wood? (There was *never* any wood around when you needed it!) How are we going to get Mamaji down to the *ghat*? Someone had to rush down to the *ghat* to be sure that there wasn't another burning in progress. It just wasn't done to have two burnings going on simultaneously. The concrete part had to be cleaned out thoroughly in advance: There was no way we could burn Bhagwan's father with the residue of some poor Indian clinging to the *ghat*.

Although the Ashram was very meticulous about the ashes of the dead, as were richer families, these *ghats* were for everybody. Sometimes someone would be burnt, and no one would bother to gather up the ashes. That would all have to be cleaned up and thrown out—into the river, because that was most convenient.

My role in this frenzy was to handle emergency requisitions and to make sure the telephone lines were open at all times. This last was no small task, since the Indian telephone service was a law unto itself. One of the Indian women would get on the phone to start calling around for *prasad*, wood, flowers—the whole thing. At the same time, a whole team of men would be sent off on bikes or in rickshaws with purses of money. The joint effort would certainly procure enough materials to meet the need.

Everybody in Buddha Hall was high-energy from the music and the singing; the rest of us were in the same state from the effort of pulling everything together instantaneously. Of course, everything had to look like it simply *happened*. Sweaty brows and messengers dropping from exhaustion were simply *not allowed*. Our frantic efforts had to appear *effortless*.

We had to muffle all the screaming and shouting that went on; Deeksha, of course, was standing in the middle of the road crying, *"Mama mia!"* and rising to her moment (which was anytime there was total chaos). With vast quantities of this-and-that to procure, and everything needed on the spur of the moment, she would be in her own dramatic element, screaming in Italian, French, German, English. There she would stand, this short, huge, beautiful opera diva, screeching, "Shantam, get the truck! Bavani, go and get that! Venu, build this!"

None of them—Deeksha, Laxmi, or Sheela—was ever satisfied that this was merely a burning. A moment like Dadaji's funeral would be a launching pad for many department heads. This would be a prime time for Deeksha to decide to put up a new building. The general pandemonium was always seen as a positive thing; people loved riding on the high energy that erupted from these events.

For Deeksha, not only would you have to supply vast quantities of flower, wood, *prasad*—but the whole menu in Vrindavan would have to be changed that morning. "My God-a," she would cry. "You can't give-a people pizza today! Not-a with his father dying!" She would haul her people out of the funeral celebration and send them into Poona to buy the ingredients for whatever items her revised memorial meal was going to feature.

Key people were always leaping on moments like this to create change—and Ashramites loved it. It was the magic of the commune all over again. In the West, if the chairman of the board dies, things tend to slack off for the day; in the Ashram it was the reverse: *more* would happen. Some of the changes might be short-term; but permanent changes would often result.

Fortunately, it was the dry season and there was no doubt that the wood would burn properly, which was always the main concern. But there were plenty of side concerns. I was running around trying to take care of as many of these as I could; Sheela was sitting cursing and swearing and demanding to know, "Oh, God! What are we going to do with Mamaji? Now she's going to be impossible to live with!"

Any event like this meant change everywhere, and one of the most obvious places for change was the situation of Dadaji's surviving family. Up to now Mamaji and the sons and all the Indian servants (since they were a high-caste *Jain* family, even though they were disciples in the Ashram, they had to maintain the old systems) around them had always lived in a separate house inside the Ashram. All of this, Sheela decided, had to change.

At the moment we had Bhagwan's father lying on the podium, having just been blessed by the now-departed Bhagwan; Deeksha was standing in the middle of this road changing menus, ordering flowers, arranging the pyre long-distance. And those of us in the office were looking at each other wondering, *What more?* The answer: *Mamaji can be moved to a new house.* Sheela and Deeksha decided that this was the only way to take Mamaji out of her grief, which would only be accentuated by having her stay on in the same house she had occupied with Dadaji.

So Deeksha, as if she didn't have enough to do already, suddenly called on one of her crews. While the mother and children were mourning in Buddha Hall, the crew went into their house—one of the smaller buildings that had been given over to the family on the lower floor, while Ashramites occupied the upper level—stripped it out, and moved them *before they returned from the cremation.* The meditation for anyone involved with this would be that it all happened *smoothly* and *without any apparent effort at all.*

The family and servants were moved up to the top of Krishna House; later, Mamaji was moved into Lao Tzu. Of course, this meant that the rooms they were going to occupy had to be vacated—and there was no such thing as a "straight swap" in the Ashram. People who were moved out of Krishna were dispersed into Vipassana and Veggie Villas. The original occupants were at the funeral celebration; when they returned from Buddha Hall to get ready to go to the burning-*ghats,* they found they had been dispossessed.

All of this was done to remind people of a main Ashram rule: Never

be attached to anything—certainly not your room; never identify with
a place. The ex-Krishna-ites would *never* make an issue of the fact that
they'd been moved out: they'd just look cool as they tried to find where
they'd been resettled. The Ashram always operated on the principle
that the minute you realize that you're overly attached to something—
stuck—it's going to change.

Things like this just made us more and more used to constant
change. We didn't question things because that was the way things
were—and there was always work waiting to be done that was more
important than useless questions.

At last Deeksha got word that all the necessary wood was in place at
the burning-*ghats*, so she alerted people that *now* they could start carrying Dadaji's body down there. Most people got up and followed the
corpse as it was carried out the side entrance to Buddha Hall; the rest
left by the main exits and joined the procession from there. There was a
maximum of noise and movement—the music continued to play, and
everybody had to retrieve shoes and bags and what-not from the security check-in.

Mamaji walked alongside the litter carrying Dadaji towards the river. Bhagwan stayed in Lao Tzu; he did not go to the burning-*ghats*. Immediately after the family walked Vidya, Sheela, and myself—
Deeksha, finishing up last details, came down on the motorbike later—
with all the other *sannyasins* singing and dancing and trailing along behind. Shantam and others were already at the riverside, stacking the
wood for the pyre.

When the funeral procession arrived the body was placed on the
pyre, which was about three feet high. Once the corpse was in place,
another load of wood was stacked on top of it. Dadaji's skull hadn't
been crushed at this point; tradition had it that the wife or whoever
was closest would do the honors. Unless you crush the skull before the
flames reach it, the head will burst from the heat. This was done, using
a heavy piece of wood, and the torches were applied. The singing and
dancing became more ecstatic.

The whole thing was so light and festive, it hardly seemed to me
like a funeral at all. The dancing and singing continued as long as the
fire burned. If people became too tired to dance, they simply sat and
sang or chanted. All along the hillside, into which the *ghats* were nes-
tled, was a sea of orange- and red-robed *sannyasins*, celebrating until
the body was completely consumed.

Whenever a burning happened, whoever you walked down with or
danced with (and you wouldn't choose: it was pure chance) would be

"bonded" to you—you would always share this close moment together.

At an unspoken moment everyone would decide the time had come to return to the Ashram. People (Deeksha's crew, most likely) would be waiting outside the gate to hand us *prasad*. After that, we would wander off for an hour or so to have *chai* and wind down from the event. But, while other departments would get some down-time, the office and Vrindavan would continue operating at full steam. The attitude was that we'd had the last hour or two off, now it was time to get on with our work.

Mamaji, the sons, and a few *sannyasins* sat by the ashes for the requisite three days. (I always thought that this was less a spiritual interval than the fact that it took about this amount of time for the ashes to cool down enough to be collected.) They sat in the open air, day and night, with only the wailing and leaping *ghat*-keeper for company—all according to tradition.

Meanwhile, all of us were sitting in the office wrestling with a new problem: we had never dealt with the death and funeral of an enlightened one before. Simply gathering the ashes and scattering them down the river seemed woefully inadequate, given the circumstances: Dadaji was not only *Bhagwan's father*, but he had reached *enlightenment*.

Those outside the crystal cave were probably thinking about these matters in a very religious light. Everybody was feeling high, thinking, *If enlightenment can happen to him, it can happen to any of us.* In the office we tended to be more down to earth about such matters. Sheela sat there and said, "So, guys, how do we honor a dead enlightened one?" She was always dead-set against the esoteric, and refused to go off on any spiritual mumbo-jumbo.

Deeksha piped up, "We'll get-a some marble." Something in her Italian background seemed to find marble appropriate to any celebration. On the other hand Sheela's way of dealing with things would be, "Let's have a good glass of scotch and get over this crisis." It was always wonderful to watch these two interact.

In their different approaches was a mirror of the different reasons people had joined the Ashram. Some were there for purely esoteric reasons, and would read a lot of metaphysical meanings into everything. Bhagwan would talk on different subjects every day, and never condone or condemn any point of view. Whatever your path is, that's your path, was the rationale.

No one had any problem with the fact that Sheela wanted nothing to do with the occult side of things, but was simply, as she would put it, "in love with this man." Of course she meant in love as a devotee is in love. I truly believe she saw Bhagwan as a god of some sort. "I don't know how the fuck I got here," she would admit, "Or what I'm doing with this crazy little Indian. I have no idea what's going on." She would even say, "I don't believe in all this spiritual bullshit," as she would call it.

On the other hand you had Deeksha, who would cry, "*Mama Mia!*" when Sheela said these things. She was much more into the esoteric side of things, and was always having dreams in which the Archangel Gabriel or others visited her. But, in point of fact, *both* of them would swoon equally when confronted by the Lao Tzu women who were *truly* into the esoteric side of things. These women were known to insiders as "the coven of witches."

In sum the Ashram was a playground for belief, theory, and exploration. It didn't matter what your attitude was toward Bhagwan or his experiment. It fascinated me—without implying any criticism whatsoever—that Sheela was here without believing any of the mystical stuff. She was there simply because she believed this man had a story to tell, and she somehow had a story with him. She would say, "Bhagwan is the first person who's brought me this close to anything esoteric."

She'd always been a real skeptic; yet, when she'd first met Bhagwan, she'd felt very drawn to him—as if there was something to be gotten from him. She loathed the stories people built around him. She'd been brought up in India—the "guru country"—and she *hated* the idea of gurus. In a sense she *had* come to Bhagwan for an "esoteric" reason, but she resisted the idea all the time. She never really understood why she was attracted to him in the first place—nor was she overly concerned with sorting this out for herself. She wanted to get on with whatever it was they had together.

The debate continued for a long time over how best to honor this enlightened one. Someone injected the cautionary note, "We'd better be careful how we handle this one, because he might declare *everyone* enlightened. In that case whatever we do for this one, we'll have to do across the board."

At this point it was decided to build a *samadhi*, a place that an enlightened one is kept. They take many different forms in India and the Orient. Quite often they are little shrines on the side of the road, though every little shrine along the road is not necessarily a *samadhi*. In Nepal, for example, it's easy to distinguish the *samadhi* from other types of shrine, because they'll have a small box inside that contains a relic of the lama or whoever it is who died enlightened. We weren't expecting any more deaths, and this *was* our first enlightened one to cross over.

We didn't anticipate a big rush on this—but, we were the first to admit, with Bhagwan you never knew.

The next major problem was deciding where to put it, since we didn't want these tombs popping up all over the Ashram. We finally decided to put it in the Jesus House garden, near the fence for Lao Tzu House. It would be placed so that it would overlook the Lao Tzu gardens.

The *samadhi* was basically a slab of flawless white Carrara marble (Deeksha's favorite). Typically, we demanded the most beautiful materials in the world—and the hardest to find. On top of that was placed a rectangular sarcophagus which would receive the ashes. And this was all created and carved appropriately between the Monday of Dadaji's death and the Wednesday when his ashes were gathered up to be enshrined. On the front of the shrine was engraved Dadaji's name, the legend, "became enlightened," and the date. It doesn't say he died: That's presumed from the fact of the shrine.

The top of the *samadhi* came off, and that was laid aside on the enshrinement day. Then there was another whole celebration and procession to go down to the burning-*ghat* and gather up the ashes and bring them back. A lot of the people who didn't work in the Ashram went down with the official group. The rest of us lined the drive all the way from the front gate to the newly installed *samadhi*. This was a big deal for many newer people, as much because they were going to be allowed into the back portion of the Ashram from which, because of security rules, they were excluded.

The people following the ashes in procession circled the *samadhi* in a ceremonial way, giving blessings and receiving them. Everybody was blessing everybody else. At the height of this celebration, the ashes, in a solid gold urn, were placed inside the sarcophagus and the lid was replaced. All this time Mamaji was sitting on the corner of the marble base, weeping, while everyone filed past the shrine one final time.

No expense was spared at this time—and it never would be spared on such projects. At the same time, however, you could count on Deeksha to have her shoppers drawn and quartered if they didn't get the best possible deal on carrots or rice.

Once the lid was in place everybody was supposed to return to work; now, however, there was the *samadhi* to be properly cared for, which meant creating new jobs. It would have to be kept cleaned, the area around it kept free of leaves, and fresh flowers would have to be placed on it every day. Back in the office we debated which department should have charge of the maintenance. It was finally decided that the cleaning department would take care of it, since they had their own handyman department, and Carrara marble has to be attended to all the time and worked with oils to keep its luster.

That much was fine, but dealing with the different departments was like dealing with rival unions. When it came to keeping the leaves off the shrine or dealing with the grounds immediately around it, the gardening department felt that was *their* responsibility. Everybody wanted to work around the *samadhi*, because it was a very peaceful place to sit and meditate. I would often go there myself for just that reason.

There was some initial friction, but we were finally able to work out an arrangement whereby the cleaning department would clean it, polish it, and maintain the vase for the flowers, while the gardening department would keep leaves off it, maintain the grounds, and put out fresh flowers each day. The whole thing turned into a ceremony every day when one person from each department would meet and the two of them would clean the vase and put the flowers in it. If they were caught making too much ceremony of it, getting too attached to the ritual, they would be replaced. Ashram "policy" discouraged anything that smacked of such ceremony. In general, people who become attached to their jobs were transferred. With a job like maintaining the *samadhi*, there was always a risk of a person getting egotistical about his or her work.

Sheela's husband, Chinmaya, died on June 11, 1980. The day before he died Sheela had been called in to see Bhagwan. When she came out and returned to the office, she was crying and crying in Laxmi's lap. She said, "He told me to tell Chinmaya he can go now."

Chinmaya *had* been sick for quite some time, and was in added misery from shingles. But he hadn't seemed that much worse to me than he had on other occasions. In any case, after about an hour of crying, Sheela pulled herself together and went upstairs to see Chinmaya. It was our understanding that she passed along Bhagwan's words, telling him he could go, that he didn't have to cling to his body anymore.

At that point, Sheela later told us, Chinmaya had turned to her and asked, "Did he really say I could go?" To which she answered, "Yes." But then she ran back into Bhagwan shortly after this, crying again, and saying she was going to ask why Chinmaya had to go. What Bhagwan's answer was to this second visit, I don't know. But Sheela stayed up all night with Chinmaya.

I remember turning to my friend Shradda while I was in the office that day and saying, "I don't believe you can just leave your body like that." But, in the Ashram, you found you really *did* believe all sorts of things. I was crying myself, because I really loved Chinmaya. I counted him one of my closest friends. The thought of his not being there was terribly upsetting. When Sheela really got to me, I could always run upstairs and he'd cheer me up. He'd tell me a joke, or tell me something about her that made her human to me. And he really *did* love her.

Bhagwan's words and everything that followed were kept a strict secret by the office staff. Even Gopa, Chinmaya's girlfriend, was not told anything—she wasn't even allowed in to see him before he left his body. If Chinmaya was going to die, then Bhagwan clearly intended himself to be the one to reveal it—most likely during lecture.

Sheela looked awful the next morning, after sitting all night at Chinmaya's bedside. I saw her briefly; then she, Deeksha, and Shantam went back into the room. This was just before lecture was starting. I don't know what happened to me at that moment; but something in me suddenly decided, "I can't be here."

I ran outside the gates. A friend of mine who lived nearby said I could use his apartment to lie down in, because he could see how upset I was. I just lay there, listening to music, my stomach in a knot. Somewhere, in the midst of these tangled thoughts, I fell asleep.

I woke up in the early morning. Distantly, from the Ashram, I heard singing. My first thought was to run back there, but I hesitated on the threshold of the apartment house. I knew someone had died, and I was afraid to find out who. I refused to face the possibility of Chinmaya's death. I returned to the room and curled up on the bed and just spaced out. *I don't want to know what's happened*, I kept saying to myself, and drifted, sleeping a lot, until evening.

When my friend came back with his girlfriend, he told me that Chinmaya had died. Feeling I couldn't stay away any longer, I went to the office.

Sheela was there: She looked like a ghost. All the life had gone out of her, it seemed. After a time, she left; when she came back, she handed me one of Chinmaya's tee-shirts from the West. "He asked me to give you this," she said. She also gave me some of his dictionaries and grammar books that we'd worked with.

After this, every time Sheela brought out a sheet of paper with anything written on it by Bhagwan, she would shred it. Bhagwan had given her explicit instructions to do this, she said.

Sheela was very weird after the death. Within a week, when I looked in her eyes I could see that her energy had changed completely.

She was empty. At the time she got a lot of insurance money.

The shock of his death reverberated through the inner circle. This was the only time it felt directionless; we all seemed to be adrift.

The next day we got a message from Bhagwan that we *must* be in lecture. Bhagwan talked at length about Chinmaya and Sheela. He told us that Chinmaya hadn't died enlightened, but that he would soon be born again as a baby who would be named Ko Hsuan, to achieve enlightenment in that lifetime. At this news all the fertile women became very excited over the possibility that one of them might become the mother of this wondrous infant-to-be. Even Sheela seemed to take real comfort in this curious story.

I simply felt very angry at Bhagwan. I resented him for not putting more energy into keeping Chinmaya alive. Then Bhagwan told "three jokes for Chinmaya," which set everybody laughing—and I hated everyone for that laughter. I felt ripped off by the loss of my friend. For the first time I felt real doubt about Bhagwan's claim of being able to tell if a person was or was not enlightened. It felt to me that Chinmaya's good humor and friendship and love for so many, after eight years of Hodgkin's disease, should have earned him more than "three jokes" in his honor and vague talk of rebirth and enlightenment sometime in some unspecified future.

For weeks afterward I had to drag myself through work. I felt hurt, confused, and angry. With Chinmaya's death everything had turned sour, and I was no longer sure who I trusted. The death that followed only added to my growing disillusion with Bhagwan, the Ashram, and my own path.

CHAPTER 20

Another Death

Bhagwan spoke often of Chinmaya in lecture and with such obvious affection that I was gradually reassured. And Sheela's grief was so overwhelming.

Sheela had to leave for the United States to take care of Chinmaya's sister, who was having a hard time functioning in the world. Chinmaya had always taken care of her. The family was tightly knit, and somewhat old-fashioned.

Sheela planned to pay a long visit to help as best she could; she also brought back tapes of Chinmaya's funeral and burning for them. The idea of going back to America seemed to give her an energy boost, because she was still pretty upset by her husband's death. I think she was also hoping that she might be accepted by his mother at last. But this didn't happen: She was still shut out by her mother-in-law. One has to wonder a bit if the tapes for a traditional Hindu cremation might have been a bitter pill for an old-school Jewish family to swallow. But Sheela never spoke much at all about her visit. She did, however, pick up Tanmayo, and she brought her back to the Ashram.

While Sheela was in America she met a *sannyasin* named Jayananda (John Shelfer), an investment banker; he became her second husband and traveled back to the Ashram with her. She had met him at Chidvilas Center, which was near Chinmaya's family. Jayananda didn't work at the center, but it was his local contact with the commune network. Everybody was very happy for Sheela, even though the man didn't seem exactly her type. But everyone felt this would help smooth the transition after Chinmaya's death.

According to reports Jayananda went with her to help finalize the purchase of the Big Muddy property that became Rancho Rajneesh. Interestingly, her reason for selecting the Ranch site was her claim that Ko Hsuan would be born there—she and Chinmaya had reportedly traveled there several years before, and he had loved the place.

Most people *failed* to recognize that Sheela was kicking into high gear her plans to move the Ashram to America. Jayananda was very much a businessman, and very good at what he did, which was investing in stocks and shares and so forth. They lived together in the commune and he became Sheela's key business adviser. Funds were directed more and more into the American stock market and other investments.

The threat of someone killing Bhagwan prompted the office to move to distinguish the Lao Tzu guards from the regular guards. At night, in *darshan*, Shiva would organize the guards for Bhagwan's appearance. Literally overnight it was decided that Lao Tzu would have its own guards, called *samurai*. (This Japanese connection seemed especially appropriate, since we saw a Japanese influence in rooms, landscaping, and a variety of other ways.) Though they had been selected individually, they were overseen by the Scotsman Shiva. All other guards were overseen by an Englishman named Krishna.

Ma Gayan and Ma Veena, Bhagwan's personal seamstresses, were given the job of making all the *hakimas*, which were the Japanese outfits for *samurai*. It was felt that fourteen guards would be enough to cover night shift and day shift.

So Gayan had to assemble assistant seamstresses to prepare the fourteen *hakimas*, which was no easy feat. The cotton poplin tunic and trousers involved hundreds of pleats, and stiff board inserts. An adept Japanese seamstress would routinely take six weeks to produce a proper *hakima* outfit. Gayan's team made the required fourteen in *one night*.

At 5 A.M. I was woken up (because this was to be another one of these "magic" things), by Bhagwan's personal washer. She had been up washing each *hakima* so it would be soft enough. But she had panicked when she felt that she wasn't going to be able to have them ready in time. So I was awakened, because these were all to be ready by 7:30 A.M. I roused Deeksha's whole crew to finish the washing. Then we had to blow-dry them to get them dry enough to iron.

It would never have occurred to anyone to say, "Forget it, we'll finish tomorrow." In the Ashram, once a decision was made, your course of action was set. There were no compromises. Even if the outfits got washed, ironed, and finished, we might be told there was no need for them. We knew this was always a possibility, but that did not make us one whit less accountable for having materials ready to deliver when they were expected.

By 7 A.M. the guys were running in to be dressed in their new outfits. Since they knew nothing about these outfits, we also had to serve as dressers. But we got the last of them ready five minutes before Bhagwan's arrival. I personally dressed Shiva, the head of the guards, at the last possible minute.

Once they were all ready—and they looked incredibly handsome in their *hakimas* of deep, deep maroon—I ran around to see how the whole presentation would be received. I was excited by the simple business of pulling this all off. And it *was* impressive, since Shiva had rearranged the whole placement of the guards to coincide with the new uniforms. They formed a line in front of Bhagwan, so no one who was a threat could get near him. All the time Shiva would continually be watching, swiveling his head from side to side.

The guards took the *samurai* training very seriously, studying the classic texts as well as taking a lot of martial arts classes. They were trained by a man who had been one of the top martial arts teachers in Japan.

You could see *chukka* blocks, martial arts weapons, tucked into their *hakimas*. They also displayed the silver weapons, like blunt swords, that were twirled around before they were used.

The majority of people looked on this as a "romantic" addition rather than a tight line of defense for Bhagwan. But, as time and paranoia went on, the very practical side of these new guards began to hit home. The whole place became more and more focused on the possibility that something could happen to Bhagwan.

Then, one day, Bhagwan blew the whole thing even further apart by saying, "If you don't love me enough, I'll leave my body." We all thought too much of him to assume he was acting as a child, using emotional blackmail. Instead, we internalized it all. I remember thinking, *My God! Can he read my mind and see that I'm rather negative these days? And if he does die, will it be from my negative thoughts?* I immediately began to change even the way I thought out of fear that, if it *was* my negative thoughts that pushed him over the edge, I might not realize my guilty role until it was too late to undo the damage. Such thinking was ludicrously convoluted—and deadly real to me. I was not alone in consciously trying to purge my mind of every negative thought, no matter how trivial. If that was Bhagwan's purpose, he succeeded admirably.

At this time, between Buddha Hall and the Chiyono cleaning hut, they erected what I called "Winnie-the-Pooh's House." This was a prototype of what the houses were supposed to be like in the "new commune." Although it was done in bamboo, it was so solidly built and so brilliantly designed (with an upstairs and a downstairs), that it convinced all of us that we were much closer to the ultimate mystery school. They moved two Indians into Winnie-the-Pooh's House—two *very wealthy* Indians. And we all accepted the fact that big money was going to help further our collective dream.

It was a curious fact of life in the Ashram that (with the exception of a dope deal or the like) very little was hidden. It was all out there in the open: favoritism, playing up to monied interests, that sort of thing. Nobody would deny this was going on—but everybody would accept that it was for the common good, so nobody would object.

The rate of growth continued faster and faster. Rada Hall, which had been serving as the Ashram boutique, now got divided up into a number of offices, which included the production of I.D. cards, dentist, architects, and darkroom. At the same time it was decided that no books would be published outside the Ashram, because it was too much hassle. So the book bindery was built between Lao Tzu and Veggie Villas. It handled the full production of books, as well as the rebinding of Bhagwan's personal library books.

Lao Tzu added another six rooms, and people were moved into these. The Lao Tzu personnel included Laxmi; Vivek; a woman whose husband was one of the largest dope dealers in Canada; Chetana, who did Bhagwan's laundry; Savita, an Englishwoman who did proofreading (not to be confused with Savita, the accountant); Pratima, who ran book printing and distribution; Hamid, an acupuncturist whose girlfriend Divya was a primal therapist; Shiva, the head of security; Haridas, an electrician; Teetha, a right-hand to Bhagwan on the esoteric side of things, whose girlfriend Maneesha, another proofreader, also taught in the children's school; the seamstresses Veena and Gayan; Asta, who cleaned Bhagwan's rooms; Nirgun, who cooked for him; Nandan, who worked between the library and cleaning; Lalita, who ran Bhagwan's library; a woman named Anurag, who did writing for the press office; Christ Chaitanya, who led meditations; a woman named Champa, who was a photographer, and her boyfriend, Daniel.

Most of these people had been with Bhagwan for a very long time, since Bombay. Only Nandan hadn't come in with the initial group.

In January 1981 there was a third death in the Ashram family. This was the death of Vimalkirti, who was the German Prince Wolf of Hanover.

Vimalkirti was a *samurai*, who stood guard outside Bhagwan's door. Before he came to Poona he had married Tariya, and they had had a daughter named Tanya—the three of them made a strikingly handsome family. It had actually been Tanya who had decided to take *sanyas* first. Her parents had accompanied her to India for a visit, and only then had taken *sanyas* themselves, and stayed on. At its height the Ashram attracted many high-ranking people from the social, artistic, business, and political worlds. It struck us as only fitting that a smattering of royalty would be mixed in.

One day the office found out that Prince Charles of Great Britain was going to be in Bombay. Vimalkirti and Charles were old friends who had grown up together, had spent summers together, had gone together to Gordon Stowe, the English school traditionally attended by the British royal family. Vimalkirti, had he lived, would have inherited his father's title. Prince Charles would often spend part of his summer in Germany, and Vimalkirti would in turn be invited to Sandringham or one of the other estates. The office decided it would be a great public relations coup to have Vimalkirti go down and visit Prince Charles.

Vimalkirti was asked to come into the office. There, Sheela informed him, "The suggestion is that you go down to Bombay, and see Prince Charles, and talk to him. Tell him what a wonderful place we have here." What they really wanted was for Prince Charles to get directly involved with the Ashram, or at least give it some verbal endorsement. One of the requests was that he get Prince Charles to come to the Ashram for a visit, because this would be very important for commune public relations.

This proposal put Vimalkirti under intense emotional pressure. The key words "the suggestion is . . ." implied that this had come directly from Bhagwan, though no one would ever say this *explicitly*. And there was his endlessly repeated dictum, "Anything you're told in the office has come from me."

Vimalkirti was totally devoted to Bhagwan, but he felt uncomfortable trading on a friendship in such a crass way. A prince simply didn't use his social connections to launch a publicity campaign. Up to this point, he had never been asked to do anything that might be termed "political" for the Ashram, and had never given any indication that he would be willing to do so. This was clearly a political maneuver, and it went against the grain.

At the same time Sheela had made it very clear that carrying out this "suggestion" would "really help Bhagwan." It was emotional blackmail, but it got to him. And Sheela was really putting the pressure on, because it was a high-stakes gambit. She had already gotten everyone in the office worked up over the prospect. I was present at the meeting, and I remember my own feeling at the time: "Yeah, drop your trip, Kirti, go and do it." I was caught up in the excitement of having Prince Charles pay us a visit.

I felt what we wanted to do was good; I don't think any of us saw any harm in at least telling people about what we were doing. We'd come so very far in such a comparatively short time that it seemed worth boasting to the world about. We *were* very proud of ourselves.

Tanya was then about eleven, a beautiful child with long, blond curly hair—everybody's dream of a princess—and was extremely excited about the plan. She began bobbing up and down, shouting, "Daddy, Daddy, I want to go!" And Vimalkirti *did* want to see Prince Charles, who *was* an old friend. But he still resisted the idea of going and pitching the Ashram to him. Finally, Kirti said simply, "You're asking me to do something that I wouldn't want *him* to ask of me."

In the end, however, he capitulated, and agreed to go down to Bombay. They gave him a yellow Mercedes to travel in. We typically got as excited as little kids at what was happening. Vimalkirti's family was outfitted in a whole new wardrobe of clothes; as usual, once this energy got started in the Ashram, it carried forward on its own momentum. Beautiful gifts were put together for him to present to Prince Charles; pictures and books, especially, that showed him all the things we were doing in the Ashram.

So, off they went. It was the first time they had been outside the Ashram since their arrival.

They were supposed to stay several days in Bombay, but they were back again in twenty-four hours. Vimalkirti was immediately called into the office, and Sheela asked how he did. He said it had gone very well, and it had been nice to see Prince Charles again—but *no, he hadn't asked him to come up.*

Since the trip had involved a new car, clothes, and so forth, it was clear that Bhagwan knew of the whole plan. And I had seen the notes Sheela took in to Lao Tzu, shortly after discovering that Prince Charles was going to be in the area. These asked specifically if we should try to do something with this fact—especially given that the Prince's old friend was an Ashramite.

I knew from my office training that if you were told "the suggestion is . . . ," whatever that "suggestion" turned out to be, *you'd better manifest it.* I don't think poor Kirti realized that he was being given no choice in the matter: He was expected to do what he had been directed to do. Period.

It's ironic. If they had just let things take their natural course, Kirti would probably have gone to visit Prince Charles on his own, talked at length about the Ashram, and maybe have intrigued him enough to come for a look around. But by forcing the issue Sheela made Kirti so uncomfortable that he was more inclined to discourage any such thing. And my hunch is that Prince Charles picked up on the stress his old friend was feeling, and stayed away from what was a sore point.

When Vimalkirti left the office he knew that he had messed up. Certain things had been expected of him, and he hadn't come through with the goods. Sheela had really laid into him. "You have no love for Bhagwan," she accused him. "You were given *one* simple thing to do in *all* the years you've been here. *And you wouldn't do it!*" This was an emotional attack that challenged his whole relationship to Bhagwan. While he may have been doubtful *before* the trip to Bombay whether the suggestion had, indeed, come from Bhagwan, or merely from Sheela, he *now* found out in no uncertain terms that he had directly let Bhagwan down. *And Bhagwan knew this.*

This last was a huge blow to him. He left the office visibly shaken.

Three days after his return he went into his *samurai* workout in Buddha Hall. Halfway through the session, he was called back to his room. So he left for a few minutes. When he came back to workout he must have looked a bit off, because the instructor asked him if he was okay. Chin said that Kirti seemed "a little subdued," but he couldn't put his finger on anything specific. He assumed that he had just been told off again.

Within seven minutes of returning to the exercises, however, Kirti collapsed. He was rushed to the big hospital in Poona, but he never regained consciousness. So Tariya was sent to call the Prince; and she found out that some crisis had just broken in Britain and he had flown out that morning.

The next day in lecture Bhagwan talked about Kirti, calling him "one of my most beloved disciples." I mean, he *really* turned on the syrup.

I liked Kirti a lot; every morning he would bring me a rose in the office. He would buy a dozen or so, and take them to various people. Though we didn't talk a whole lot, I felt I knew him pretty well. What struck me most about Kirti was his innocence. He was very kind, very gentle—almost childlike, for all that his manner and his walk were every inch princelike. But this never came across in an aggressive way; he was a charming, *gorgeous*, delightful person. The fact that the Prince of Hanover brought me a rose every morning only added to my perception of the fairy tales I was living inside the Ashram walls.

His mother and brother were called next. His mother was in India, visiting with Indira Gandhi in Delhi under the auspices of some women's international charity effort. Kirti's brother was traveling with her, so they flew down together.

The official diagnosis was that Vimalkirti had had a cerebral hemorrhage caused by an aneurism in an artery at the base of the brain. In a normal situation the parents of the sick person (he remained in a coma seven days) would have stayed at the Blue Diamond Hotel in town. Even if they'd been invited by the Ashram, the understanding would be that they took care of themselves. It was not policy for the commune to house such people. However, when the mother and brother arrived, they were immediately put up in the Ashram. The brother was put in Veggie Villas, next door to my room; the mother stayed in Krishna House.

The mother and brother were both clearly under terrible stress, going to visit the hospital every day. When they returned, they were given guided tours around the Ashram. They were given books and told what a beautiful person Kirti was. Tariya and Tanya were there, of course, and it was a sad reunion, since it had been years since everyone had been together. But this added to the overall stress.

Bhagwan personally sent the mother and brother a number of gifts. Clearly, the mother wanted to use all the time she wasn't at the hospital to learn about this part of her son's life that was totally unknown to her. And the Ashram invited that at every point. She was very open, and very vulnerable. Everybody she talked to kept telling her how wonderful her son was and how much they loved him. She felt surrounded by this love, which was real—people really *did* feel this for Kirti. Although the office and Bhagwan had manipulated their arrival, what they were being fed was genuine enough. And she was *not* being exposed to the office, where she might have picked up that something less than honest was at work. She saw only the positive side of the Ashram.

The mother also heard how devoted Vimalkirti was to Bhagwan and the Ashram. When she was asked by the doctor for permission to perform an operation that might relieve pressure on the brain, she was told (as was the brother) that Kirti had specifically said he never wanted any kind of surgery or any kind of drugs or whatever. I believed this to be the truth.

Puja was the one who was taking the brother around all the time, and she was also the one who kept stressing that Kirti didn't want this and didn't want that—and how important it was to respect his wishes.

They began to really pay attention to her and to depend on her because she was a nurse. When she'd talk about a procedure they'd trust her completely—something that many of us didn't.

They went to the hospital for a few hours each day and just sat with Kirti. But what really astonished everyone was that *Bhagwan* went to the hospital to visit him. Immediately, a whole energy phenomenon went through the Ashram, since it was presumed that if Bhagwan went to see him Kirti must be going to be enlightened. His family had been around the Ashram long enough to be impressed by just what an event it was for the Master to visit his ailing *sannyasin*.

On January 10, 1981, Bhagwan was sitting on the podium when Puja came in and gave a finger-sign to Vivek, who faced Bhagwan in lecture. Vivek, in turn, signaled to Bhagwan, who turned to us and announced, "Vimalkirti has just left his body. I saw Vimalkirti a day or so ago, and I know that he is now enlightened. He"—meaning the body—"will be here in about half an hour, so just wait and celebrate and dance. I'm going to go now."

The mother and brother were sitting in lecture, and they both began to cry. Immediately, Arup hugged and comforted them. Then Puja came over and began hugging them both. At that moment the son got up, marched over to office, and said, "My father's coming and you've got to do an autopsy."

I was in the office when Puja followed him there. She told him to relax, go back to the hall, and everything would be fine. Besides, she added, there wouldn't be any point in doing an autopsy, since Vimalkirti's skull had already been crushed before bringing it to the podium. Since it would be upsetting to do it at the burning-*ghat*, they had decided to prepare the body ahead of time.

Everyone in the office knew that the father had specifically requested an autopsy. The brother started to argue at that point, saying, "No, no, you must do an autopsy." I was then told to leave the room, and did so.

When the brother was able to pull himself together, he went back into Buddha Hall to celebrate, as he was instructed to do. When the body arrived Vimalkirti's wife and daughter sat on the podium with the "enlightened" corpse.

Then Bhagwan returned and blessed the body, which was covered in flowers. Everyone was feeling high from the fact that "one of us" had attained enlightenment. I was told to stand near Vimalkirti's head, which was bound in a red cloth, during the blessing and celebration in the auditorium. Everyone came up to be near the body for a moment:

We didn't feel the distance we had from Dadaji, because this was someone we had known and loved and worked and laughed with.

I left a short time after Bhagwan. I was feeling upset by the whole
idea of death and burning. I was walking around the gardens near Buddha Hall when I bumped into the old Scots gardener, Paritosh, who
was about seventy-three.

"What ya doin', lassie?" he asked.

"I don't know," I said. "I guess I'll have to go down to the burning."

"Oh, well, come 'n' have a wee dram with me. I've got some shortbread. Let's go up there, 'n' when they've got the body down there,
we'll just zip down in a rickshaw." Since everybody would be following the body on foot, we would have plenty of time for this break.
And, to tell the truth, I was beginning to think there was no way I
could face the smoke and the smell and the despair of the burning-
*ghat*s that day.

Paritosh opened a fresh bottle of scotch, poured us each a glass, and
put out a plate of shortbread biscuits. We just sat and talked about Vimalkirti's death.

One drink led to another, but we kept our wits about us enough to
hire a rickshaw and get down to the burning. There I witnessed Deeksha's great *faux pas*. The funeral was a big press event·because of the
connection with the House of Hanover. For some reason the wood was
damp, and it didn't want to catch fire. To help things along, Deeksha
poured kerosene over the pyre, which is *totally* sacreligious in Hindu
eyes—and it stinks terribly. The fire blazed up, though. She was not allowed to have anything to do with burnings after this tactical error,
which gave an element of black comedy to the whole grotesque event.

Vimalkirti's mother got on the phone as soon as we returned to the
Ashram and intercepted the father en route. She told him that the
burning had already taken place and there was no need for him to
come. So he never did visit the commune.

Unlike previous cremations, the rest of the day was turned into a
holiday for everyone. So I was able to keep to myself, which is what I
needed to do.

The mother and brother stayed on a few more days, while another
samadhi was built for Vimalkirti's ashes. Everyone assumed that it
would be placed next to the shrine to Bhagwan's father. But Bhagwan
suddenly decided, "No, no, no! Vimalkirti must be buried *in my garden*." So the *samadhi* was placed inside Lao Tzu, which added excitement to the overall celebration and happiness, because few people had
ever been inside the Lao Tzu grounds.

All the festivities were videotaped. The mother, brother, wife, and daughter stood by the *samadhi*, and everybody, Ashramite or not, went into Lao Tzu and walked around the shrine and dropped rose petals on it. As ambivalent as I felt about the circumstances, I was caught up in the beauty of it all and got a real energy hit from it.

Afterward, the mother and brother left, but Tariya and Tanya stayed on. They later moved with the Ashram to the United States and a lot of bad publicity was generated.

When Vimalkirti's mother and brother had gone, the general consensus was that the incident was closed. We believed Vimalkirti was enlightened, and that was enough good to outweigh the sadness of losing him. Everyone felt that, with two enlightened people having passed through the Ashram, things would continue to improve when the "new commune" came into existence. There was a prevailing air of optimism.

I kept pushing aside the sense of strangeness that three deaths had occurred within a year of each other. For most people, however, these deaths became merely part of the ongoing life of the Ashram. We formally remembered them all each September, on the anniversary of Dadaji's death.

By this point I had been working for Sheela for quite some time, but I was becoming disillusioned. Since Laxmi had failed to find the "new commune"—it was now an open secret that Saswad was never going to be the hoped-for mystery school—people were looking to Sheela to find it, and she was assuming even more authority as a result. Laxmi was aware of this, but Bhagwan was giving Sheela freer rein and Laxmi's options were limited. The focus of interest was in the West, and Laxmi was out of her element in the Western business and social world.

I was always fond of Laxmi. One time, while I was helping her pack her bags for a two-day trip, I said, "I wish I was going."

"Oh, you want to be near me?" she asked.

"Yes," I said, "Sure. I'd like a change."

"Fine," she said, "then you come and work for me."

And when she came back, she asked me, "Do you still want to work for me?"

"Yes," I said.

"Then," she told me, "you can take care of me, take care of my room and my clothes."

So, for a short time, I left off working for Sheela and began working for Laxmi, as a kind of glorified maid. I'd wash her clothes in special soap, and hang them up on the roof of Krishna House to dry.

But one day, as I was coming downstairs, it really hurt me to put my foot down on the step. I got down the stairs and sat down in Laxmi's room because of the pain, only to have Puja walk in. She took one look at my leg and said, "You've got to get straight to the hospital." So I went to the medical center with my little note from Puja telling them that I was supposed to be there.

They put me through a number of tests and discovered that I had thrombosis, a blood clot in my leg. I was put to bed immediately. I remember thinking at the time, *I don't know if I ever want to get up and work in the Ashram again.* After I'd been there a few days Puja came in and asked me how I was. I said I was fine. Then she said, "Bhagwan wondered how you were." I repeated that I was feeling fine, but I said I wanted to send him a note to this effect, which I did. I told him it was going to take a little time for me to get better, and I added that I would really like to go back to the West. "What do you think?" I concluded.

He sent me back word, "Fine: go back to the West. And if you don't like it, remember that this is your home, and just come back."

All this time I hadn't spoken to Deeksha or Shantam. But when it was time for me to have my leaving *darshan*, Deeksha was in Sheela's office. She spotted me near the front gate and ran out to me. She was warm and loving, and asked, "Why did we agree with all these people not to talk to each other for so long? I really love you, and I have to tell you so much that's happened." I was delighted to have my old friend back.

I had come to the hard decision that the Ashram was no longer the place for me, and it was time for me to leave. Deeksha didn't understand this; she was acting as though this was only a temporary return to the West.

I went up, took a bath, and slept for a while. Deeksha woke me up and said, "It's time for your *darshan*." She had packed me a whole suitcase full of new clothes, with a beautiful new dress for *darshan*.

During *darshan*, Bhagwan didn't talk: He just touched me. When I came out Deeksha said, "Oh, great: Now we can celebrate and have a party." She had invited some friends and we had a great time. Much later, she put me to bed in her room in Lao Tzu; before I fell asleep, Shantam came up, and we talked for the first time in years. A few other people also came by to visit.

Leaving Sheela was particularly hard. We just sat together and held hands. She said, "Wherever I am, wherever this Ashram is, is your home. When you're ready to come back, then just come back."

When I got up the next morning Deeksha had presents ready to give to my parents and my sisters, one of whom was getting married about the time I was returning. She had already arranged for one of her people to escort me to Bombay, and had made arrangements for me to stay in the Oberoi Sheraton there.

I was resting on the bed because of the thrombosis, when three of my best friends—sent by Deeksha—turned up. We had a lovely farewell party. They went with me to the airport and waved to me until we were airborne. Then I was on my way back to London.

Part 4

THE UNITED STATES: RAJNEESHPURAM

CHAPTER 21

Kalptaru Centre

The thrombosis and my sudden decision to leave India left me feeling uncertain, scared, and excited all at the same time. But what really hit me was the shock of awakening to the outside world.

It didn't get to me all at once. My parents met me at the airport in London, and we had a happy reunion. It was clear from the first that they felt I had done something positive with my life. I expected everybody I met would be just as understanding. I felt very confident once I was in the hospital at Hereford, where my condition was quickly stabilized.

My parents visited often and talked constantly, catching up on all the years apart. Soon, however, I grew weary from the stream of words—such a contrast to the Ashram and its emphasis on only speaking "the needful." I was physically and mentally exhausted, and clearly in need of a good long rest.

When the doctors approved my release, my parents took me to their house in Hereford. Once I was settled in a stream of well-meaning, curious friends and relatives began dropping by. In short order I felt like some exotic creature in the zoo: a being from an alien country, following a strange religion.

The endless idle chatter got on my nerves; I found it incredible that people could run on so about such trivial things. Within a few days, I began to think of my brain as a scrambled computer, overloaded with memories, new impressions, and words, words, words. I saw just how flooded we can get outside of a place like the Ashram. The sheer physical *muchness* of things was overwhelming. In the medical center in India, for example, there was little talking, bare walls, piped-in music, and extra care given to each patient. The hospital in Hereford, by contrast, seemed crowded with machines, noisy, and impersonal. Even my functional room there seemed full to bursting with things. Voices sounded brutal. I never believed the doctors were telling me what was really going on, while in Poona they would tell me as much as they knew. I must say, though, that the care and attention was extremely good, and these feelings had come from my own homesickness.

I felt gawked at; I felt the world was, if not outright hostile, at least cold, clinical, prying—only interested in me as a novelty, not as a person. All the programming I had picked up about "we" and "they" came into play in my mind. I was making the classic error made by most people who decided to pack it in and leave the Ashram cold turkey: I thought I would adapt immediately to the world outside the commune. After all, I had been raised in it.

In fact, I had become a very different person in those years between leaving my mind and shoes at the gate and reclaiming them as I left. And with the mental baggage I had brought along from Koregaon Park was a strong residual dose of paranoia, which was reinforced everywhere I turned. Even my parents were, out of love and concern, smothering me with words and trying to draw me too quickly out of the shell the Ashram had encased me in. I needed time to peel away layers of ideas and conditioning gradually; instead, I felt everybody was going to yank the bandages off suddenly, and I was afraid of how much of me was going to come away with them.

I began to think about going back to Poona. I felt torn: Reentering the world *was* exciting in many ways; but a big part of me wanted to cut and run back to Bhagwan. My parents had made every effort to make things comfortable for me. In the two weeks that I was in the hospital they had my old room done in white, with a cream carpet, very reminiscent of the Ashram. I thought that was very insightful of them.

I kept to myself more and more, reading, writing poems, listening to music. I felt somehow superior because I didn't have to talk. My ego, freed of the constraints of the Ashram, began to feed on all sorts of foolish ideas. But, underneath it all, I felt incredibly lonely for the people and lifestyle of the commune—and that feeling of being taken care of.

When I began to get out of the house on short shopping trips with my mother, my disorientation grew. In the shopping mall the clatter, the crowding, the masses of goods in *so many different colors*, and especially the fluorescent lights, pounded on my senses. I couldn't wait to leave, and I told my mother I wouldn't go back again.

I was estranged from the world around me. On one level I was beginning to see how isolated I had been—and a voice inside me was sounding the alarm about the way I'd been in the Ashram. But the voice I listened to said, *This world is crazy. I really don't want to be here.*

What amazes me now is that before the Ashram I had always been so independent; I had always felt there was only me, and whatever I got myself into I had to get myself out of. Now I felt able to trust myself least of all. I had lost the ability to function outside of the Ashram. Somewhere along the line I had lost a huge part of my individuality. But I wasn't seeing it that logically at the time: My mind was twisting it to say, *My God! The Ashram was right. I can't survive here: I'm too vulnerable.*

After only a few weeks at my parents' home I turned to them and said, "I can't be here; I've got to leave." Once they saw that my mind was made up, and having been assured by the doctors that my leg was healing nicely, they agreed with my decision.

So I went down to the Rajneesh community at Kalptaru Centre in North London, near Camden Town. At this time it was the largest center in the world for Bhagwan. It was run by a woman named Poonam.

The minute I walked through the door of the center, the isolation and vulnerability began sloughing off. All these people came up and greeted me warmly, and touched me and hugged me and asked me how I was doing. I didn't recognize most of them, but they knew me from the Ashram office. I had an immediate sense of belonging. I didn't question how relieved I felt or why, I just *relaxed* into it. It was as though I'd been hungry for weeks and was being fed again.

I saw Poonam and explained my situation to her, telling her that I had made up my mind to return to India once my thrombosis was cleared up. I was still checking in with the doctors on a regular basis. They hadn't discovered the cause of the disorder but were treating it with an anticoagulant. And I had to wear elastic bandages and support stockings all the time.

In the meantime I wanted to work, and Poonam was delighted to help out. In the Ashram, when you leave, you surrender everything you've managed to get: food pass, housing, whatever. If you choose to come back there's no guarantee you'll be given anything like your old job or benefits. So I was expecting to take just any old position at Kalptaru.

I didn't realize, however, that hero worship was rampant in the centers and communes away from India. Anybody who had lived in the Ashram—and *particularly* anybody who had worked in the office— was like a king or queen to the other *sannyasins*. They were starved for news of the Ashram and Bhagwan. It was like old friends running into each other in a distant corner of the world, and filling each other in on the news from home. This was one of the most stimulating things about being a *sannyasin*. I "got it" the minute I walked into the center: They sat me down, gave me something to drink, and made a fuss over me. Because of my previous position in the office, I was given to understand that things would automatically be taken care of for me.

Right off Poonam said, "We have a space at Oak Village," which was one of the residential sections of the center—one of several houses attached to Kalptaru. People would either donate a residence outright when they joined, or open their homes to however many *sannyasins* they felt they could accommodate.

Kalptaru did a lot for the Ashram—though I didn't find out *how* much until I had started to work there. It was one of the biggest liaisons for press releases. Kalptaru would sometimes be instructed to do certain things in the way of publicity events, such as sponsoring a stall on behalf of the Ashram at the world exhibitions regularly held at Earl's Court. It was much more highly organized than most other centers.

I knew it was going to take a few more weeks to clear up my illness. And Poonam was very generous in letting me be there, because you weren't encouraged to be in the Ashram at all if you were sick. If you left for a medical reason, you were supposed to be completely well before you returned. Although you'd be well cared for if you got sick in the Ashram, you were always scared that things would change suddenly, and you'd be sent packing as soon as you were able to.

So I moved into Oak Village, and Poonam started me working in the office. The day I went to start work, she just waved her hand over the office area and said, "Take it over and rearrange it and redo it."

I started revamping office procedures, and had a number of people working directly under me. I began to realize just how much influence the Ashram had at this center. Previously, I had thought of Kalptaru and the other centers as far more independent. Now I saw that it organized the transport of a huge amount of items to Poona—acting really as a clearinghouse for such goods as videotapes, typewriters, calculators—shipped from all over Europe.

Though Poonam was officially just a "center leader," she actually had the kind of authority that Arup had in the Ashram. If somebody wrote to Bhagwan and the office didn't want to write a reply for some reason, Poonam would deliver a verbal response. She would be contacted by the office in Koregaon Park and told to call the person in (assuming the person was within a reasonable distance of Kalptaru).

So I worked upstairs at Kalptaru, with six people under me, which let me see how thoroughly Sheela's training had taken root. When I worked with Sheela and Laxmi, I had people under me, but it was very different in the Ashram. There it was emphasized that, even though I was Sheela's secretary, I was "a nothing"—because there were not supposed to be higher ranks or lower. Now, away from the Ashram, I found that people had a very different idea of what Poona was like, and that being Sheela's secretary was really something special.

These people couldn't do enough for me, and I *indulged* myself in this. Since everybody did exactly what I said, and carried things out to the best of their abilities, it was easy to make what was already a pretty efficient operation into an even more effective one. I simply transferred what I'd learned in the office in India to Kalptaru.

But what I really got off on was the fact that *I* was now being treated in the way I would treat Sheela. Part of my joy in working with Sheela was that element of devotion, because taking care of someone else made it easier to drop the ego and feel you were moving along the path to enlightenment. Now I was on the receiving end of such devotion—and I saw that people *wanted* to be devoted in the same way I had. It was a pleasure not to have to think about things, because someone would always have a cup of coffee at hand for you or something to eat.

My ego really got into the fact that these people wanted to wait on me. And having the little details taken care of automatically certainly made it easier to work. I noticed that I was much clearer about things, able to give my undivided attention to important matters. Within twenty-four hours of being around *sannyasins* and around the routine that we all seemed to want, I felt the confusion and uncertainty of the preceding weeks evaporate. I felt I was back in my element and functioning at tip-top level.

It was a relief to be away from frivolous talk about the weather or fussing about social niceties; it was a joy to keep my mind on one thing. I was used to working long hours with never a day off. The people around me found this impressive, because they were still living in the West and very much attuned to Western business hours and weekends as holidays and that sort of thing. Since they were not living in the Ashram, where everything was routinely taken care of, they had apartments to maintain and lives to live outside the center. Though there was some initial resistance when I began to expect them to work as much as I did, in the long run they really liked to work that much. The fact that this was the way we did it in the Ashram made it very appealing: People liked the idea of putting themselves as much in tune with the rhythms of Ashram life as possible.

Although these *sannyasins* were apparently living in the world, they really weren't. They created their own illusion. At this point, no one had anything to do with non-*sannyasins*. On one level, of course, we were told that the world was not a good place: It was filled with distractions. But, in another way, I have to confess that a lot of them felt superior. They tended to look on the average person in the street as an "unsaved soul." We would put down born-again Christians, yet we were functioning in many of the same ways—except we had no organized program of outreach to bring in converts.

But we were so invested with the idea that we were "right," that each of us living in the larger world became a message in his own light. The word got out so effectively, because there was no overt pushiness, no obvious attempt to draw in converts. We were thoroughly indoctrinated with the idea that we were better, but we didn't put this across in any crude way, such as going door-to-door or handing out pamphlets on street corners. The very fact of our discretion and refinement I think was what drew so many intelligent, affluent people to take *sannyas*. The core group in London, for example, was made up of very successful businesspeople. And this would have its own chain-reaction: When people found out that a lawyer or doctor they'd been going to for years was a *sannyasin* (probably because he'd begun to wear red all the time), they'd be open to finding out more. They weren't threatened, because this was someone whom they might have known in a business way for years; at the same time the fact that a clearly successful professional was part of such a group made people want to find out more. The number of *sannyasins* who had already "made it" in their careers was a strong, if subtle, endorsement of the group's values and dynamic.

Bhagwan's message appealed to such an evidently upscale group because it was so inclusive. Because he talked about all the great masters, from Lao Tzu to Jesus, in such a vivid way—he was a brilliant storyteller—he brought them alive. And he used reverse psychology very effectively, always protesting, "I am not a master; I'm your *friend*. I can't give you anything; but, if you listen, you might learn something for yourself."

In my observation a highly intelligent person will not follow a religion or sect that says, "You are a sinner; and if you come to us, you can repent." You listen to that and say, "I'm not *that* much of a sinner; I don't need to repent *that* much." Bhagwan would say, "I don't want anything from you at all." And, by appearance, it would seem that he didn't. You didn't feel you were being conned the moment you entered.

Moreover, there was no such thing as "sinner." Whatever you had done you'd done, but "Drop the past and be in the moment" was the operative rule. Most people *want* to be able to leave their pasts behind and start with a clean slate.

Bhagwan's message also appealed to the wealthy, because it reassured them that they could be valued for themselves, whether they chose to keep their money or give it away. Money in itself was certainly no drawback, so long as you felt it wasn't interfering with your personal spiritual quest. In the Ashram it seemed that everybody was treated equally; you could have millions of dollars and *still* be assigned to cleaning toilets. And a large number of millionaires happily cast their lot with the Ashram *on the Ashram's terms.*

It's ironic that so many people who had really made it wanted to come into a place where they'd be told what to do. Of course you never *told sannyasins* in advance that this was what was going to happen; but once in the Ashram they adjusted quite happily. The Ashram's take-it-or-leave-it, it's-all-the-same-to-us attitude, which signaled a disinterest in worldly goods, appealed to people who had probably found themselves fighting off hangers-on and con artists and phonies ever since they made their money. It was more reverse psychology, and it worked.

Gurdjieff used this ploy very effectively. A very wealthy woman in Paris once came to him to be his student. He said to her, "Give me all your jewelry and money." She said, "Oh, you're just a fraud!" "No," he answered, "I'm just unburdening you." And she did give him all her wealth. Then, three days later, she reconsidered. She said, "Somehow, you hypnotized me, and you managed to take all my money away." Gurdjieff just said, "Take your money and never come back." That made her want to be there more than anything.

And this is how Bhagwan would work. A woman from California came to the Ashram and wanted to donate a million dollars. I was sitting and watching when Sheela said to her, "Well, do you really think you're ready to give that? You must realize that by doing this, you're dropping the past." "Yes," the woman said, "I know." Then Sheela said, "Well, I don't feel you *are* ready to do this. I think you need to go out and spend it or do whatever you want to do with it. You're making such a big deal about donating it, that you're doing it with too much ego." The woman began to cry and insisted, "But, I really want you to have it." And Sheela kept saying, "No, don't bother." This went on for a while, then Sheela abruptly said, "How much do you have in all?" "Oh, I don't know. . . . About five or six million dollars, I guess," the woman replied. Sheela said, "Yeah, you see: You make this big deal about giving me a million dollars, but to you it's nothing. So, really, you haven't sacrificed anything."

She wound up getting *every penny* of the woman's money. In the end the other woman was actually *forcing* her money on Sheela.

Yet, for all this talk of manipulation and reverse psychology and so forth, people *really did get something from it*. Clearly, the whole idea Bhagwan represented wouldn't have caught on or lasted if people weren't getting anything from it.

New *sannyasins* also came in through groups. A lot of group leaders were already well known on the therapy circuit. They went to Bhagwan because he was allowing new groups to experiment with the most radical ideas, including the no-limit groups in which participants would have to sign a release in advance in case they were injured during the course of such a no-holds-barred session. This was actually what was behind rumors of "underground torture rooms where bones were broken." In point of fact the Ashram had rooms below ground level which were padded to prevent injury; this was where the no-limit encounters were held. One woman broke her arm during an intense session, but to my knowledge, that was the only serious injury connected with these groups.

At this time, a variety of encounter groups were available to people in the West. But they had clear-cut limits, and somebody could always turn around and sue if anything got out of hand. In the Ashram you signed a release absolving the Ashram of responsibility before taking *any* group. And people were eager to move into these new frontiers. Therapists were able to break all kinds of new ground in understanding the mind and group dynamics—the sort of thing an individual therapist would never be able to try alone.

Remember the joke, "Who's the psychiatrist's shrink?" In the Ashram it was Bhagwan, "the ultimate shrink." Therapists could go as far as they wanted with these groups—and they'd effectively be putting themselves through the group at the same time. They could go with what happened in a way that would not be possible elsewhere. In the West, the leader of a psychodrama group can't afford to lose control. In the Ashram it was understood that therapists were also working on themselves.

At Kalptaru it amazed me to see how many people did groups, because the English tend to be reserved about such things. Encounter groups were always much more popular in Europe and America. A lot of people who came to take a group ended up taking *sannyas*; incredible numbers came either directly through the group or from word-of-mouth the groups engendered.

The Ashram also counted on snob appeal to attract new people. In London, for example, the Hare Krishna people run a popular restaurant that is very good and very cheap. Bhagwan used the opposite tack: everything was expensive, which had a cachet that appealed to a whole class of well-heeled people. As an extreme example, it cost *$1,000* to have dinner at the center in Hollywood, California. For your money you got dinner, two videos, and a disco afterward. And people would crowd the place. The "Hollywood crew" were the best-known therapists in town—all of them had taken *sannyas* and moved up from $200-an-hour sessions to $1,000 an evening.

Bhagwan was an amazing mass-marketer. Most religious organizations go through one channel to get their adherents—the Mormons, for example, have a particular line of media advertising and use their missionaries in a certain way.

In the Ashram there were as many different appeals as there were *sannyasin*s. Anyone who opened a center signed a release in advance that distanced the Ashram from any negative fallout, while giving them permission to present themselves and that center to the world in any way they choose. Thus, if you're wealthy, you charge $1,000 a night. On the other hand there were centers in other parts of London or Wales where it didn't cost anything to have dinner, because that would be *their* way of doing.

The Ashram relied on individuals, using their own creativity, to attract people—though this was never an official program. The Ashram never appeared to be telling anyone what to do. This was the brilliance of the approach, because people put *more* energy into what they felt was their own effort all the way. Because nothing was ever *asked* of them, people would send part of what they made to the Ashram. They would choose to send it, and be all the more generous because the giving was spontaneous. Had they been told they were *obliged* to send "x" amount a month, "x" is all the Ashram would get.

*Sannyasin*s always got good press from the fact that they were very hardworking and very creative: These were things Bhagwan particularly encouraged. Nor, in those last open days, were devotees hesitant (with some obvious exceptions) to talk about what they were doing with anybody who seemed interested. And that openness and candor were attractive. So a businessman who was successful could join and feel very comfortable talking about his achievements—since the fact that he was successful *and* had taken *sannyas* reflected favorably on the group as a whole. That's certainly different from someone in a Christian sect who would be more apt to shy away from boasting about worldly success or relishing the fact that he or she had "made it."

Bhagwan was able to offer a "multidimensional philosophy"—he was careful to distinguish his teaching from a "religion" at this point— that spoke to people at all different levels who were pursuing a variety of goals. It could be all things to all people. A successful man would be told, "Fine, you've made it, now let's see what you can do to center yourself." He wouldn't be told to give up his business. You could have your cake and eat it too. It was very similar to the Oriental idea that the wealthy would patronize a monk to pray for them. You didn't have to give up anything to be in Bhagwan's religion—which wasn't really a religion anyway. And you *did* become part of a network that gave both emotional support and helped financially better the situation of its members. *Sannyasins* always gave priority to businesses run by other *sannyasins*, and gave each other preference in hiring.

Bhagwan emphatically stated that what we were involved in was *not* a religion, and this appealed to people who would be the first to decry anyone who joined a "cult." As a matter of fact we joined a cult precisely because it *wasn't* a cult. It was marketed as being a "philosophy," which also gave it an intellectual appeal. Everything seemed very open, free of dogma, and creatively involved in everything from business to art. It really did offer something for everyone.

This is not to say that only upscale people were allowed into the community. It was never limited in that way. A street person who wandered in would be invited back. He'd be told to come every day and meditate for an hour. In the meantime they'd write to Bhagwan for his *sannyasin* name, and when that came by return mail, Poonam would give him a *mala*.

If a person was very scruffy, Poonam or I would sit down with him and say, "We're glad you've found Bhagwan . . . maybe it's time for you to start taking better care of yourself. I can see your clothes aren't so clean, and it's a good thing to work on the outside of ourselves while we're working on the inside. So the suggestion is that you start really taking care of yourself . . . " and so on. You wouldn't insist that someone go out and get a new wardrobe, but you might suggest that there was a good, economical clothier in Camden Market, and maybe he'd like to pick himself up some red or orange things. You'd urge the person toward a cleaner, simpler way of dressing, insofar as his budget would allow. You'd try to keep people striving for a little higher level than the one they were at—but not so much pressure that they would run. We were always looking for that balance point.

And there would usually be a noticeable improvement in a short time. *Sannyasins* tended to inspire each other. Even today, that part of the support network is still in place; *sannyasins* stick together and help each other out. For someone who wandered in off the streets, *sannyas* was a godsend, because there were all these people who probably already had businesses or such, and they all employed each other. A businessman who had taken *sannyas* would always call the center first if he needed a typist or whatever, hoping to fill the position with a *sannyasin*. This system of patronage also encouraged an isolation from the non-*sannyasin* world.

While I was at Kalptaru I stressed what I had learned at the Ashram: Present yourselves in the very best light. Since you're in the West, play the game of the West the best that you can. Whatever your job, do the best you can at every minute. That's how *sannyasins* made a name for themselves: hard work, care, and an insistence on taking care of something *now*, not later. People learned that businesses we were associated with gave the best service around. Perfectionism reflected favorably on both the person and *sannyas*; we were quick to distance ourselves from the "spiritual air-heads" (as we called them) of some of the then-popular cults around. Outsiders found us the easiest, most efficient people to work with: We offered a stance of spiritual awareness and business savvy.

London gave me a wonderful opportunity to see the way centers were run. It helped to refine my organizational skills, and my ability to keep my eyes and ears open so that I grasped the whole picture—not just the segment under my direct supervision.

By May 1981 my leg had healed. I said to Poonam, "It's time: I've got to go back to India." At that point I'd been away just under five weeks, but I was desperately homesick for the Ashram. And I felt I was never going to be able to attune myself to the world outside; dealing with all of its stimuli and diversions exhausted me every day.

Poonam said, "No, I really want you to stay here. We need you to help run the center." But I was very clear that I wanted to go back. I didn't know it until afterwards, but Poonam telexed to Sheela, saying, "I really need her to stay: Please don't tell her that she can come back." Sheela telexed back, "Avibha can do anything she likes. If she wants to come back, there's a home for her here. But tell her to wait a few days: There might be some other news."

Several days later I heard that Bhagwan and Sheela were in America. Kalptaru was deluged with phone messages about what had happened. Sheela, Laxmi, and other key corporate officials resigned from the board of directors of the India-based Rajneesh Foundation. *Sannyasins* knew in the Ashram that Bhagwan had left on May 31, 1981, but no one told the people living there that he had gone to the United States. (He arrived in New Jersey on June 1.) So everybody in Poona continued working, assuming he'd merely gone for an unusual but temporary visit to Bombay or somewhere else in India. They didn't realize until about ten days after he had gone that he was in America.

In London we heard it from the Swiss center, because Bhagwan's plane had to stop in Switzerland en route to New Jersey. At this time the official line was that he was sick, and had gone to America for an operation. His medical visa was later (after considerable legal entanglements) converted to one granting him status as a "religious teacher."

Shortly after that another telegram came saying, "Tell Avibha to come to New York." Something told me that this was no short-term visit. I instinctively sensed that Sheela's efforts to engineer a permanent move had finally paid off.

I'd known for a long time that the move to America was coming; what surprised me was the speed with which the final move was made. Deeksha had told me before I'd left that they had bought a "castle" in Montclair, New Jersey. It had been purchased toward the end of 1980, while she was on a visit with Sheela to "have dental work." It was an actual castle that had been transported from Europe, stone by stone, in the 1920s.

A number of reasons for Bhagwan's precipitous departure have been put forth. The Indian government revoked the tax-exempt status of the Rajneesh Foundation (the legal shelter for the Ashram), denying its status as a charitable organization and reassessing tax liability going back to 1974, the year it was founded. This appears to stem from charges that the amount of money accumulated by the Ashram was in no way reflected by any visible public charity programs. A second consideration was the supposed inability to find a large enough chunk of property in India to house the larger dreams of a "new commune," which Oregon residents later feared might ultimately shelter 100,000 people—though this was vigorously denied by Sheela and Bhagwan.

Bhagwan and his entourage flew out on Pan Am Flight 001, from Bombay to New York. The entire upper cabins of the 747 Jumbo Jet had been reserved for them. Cleaners from the Ashram went to Bombay to deep-clean the cabin; special food was prepared; a full complement of medical equipment, including oxygen, was supplied; and the whole cabin was draped in white terry cloth to reduce the chance of irritants. The pilots and stewards agreed to shower and shampoo with scentless soaps the night before the flight.

Bhagwan was met at Kennedy International Airport in New York by a fully cleaned and sanitized black Cadillac limousine. He emerged from the plane wearing the unprecedented outfit of white kimono and black-knit stocking cap—heralds of changes to come. He was immediately whisked off to his hilltop retreat in Montclair.

Laxmi stayed behind to run things in Poona and oversee closing down the Ashram. She nearly went crazy. She had never been so separated from Bhagwan since she'd met him. Even while she'd been off looking for the "new commune," he'd never been half-a-world away. But she continued working because that was *his* wish; and, over the years, she had brainwashed herself to believe that whatever he did was right. She would never let anyone in the Ashram see that she was disoriented in any way by this upheaval. She felt that she was an extension of Bhagwan, and that kept her functioning at the time.

Typically, secrecy was the order of the day. Of the maybe five hundred people left at Poona, probably only twenty would know that Bhagwan was going to stay in America. Maybe two hundred would know they had to close off different sections of the Ashram because these divisions were going to be transferred to America, though their understanding would be that Bhagwan was coming back. The rest, like the people in Vrindavan or Miriam, would have no idea at all that Bhagwan wasn't coming back or that things were changing dramatically in other areas.

Bhagwan's flight to America stirred everybody up. Before this, just the threat that he might leave his body had caused near-panic among *sannyasins*; for him to have suddenly jetted to America underscored just how easily he might disappear from their lives forever. It brought home just how attached we were to him; he'd brought us all together and made us a close family, and now we suddenly felt like children whose parents had just abandoned us.

People went crazy—though in Poona they just kept working along until they had given the place a final cleaning, had bundled off Bhagwan's library books and furnishings, and so on. Then they left—some went home, others tried to hook up with Bhagwan in America. Agents of the Indian government came down, claiming the Ashram owed money for taxes and equipment they had tried to bring in illegally that were being held by customs and so forth.

One curious thing: About three weeks after Bhagwan left the building that housed the editorial offices and printing press burned to the ground. None of us to this day have any idea why the fire started. I wondered at one time if it was for insurance purposes, but that hardly seems likely given the amount of money involved. More recently I've thought that there might have been a lot of documents there that, in someone's opinion, were best destroyed.

There was never any doubt that it was arson: The fire was started by a *sannyasin* who had explicit instructions from the Ashram. Later, when I visited the castle, I was told this had happened; but that was all. I knew the *sannyasin* who had torched the place, but he never had any idea why he'd been told to do it. Since it was not information I had been privy to from the first, I would never presume to *ask* about it. I can only assume the instructions came directly from Bhagwan: Sheela, no matter how much authority she had, wasn't about to have a building burned down on her own say-so. Much later, when she was in prison in Oregon, Sheela continued to insist, "I only did exactly what he told me to do." And that was pretty much my observation all the time I was working for her.

For about six months the majority of *sannyasins* thought that Bhagwan really *had* gone to America because he needed a back operation. The fiction of a "back ailment" soon began to crumble when newspaper stories featured Bhagwan's delight in learning to drive the roads around Montclair. This was Sheela's first major fumble: She had brought Bhagwan into America on the pretext that he was ill; so his visa was a tourist one, with a rider stating that he was here for medical treatment. I think Sheela believed that this was the only way she could get him into the country. It seemed clear to most of us that the American authorities would *never* have refused him entry had he applied as a "spiritual teacher." But she saw that as too threatening.

A majority of *sannyasins* began to accept that this was just another step in the game—although few had any idea what the larger plan was. They continued to trust, just like Laxmi, who was still closing down operations in India. I think most, like myself, thought that when you looked at all that we had achieved in Poona, having the United States as a gameboard could only bring about something truly magnificent—the ultimate mystery school, but more magical than any of us had dreamed of.

Massive celebrations by Bhagwan's disciples in New York, Amsterdam, Sydney, Berlin, and San Francisco throughout the following year kept the sense of purpose and vitality growing around the globe.

In London, while I was at Kalptaru, I ran across Swami Vijen, whom I had known slightly in India. Some Ashram policies were clearly unchanged in spite of the move: Though Sheela had wired me to come to New York, the Ashram would never dream of sending an airline ticket along with the directive. You were always responsible for getting that end of things together on your own.

Vijen had worked with me in the office at Kalptaru, and he was so sharp that I thought he'd be a real asset to the Ashram in America. So I invited him to come along with me. Again, I'd never been told to recruit people or anything like that; it was up to us to take the initiative in matters like that. The fact that he was well-off also made him the ideal traveling companion, since he paid for everything along the way. It was automatic that a *sannyasin* with money paid without asking in situations like this. He'd look upon paying my plane ticket as his gift to Bhagwan.

So we arrived in New York and checked into a hotel. And I was immediately caught up in one of those endless little games the Ashram would play to keep you loyal. By now I was feeling acutely just how cut off I'd been for so long; all I wanted to do was get back into the "womb" of the Ashram.

Even though I had held the position I did, and had been directed explicitly by Sheela to come to New York, I would never presume to go to the Ashram uninvited. Even somebody like Vidya would call and wait for further instructions. So I called from my hotel and was told by Ma Geeta, who was an assistant to Arup, that it wasn't possible for me to go to the castle. "Just wait," she advised me, "and you'll be told what to do."

I was crushed. *My God*, I thought, *I can't go back to the Ashram.* I immediately turned it back on myself, momentarily forgetting that this was a classic pattern that I had come to know so well in India. Now, if I had totally panicked and lost my center, I would never have gotten back into the Ashram. It never mattered what your position was, you could always find yourself back at square one—just as in the game of *leela*.

So I sat and waited and went through a lot of head trips: *What am I going to do if I'm never allowed back? How can I stand being cut off from Bhagwan when I love him so?* At this point what I had already begun to discover became crystal clear: My whole freedom with Bhagwan was gone. It frightened me that I no longer looked on him as just a man who was a teacher with a lot to offer.

Now, in the uncertainty of my New York hotel room, I realized that

I was looking at him as a kind of *god*, as my ultimate security. The last shreds of my independence were gone—but I didn't see this as the result of having been indoctrinated over the years in Poona: I thought it all arose out of something that had always been inside me. It shocked me to feel so unable to stand on my own any longer; and, paradoxically, this pushed me further and further toward the Ashram.

I went through days of hell, waiting for the call that never came. I never even wanted to leave my room for fear that the Ashram would phone and I'd miss the call. I knew them well enough to know that they might call; and if they didn't connect with you that one time, they might never try again. They were always keeping you on a string, and the results were very effective from their point of view. It certainly impressed very successful people who were *never* kept waiting in other circumstances. The Ashram made it clear that it was up to *you* to keep knocking on the door.

During this time the New York center had taken responsibility for me, because of who I was and because I had been told to come to New York by the Ashram. If I wasn't comfortably off in the hotel, they would have arranged a room for me. However, they arranged for making phone calls or doing typing or whatever since, all this time, I was doing things for the Ashram. I had brought a lot of information from Kalptaru that needed to be processed and passed along to the Ashram, since the heart of the office had transferred with Sheela. A lot of this had to do with highly placed people who had taken *sannyas*, and who could be relied upon to help get the Ashram favorable publicity and bring even more people to Bhagwan.

The call finally did come through a few days later, but it certainly wasn't what I was expecting. "You're *not* going to be coming to the castle," Geeta told me, "You're going to be going up to Sambodhi"—which was a center in Boston—"and once you're settled in, we'll call you again."

Everything had changed, I realized. One minute, it was Laxmi, Sheela, Vidya, and Arup who were running everything; now it was Sheela and Deeksha who were in control—the latter actually administering the castle, the former handling all the business being conducted from Montclair. My overwhelming sense of disorientation was intensified by the vast difference between India and America.

Unable to see any other options, I took Vijen in tow, and the two of us dutifully trundled up to Boston.

CHAPTER 22

Sambodhi Center

The move had shaken things up. Procedures were a lot more decentralized than they'd ever been before. Even though Bhagwan was established in Montclair, New Jersey, some center business and some people taking *sannyas* were still being processed through the Ashram in India.

For a brief time *sannyasins* bought the fiction that Bhagwan was ill and in seclusion. But then came the newspaper stories of his driving lessons, of his trip to the New York center. And people did love to hear of the day-to-day antics that he would get up to. In India he had always been fairly predictable: He drove to lecture at the same fifteen-miles-per-hour through the gates of Lao Tzu to Buddha Hall; he walked at the same pace to the podium, lectured for exactly two hours, and wouldn't be seen again until *darshan*. Suddenly, he was in the media; and devotees chuckled over all these little escapades that made him seem so human.

Bhagwan had said, "If you need to lie, or if you need to do things to get to another end, that's fine." So everybody was used to hearing one story after another—often flatly contradictory—to rumor and gossip; so although they initially reacted with worry to the story of Bhagwan's medical problems, they were just as quick to accept that, based on newspaper reports, he clearly was in fine fettle.

Everything that Bhagwan did was looked on, ultimately, as a divine joke. Bhagwan once commented (*The Secret of Secrets*), "I am consistently inconsistent; that's the only consistency that I have. And I have infinite freedom; a consistent man cannot have infinite freedom. I can play, I can joke, I can enjoy shattering your egos, destroying your structures. I'm not serious about these things. I dare to play, to try first one thing, then another. My statements are like the actors on the stage: let them contradict each other; they are not there to tell the truth, but to provoke it; to discover it."

So people just laughed at his antics, and were happy that he was all right. Much later, when all this talk about attempted murder and other improprieties came to light, and Bhagwan was implicated, many were quick to say, "If he was, then I guess he knew what he was doing." They managed to read a higher spiritual significance into everything he did—which was, in many ways, his ultimate defense. Some people might see duplicity, corruption, "wickedness"; but the "true believer" knew that there was a deeply spiritual message—though it might not be evident to any but the most adept Bhagwan-watcher.

We had all practiced this cunning quality to some extent, believing that anyone who looked beyond this could enjoy the joke behind it. We had agreed from the moment we walked through the gate to play "the game." If we could be cunning, yet still feel good about ourselves, then we would have to allow that Bhagwan was often creating a joke that—because he was master of the art—might be so complex and subtle few, if any, would ever grasp its totality.

The great loss in the wholesale abandonment of Poona was the abrupt end of what was effectively an entire town built by Bhagwan. It was in many ways a truly magical place, where creative people could have their immediate needs taken care of so that they would be unhindered in their pursuit of ever-more-creative projects; it was a place that managed to feed, clothe, and house a substantial number of people, without bureaucracy; it was self-supporting, quick to use and develop low-cost, high-efficiency sources of food (such as hydroponics), health maintenance, and energy (such as wind-turbines); it was steeped in a spirituality that avoided dogma and judgment; its citizens lived well, enjoyed the trappings of wealth, from marble pathways to *malas* of fine woods with gold edgings, yet managed to get along without personal money.

Bhagwan gave guidance but laid down no "laws." He also provided an arena in which we could explore the powers of our minds—often with startling results. There were times when I found myself able to move into another's personality completely, so that I didn't know if I or she had done something. He taught us how to give and get psychic energy individually or collectively. He challenged us to push ourselves to the limit—then keep going. In many ways it was utopian—*and it worked.*

The Ashram tried to recapture this and improve upon it in America, but the perfect wedding of a time, a place, a group of people can never be captured again. For a short time the Ranch in Oregon gave the promise of the "new improved" Ashram. But the whole adventure was doomed from the moment those two chartered planes took off from Bombay on the first leg of the journey to disaster.

It seemed quite fitting that the transport of the "magic kingdom" to the United States began with the establishment of a new base of operations in a castle. Sheela originally found the castle on one of her visits to New Jersey, and Deeksha fell in love with it the moment she laid eyes on it. And it truly was a fairy-tale place. It had been a German or Hungarian castle, transported piece by piece by boat to America. Known as the Kipp's Estate, it was an imposing, three-story stone residence perched on a 120-acre hilltop estate overlooking New York City. The grounds were lushly wooded; the interior was magnificent, with the original stained glass, carved bannisters, wooden floors—everything. It was completely refurbished by *sannyasins* from Chidvilas Rajneesh Meditation Center to include extensive medical facilities and an electric chair lift to assure that Bhagwan didn't have to walk up the front stairs.

Then Deeksha, in one of her characteristic frenzies, went in and smashed it all. She sheetrocked the walls and covered the floors with linoleum and utterly buried its antique charms. Her rationale for this was that it would avoid letting anyone become too attached to the place.

The story, as I heard it later, was that a *sannyasin* was standing on the landing of the main staircase one day saying, "What beautiful stained glass." And Deeksha ran down to the tool shed, picked up a mallet, walked up, and smashed the window to pieces in front of the person. Her lesson was, "Drop this whole attachment." If the person could have simply looked at it and admired it without putting it on a pedestal, Deeksha might not have felt so compelled. But she was making a graphic point about one of Bhagwan's basic teachings.

When she first punched the window out there was still a large fragment left, which prompted the *sannyasin* to say, "That's so beautiful, let's at least save this much." At which point Deeksha reduced even the slivers to smithereens. She wasn't a totally crass being; she loved beautiful things, but she was always watching herself to keep from getting too attached. She felt she was simply giving someone an object lesson in an area she knew only too well. One of my *sannyasin* friends gave away a diamond-and-ruby bracelet on impulse to someone who admired it just to make the same point; in reality, it's *nothing*, it's illusion, metal and rocks.

Of course the immediate question is, If this is the teaching, where do the eighty-three Rolls Royces fit in? The answer is the same: One or none or eighty-three, they're still *nothing*. It was Bhagwan's way of pointing out the foolishness of somebody who owned, say, one Silver Shadow, riding around saying, "I'm really something because I own this car"—rather than concentrating on the more important aspects of the inner life. The fleet of Rolls Royces was a joke, running from one in gold leaf to one hand-painted in psychedelic swirls right out of the flower-power 1960s. There *was* a practical side to the Rolls, of course: It's a car that's comfortable, quiet, easy to drive. The fact that it costs anywhere from upwards of $50,000 is irrelevant.

So this is how Bhagwan and the others came into America, the consumer capital of the world. People here attach a great deal of significance to money and the objects it can buy. Bhagwan came in and bought a castle, a ranch, Rolls Royces; everybody had a *Mont Blanc* pen and a *Cartier* gold pencil—just to show that *it didn't matter*. If it worked better, that was its value, not the fact that it was made of a certain metal or had a certain status attached to it. If a Honda Civic had felt as comfortable on the road, Bhagwan might as easily have driven one of these. This was the "gusto" they brought to America.

The ultimate justification of the move was the fact that Bhagwan had said, years before any of this became even a possibility, "The seed will be planted in England, and will flower in America." Before, that had always been taken in a more abstract sense; once the move was in place, however, everybody looked again at those words and said, "Oh, sure this is what he meant all along." Sheela certainly found this a convenient quote to hark back to in justifying the move to America.

In Poona (except for the office staff, who worked up to eighteen hours a day) the average work day would be ten hours a day, seven days a week. During the last eighteen months they had one day off a week, which was a major innovation. Of course it wasn't a hard-and-fast rule; if something came up, you worked right on through with no questions asked. If you lost a day off, you didn't automatically get compensatory time: It was gone. Nobody rearranged schedules to adjust for overtime.

When Bhagwan came to America Sheela said she wanted to drop the whole "dictatorship," so that people would be working in the Ashram because they wanted to be—not out of any guilt trips. She was giving this kind of P.R. talk to people in the castle—then apologizing that it couldn't be given to them right away, because they all had to work harder to establish the commune in the United States. So the people in the castle were working pretty much every minute that they weren't asleep, because they were such a comparatively small group with such a large amount of work to be done.

Many of the people who had bought "rooms" in the "new commune," and had given everything they had, returned home with nothing. They were streaming back in droves, to piece together new lives for themselves. But everybody believed that at some point, sooner or later, they'd be called to the Ashram. These *sannyasins* trusted that a way would be found for them to be near Bhagwan. People waited, and waited, and *waited* for years—people are *still* waiting—for the summons that has never come.

Those who were at various centers were going whacko—with only the idea of *leela*, the game—to provide them something to hold onto. People steadfastly refused to see things in the light of mistrust or disillusionment: This was *the Master*, and he was just playing a divine joke on us all. Even people who had given everything they had for a room in the "new commune" were sitting back and laughing. Which, considering that you might well have been a wealthy doctor who suddenly found himself in a squat in London, was probably as healthy a response as any. This is life, we told each other. This is the game.

The castle was separate, but only up the hill from Chidvilas center. The staff there fleshed out the fifty or so *sannyasins* who had accompanied Bhagwan and Sheela and Deeksha to the castle.

Once people knew that Bhagwan was in America, they flocked over, and were staying in every available room around Montclair, hoping to be near him or maybe see him drive by.

The "art of the Ashram" in instilling the utmost loyalty in people is hard to pinpoint other than by example. Here Bhagwan walks out of the Ashram. If this had happened in normal life, people would have been disillusioned and left on the spot. It's hard to imagine them staying behind to clean up the mess left by a guru who's just left them flat. But the Ashramites stayed on, following Laxmi's instructions, helping break down and box up whatever materials were left in Poona that were "needful" for the United States venture. They kept on until they dropped in their tracks, and the Ashram was utterly dismantled. And all the time they *knew* they weren't going anywhere; there was no promise whatever that they were going to America. In fact, the day the place was shut down and the "Munchkins"—the rag-tag bunch of people from Bombay who were invited to live in it in return for keeping up the grounds—moved in, they were turned out on their own, without a ticket out or a *paise*. Most went back to their country of origin to join the others waiting for the apocryphal invitation to come to America.

It was a bitter irony that most of us were so busy living in the moment that we forgot to prepare for the future. While many who were once successful in business or whatever were successful again, some have never made the transition back—and more than a few either broke down or gave up completely and chose suicide.

The Ashram went up for sale but, to date, it's still owned by Rajneesh International. Saswad, apparently, is also still owned by the Foundation, as is a huge commune in Nepal, near Katmandu, which is overseen by a skeleton staff. Why it was built and when Bhagwan intended to use it remains a mystery. I only stumbled across it some years later, while on a trip to the area.

Although I was dreading it, Sambodhi Center near Boston turned out to be a joy in many ways. The message I had received just directed me to go the center. It told me nothing about it, and nothing about what I was supposed to do once I got there. I had already made up my mind that it was going to be some piddly little center filled with people who'd never been near the Ashram, and all I was going to be doing was breaking them in again. I was expecting the London mentality all over again, and I just didn't have the energy to deal with that sort of reorganizing.

But when Vijen and I drove through the gates of the center my only thought was, *This is an incredible place!* I could feel it from the first moment I got there. I was greeted by Stephen, who had been in charge up to that time, and we hit it off from the start.

The house itself had been built by Stephen as a Gurdjieff work project—which was a funny connection for me. The site was about two miles from the ocean, in Essex, which is some two miles outside of Boston.

At the time it was built there was nothing on the spot except trees and stones. The "exercise" for the Gurdjieff disciples who owned the land was to build a house with ten bedrooms, a large kitchen, a large living area, an office, a meditation room, and a photography studio. It had to be built in six months, without a penny exchanging hands for building supplies. They were not to be put in jail, either, so this ruled out even the thought of stealing necessary items. Nor could they directly barter for things.

The design of the house was up to Stephen and one other man, with the stipulation that it had to be glass and wood. Those were the only two materials allowed in the structure, with the exception of metal for water pipes and electric wiring. Of course that meant no nails in the joining of the wood, which made the project truly staggering. The only wood they were allowed to use was the timber already growing on the land, which meant cutting, curing, and milling it themselves. They could get jobs to earn money to buy things, but they couldn't pay anyone else to work on the place. The stipulations also called for a maximum of two hours sleep in a twenty-four-hour period. (They learned to sit for ten-minute stretches, practicing total relaxation, since two-hour stints of sleep just didn't rest them.) The only water was underground, so this meant they would have to dig a well.

The house was gorgeous. Stephen and his friend had gone far beyond the minimum the project rules demanded—which is typical of Gurdjieff students. Every window looks out onto a breathtaking view, like a framed painting. Once I heard the story I realized what a gift Stephen was—clearly he was a man who could go far beyond himself. I sensed he would be a terrific help to me at Sambodhi. We had some great discussions during my stay there.

Stephen wasn't used to—and, to tell you the truth, I was still pretty green at this—organizing other people on such a large scale. My project—which really became *our* project—was to build the commune back up to peak capacity and create the money so they could live, while we set up a major media event.

This last was a proposed World Celebration, which Geeta had sprung on me by phone—she had now shifted loyalties from Arup to Sheela. They had given me five weeks to conjure up a major media event that would attract lots of attention and let the world know that Bhagwan and company had truly arrived. They wanted me to get movers and shakers from the alternative world there for the celebration.

When I got to Sambodhi six people were living in the house; Stephen had built a separate little house for himself that I nicknamed "The House at Pooh Corner." I immediately started calling all the *sannyasins* in the area to say that I was offering free room and board in exchange for work. I estimated that I'd need a total of sixty people: thirty to arrange the festival, and thirty to create industries to get money to support the whole venture.

Working with Stephen was a thorough pleasure. If I said, "We need to build some kind of a dormitory in the next forty-eight hours to house these extra people," he'd get the job done. It was primitive: A lot of 2-by-4s and plywood; but it was ready on time. I bought most of the supplies on credit at first, since we had almost no cash. It was a typical Ashram approach—procure the goods, get what you needed built, *then* figure out how to pay for it.

The six people who already lived in the house were very resistant to my directions. Most *sannyasins* are individuals by nature—but this group was determined to set its own course for following Bhagwan. It led to a lot of head-butting to get them to contribute energy to the festival. One man, who had always been the gardener for Stephen, really balked when I explained he now had to grow food for sixty people. "Well, I don't know that I *feel* to do that," he told me. And I said, "It doesn't really matter *how* you feel, my dear; if you can't do it, you'll have to leave."

I was the first person who really gave them a taste of how the Ashram was run. But I simply didn't have time to work through everybody's problems by slow degrees: I needed buildings built, vegetables planted, and a festival pulled off. After that we could have time for group encounters. I'm afraid I was a bit of a Red Queen, threatening "Off with their heads!" every time someone slacked off. To tell the truth, I got so I was almost eager for them to get out of line enough so I could kick them out and replace them with my own people, who would have been a hell of a lot easier to deal with.

Watching myself in Sambodhi, I saw an "ogre" side to me that I had never dared let emerge in the Ashram. There it was Sheela, not me, who had been under the real pressure to make things happen. When I look back at myself under those conditions, I can appreciate a little more how Sheela could have done some of the things she did, things that Bhagwan directed her to. And his threat that he was going to leave his body if she didn't come up with the goods was a lot to handle. Of course she does seem to have taken it to a further length than most people—though there were times *I* felt I could murder some of these old farts who refused to cooperate.

There was some initial challenge to my authority, but I was clear enough and centered enough to override it without too much problem. Actually, I could have gone in there as a total imposter, since I swept in on my own say-so. When the gardener questioned me I told him to call the Ashram if he wanted proof. At that point he backed down, not daring to risk it; because if I was right he'd be out on his ear for making such a call.

We held the festival as scheduled on the Sambodhi grounds. It was quite successful; we even managed to get it covered in *Life* magazine. The theme was simply the first celebration for Bhagwan in America, but the subtext was to let people know about *sannyas*. We weren't making any official statements about Bhagwan being in America permanently, because they were still working on his visa.

It lasted four days. We had a band, with singing and dancing—*sannyasins* have always created very good music. We had some groups going on, special Sufi dancers, displays of books and tapes. The image we wanted to give was of the celebration that was *sannyas*. We wanted to show that even though we lived together, we weren't hippies; we had a viable alternative way of thinking to offer—though we might very well be driving an Alfa Romeo or BMW. Again, we were stressing that we had an alternative spirituality, but we were not a religion.

Because there were no celebration days set any longer, people were really looking for some way to meet again. Even today, all you have to do is advertise a big *sannyasin* party, and hundreds of people will run, drive, or fly in for it, because we don't see much of each other any more; but we still remember the old communal spirit, in spite of everything that's gone down these past few years.

Over the four days we had about 750 people. They paid $50 to get in at the gate, $500 to stay the full time. As I mentioned, we got some very good press coverage out of it. It gave us enough money to put back into Sambodhi to help it grow. After the festival we even moved in a few more people. Gradually, a lot of the people who had worked most intensely to get the festival going dropped off. But newcomers drifted in, so we drew up plans to expand.

The center continued to thrive. Later on the Ashram provided a color processor, so that they could do the photographs for Bhagwan's books. Eventually, the color processor went back to the Ranch in Oregon. It never really got off the ground as a center; it was too far outside of Boston to support itself. The last I heard Sambodhi was reduced to being merely a house where people stayed from time to time, although knowing Stephen, he will have it blossoming into yet another form in no time.

On August 29, 1981, Bhagwan flew to Redmond Airport in Central Oregon, then traveled on to the Ranch near the town of Antelope. The Ranch had been purchased on July 10, 1981, by Bipin Patel, Sheela's brother. Sheela had already moved there and taken half the people from the castle with her, and set up temporary headquarters in Antelope. I soon discovered that they were actively recruiting new *sannyasins*, while excluding the old. This was the beginning of a real split within the community.

I think the scale of the venture escaped a lot of people. The Big Muddy Ranch, as it was known before Sheela acquired it for the "new commune," was a 64,000-acre ranch sprawling across two counties, Wasco and Jefferson. The purchase price was about $6 million. Not long after they arrived the Ashram arranged to lease an additional 18,000 acres from the Bureau of Land Management.

Rancho Rajneesh had a total land area in excess of 100 square miles. Located in the high desert region twenty miles from Antelope, it included valleys, hills, meadows, and creeks, and was bordered by the John Day River (later renamed the Radha River). In the 1930s the ranch had extended to 110,000 acres, supporting 32,000 sheep and 1,500 cattle.

By the time it was acquired by the commune it had been overgrazed, much of the land eroded, and a lot of the place was a waste of juniper, sagebrush, weeds, and wild grass. It also held deserted homesteads, rusting farm equipment, collapsing outbuildings, and some repairable corrals for cattle and sheep. And it did have about a hundred underground springs to supply water for humans, proposed dairy animals, and crops.

This parcel of worn-out land was a far cry from what it would shortly become under the ministrations of hundreds of *sannyasins*. Nor was the weather helpful—the first workers to arrive that summer had to put up with weather that could turn from freezing to blistering, from rainy to cloudless, from still to suddenly gusting winds—sometimes within a single day.

It was purchased in the name of the Rajneesh Investment Corporation, a wholly owned subsidiary of the nonprofit Rajneesh Foundation International, a "charitable organization." The property was actually mortgaged to Rajneesh Savings International Limited, a London-based British corporation. Some years later *The Oregonian*, in its series of investigative articles, charged that Sheela and Bipin Patel, her non-*sannyasin* brother, had personally profited from the transaction.

When Rajneesh came he was officially paying a "visit" to the place (which would last four years). The formal reason given was to get him away from the heat and humidity of New Jersey to the drier, more healthful climate on the Ranch. Sheela was reportedly surprised that he had accepted the invitation.

Though *sannyasins* around the world tracked Bhagwan's every movement and longed to be near him, people wouldn't dare just "turn up" at the castle or the Ranch. They waited to be called back into the community. For the majority this never happened. As usual, no explanations were offered—people had to take things on trust. It was widely assumed among *sannyasins* on the outside that this was being done so that people accustomed to Western business ways could get things established—then, everybody else would be invited back.

I got fed up with running Sambodhi center, and just left, traveling to Woodstock, New York, with Sudhas, another *sannyasin*, whose home was there. When we arrived I phoned the Ranch to let them know what I had done, and to await further instructions.

CHAPTER 23

Woodstock and Long Island

While I was staying in Woodstock I heard that Laxmi had been ousted from the Rancho Rajneesh on grounds of "negativity." For a time she went to Ashland, where other *sannyasins* who had been dismissed from the Ashram put her up.

Deeksha and Shantam were also forced to leave soon after this. Deeksha's ouster had been more gradual. Sheela had demoted her to a common worker, but Deeksha had endured it as long as she could. She kept working, though it was said she was suffering from breast cancer and was very ill. Finally, she burnt both her arms in the kitchen and decided that it was suicide, not surrender, she was practicing. So she left and was en route to Switzerland for medical treatment when I caught up with her.

Letters were then issued from the office announcing that these persons were "dead" in the eyes of Bhagwan, and that "anyone supporting Deeksha or Laxmi is not a *sannyasin*: This person is dead."

Since Laxmi and Deeksha were the ones who had taught Sheela so much, they were the only ones who could challenge her at the Ranch. As such, their abrupt dismissals—for "personality conflicts"—were clearly because Sheela felt threatened by them.

I was working two jobs at the time: One in Woodstock, working for an oral surgeon; one in New York, where I was still doing (at long distance) some stock investing for Sheela. There was no reimbursement for my time doing the actual investing or research involved. We were still operating under the old rules as far as that went. During part of the week I resided on Long Island, where I was sharing space with another *sannyasin*, Rakesh ("Rocky"), who also worked in New York.

Laxmi initially came to Woodstock, completely broke and supported by friendly *sannyasins*. Later she came to Long Island. Deeksha and Shantam also came to the Long Island house, where they filled me in on the details of the preceding several weeks.

A lot of people questioned Laxmi's dismissal. When she was given the message to leave, she sent her own message in to Lao Tzu (that name was continued at the Ranch) and asked, "Is this true?" The reply was, "Yes. Why are you doubting the office word?" She was getting thrown back in her face what she had always said in Poona.

She left the Ranch and traveled around, saying that Bhagwan had told her to gather the old *sannyasins* and raise money to start another commune. Bhagwan, she said, would either travel between the two, or stay permanently at one. All the old ones who were hanging around felt this made real sense. Since Sheela was running the show with all new *sannyasins*, Laxmi, representing the earlier group, seemed the logical person around whom a second commune would be built.

Nobody ever doubted for a minute that Laxmi was telling anything but the truth. In the *Sound of Running Water*, Bhagwan specifically refers to her as "empty" and adds, "whatever she says is my word." So when she started soliciting donations she was actually seen as a kind of saint, gathering up the "homeless and hungry" who desperately wanted to get back to the Ashram and Bhagwan.

The *sannyasins* who believed Laxmi were quick to believe that somehow Sheela had engineered the whole thing. That much isn't true, I know: I was with Laxmi part of the time, and she was out and about and very clear that she was rounding people up for this latest "new commune."

She flew back to the West Coast to continue her fund-raising there. And the next thing we heard was that she had made it all up and was now in disgrace. This news threatened to swamp a boat that was already rocking. She had been summoned back to the Ranch, and she had gone back. Even though she was disgraced, all she really wanted was to be back where Bhagwan was. She was put in a trailer off in the middle of nowhere, and not allowed to do any work. Sheela had even managed to get Vivek out of Lao Tzu and down to the office as an office worker. By this point people were becoming numb to the steady stream of surprises issuing from the Ranch.

Shortly after that Deeksha flew back to Switzerland.

With each passing day, I was seeing more and more clearly that Rakesh depended upon the Ranch.

Now, just before the First World Annual Celebration to be held at the Ranch, the Ashram let it be known that *sannyasins* who were American citizens, or who had green cards, could apply to be considered to come for three months in advance of the Festival to help work on and through the celebration. A specified amount was to be paid for the privilege. This was the start of people paying to work at the Ashram. A new twist, that.

So Rakesh started calling to find out if he could come back to the Ashram for at least this limited amount of time. He kept contacting Vidya, and she kept saying, "No." Because relations never had improved between Vidya and myself, there was no point in my adding my two cents' worth. Rakesh wouldn't let me call Sheela, for fear it would mess things up. Which it might well have: if you didn't take the bull by the horns yourself, you'd probably raise more questions than you'd resolve. It was just unfortunate that Vidya was the contact person for this particular project.

At the time most of the energy on the Ranch was going into establishing the "spiritual co-op," putting up A-frame houses for people to live in, and preparing for the festival. They had brought in a lot of really nice house-trailers for Ashramites, and they were building rooms in which encounter groups would soon be held. The first ones would be held at the Festival.

Heavy equipment quickly excavated or improved what had been mere jeep trails, turning them into first-class roads paved with red gravel. They brought two tractors to clear the long-disused fields of brush, weeds, and the accumulated debris of years of neglect, and to break up the soil. The first crop was a 150-acre patch of sunflowers, which grew faster than weeds, and provided "green manure." It also turned out to be a cash crop, providing a windfall $800 when some was sold as high-protein food for local dairy cattle.

Among the first structures raised were a chicken coop for 700 laying hens, a barn and corral for horses, several greenhouses, and a 15,000-square-foot storage building. Subsequently, 1,200 acres were prepared and planted with winter wheat and barley.

In short order fifty-four prefabricated homes were installed, trailers were brought in, and Magdalena Cafeteria was built. It was a spacious facility with the most modern equipment and became, temporarily, the heart of the budding community.

From the first an ongoing effort was made to fuse organic farming methods and modern technology. They applied many of the lessons gleaned from research in India under various Ashram-sponsored research programs.

The Ashram also took over a place called Geetam, a large center in the Lucerne Valley of California. Having the Ashram take over a center was an unusual move. All the group leaders were operating there, and

bringing in a huge amount of money. It had once been a resort property, so it also had hot tubs and extras to offer. Geetam had been owned
by *sannyasins* for several years, and had been a center during this time.
Now it was pressed into expanded service in order to keep groups going, without having them in the way of the construction going on at
Antelope.

Also, because they were establishing a city in Oregon, the Ashram
didn't want any hassles. Often, people participating in groups didn't
have valid passports, and they didn't want anybody on the property in
Oregon who wasn't absolutely legal. The federal officials were paying
surprise visits to be sure everything was in order, and no one wanted
to risk the least infraction of any rule.

The Ashram had another center called Utsava, in Laguna Beach,
California, which was a former church. Rajneeshpuram (the "City of
Rajneesh"), Geetam, and Utsava were all formed at the same time,
when Sheela discovered that the tax laws and the immigration laws
would probably be easier for the Ashram if they became a "religion." A
nonprofit organization attached to a church has certain protections,
and ministers without green cards are more likely to be let stay.

Utsava was one nonprofit center in California, owned by the Rajneesh Foundation International (RFI). It was later attached in a court
case involving funds allegedly misappropriated by Sheela—which case
was lost by the RFI.

At this time a letter signed by Sheela was sent out stating that, "We
are now no longer called *sannyasins*, we are now called *Rajneeshees*. You
are no longer just with a teacher named Bhagwan; you are in a religion
called *Rajneeshism*." The letter went on to stress that if anybody stopped
us to talk about it, we must say that we are a "religion." The letter also
stated explicitly that this was for tax purposes, and requested all copies
be destroyed. However, some people hung onto them, and copies can
still be found. A lot of people reacted very badly, but most went along
with it.

It was just about this time that Kalptaru Centre and Oak Village
combined their resources to purchase Medina, near Ascot, in England.
This was the first large-scale European commune that was formed. It
was peopled primarily by ex-Ashramites, and it was to set an example
of how Rajneesh people could function. Originally, about thirty-five
people moved in—this included children, so they formed their own
school. They also formed their own businesses, and planned to grow
their own food and become totally self-sustaining—just as the Ranch
was in Oregon.

Another commune was begun in Australia, the seeds of which had been planted in Poona. When they were looking for the "new commune" an Australian man said he had some property in Western Australia that he would be happy to donate to the Ashram. They didn't want it at the time, but asked him to hold onto it. When they got to America they authorized the foundation of a commune there. It provided a place for a lot of those who had been abandoned at Poona.

None of these communes were owned by the Ashram, because the Ashram was nonprofit. So it began setting up a number of foundations to get through these problems. Medina was a corporation unto itself, as was the Australian venture. These paid their own way, paid their own taxes, and would "donate" money to the Ashram.

Once these two "legal" communes were under way, another *unauthorized* center was formed in the south of France by an old *sannyasin*. He had been kicked out of the Ashram several times, and had always been invited back by Bhagwan. He surprised everyone, because he had only been a rolfer in the Ashram; now, suddenly, he became a businessman and got a lot of people to invest in purchasing an incredible castle.

Because of its situation and its beauty, it attracted a lot of older, more creative *sannyasins*. They started their own groups; they had their own jewelry department, their own investment corporation, and so forth. But proper procedure said that you had to request formal permission to go and live in any center or commune. Everyone who wound up there had already tried and been refused permission to enter the Ashram in America, or Medina in England, and so forth. They were "rebels." Even though the Ashram had no legal or financial control over them, Sheela was able to use emotional blackmail very effectively in closing it down. She simply went in and said, "You people are destroying the plan that Bhagwan has." That was enough, since the *sannyasins* who had gone there were still very devoted to Bhagwan.

In Germany there was a center called Purvodiya. It had been dormant, with only about fifteen people in it, for a long time. Now it took off and became the nucleus for another authorized commune.

The growth throughout the world paralleled the growth of the Ranch. More and more the *sannyasins* worldwide were being counted on to donate money to the Ashram. The Ashram would never write a letter saying, "Anyone who's a *sannyasin* will now donate ten percent of his salary." You'd get precious little with such a tactic. Instead the Ashram would was send out a letter saying, "Now we've got the new commune. Bhagwan has this vision: He really wants everybody to come and live here and be here. And to do this, we need to build more housing. But we're waiting to see you all. If you can spare anything, please send it."

The money really began to roll in. The First World Celebration was a huge success. The Ashram had been in America for under a year, but already a tremendous need had grown up in *sannyasins* everywhere to get back in touch with each other, if only on the limited basis of a celebration. So people came into Oregon from everywhere around the globe—roughly 17,000 of them. The cheapest price you could pay for the four days was $600—and this was if you had your own tent. That included two meals a day, but no drinks. If you stayed in an A-frame, that brought the cost up to $750. To stay in a trailer—with several other people—upped the ante to $1,000. Your own private room in a trailer for the four days was $1,500.

Groups were also being held. And anyone who had taken *sannyas* in this interim period was going to be required to take some groups. The groups went up in price dramatically from what they'd been in India. The average cost was now $100 a day.

The celebration itself lasted three weeks. The longest anyone was allowed to stay at this celebration was twenty-one days, and it cost a *fortune*—but people would pay, because they just wanted some time at the Ranch. The celebration itself lasted three weeks. People who had come to work before and through the festival paid fees that averaged out to about $1,000 a month for the length of their stay. They were expected to work at least a twelve-hour day—and they dropped like flies, because it was very hot in Oregon.

When Rocky was refused permission to participate in this pay-to-work arrangement, I decided that was the last straw. I said, "Look, Rocky, you're miserable. I certainly can't be with you." He had become depressed.

So we bought a Dodge Tradesman van with windows all around and completely gutted it. I put a bed in it, a futon, some indoor plants, curtains—I went whole hog with the thing. Rocky went home to Canada for three weeks while I did the work. Then I gathered him up, put him in the back of the van, and we drove from New York to Oregon. I didn't tell anybody what we planned; Rocky was frightened and kept saying, "They'll take our *malas* away for this." My answer was, "You're better off dead than living like this: Let's at least *try*."

At the very least I planned for us to stay out the festival; but, if it could be engineered, I hoped both of us would be able to stay on permanently at the ranch.

CHAPTER 24

Rancho Rajneesh

We arrived in Antelope, the little town outside of Rajneeshpuram—
"The Sacred City of the Lord of the Full Moon." At this point they'd
gotten about halfway through the takeover. When we got there we
found a building marked RECEPTION, which meant Reception for the
Ranch. We went up and said hello to the woman who had been Vidya's
assistant back in India. I saw several other people I recognized, so it
was a pretty happy reunion all around.

I was greeted quite warmly, but the whole vibe toward Rocky was
very negative; they were really doing a number on him. It was the
same trip they were doing to a lot of older *sannyasins*, putting them
through the wringer again. This was all part of the game: One person
would be gushed over, which only magnified the isolation of the
other.

I said to Vidya's former assistant, "Look, we're paid up for the festival," and there wasn't much they could do about *that*. But this was two
weeks before the opening of the celebration. Homa just said, "Well, I'll
have to call and see what they say." So she called up to the Ranch. Back
down came the message, "No, you've done wrong. You shouldn't have
come. And you've come two weeks early. You can't expect us to take
care of you." And so on.

"Fine," I said, "We'll just go and come back in two weeks."

We had turned to go back to the van, when this woman said, "Wait,
Bhagwan's going to drive by in a moment." He would drive every day
from the Ranch, through Antelope to Bend and back again. He loved to
drive. "People stand on the side of the road and *namaste* him as he
drives back," she explained.

So we walked down the road and stood and waited for him. I'd always felt an excitement when I saw Bhagwan, but it wasn't there this
time. On the other hand I really felt the charge in Rocky as he went

totally into *namaste*. It seemed like he had the energy I had once had in the same situation. Now I was standing there, just feeling *nothing*.

Down the street came the Rolls, and Bhagwan actually stopped to say hello, because he recognized us from the Ashram in Poona. After a moment he drove on. I felt weird, because I felt nothing. I was also checking on how I felt about the fact that they had said I couldn't come into the Ashram two weeks before. And I realized that hadn't bothered me either. In actual fact I *didn't want to go*. I was quite happy to go off and camp by a river or whatever.

We walked back to get in the truck and the former assistant came running after us, saying, "Vivek just radioed in to say Bhagwan said to go on up to the Ranch." Here was another example of that push me–pull you thing. Rakesh had just gone from total expectation to the pits to being built back up again.

So we drove into the Ranch. We had to go through security, which included four observation posts along the route—each manned by two members of the private security forces—while we were still outside the Ranch. There were seven additional posts within Rajneeshpuram City limits. They searched everything and ripped everything apart. They went all through the van, with dogs that sniffed it. They were really worried that during the festival people would bring drugs in, and the federal agents would come in and discover this. That would ruin this event. Other contraband included firearms or explosives; incense, candles, and matches; meat or fish; and mail, which was to be properly routed through Ranch channels before being delivered to *sannyasins*.

I saw more and more people that I knew manning these checkpoints, so I began to get excited. We paused near a marble cube, which read,

> The City of
> Rajneeshpuram
> Welcome to
> You

Nearby, flags of the United States and the City of Rajneeshpuram were fluttering in the mild breeze.

Once we were in the Ashram we were told to park just inside the last checkpoint. But I said to Rocky, "I don't want to park out here with all these weirdos"—because they had all these new people—"I want to be with people that I know." So I drove through.

Although there were very few older *sannyasins* on the Ranch, our faces were so familiar that no one thought to question us. It was just Rocky and Avibha who were driving around the Ranch. Things hadn't been established long enough for everybody to know who belonged and who didn't.

Some of the people we saw had paid to work; some were there because Sheela had let them stay. And some had paid enormous amounts just to be there, because they'd been told they couldn't work.

We stopped in the main town center and just walked around, taking in the scope of this city-in-the-making. We checked out Devateerth Shopping Mall, which offered a Zorba the Buddha restaurant, Rajneesh Deli, Rajneesh Photo Supply, Rajneesh Hair Design, and a boutique advertising European designer fashions; the post office; and Rajneesh Mandir Hall, which was the Buddha Hall of Rancho Rajneesh. It was a huge structure with a flat roof supported on colonnades that reminded me of pictures of the Temple of Karnak in Egypt.

The hall became quite a sore point in growing disputes with locals who complained that the structure had originally been designated as a "greenhouse" on application to the local zoning board. This was all part of the steadily deteriorating relations with Oregon locals, which had prompted so much beefing up of internal security. Things had gotten off to a bad start from the very first when the residents of Antelope, discovering that permission had been granted by county authorities for fifty-four mobile homes to be permanently installed on the Ranch, had contacted the environmentally concerned "1000 Friends of Oregon" in August 1981. The question of alleged land-use violations continued to haunt the Ranch in the form of political and legal maneuvering until the collapse of Bhagwan's Oregon experiment.

At the time the office simply explained that the structure hadn't proved workable as a greenhouse, and so it was converted to an assembly hall. It sprawled over 2.2 acres (some 80,000 square feet), and was the gathering place for silent meditations in the presence of Bhagwan (who was still maintaining silence), as well as the heart of celebration days and other festivals.

We were also shown the crematorium—the Western solution to the burning-*ghats* near Poona—which reportedly cost somewhere over $50,000 and could accommodate a huge crowd for the funeral of a *sannyasin*.

The scale of things planned and already underway was incredible. The place had its own radio network; by spring 1984 the Rajneesh Buddhafield Transport system had 115 buses, 40 drivers, and a 5 A.M. to midnight shuttle service, making it one of the largest public transportation systems in Oregon. Comprehensive, ranch-wide pest-control efforts kept the countryside remarkably free of these creatures—and healthy, as a consequence.

Ongoing conservation and reclamation projects to upgrade the land ultimately included building 200 siltation dams on creeks, planting over 1 million trees, and erecting miles of deer fencing to protect crops. Hunting was strictly prohibited—not even predators could be killed. More inventive, nonlethal methods of wildlife control were inaugurated. Deer were caught and moved to outlying areas. The Ranch imported several emus, the Australian ostrich-like land birds, which were good for keeping coyotes, bobcats, and hawks at bay.

Things were always done with an eye to preserving or enhancing the natural beauty of the area. Structures relied heavily on wood or were painted earth tones to help them blend into the surrounding vistas.

One of the most impressive projects was the construction of the 80-foot-high, earth-filled Gurdjieff Dam, which created Krishnamurti Lake. It had a 330-million-gallon capacity, which eventually offered swimming and recreational boating facilities.

Finally, somebody came up to me and said, "Oh you must go and see Sheela: she's asking where you are."

We walked down to Jesus Grove, which was where we were told Sheela and all the "witches" lived. We walked behind the trailer—actually, three deluxe mobile homes joined together in a triple-wide arrangement—where they all lived, and discovered Sheela presiding over a wedding. Now that Rajneesh was a religion, she was functioning as a priest—as well as still serving as personal secretary to Bhagwan and president of the Rajneesh Foundation, which had been resurrected as an Oregon-based concern.

All these people had been given titles as functionaries in the new religion, and were really into it. Sheela could legally perform marriages—Bhagwan had provided a manual of ceremonies for all rites of passage, from birth to death. Much later, during a trial involving Rajneeshees in August 1984, an Oregon court recognized the right of witnesses to take their oath of truth on the book *RAJNEESHISM: An Introduction to Bhagwan Shree Rajneesh and His Religion*—rather than the Christian Bible, which further attested to the growth and legal standing of Rajneeshism. (Bhagwan declared an end to his religion just before his expulsion from the United States in 1985.)

It was a very warm reunion. Right in the middle of things, Sheela cried, "Avibha!" and just dropped everything. It was a nice exchange. At that point I didn't push the Rocky thing.

We went back into town and I moved the van behind the bakery, so none of the guards could see it.

The guards made me uncomfortable, even though I'd known many of them for years. Rajneeshpuram was a real city, so they had a proper police force trained by the state police. As soon as they had gotten in their police cars, they took "cop" roles. We fed it back by treating them with the same uneasiness you might treat a policeman with. It was all rather intimidating.

I later learned that there were something like 150 security people, who constantly monitored all comings and goings on the Ranch. Ten full-time and thirty-five part-time officers were authorized by the state of Oregon. The rest were private peace-keeping forces. All were there because of increased talk of violence. Eventually, anyone without proper I.D. needed a day pass or an armband to go anywhere outside of a few of the more obvious "tourist attractions." Neighbors began to refer to the Ashram as a "police state," which hardly improved matters.

I knew from that first moment I saw Bhagwan that I didn't want to stay. And, to tell the truth, I was sick of working so hard. Part of me just wanted to go off and "be free," whatever that meant.

Rocky went to ask if he could work, and he was told to go work in the bakery. I was told to coordinate the various tents that would sell supplies. They had playing cards with Bhagwan's picture on them, lucite bottle openers with Bhagwan's picture in the middle of them, cups and place mats with Bhagwan's face on them—all sorts of memorabilia, rather done up like the "Strawberry Shortcake" items. The only thing missing was that the clerks hadn't been told to say, "Have a nice day." When they opened the bank on the Ranch, even the checks had his face on them.

I was told to make sure that the people who were training on the computerized cash registers were learning properly. All in all it was the ideal job for me, because it let me float around the Ranch and just take everything in. But I can't say I liked a lot of what I discovered. I no longer had any sense of what all this was leading to. And the people around me seemed increasingly regimented and depersonalized.

Then they started making announcements that people who had green cards—whether you were in this three-month plan, or had just come up for the festival—could request to stay. So Rakesh, who had a green card, went up to the office and put in his request to stay. The procedure was to file your request on one day, and you would get your answer the following day.

The next day the answer came, "No, you can't stay." I remember we sat for a long time in the van, and he was driving me nuts. All he wanted was to be at the Ranch; and, really, it was the only place he was going to be able to function. I was also thinking, *If I'm going to get away from here at all, I can't get away with him, because he'll always pull me back, because he can't function.*

So I said, "Rocky, this is it: We're going to have to go together and see Sheela. You've just got to stay, because you can't eat or sleep."

We went over to her trailer at about 11:30 P.M. Sheela wasn't there, so I was poking around her trailer. Vidya walked in and said (in her South African accent, which always grated on me), "What do you think you're doing here?"

"We're waiting for Sheela," I said.

"Why?" she demanded.

"None of your business," I answered, "I'm just here for a visit." I was already out of line, because she was such a bigwig in the office.

"No you don't!" she snapped, "You want to ask if he can stay, don't you?"

"Yes, you're right, I do."

"Well, you already asked me," she said, turning the attack on Rakesh, who was shaking, "And I already told you no."

He started to agree, but I cut across him and said, "Yes, so I'm going to ask Sheela, because I don't understand why you said no."

She retreated to the party line then, saying, "It's not your position to understand or not understand."

I just looked at her and said, "That's bullshit! I know all about this. Remember who you're lying to. *What's your reason for not allowing this person to be here?*" Rakesh had been a good rolfer in the Ashram for eight years, seven days a week, ten sessions a day, at $50 a session—he had made the Ashram a *lot* of money.

Rakesh told me to shut up at that point, because he was afraid I was really finishing things for him. He thought he'd get further with her himself. At that point Vidya turned to Rakesh and said, "You've always been negative. You were always sick in Poona. You have a bad back."

Rocky just stared at her, then said, "Vidya, you've got the wrong person. I wasn't sick a day in India. And I *never* had a bad back. I don't know why you're saying this."

"You're just reacting," she said, "You don't remember."

"Leave him alone!" I shouted. Just then Sheela walked through the door to confront Vidya and me in a near-catfight.

Strangely, Sheela and I just began to chat. I explained why we had come, and I said, "I just don't understand why you won't let him be here. Anyway, he's good; and he's proved that he works hard."

And Sheela said, "Oh, that's no problem at all. He can stay *as long as you do.*"

And I said, "I don't want to stay. I think it's time for me to go off and be on my own." But I didn't want Rocky to hear this, because he wouldn't have stayed if he didn't think I was going to be there too. So I said to Sheela, "I don't want to stay at the moment, but I'll go and get my green card."

And she said, "There's no need to do that: We can get around it."

But I insisted, "No, let me go get the card, and I'll come back. But Rocky can stay here in the meantime."

"How long will it take?"

"A few weeks."

"That's fine," she said.

"Or, maybe a few months."

"That's okay."

"Well," I joked, "It might even take years to get all the permissions."

"That's fine, as long as it takes. I just want you to remember you always have a home here."

I thought to myself, *This is incredible.* I had never been given *this* much freedom with her before. Then I went back to Rakesh and assured him, "Everything's fine; you can stay. I'm going to go and get my green card, and I'll be back in a few weeks." But I knew the time had come to begin playing the game on *my* own terms.

And that was fine with him. So we stayed through the Rajneeshpuram First Annual World Celebration, which ran from July 3 to 7, 1982. It was a major national and international success, with an estimated attendance of six thousand *sannyasins* from all over. And we had a great time—we were with a lot of old friends, and Rocky was happier than he'd been in months. As always, no one could accuse anyone of skimping when it came to staging a major event: On one afternoon low-flying planes showered rose petals on Bhagwan's car and everyone lined up along the road, waiting for a glimpse of the Master.

During this period I had several meetings with Sheela, and found just how much she was changing. Outwardly, she seemed more and more concerned with paranoia and politics. Even more distressing, I had the sense that the person I knew in India was gone. The new Sheela I was seeing was hard, withdrawn, nervous, a black, dead monotone. Everything was telling me it was time for me to leave.

I planned to drive the van down to San Francisco, sell it there, then fly back to New York. I said good-bye to Rocky, and off I went.

It takes about an hour to get from the town of Rajneeshpuram out to the road that takes you back to Antelope. Rajneeshpuram is in a valley, and you have to approach it by a very windy road. As I was driving along I began to sing, 'It's a Long, Long Way to Tipperary."

I was holding my *mala* in my hand; it was the first time I'd taken it off in all these years. And I suddenly pitched it out the window. I hadn't consciously thought about dropping *sannyas* or whatever it meant to let go of my *mala*. But I realized that the further I was from that place, the lighter I felt.

Looking back, I think one of the biggest mistakes Sheela—and, by extension, Bhagwan—made was to divide people up; she didn't create it so everybody could move in at once. And from that a rift was created. Even though most of us had a hard time adjusting, we could smell freedom through the cracks in what had once been a unified front, a smooth, insulating wall around us. It was only by coming out that we could realize just how tight it had been.

CHAPTER 25

Cold Mountain

I drove down to Ashland, where I met Tathaghat, nicknamed "T." He was a *sannyasin*, one of Bhagwan's first bodyguards, and he was later to become my husband.

At the festival he, Ma Yoga Chetana (Arup's assistant), and Ma Yoga Krishna were all accused of "negativity" and had their *mala*s taken away. This was the first time—other than with Deeksha and Laxmi, which everyone tended to regard as a great joke—that such a thing had occurred.

This is what happened: Amongst all the Bhagwan souvenirs in the shop were a number of bumper stickers. T. had picked one that said, "Above all, don't wobble," which is a Zen koan. Next to the passage was a circle with Bhagwan's face. T. had a mobile home with a window space just right for the saying itself, but too small for the whole sticker. So he decided to cut off Bhagwan's picture. He asked the woman in the store if she had a pair of scissors. She said yes, so he clipped off the portrait. Then he turned with the picture that was left, handed it to her, and said, "Here, would you like this?"

She immediately called the office and told them what happened. T., Chetana, and Krishna all got called into the office because they'd gone into the store together. This wasn't their first "offense," though; his clipping the portrait was simply the last straw. It was their house in Ashland—all three lived together—in which Deeksha and Laxmi had stayed when they had been kicked out. And Sheela had never liked T. even at the best of times. Chetana had worked for Arup, which automatically made her offensive—because Arup was always considered a rival to Sheela. And Krishna was one of the those whom Sheela didn't like on principle.

They were hauled into the office. There, ironically, they had Bhagwan's portrait cut off their *mala*s—which was what their crime had been.

These three people had been with Bhagwan almost from the first. Chetana had been there since Bombay; T. met them in Poona in 1974, when they first arrived; and Krishna had been there for quite a number of years. Susheila (of Nutella fame) did the *mala* honors.

The *mala* was something Bhagwan gave you, so this action made people wonder: Who, exactly, did the office think they were to take this away? It really hit hard.

But, regular as clockwork, the announcement came from Bhagwan via Vivek (because he wasn't speaking publicly at this point), "Whatever happens in the office, I know about." But for the first time a lot of people began to say, "Oh, I don't believe it. He must be drugged." No one doubted that Vivek had carried anything but an accurate message out of Lao Tzu.

From there, it became a regular thing. At the drop of a hat you could have your *mala* taken away.

They returned to Ashland, then the two women went on to San Francisco. But T. was still in Ashland when I arrived. In Ashland I was suddenly surrounded with a number of members of what I had considered "the fast-lane group" at the Ashram. They invited me to go whitewater rafting with them, and I had a fine time.

I stayed there a few days. I knew I hadn't the least interest in getting a green card, because I didn't want to go back to the Ranch at this point.

I went down to San Francisco for a visit, returned to Ashland, and decided to stay. And it was a few weeks of real bliss. I wasn't a *sannyasin*; I was just enjoying myself. I walked into a store and realized that for seven or eight years all I had seen were red or orange clothes. It was actually tiring to take in all those colors and designs. I now had to consider *all* of this—and that was in just one store. Before, everything—down to towels and underwear—was red. Now I had to start awakening *taste* again.

Once I got out of orange clothes I began to discover foods I hadn't tried in years: eggs, fish, cheese. It took my system a long time to adjust to digesting these foods. I spent those weeks just experimenting.

Then I got a phone call from Sheela. She said, "I heard you had stopped in Ashland. Aren't you going to go on to New York? Aren't you going to get the green card and come back?"

I lied and said, "There was a bit of a problem with the green card, but I'm here sorting it out. When I get it sorted out, I'll let you know."

Then she said, "Would you look around and see what land is available? We're thinking of opening another center there." She also had other people making similar inquiries at the time. So it began with funny little things like that, which came to nothing but let her pull on me from an old friendship stance. Even though I didn't want to be a *sann-yasin* any more, I still loved a lot of these people—Sheela included. So I slipped into this kind of trap.

I did a lot of little jobs for her, quite happily.

T. and I decided to get married. We bought the ranch in the valley in Oregon, and nicknamed the place "Cold Mountain," after a line in one of the "Cold Mountain" collection of poems by the T'ang poet Han-Shan. The collection is an early and very important work of Chinese Buddhist poetry; it is considered a classic of Zen literature. In these verses "Cold Mountain" is a symbol of enlightenment and peace. My favorite line has always been, "the path to Cold Mountain is laughable." At that point in my life I felt I needed a good laugh more than anything.

In the *sannyasin* world things seemed to be becoming more balanced. The Ashram was opening restaurants, which featured vegetarian dishes, fresh-baked breads, and extravagant desserts. These restaurants, Bhagwan said, had to be named "Zorba the Buddha." This whimsical-sounding name came from a concept that Bhagwan often harked back to over the years. In *The Perfect Master, Volume II*, he explains,

I am trying to create here not Zorba the Greek but Zorba the Buddha.

Zorba the Greek is the very foundation of Zorba the Buddha. Buddha arises out of that experience. I am all for this world, because I know the other world can only be experienced through *this* world . . .

First become a Zorba—a flower of this earth—and earn the capacity through it to become a Buddha—the flower of the other world.

The first restaurants were opened in Antelope, Portland, and The Dalles. When the Ashram bought a hotel in Portland, it opened the restaurant in the hotel. They decorated all the rooms in the hotel like the rooms in Poona, and the place became extremely popular. It had big, big plants, cream walls, a few shelves, a generous wardrobe, nice beds—but it didn't have froufrou. And there was original art, like Japanese calligraphy provided by Ashramites. It really was quite gorgeous. And the restaurant, though vegetarian, and so something of a novelty, was first-rate and quickly became very successful.

Soon after this the Ashram rented space in Portland for what was shortly to become Zorba the Buddha Rajneesh Disco Nightclub—another financial goldmine. All of these facilities were open to the public. Initially, people were a little skeptical of the hotel, because nothing was cheap—it was $100 a night but it wasn't like the Hyatt, there was no room service or any frills. But people went for it; anything the Ashram tried a hand at seemed to make money . . . and it was creative enough to always look for still other ways to use one money-making operation as a springboard for another. The restaurants became a chain—and even provided the recipes for a successful cookbook. By early 1983 the office claimed to have put an estimated $35 million into the Oregon economy—and the 1984 Third Annual World Festival reportedly netted the Ranch around $10 million.

The disco took off. The music was great, and the men and women who worked there were (as usual) attractive *sannyasins*. Only the most beautiful people were selected to run the disco and the hotel.

Not only was the general public coming in to dine, dance, maybe spend a few days, but *sannyasins* were coming in and *loving* what they were seeing. This was very different from the way we lived in India. And these places provided nice environments for getting back in touch with each other, since the Ranch provided permanent homes to only a relatively few disciples.

The Ashram soon opened discos all across the world. And that one enterprise has probably brought in more money than any other single venture. If you speak to a German or Dutch person you'll find these discos are still popular—because the design is striking, the music is always current and highly danceable, and they are smoothly run. Any business the Ashram had a hand in was a model of efficiency—it was one of the more amazing achievements of the *sannyasin* world that it could have utter efficiency without bureaucracy. This is one of the characteristics that makes many ex-*sannyasins* such powerhouse achievers in the business world today.

About three months after the First Annual World Celebration the Ashram shut down Geetam and brought all the group leaders up to the Ranch. Now it began sending the group leaders to other centers around the world, which gave a feeling of cohesion to the global network. It emphasized the fact that, though people in these other centers were at several removes from the Ranch, they weren't cut off completely. The fact that many of these group leaders were so close to Bhagwan made people outside the Ranch feel closer to Bhagwan. This type of outreach kept people on a string—and it also kept money filtering back to the United States from people who couldn't afford to come to America to take groups. A new center was opened in Holland, continuing the pattern of world growth.

Sheela kept dangling the possibility that Cold Mountain would become a center. T. was happy about that. He felt very cut off and isolated, as though part of himself had been cut away with his *mala*.

The Ranch was enjoying boom times. The Ashram set up its own bank—much more sophisticated than in Poona, where funds had been strictly held as cash and withdrawn as cash. Now there was a completely computerized facility in place within six months of the celebration. People were actually put on a Rajneeshpuram banking card. Your money was noted on a computer chip on the card, and deducted as you spent it. In the meantime the cash was used for investing.

All of these assets were frozen when the Ashram closed. The place was not a legal bank. Krishna Deva, the mayor at the time, testified that racketeering had been involved, which was enough for the federal authorities to step in.

But in those earlier, more optimistic days, the Ranch was becoming self-sufficient. Everything was taken care of for you if you lived on the Ranch. Now there was Rabiya Dairy Farm, which housed fifty Holsteins, and had such sophisticated equipment as a methane digester for production of fertilizer and gas; six greenhouses to supply vegetables, herbs, cut flowers, and seedlings for transplanting to the truck farm; beekeeping facilities; and much more. On the drawing board were grandiose plans for expanded production of oats, barley, and winter wheat, which provided both grains for Ranch use and surplus used as cash crops.

Rajneeshpuram was turning into a bustling community. It had a medical center, an elementary school, Chidvilas Rajneesh Meditation Center, a swimming pool. Eventually, Bhagwan was one day able to vary his routine—driving his Rolls Royce into Bend, Oregon, and returning by taking a 70-horsepower speedboat for a cruise around Patanjali Lake.

But there were also bizarre developments. A year after moving to the Ranch, the office inaugurated a system of regulating sexual favors, because they had become obsessed with reports of new strains of a penicillin-resistant "super gonorrhea." New arrivals had to wear an orange bead on their *mala*s until stringent testing for venereal diseases proved negative. Later, the AIDS scare produced rubber gloves and condoms to assure safe sex.

This also encouraged spying because, if a person failed to report a sexual encounter, someone else was obliged to tell. "It's not telling on someone," people were told. "It's for your own good. And it's a loving gesture, because we don't want to encourage people to be dishonest." Some of these lines, I must admit, raise a giggle with many former *sannyasins*.

Then people were given a brass marker with Bhagwan's signature embossed on it, which was designed to be clipped to your *mala*. On the back was your number, showing you were a full-time, absolute Ashramite—one of those entitled to live on the Ranch. The number corresponded with the master files in the office.

Throughout 1982, long before Rocky and I had arrived at the Ranch, the tiny town of Antelope (with a pre-Ranch population of about forty) felt threatened by the "red tide." As early as December 1981 the 1000 Friends of Oregon group had filed a lawsuit against Wasco County for approving a future election on the question of incorporating Rancho Rajneesh. The contention was that such conversion of farmland to urban purposes was a clear violation of land-use laws.

As tensions increased non-*sannyasin* residents of the Antelope area began to fear that their town and their lives were going to be taken over by the influx of "cultists" who were living in the city as voting residents. While Sheela (who was undisputed spokesperson for what *Oregon Magazine* called a "multimillion-dollar international corporation") tended at first to dismiss these people as "noncreative" obstructionists, the Antelope City Council decided to hold a vote on disincorporating the town and turning back zoning and permit authority to Wasco County.

By the time of the election in April, however, 55 *sannyasins* had moved into town and were registered to vote—so they effectively quelled the dissolution bid. This, however, kicked off the first round of legal suits over the status of Antelope's new voters. And each week seemed to bring new charges from both sides. Sheela, characteristically, was always ready to stir things up. "What rumors do you want to hear?" *Oregon Magazine* quotes her as asking during one interview, "A lot of them I started myself. It's a perfect way to keep useless minds occupied."

Additional fuel was provided by the film *Ashram* by Wolfgang Doborwolny, a German ex-*sannyasin*, whose film on the Poona experience focused on sex and violence during encounter groups, including a graphic depiction of what was called an attempted gang-rape of a female participant. Though the film was shown in Portland, a large number of Antelope citizenry made the four-hour drive to see the film for themselves.

Fearing a complete takeover, the Antelope City Council deeded the Community Church to the Eastern Diocese of the Oregon Episcopal Church. The vote at Rajneeshpuram in May 1982 was 150-0 in favor of incorporation. A circuit court overruled 1000 Friends of Oregon's request for an injunction against the incorporation pending outcome of the lawsuit. This motion was denied, but the court warned that a decision unfavorable to the Ranch could force dismantlement of the whole city.

When Sheela sued an Antelope resident for libeling her during a joint appearance on the "Merv Griffin Show" in July, many locals became considerably less vocal. In August Rajneeshpuram installed its first mayor and other officials, and things began growing even faster.

For a while local opposition held up a business license for mail order publications; a requested permit for an 18,000-square-foot printing plant to employ 111 workers; and some housing permits. In regard to the latter issue Sheela reportedly said, "If I can't get more housing permits, I'll get the best lawyer in America to contest the decision." Matters peaked when city council meetings became media events, with NBC vying with the Ranch's own videotaping equipment for coverage.

The fear that the Ranch, with its incredible resources, would simply sweep them aside kept the Antelope citizenry united in their opposition to the Rajneeshees—and pinning their hopes on the as-yet-unresolved land-use suit. Sheela added spice to matters by accusing city officials of Antelope of "secret meetings" and a variety of other infractions, including tampering with Ranch mail. While nobody accused the red-clothed disciples of violence, Antelope citizens felt threatened by the increasing number of Bhagwan's followers pouring into the area. And there was also some resentment of these johnny-come-latelies who were clearly determined to tell local farmers what proper land management was all about. One charge that crept in again and again was "arrogance"; it seemed to cling to Sheela in particular, but it was a blanket resentment big enough to cover everyone living at Rancho Rajneesh.

On October 14, 1982, Bhagwan, accompanied by Sheela, went to Portland to be interviewed by U.S. Immigration and Naturalization Service (INS) officials who were reviewing his application for "permanent resident" status as a religious leader and teacher. He was greeted at the downtown offices by a throng of sannyasins who had bused in previously. They mixed with journalists and television crews from several networks in greeting Bhagwan when his chauffeur-driven white Rolls Royce brought him from the airport.

On their return from Portland, Sheela reportedly said, "Let us all pray that a Master of this quality and sensitivity never has to be subjected to this kind of procedure again anywhere in the world." An ironic comment, given the subsequent bizarre turns of event that

brought Bhagwan up against the INS—and plenty of other federal and
state officials.

In November, while Bhagwan's request for status change was pending, Rajneeshees were elected to four of seven seats on the Antelope
City Council—certainly confirming many people's fears of a takeover.

But, in Rajneeshpuram, this was overshadowed by the dismaying
news on December 22 that the INS had denied Bhagwan's petition to
remain in America as a religious teacher. This set in motion a worldwide series of peaceful demonstrations in January, February, and
March 1983—in Sweden, India, Japan, Australia, Germany, England,
Italy, Spain, the Netherlands, and across the United States—demanding U.S. resident status for Bhagwan. Things were suddenly very unsettled at Rancho Rajneesh, pending appeal of the ruling.

Things were becoming unsettled in other quarters, also: People who
had had *sannyas* taken away were first looked on as heroes—it was assumed that Sheela had gotten carried away, and that Bhagwan would
eventually set things to right. Which, of course, he never did.

Changes continued at a furious rate. A press release was issued that
said you didn't have to wear orange and a *mala* to work, because it
could make getting a job difficult. However, if other *sannyasins* saw you
on the street without your *mala*, they would actually call the Ashram
and tell. Somebody ultimately called about *me* and said to Sheela, "Do
you realize she's not wearing a *mala?*" "It's none of your business," was
all Sheela said, "Why are you bothering me about this?" Then she
called me and said, "I hear you're not a *sannyasin.*"

I just laughed and asked, "What does *that* mean? I am what I am; I
haven't changed." "That's what I thought," so she said, "It's no problem with you." "But I don't understand why it's a problem for anybody." I reminded her that Bhagwan had said we wore the orange and
the *mala* to surrender. *Not* to surrender to something *outside* ourselves, I
pointed out, but as an expression of freedom. It was a way of saying, I
surrender to *myself.* And it shouldn't be a big deal whether I wear orange or blue or whatever: but, to drop the ego for a while, I'll wear one
color. It was simply a way of dropping the diversion of always looking
out—nothing more. "Why are you all making a big deal of the fact that
I'm going out and wearing other colors?" I kept pushing. "Of course,
you would see it that way," she said, "But other people see it as meaning
you're not surrendered to Bhagwan."

This led us back to our old argument over what this surrender to
Bhagwan *really* meant. He always said "freedom," and now he seemed
to be saying, to be free of yourself you had to put yourself in chains.

We didn't resolve anything. Finally, Sheela said, "Well, it's okay with me: I won't send a letter out about you being dead."

"Well, in a way, I'd rather like it if you *did*," I said, "Because it's all too cuckoo to me."

This was the first of many such conversations we had over the next few years.

During this period people like Semendra, who was a popular group leader with an entourage of women, broke off on his own. Within the *sannyasin* world there began to be a definite split into "Sheela" factions and "Laxmi" factions. Arup had developed her own "school." T. had his own admirers outside the Ashram. People began to look to these other leaders for direction, because Bhagwan was in silence, secluded in Lao Tzu, only emerging to take his regular drive each afternoon.

Women had always run the departments. Now Sheela came up with the idea that department heads were to be called "Mum," as in "mother." And *sannyasins* were to *think* of these people as their mother.

When we were in Poona we had had bare rooms, and we liked it. We worked very hard. We didn't have Nutella, we didn't have *umibushi* plums—but we were freer. We were funky; we joked and laughed; it was easy to lighten up the whole thing.

At the Ranch people were also working very hard, but they were living in luxury trailers with custom-fitted interiors, with fine carpets and beds and all the extras—the Ashram even supplied houseplants. People had proper rooms for the first time; they had nice clothes; they had a lot of things that were taken for granted in the outside world—but the lines were clearly blurring.

All of this brought a lot of energy to the Ranch. People might go home exhausted from the day's work; but they could look around and say, "We're making it. We're *really* making it." Rajneeshpuram was becoming a city: By the climactic last moments of 1985 the Ranch boasted numerous first-rate roads, schools, banks, a series of office buildings, a counseling complex covering nearly 22,000 square feet, and an airport big enough to service the jets of Air Rajneesh.

Sheela would give pep talks: "You're doing really well; it's really growing; but we just have to work a *little harder*." This, to people who were already working eighteen hours a day. She felt she had to keep hammering away at resistance.

In India we didn't hear any of the news from outside, so we didn't hear much of the feedback about us from the world at large. We were behind the four walls, and that was that. At the Ranch Sheela saw to it that the *sannyasins* heard the input—the *negative* input. They now had televisions all around Rajneeshpuram that were equipped with VCRs. All hostile television programs about the Ashram were videotaped and played back on these machines. All negative press releases were duplicated and posted on the communal bulletin boards. The *sannyasins* on the Ranch were getting the overwhelming impression that the world did not like them.

And there *was* plenty of bad news: Portland radio station KMJK, during Valentine's Day Week of 1983, broadcast a series of two-minute excerpts from interviews with an ex-*sannyasin*, Prem Gatama, titled, "Better Dead than Bhagwan Red: Confessions of a Rajneesh Refugee." Needless to say, the comments were very negative—though Prem Gatama later denounced the program's "sensationalism," claiming his remarks were often misrepresented.

That's when the Ranch started buying guns for self-defense. First people were deluged with this external negativity; the next thing they saw was the guards coming into lecture with M-14s. Although Bhagwan was not talking during this period, he would come into hall and sit in silence for an hour and a half. The justification for this weaponry was the "negativity and hostility" that was coming from the world outside.

The growing Ranch peace-keeping arsenal reputedly included CAR-15s and Uzi Model Bs. Even Sheela turned into a "pistol-packing Mum," displaying a sidearm for newly arrived Rajneeshees and press photographers.

More and more, the average *sannyasin* who made jewelry or milked cows was being convinced that people outside would like to hurt them or kill them. At the same time they could *see* that the people *inside* were beginning to arm up. It became a very freaky time for most people.

I went up for a couple of weeks at this point, and stood one day on the side of the road, waiting for Bhagwan to drive by. A person was walking behind his car, carrying an M-16. This guy was shaking so much that I turned to Chin and said, "I wouldn't want to faint in this heat, because that guy would probably just shoot me. He's so ready for anyone to make a move or try to kill Bhagwan."

Bhagwan kept a low profile during all this—unless being stopped for going 68 miles per hour in a 55-mile-per-hour zone constitutes "high visibility."

The paranoia was also being fed from the inside. The old lecture that Bhagwan had given in which he said one of his own *sannyasins* would kill him was kept uppermost in everybody's minds. Everybody became suspicious of everybody else.

Things had changed so much that no one would dare stand around and gossip the way we had done at the back gates of Poona. And you certainly wouldn't knock a fellow Ashramite or any aspect of Ashram life. If you even said, "I had an awful day," you risked being called into the office and told that you were being "negative," and if you didn't like things as they were, you could leave your *mala* on the desk and get out.

People didn't realize that there were now bugs on every table in the dining commons. They would have conversations, say something indiscreet, and get called on the carpet. Their first reaction would be, "Who told on me?" If you went to the office and demanded to know, you'd be told that so-and-so had been "loving enough to tell that you had done this." Of course, you'd go back and hate so-and-so. In this way the office opened rifts between people and prevented any loud clamoring for change or, at least, full explanations.

Reporter Jay Maeder of the Miami *Herald* described Rajneeshpuram, at the peak of the paranoia and uncertainty, as "a dark-souled, us-against-them kingdom, full of beaming, soft-singing spiritual storm troopers, whose high priests daily drum into acolytes that the world outside is a savage forest full of predators who mean to destroy them."

A bit melodramatic, but not all that far off the mark, I'd say. I was glad to be out of that "kingdom" and on my own.

I was now fully established at Cold Mountain. Deeksha was in Switzerland. Laxmi was still in disgrace on the Ranch. Sheela was getting such hostile publicity that everyone was shocked (though she often manipulated these responses from the press in order to say to the commune at large, "See, I told you so, they're out to get us").

She even made national headlines when she blasted critics of the Ranch, taking particular aim at Oregonians who were attempting to block the commune's takeover of Antelope. She accused Bhagwan's critics of being "full of prejudice." On one occasion, she accused them of being "fanatic" and out to "torment the people."

You could call in to the Ashram, but everybody knew that phone conversations were tapped. Sheela's recent conviction in federal court included a sentence of four and a half years for wiretapping, and Puja was also sentenced for wiretapping. The rationale for the tapping was to discover if there were any *sannyasins* who were working for the federal government, which people tended to accept as unpleasant but necessary. The rumor was spread that there were "terrible criminals" inside the Ashram—a fifth column out to destroy it from within.

I'd call up and unthinkingly blurt out, "My God! How can you guys stand behind this shit?" And I'd get back a vague, "Oh, you're just being negative. You've been away too long: You don't understand Bhagwan." All they were hearing from me—from any outsider—was negativity directed at them from the non-*sannyasin* world. They were not seeing the Ashram as a major source of a lot of their own feelings of insecurity and fear. I could feel them slipping away, mistrusting me, making me a part of the growing conspiracy that included everyone outside the Ranch—and a number of shadowy figures in Rajneeshpuram itself.

The centers around the United States and the world were taking off. People with green cards could stay in the Ashram if they passed whatever "screening" the office imposed.

Then Sheela began sending Ashramites to various centers around the world to work. It was set up as an exchange program. The Ashram might send ten people out to a center in Germany or Australia. In return, the center would be able to send maybe four of their own people back to the Ranch. Each center supported the ten visitors totally—though the understanding was that they would work as hard for the center as they did in the Ashram.

By doing this Sheela saw to it that the communes became much more productive. The people who came from the Ashram were used to working eighteen hours a day. Ten people, coming in with *that* kind of energy, would redo a whole commune in no time and have it operating at peak efficiency—and generating real money. And all of this *really* strengthened the ties between the outlying centers and communes and Rajneeshpuram—just as the exchange of group leaders did.

About half the expenses for all this "tie-binding" were absorbed by the Ashram. This was a dramatic change: *Sannyasin*s had never had real financial support from the office before.

The Ranch was also making clothes to sell to the mass market. These clothes were in all colors—not just red-orange—though the clothes that were brought in for sale still fell into the familiar spectrum. Once again, it was a case of the Ashram making money from whatever it touched.

To the surprise of many, Sheela began to travel. She went to Australia, Europe, and India. This triggered some press speculation that she was searching for yet another "new commune." She strongly denied these rumors.

And she never lost control of things, no matter where she was. She knew how Laxmi had lost the reins during her trips in search of the "new commune." Put more simply: She knew just what she had done to seize control of the Ashram, and she was careful to make sure nobody turned the tables on her. It was made clear, before her departure, that nobody else would carry messages in to Bhagwan. She arranged to conduct all necessary business by phone.

(Laxmi's control broke down because she was far too independent. She didn't build up a strong alliance around herself. Although Sheela and Arup were under her, she pretty much expected them to do their own things. Sheela, on the other hand, would *never* let anyone do a complete job. She would always arrange things so that she would have to be consulted to find out how all the pieces ultimately fit together. She was quite ingenious in this way.)

They became quite a mobile bunch: Even Vidya traveled somewhat. Puja never left: She seemed to be Sheela's alter ego on the Ranch—particularly when Sheela was off on a junket.

Sheela and I kept in touch by phone during this period. The change in her attitude was dramatic. In our first conversations she had laughed at my not wearing orange. Now that gradually gave way to talk of a coming "bloodbath." She seemed increasingly to be losing her perspective. I was becoming more and more a confidante and mother-confessor to Sheela, who at one point bluntly admitted to me: "I'm losing it."

CHAPTER 26

Uncertainties

I had become involved with a woman named Pat Lear in a lawsuit involving the distribution of three small volumes of Bhagwan's sayings, entitled *Sex, Love,* and *Prayer,* which she had published under her own imprint. I had drawn up the original contracts while in India; but now the Ranch wanted to discontinue the arrangement because Pat had dropped *sannyas.* Since the requirement of being a *sannyasin* had never entered the original agreement, I agreed to testify on her behalf.

She introduced me to an INS official who was investigating the Ranch. I didn't realize, until I'd been working with her for a time, that she had planned that I was going to work with the government. In fact, it seems now, she had an elaborate plan that I wasn't aware of.

I called Sheela to let her know I was going to testify on Pat's behalf in the book distribution dispute. "Fine, great, good luck," was all she said.

Out of the blue Deeksha called me from Switzerland. She advised me to get involved with the case, as she was. She had given information, but refused to testify. How, exactly, she came to be involved with the INS has never been made clear to me. However, she assured me the INS agents were good people to work with.

So began a relatively short—but certainly *instructive*—experience with the U.S. government.

From the first I was very wary of getting involved. But Deeksha's call had turned my thinking around. She made it clear that she was working with the INS and some other federal people, as was Shantam. "It would be good for you to work with them too," was how she had phrased it.

At one point I argued with her. "Deeksha," I said, "This is *Sheela* that we're talking about!" I knew that even though they had fallen out over the Ashram at one level, they were still very close. "How can you do it?"

Deeksha said, "It's not *Sheela*, it's *Bhagwan!*" Deeksha and I were in agreement then, and I think we're still in agreement: If the term "evil" means anything, Bhagwan certainly played the major part—not Sheela.

Deeksha said, "If you act now, things won't get out of hand and people won't die." And what she was saying made sense. I remembered how startled I had been when Sheela had told me on the phone, in regard to a question of a possible Ranch-wide sweep by government agents to check for green-card validations, "If we have to have a blood-bath, we'll have a bloodbath. And if all these people have to die, then they have to die." I felt the response was excessive.

I was bombarded with information on all sides. In the end the best solution seemed to be to work with the government.

But after I worked with them for a short time I was convinced that they were as corrupt as anyone else. At that point I told Sheela what I was doing. From then on I would pass along to Sheela whatever information they were giving me; she would tell me what she wanted them to hear. And things would go back-and-forth in this way. Pretty crazy—but *what* connected with the Ashram doesn't have that element of loony-ness?

At this time I became an intermediary in the purchase of a Lear Jet for Sheela. At the same time, I found out that the Rolls Royces at the Ranch—all eighty-four, at latest count—were *leased*, so that money could be diverted elsewhere.

Earlier, a few *sannyasins* had arranged for the purchase of a jet through an organization that resells such aircraft. The one they acquired turned out to be one that formerly belonged to Mohammar Khaddafi. It became involved in a smuggling operation in Latin America, and a comedy of errors followed. The registration number, which had never been changed, alerted the local government that a high official of a foreign nation was visiting. Out of courtesy they decided to greet the plane upon landing with full fanfare and a military escort. The dope smugglers, faced with the unexpected appearance of the military, abandoned the $8-million plane and its cargo on the runway, and left it as salvage to the surprised government. This story, which never hit the wire services, is an inside joke among those in the know about aircraft registry.

As a result of this fiasco I became involved in purchasing a replacement plane for the Ranch.

Unlikely as the earlier incident was—the stuff of Hollywood slapstick—it was only a small part of the increasingly black comedy that had Rancho Rajneesh as its backdrop.

If Bhagwan's legal status (still under appeal to the INS) was unresolved, so also was the Ranch's. The whole can of worms that was Rajneeshpuram's legal status (or lack of it) was reopened when the Oregon State Court of Appeals bounced the question of the legality of the incorporation of the Ranch back to Oregon's Land Use Board of Appeals. The threat of having the developing city declared illegal hung like a pall over the ongoing efforts to turn the place into a paradise on earth. But Rajneeshees (like the *sannyasins* they had formerly been) characteristically waxed optimistic, and went on with the work.

Still, they were playing the game of local politics with a vengeance—and scoring points! In the November elections the year before (1982), Rajneeshees gained control of four of seven seats that had come up on the Antelope City Council. In January 1983 they used their majority to appoint two more Rajneeshees to council positions that had become vacant. With six of seven seats (a clear majority, that!) they signed a series of service contracts with Rajneeshpuram enterprises. The cost of these services drove local taxes up, and drove many local farmers out—they sold their properties to Rajneesh Foundation International. The City Council also filed suit to wrest control of the Antelope Community Church—a striking, white clapboard affair worthy of a Grant Wood painting—to the town. The case actually dragged on until the following year, when the courts decided *against* the Rajneeshee-controlled City Council.

The game moved on to higher stakes, and the markers became more sophisticated. In 1983 the commune extended its influence in a new way into Salem, Oregon's capital, when it employed the services of a veteran lobbyist who had previously represented such concerns as Nike, Teledyne, and Allstate Insurance. But the results were decidedly mixed. Deciding the personal touch was the better route, the Ranch sent Rajneeshee lobbyists to confront the politicians directly. But, if their earlier efforts had been a mixed bag, the latest *putsch* had decidedly negative results. Conservative politicos did not take kindly to the orange-and-*mala* presence in their midst, and my overall impression is that little (if anything) was gained by this particular maneuver.

In May the disciples offered to vacate Antelope and leave the township to its own devices, if the state legislature would pass special legislation establishing Rajneeshpuram's legal status once and for all. The proposal was shot down by legislators.

In the ever-flourishing climate of paranoia that seemed to me (on my increasingly rare visits) to cling to the Ranch like the smell of the burning-*ghat*s in Poona, attitudes began to make bizarre turns.

The press, which had been welcomed by Bhagwan in Poona (even "bad publicity," he had once assured his *sannyasins*, "is going to help my work"), was increasingly viewed as hostile and a threat to Rancho Rajneesh's continued existence. In June two journalists were arrested by the Rajneeshpuram Peace Force. One was charged with trespass; one with illegal taping. Both were known to have published unfavorable articles about Bhagwan, Rajneeshism, and the Ranch. (A Wasco County Grand Jury dropped the charges a few weeks later.)

Sheela, who all along had been warning of possible violence to Bhagwan or his followers, had a graphic validation of her dire prophecies when, in July 1983, several bombs ripped through Hotel Rajneesh in Portland. The damage was estimated at $200,000. A man from California was accused of the crime, which only intensified the Ranch's feelings of a noose of bigotry and hostility tightening around them—Sheela played this to the hilt, of course—and led to even more stringent restrictions on traffic into, and out of, Rancho Rajneesh.

On the legal front the Gordian knot of the Ranch's status became even more entangled when the Oregon Land Use Board of Appeals decided that Wasco County had not followed correct land-use procedure in authorizing the incorporation election at the Ranch. The whole issue was thrown back to Wasco County. The matter seemed no nearer a solution than it had two years before.

Things seemed to be heating up on lots of different fronts: A group of long-time, highly vocal Antelope residents claimed that Rajneesh private security forces were conducting surveillance of them that constituted an invasion of their privacy. A month later the City Council contracted for police patrols from Rajneeshpuram to operate in Antelope. Although there was no clear connection between the protests and the new police arrangements, the situation between the oldtimers and the upstart Rajneeshees continued to deteriorate.

Around the same time the Oregon State Attorney filed suit against the incorporation of Rajneeshpuram on the grounds that it violated constitutional provisions for separation of church and state.

The year 1984 began auspiciously enough. In February the news was announced that the INS officially recognized Bhagwan as a "religious teacher." Celebration swept Rancho Rajneesh, culminating in a gathering at the assembly hall, Rajneesh Mandir, where Rajneeshees danced to wild Russian gypsy music and were served such goodies as champagne, slices of a 225-pound chocolate cake, fresh strawberries, and grapes.

This event overshadowed a curious, startling revelation, which had come about on February 9. Swami Swarupananda, Sheela's father, told the commune that he had *adopted* Bhagwan when the latter was four years old.

The story, reported in the *Rajneesh Times*, claimed that Bhagwan's parents had consulted an astrologer shortly after the boy was born. They were told that Bhagwan would be dead before he was seven years old. But, the astrologer told the obviously upset parents, if they disowned their child his fate could be avoided. Then, the astrologer assured them, the boy would be a world leader.

Bhagwan's parents tried to ignore the prediction, but the boy suffered several near-fatal illnesses in his first few years—and, though he survived, his parents became convinced of the truth of what the astrologer had told them. Dadaji shared this fateful information with his good friend, Swami Swarupananda, who offered to adopt the young Bhagwan to avert tragedy. This was done immediately (with the truth of the astrologer's prediction there for everyone to see!). The two families agreed to keep this arrangement a secret.

The reason for "going public" with this information at this time was another ploy to get Bhagwan's legal status in the U.S. changed— his adoptive parents were naturalized citizens, with American passports. This all tied in with later investigations on the part of the immigration officers that revealed substantial property holdings on the West Coast had been purchased by the Patel family—Sheela's family— largely in the name of "Acharya Patel." According to documents on file with the immigration office, Bhagwan and "Acharya Patel" are one and the same person—as Sheela's father attested when he claimed Bhagwan had been legally adopted by the Patel family years before.

This good (if rather too "magical") news was enhanced with the additional encouraging news that a three-judge panel of the State Court of Appeals had reversed the Land Use Board of Appeals ruling that the incorporation of Rajneeshpuram was improperly carried out.

But the good news was quickly offset by the bad. A full Court of Appeals hearing three months later reversed the panel's findings and ruled the incorporation improper. The threat of dismantling Rajneeshpuram loomed larger than ever before. The press printed a number of stories about the building of an arsenal at the Ranch.

Around this time I found out that the INS and the United States Attorney's office were conducting a joint investigation into alleged criminal activities at Rancho Rajneesh. Feeling trapped in a web of circumstances, and trusting nobody, I took T. and left abruptly for Katmandu. There we discovered, quite by accident, that Bhagwan had established a complex at Pokhara in Nepal. We had been talking with someone, and got onto the subject of Rajneesh. "Oh, *Rajneesh!*" he cried, "They're building a huge city here."

I looked at T. and he looked at me, and I said, "Ahhh! They're leaving America . . . "

Our informant volunteered to show us the place. So we hiked over there.

It turned out that an old friend of T's was running the complex. Oddly enough, he had been kicked out before by Sheela.

Sure enough, they had built a house for Bhagwan. It covered some 2,500 acres, included dormitories like those in Poona—very similar in design to Vipassana-Go-Down—and a swimming pool for Bhagwan. It had been in existence some three years, during which time they'd learned to grow appropriate crops, so the place would be self-sustaining in terms of food. Eventually, it would be able to shelter a large number of people.

None of us could figure out who was footing the bill for all this construction. Checks to support the place, according to what our friend told us, were drawn on a variety of banks—but none were directly connected with Rajneeshpuram or any of its far-flung operations. They came from private parties, which wasn't that unusual: It had been standard practice to have *sannyasins*, from time to time, use their personal checking accounts to handle Ashram business. There was no consistency to the times the checks were issued, or in the names of the various "donors." It was all very mysterious. Our friend had only been told at the outset to build this commune, and that he would be getting a given amount of money in different payments. So he commenced the work.

When we visited about fifty-five people were working there. My first impression was that Sheela didn't know about it. But then, just before we were to leave, our friend got a telegram saying that Sheela was on her way to visit. So she did, indeed, know of its existence—though she'd never indicated it to me in all our years of working together.

This may well be where Bhagwan is going to end up when all the dust from the collapse of Poona-Antelope settles.

At the end of the vacation we returned home, hoping that things would have quieted down enough that we could be left in peace. I wanted nothing to do with the Ashram or the government.

That, however, was not to be.

Upon our return to Cold Mountain we found that things back at the

Ranch had been anything but quiet—or dull.

In August a Wasco County executive had nearly died from food poisoning, after having been given a glass of water by someone from the Rajneesh Medical Corporation. Subsequent medical examination turned up evidence of a "highly toxic substance" concentrated in his kidneys.

Relations with Antelope residents had bottomed out when Rajneesh police entered the home of a local resident (reportedly without a warrant). They charged him with "menacing" conduct over some anti-Rajneeshee signs he had put up. (I heard that these were "Jesus loves you" signs posted around the recycling center.) He was handcuffed, dragged out of his house in the middle of the night, and jailed. (The Wasco County District Attorney quickly dropped all charges.) Shortly thereafter the name of the town was officially changed from "Antelope" to "City of Rajneesh."

I found out that Sheela had been talking for a long time about taking over the reins of Wasco County government in the upcoming November elections. She was going to do this by importing large numbers of junkies and the homeless—an action which would, on the surface, be attributed to Bhagwan's benevolence—who would be registered as local voters. These, it was presumed, would happily vote in favor of the Ranch in return for food stamps and other guarantees the Rajneeshees would provide—once the Ranch had control of the Wasco County offices.

This actually came to pass in September 1984, when the just-created Rajneesh Humanity Trust began busing in street people from all over the United States—more than three thousand, according to some estimates—under something called the "Share-a-Home Program." This program was inaugurated on September 16, 1984. The avowed reason for its existence was "to share with some people who have been less fortunate than we have." At the outset it guaranteed the newcomers room and board, a work-exempt status on the Ranch, and a ticket home if things didn't pan out.

Not a few Oregonians looked on this as a blatant attempt to seize control of county government, since two of three Wasco County Court seats were up for reelection—a situation which could have had a long-range effect on the Ranch's land-use problems. Cries of "voter fraud" led to the initiation of special restrictions on voter registration. But the Wasco County citizenry's worries were unnecessary: Internal problems caused the program to collapse almost as rapidly as it had begun, with the new arrivals being bused out of Rajneeshpuram and left to their own devices in such local cities as Bend, The Dalles, and Madras.

That same month there was a widespread outbreak of salmonella food poisoning in and around The Dalles, which ultimately affected more than eight hundred citizens—quite a number of whom required hospitalization. I had heard speculation about a plot to smear the hands of "greeters" at county preelection meetings with salmonella bacteria to infect the Ranch's political opponents or use the same "biological warfare" techniques to infect salad bars in The Dalles and elsewhere to incapacitate potential anti-Rajneeshee votes in the area.

The timing seems off (this was two months before the election, remember), but the story seems hardly less bizarre than later press reports of finding secret "biological warfare labs" on the Ranch when all hell broke loose. It seems hard for me to see Sheela as Lucrezia Borgia—even now, given her recent convictions, which the July 23, 1983, edition of the *San Francisco Examiner* stated included a four-and-a-half-year sentence "for tampering with consumer products, involving the salmonella poisoning of dozens of people eating in restaurants in The Dalles."

Later, Rajneeshees let it be known that the proximity of the "Share-a-Home" program and the county elections was a "coincidence." When questioned by the local press Sheela attempted to dismiss the whole thing as a "joke," but none of the locals got the humor of it. Always quick to throw fuel on the fire, Sheela persisted in making statements to the effect that Wasco County was "so fucking bigoted that it deserves to be taken over." Hardly the sort of thing to win friends and influence people county-wide.

In a last-ditch effort to affect the elections, the Rajneeshees boycotted federal, state, and county elections on November 4. But the outcome was decidedly negative as far as Rancho Rajneesh was concerned: Three people who were extremely critical of Rajneeshism were elected to the county commission, and retained their seats in spite of a formal Rajneeshee challenge of two thousand votes. (This challenge was quickly quelled by the Mayor of Rajneeshpuram, Krishna Deva, who gave priority to "peaceful coexistence" between Rancho Rajneesh and the other residents of Wasco County.)

Shortly after the election debacles, Sheela took off on one of her junkets. In December she married Dhyan Dippo, in Zurich, Switzerland, and then went on to Nepal.

I couldn't help but wonder if her trip to Nepal had anything to do with that large, empty, waiting commune high in the mountains. Was another move blowing in the wind? I suspected it: Over the years I had learned to read revealing patterns in the movements of key players in the Ashram—much the way one might chart the migrations of a flock of wild geese or, in this case, lemmings headed for the brink of disaster.

CHAPTER 27

Last Days

The year 1985 literally began with a blaze. Fire, which authorities quickly ascribed to arson, broke out in January in the Wasco County Planning Office where all the records of land-use cases relative to Rajneeshpuram were stored. Charges that Sheela was implicated were borne out by a court order on July 22, 1986, in conjunction with her sentencing in federal court in Portland, that she "pay more than $69,000 in restitution for an arson fire," as reported in the *San Francisco Examiner*, July 23, 1986.

Charges and countercharges flew between pro- and anti-Bhagwan partisans, and the press had a field day. Anything became grist for the anti-Bhagwan mill, as reports fired up concerns about what was *really* going on inside Rancho Rajneesh. Such items included speculation about *why* the commune had such extensive medical facilities—including an estimated twenty doctors, fifty nurses, full paramedical support staff, fully equipped medical laboratory, X-ray machinery, and two ambulances—to serve a population of roughly five thousand. Were they expecting violence? A major epidemic? Civil war? Other articles indignantly pointed to the emphasis on abortions, sterilizations, and the fact that no children had been born at the Ranch since its inception. (This last point is accurate, as far as I know.)

This was indicative of a year marked by increasingly bizarre events and a split between Bhagwan and Sheela that hastened what many already saw as a doomed "experiment." Already, a federal grand jury was investigating charges of "racketeering" and criminal violations of U.S. immigration laws by the Ranch.

I had compulsively called Sheela shortly after I returned with T. to Cold Mountain. I could never seem to help myself: I would always have to pick up the phone and just tell her I was around. And every time I did that, I'd get dragged into something else.

I spoke with her often during this time, but she never indicated she was going to leave. She said she was feeling "overwhelmed." Bhagwan kept pushing her, and she was doing, doing, doing everything she could. He had no sense of the reality of things: he just expected the world to pay homage to him.

Then I got a series of increasingly confused calls from her. Things were falling apart on the Ranch, and reports of an imminent collapse began filling the newspapers. What was anyone to make of her declaration that anyone who died within a twenty-four-mile radius of Rajneeshpuram would be assured "enlightenment" automatically? Not only did it seem to pervert the whole notion of enlightenment, but it smacked of *jihad*—a Moslem holy war waged against persons not of their faith, in which anyone who died in the name of the prophet was instantly translated to paradise.

Still, there was an increasingly consistent pattern to such remarks. It seemed a logical extension of her comments noted in the *San Francisco Chronicle* on July 5, 1983, when she threatened to "paint the bulldozers with my blood" if they ever came to level Rajneeshpuram. At the same time she claimed to have the unquestioning support of all Rajneeshees on the Ranch, who would be "willing to die for human freedom." And, during the Third Annual World Celebration at Rajneeshpuram, she had promised to resist "fascist forces" to the "very last drop of our blood."

That June, in what I saw as a last-ditch effort to maintain control of a rapidly deteriorating situation, the Ranch filed suits against county, state, and federal officials—including INS officers and U.S. Attorney General Edwin Meese—charging them with conspiring to violate Rajneeshees' civil rights and requesting a cease and desist order. The suits came to nothing.

Things began happening with greater and greater rapidity. The Oregon Supreme Court served up a split decision, finding on the one hand that the incorporation of Rajneeshpuram was properly carried out, but bouncing (yet again!) the issue of whether or not questions of urban-versus-agricultural land-use were correctly addressed back to the Land Use Board of Appeals.

At the same time the citizens of Antelope formed the Antelope Defense fund, charging the Rajneeshee-controlled City Council with misuse of its powers and launching a statewide initiative petition to put the Antelope disincorporation issue on the November 1986 ballot.

In September the Oregon Supreme Court handed down a decision indicating that Wasco County land-use law had not been properly consulted in key Ranch maneuvers. This opened the possibility of a future order to stop using—or actually dismantle—many Rajneeshpuram buildings.

Suddenly, Sheela left. On September 14 she resigned her position as head of Rajneesh Foundation International and left Rajneeshpuram— as did Ma Anand Puja, Director of the Rajneesh Medical Corporation; Ma Prem Savita, the financial manager; Krishna Deva, the Mayor of Rajneeshpuram; and many other key officials.

Sheela immediately flew to Seattle via Air Rajneesh. From there she caught a flight to London, then Frankfurt. Her final destination was Zurich, Switzerland.

On September 16 Bhagwan appeared at press interviews where he accused Sheela and her cohorts—what he called her "gang"—of attempting to poison Michael Sullivan, the Jefferson County District Attorney, and William Hulse, Wasco County Commissioner; of drugging the street people who participated in the abortive Share-a-Home fiasco; of spreading salmonella poison in The Dalles; of poisoning The Dalles's water supply; of wiretapping; of arson at the Wasco County planning office; of stealing up to $55 million from Rajneesh organizations; of plotting to bomb the Wasco County Courthouse; of attempted murder of his personal physician, dentist, and caretaker. Later, he even accused Sheela of trying to murder *him*. The newspapers were quick to point out supposed similarities to Synanon or Jonestown—where apparently high-minded beginnings had turned to bizarre violence.

Bhagwan replaced Sheela almost immediately with Ma Prem Hasya, who took over the reins as his personal secretary and president of the Rajneesh Foundation International. A former Hollywood film producer, Hasya was quick to accuse Sheela of being disruptive, and to charge Puja with miscoding and misusing test results.

Hasya immediately changed the name of the secretarial living quarters from Jesus Grove to Sanai Grove. She set to work to smooth things over and help keep Bhagwan's "experiment" going.

Bhagwan himself attempted to do major fence-mending throughout the summer of 1985—apparently to offset the increasingly adverse publicity that culminated in a devastating series of articles in *The Oregonian* beginning on June 30—timed to coincide with the opening of the Fourth Annual World Festival at Rajneeshpuram. He gave a series of press interviews, including an appearance on ABC's "Good Morning America."

He claimed that Sheela had turned Rancho Rajneesh into a "concentration camp" and had willfully antagonized local residents—all without his knowledge. To show just how guiltless he was, he urged a swift criminal investigation of all the charges. Investigators subsequently turned up enough evidence of wiretapping to secure eventual convictions for both Sheela and Puja.

On September 30 thousands of copies of the *Book of Rajneeshism* were burned in the crematorium as Bhagwan declared the end of Rajneeshism as a "religion." Around the same time he announced that his disciples no longer had to wear red-orange clothes or *malas*.

Bhagwan also expressed a desire to smooth over relations with Oregonians, and to have his disciples leave Antelope. But the damage was done: mending was not good enough: the whole system of fences had collapsed.

Sheela, interviewed in West Germany, retaliated, claiming her life was in danger because of what she knew about the Rajneeshee organization. She also accused the new regime at the Ranch of being heavily into drugs, and charged that any cash shortfalls were Bhagwan's fault, since he had become far more interested in expensive cars and jewelry than in his disciples. On October 28, Sheela and Puja were arrested in West Germany and extradited to the United States. They were charged with the attempted poisoning of Bhagwan's doctor, Swami Devaraj, a "commune rival," with a syringe injection of adrenalin.

Devaraj claimed that just before lecture, while he was seated in Mandir Hall, Shanti Bhadra, one of Sheela's assistants, had come over and given him a hug. At that moment he'd felt a prick in his arm. Shortly afterwards he became violently ill, but *insisted* that he be taken to the hospital in Bend—*not* to the Ranch's clinic. (Shanti Bhadra later was convicted of the attempted murder of Devaraj.)

This incident brought back to my mind a confused incident from the years at Poona. One time, when I was just completing some financial reports for Sheela, Shantam came over and hugged me. I suddenly stopped working; my hands dropped to my sides; my mind went blank. My friend Shradda came over and asked what the matter was.

"I feel like I've just shot up," I said, and showed her the rash that had suddenly appeared on my arm. I felt dizzy, confused, sick to my stomach. Shradda got me up from my desk and started me walking to clear my senses, but I kept going off my head more and more.

"Is this what they mean by 'flashbacks'?" I remember asking her at one point, wondering if I was undergoing some weird delayed reaction to my drug problems years before in Oxford.

Then I really went off my rocker, beginning to call to the birds in the nearby trees in what I regarded as quite fluent bird-talk.

Shradda got me to bed, and had the clinic's doctor look at me. I don't remember much of anything clearly—though I always had vague memories of Sheela sitting on my bed, telling me over and over, "You must forget"—meaning that I must forget the bank work that I had been doing just before the dizziness hit me.

When I came out of it I was unable to sort out dream from fact, and let the matter go as a "touch of fever." But this mystery was cleared up very quickly, as we'll see.

Law officers, investigating on the Ranch, turned up a wealth of evidence against Sheela, Puja, and others. Simultaneously, INS officials were stepping up their investigations of twenty-five to thirty alleged cases of "marriages of convenience" between U.S. citizens and foreign nationals to help the latter gain entrance to, or remain in, the United States—in clear violation of immigration laws. As investigations continued Bhagwan (never one to miss a P.R. possibility) stated that he would let himself be interviewed by police *only when television cameras were present*.

Shortly after that Hasya called me on Bhagwan's behalf, and I went up to try to help sort out the documents left in the office. On that visit I realized that Bhagwan was totally corrupt: He had set the whole thing up.

I arrived after everybody—the Ashram, TV, the local citizens—had pulled Sheela apart. Bhagwan suggested that we use hypnotherapy to help me remember all the different things they needed to know. He hoped I could supply him with all the bank account numbers, property holdings, and financial statements. He was claiming that Sheela had charge of all such matters, and left everything in disarray.

So I signed something, and we began taping. One of the things that came up was that time, years before, when I'd gone off my rocker. It had really been the result of drugs Sheela had directed to be given to me to set me up for hypnotherapy to make me block out what I'd learned about certain financial arrangements.

After that, not knowing *what* might come up—something previously unremembered, but compromising—and no longer trusting my own memories of the years working in the Ashram office, I insisted, "You have to give me the tapes."

We did one lot of taping; but the next day they told me that the tapes had "disappeared." So I said, "That's it." I knew the game—*their* game—was still very much afoot. Through it all everybody was blaming Sheela, but I saw that it was Bhagwan at the center of things. If I ever had any doubts, I no longer did. He *must* have been the person who had contrived it all: The person who had been giving directions from the start.

On reflection I realized my role was all bullshit anyhow: He must already have known all the information. But he was playing the game of making it look like everything was Sheela's doing, and he didn't know any of it.

On October 6, 1985, Bhagwan was served a summons to appear before a federal grand jury—but he managed to obtain a thirty-day delay. Toward the end of the month he fled the Ranch by plane. He was arrested in Charlotte, North Carolina, en route to Bermuda.

He was charged with thirty-five violations of immigration law and with unlawful flight to avoid prosecution. Eleven days later he was released on $500,000 bail, and returned to Rancho Rajneesh. In Portland he pleaded guilty to two federal immigration charges, and paid $400,000 in fines and court costs. He was expelled from the country in November, after promising not to return for five years. He admitted that coming to America had been a "mistake." He advised all *sannyasins* who were not United States citizens to leave Rancho Rajneesh, and ordered those remaining to begin dismantling the commune and selling its assets.

Just in time for Christmas, on December 10, 1985, a United States District judge ruled that the incorporation of Rajneeshpuram was illegal, since it violated the First Amendment clauses guaranteeing separation of church and state.

The "experiment" in America was finished; most *sannyasins* were gone from Rancho Rajneesh within a week.

Some stayed on to close down the operation and arrange for its upkeep and eventual sale. Early in 1986, when Bhagwan was residing in Greece, an announcement was made that too many people were at the Ranch—far more than were needed.

For the first time ever, the Ashram *gave* money—$1,000 a person— to those who had to move on. However, rather than setting them free with a stake to start a new life, those disbursing the funds let it be known that Bhagwan was in Greece and had extended an open invitation to these refugees from Rancho Rajneesh to join him there.

So these people dutifully set off on yet another wild goose chase. By the time most of them arrived—now penniless—Bhagwan had departed for his next port of call.

From May 4 through May 11, 1986, the Rajneesh Neo-Sannyas International Commune in Oregon announced a sale of its assets, promising, "Everything reduced below cost. Used merchandise, incredibly well maintained. Bulk sales only." Among the items to be liquidated:

- *AIRPLANE:* Convair 240 S/dU 31. Excellent airframe. Heavily equipped: dual RMI's, auto-pilot. $155,000.
- *MACHINE SHOP:* Fully equipped including Van Norman Milling Machine No. 12, Bridgeport Universal milling machine, and Herter lathe JH-1752. Asking $14,000.
- *MOBILE HOMES/MODULAR UNITS:* Double-wide, Golden West mobile homes & Boise-Cascade modular living units. 7-24 bedrooms each. Totalling 308 bedrooms. 0-16 baths per unit. From $18,000 per unit. All $750,000.
- *MOBILE RESTAURANT KITCHEN TRAILER:* Fully equipped. 2 grills. 2 stockpot stoves, deep fryer, ice maker, dishwasher, New Ansul system 14' x 30'. Excellent condition. $25,000.

Other items offered included clothing (70 percent new); a complete beauty salon; appliances; satellite TV equipment; video and videotapes; communications equipment (two-way Motorola radios); living room, bedroom, outdoor, industrial, and other furniture; office supplies; professional sound equipment; photo and graphic arts equipment, film, and paper; gambling tables; and place settings for twenty thousand people.

The centerpiece of the sale was, of course: • *100 SQ. MILE RANCH:* Includes incorporated urban area that will accommodate and service 5,000 people. Price: $40,000,000.

"All sales final," the ad warned.

To date, parties interested in the last comprehensive item have been few. On July 25, 1986, the *San Francisco Chronicle* commented that

a real estate company is now offering the former Rajneeshpuram commune for sale for $28,500,000 cash, a reduction of 35% from the $44,000,000 that had been asked for the 64,229-acre ranch. . . . The Rajneesh Investment Corp. put the central Oregon ranch, its 295 buildings up for sale last winter after it announced the commune was closing. . . . The sect bought the ranch in 1981 for $5,750,000.

On August 13, 1986, a *San Francisco Chronicle* article by Paul Liberatore, datelined Antelope, commented:

The Bhagwan is gone, but bitterness lingers in this speck of a town that the Indian guru made famous.

"There are scars in this community that may never heal," said Margaret Hill, a former mayor. "The toll on peoples' health and finances was tremendous. I wouldn't wish it on anyone."

The "City of Rajneesh" is now "Antelope" again; "Melvana Bhag-

wan" is now "Main Street" once more. The recycling center is dismantled, the Zorba the Buddha restaurant in the town is for sale, and the
local citizenry have raised a plaque reading:

Dedicated to those of this community who throughout the Rajneesh invasion
and occupation of 1981–1985 remained, resisted and remembered. . . ."The only
thing necessary for the triumph of evil is for good men to do nothing." (Ed-
mund Burke)

The *San Francisco Chronicle* article concluded:

Tourists from all over the world still flock to the commune, but there isn't
much for them to see.

At Krishnamurti Lake, where hundreds of Rajneeshees once swam, sailed
and sunbathed, moss is taking over and the deer have the water all to
themselves.

Where there had been music and laughter, there is only the whisper of
wind and the sounds of birds.

An earlier *Chronicle* article on July 31, 1986, stated that Bhagwan returned to India from Portugal on a private plane, having been denied
permission to settle in Nepal, Greece, Britain, the West Indies, Fiji,
Spain, Uruguay, and other countries. Rekindling his old antipathies for
his native India, Bhagwan, according to newspaper reports, complained bitterly of nearly two hours of extensive questioning he under-
went at the airport in Bombay. Confined to a wheelchair due to an
apparent back ailment, he stated, "I was treated like a tourist, despite
having an Indian passport. This is not a country to be in for good."

The wirephoto showed him wearing what was described as "a glit-
tering green robe and a diamond-studded cap," so it seems to me that
he's managed to hang onto a little of that sparkle and sass that clung to
him when he billed himself as "the rich man's guru."

Many people see the whole American adventure as an unmitigated
disaster, and count Bhagwan out of the game. But he has always been a
master of surprises—so I wouldn't be surprised if he has one or two
more up his sleeves. Many *sannyasins* around the world still believe he
does.

To those who say he failed in his ultimate goal, Bhagwan would
probably respond in this way, as he did to a *sannyasin* in lecture (quoted
in *The Goose Is Out*):

"There is no ultimate goal. . . . There is nothing ultimate anywhere;
the immediacy itself is the ultimate. And there is no goal: the pilgrim-
age itself is the goal. Each step is the goal; each moment is the goal."

To charges that he has failed as a guru, I can imagine him smiling and saying:

"The Master really makes trust almost impossible, but when it is impossible and still you trust, then it works; *only* then does it work. If the Master makes trust very simple and possible, if he fulfills all your ideas of being a Master, then trust is cheap, very cheap . . . meaningless, too" (*God's Got a Thing About You*).

Finally, in response to the charge that his experiment is over and done with, I can imagine him responding as he responded to an attack by a Christian theologian:

"He says: the moment Bhagwan dies, his whole movement will disappear like a soap bubble. . . . I live now, I am not interested in the future at all. How does it matter whether my movement disappears like a soap bubble or not? I love soap bubbles! They look beautiful in the sun. And they should disappear so that a few other people can make other soap bubbles" (*The Goose Is Out*).

His next move in the game is anybody's guess.

Sheela and Puja were sentenced on July 22, 1986, in the U.S. District Court in Portland, Oregon. They entered the Federal Correctional Institution near Pleasanton, California, in the San Francisco Bay Area, to begin serving sentences on Friday, July 25, 1986. Ma Shanti Bhadra accompanied them.

On July 26, 1986, The *Contra Costa Times* reported,

The former cult leaders . . . entered the barbed-wire compound of the prison at 6 P.M., with their hands and legs shackled in chains.

The three women, who until last year were part of the inner circle of the Bhagwan's central Oregon commune, Rajneeshpuram, were sentenced in Portland, Oregon, Tuesday morning.

Sheela, 36, also known as Sheela Silverman, was sentenced . . . for charges that included attempted murder, assault, arson and wiretapping.

Ma Anand Puja, 38, also called Dianne Onang, [was sentenced] . . . for attempted murder and assault . . .

Ma Shanti Bhadra, 40, also known as Catherine Elsea, received a . . . sentence for attempted murder.

The three, escorted by two federal marshals, arrived in an unmarked white van from Portland.

The women, who as leaders of the Oregon cult were more accustomed to traveling in limousines, appeared subdued as they walked to the prison, gazing straight ahead and not stopping to answer questions.

For all the talk of a "subdued" Sheela, I think I know her well enough to make this warning: Don't count her out of the game quite yet. She will actually be serving only four and a half years, and she's still a fairly young woman.

As for me . . . I find myself turning toward a new life.

There is still a long way to go on the path of self. Probably the most important thing I've learned from what has gone before is that there are no "short-cuts to enlightenment"—just a delightful dance into the dawn with no turning back.

Welcome to the Carnival . . .